LONDON AND PARIS AS INTERNATIONAL FINANCIAL CENTRES IN THE TWENTIETH CENTURY

London and Paris as International Financial Centres in the Twentieth Century

Edited by

YOUSSEF CASSIS
ÉRIC BUSSIÈRE

OXFORD
UNIVERSITY PRESS

This book has been printed digitally and produced in a standard specification in order to ensure its continuing availability

OXFORD
UNIVERSITY PRESS

Great Clarendon Street, Oxford OX2 6DP

Oxford University Press is a department of the University of Oxford.
It furthers the University's objective of excellence in research, scholarship,
and education by publishing worldwide in

Oxford New York

Auckland Cape Town Dar es Salaam Hong Kong Karachi
Kuala Lumpur Madrid Melbourne Mexico City Nairobi
New Delhi Shanghai Taipei Toronto
With offices in
Argentina Austria Brazil Chile Czech Republic France Greece
Guatemala Hungary Italy Japan South Korea Poland Portugal
Singapore Switzerland Thailand Turkey Ukraine Vietnam

Oxford is a registered trade mark of Oxford University Press
in the UK and in certain other countries

Published in the United States
by Oxford University Press Inc., New York

Oxford is a registered trade mark of Oxford University Press
in the UK and in certain other countries

Published in the United States
by Oxford University Press Inc., New York

Reprinted 2006

ISBN 0-19-926949-1

Preface

This volume originates from the third Anglo-French business history conference, organized by the Business History Unit at the London School of Economics, on 4–6 April 2001. A first conference, on 'Management in the Age of the Corporate Economy, 1850–1990', took place in September 1992 (the proceedings were published in Y. Cassis, F. Crouzet, and T. Gourvish (eds.), *Management and Business in Britain and France: The Age of the Corporate Economy* (Oxford, 1995)), and a second, on 'Les Stratégies de commercialisation et de marketing', in Paris in October 1995. The need was felt by scholars in both countries to compare the financial sector in Britain and France from a business history perspective, and the theme of 'London and Paris as international financial centres, 1890–2000' was chosen for the third conference.

The editors would like to thank the many people who have helped them in their endeavours. They are particularly grateful to Kathleen Burk, Forrest Capie, François Crouzet, Patrick Fridenson, and Terry Gourvish for chairing the conference's five sessions, as well as to François Caron, Maurice Lévy-Leboyer, Piere de Longuemar, Roger Nougaret, Geoffrey Owen, John Plender, Geoffrey Wood, and the others who attended the conference and enhanced the quality of the debates. They are also grateful to Pascal Boris (BNP Paribas), David Green (Financial Services Authority), David Kynaston (London), David Lascelles (Centre for the Study of Financial Innovation), Philip Mallinckrodt (Schroder Salomon Smith Barney), and Frédéric Périer (Paris Europlace) for participating in the round table, chaired by Martin Dickson from the *Financial Times*, which provided a highly stimulating conclusion to the conference. Dr Christophe Revillard, of the University of Paris IV, skilfully edited the final manuscript, Dr J. C. Whitehouse translated Chapters 3, 11, 13, and 15, and Mr Owen Leeming Chapter 5, from the French. Sonia Copeland efficiently dealt with all organizational issues. The editors would also like to express their gratitude to the funding organizations which generously supported the conference, namely the Bank of England, the Banque Vernes Artesia, BNP Paribas, the Caisse des Dépôts et Consignations, the European Association for Banking History, Euronext, and N. M. Rothschild & Sons.

Y.C.
E.B.

April 2004

Contents

List of Figures

List of Tables

Notes on Contributors

MAE BAKER is a lecturer at the University of Leeds.

HUBERT BONIN is a professor at the Institut d'Études Politiques de Bordeaux.

ÉRIC BUSSIÈRE is a professor at the University of Paris IV.

YOUSSEF CASSIS is a professor at the University of Geneva and a visiting fellow at the Business History Unit, London School of Economics.

MICHAEL COLLINS is a professor at the University of Leeds.

P. L. COTTRELL is a professor at the University of Leicester.

OLIVIER FEIERTAG is a professor at the University of Rouen.

NIALL FERGUSON is a professor at the University of Oxford.

MARC FLANDREAU is a professor at the Institut d'Études Politiques de Paris.

FRANÇOIS GALLICE is a researcher at the University of Paris X-Nanterre.

RANALD MICHIE is a professor at the University of Durham.

ALAIN PLESSIS is a professor emeritus at the University Paris X-Nanterre.

RICHARD ROBERTS is a reader at the University of Sussex.

SAMIR SAUL is a professor at the University of Montréal.

CATHERINE SCHENK is a senior lecturer at the University of Glasgow.

ANDRÉ STRAUS is a research fellow at the CNRS.

1

Introduction: Comparative Perspectives on London and Paris as International Financial Centres in the Twentieth Century

Youssef Cassis

Throughout the 'long nineteenth century', London and Paris were the world's two leading financial centres. Whether an international financial centre is defined as a cluster of financial service providers serving the requirements of either a region, a continent, or, indeed, the whole world, or as a central location where an area's financial transactions are coordinated and cleared,[1] the British and French capitals were at the forefront in fulfilling these tasks. Their financial markets were ahead of those of other European centres—Amsterdam, Brussels, Hamburg, Frankfurt, and, from 1870, Berlin—as well as New York. This hierarchy changed during the twentieth century with the rise, first, of New York and, later, Tokyo. Although London, Paris, and New York competed during the 1920s, New York's global dominance had become clearly established by 1945. While London from the 1960s re-emerged, and Tokyo from the 1980s emerged, as global financial centres alongside New York, Paris, despite some attempts during the 1960s, remained in the 'second division', behind Frankfurt and Zurich in Europe, and Hong Kong worldwide. Only in the closing years of the twentieth century did Paris appear capable of re-establishing itself as a prime European financial centre.

The destinies of the two centres thus followed parallel courses until the 1950s, thereafter diverging, although significant differences, and similarities, can be observed during both eras. The main differences during the first sixty to seventy years surveyed by this volume, say from 1890 to 1958 (and even earlier during the nineteenth century), were a matter of size and international outlook. London was always the larger, by a significant margin. There are no available statistics for the magnitude of international financial centres, especially before 1960, and, indeed, no clear criteria regarding the basis on which to rank them. Nevertheless, all the suggestive indicators for 1913, a convenient vantage point for an approximate quantitative comparison between the two centres, clearly point to London's advantage.

In terms of financial capacity, Britain was by far the larger exporter of capital, with a stock of foreign investment reaching some $18.3bn. (about 42 per cent of the world's total) as against $8.7bn. for France (20 per cent and second only to London).[2] Many more foreign issues were floated in the City, whether for governments or private companies, than in Paris, and London's banks, primarily the merchant banks, were more likely to lead international syndicates. The bulk of world trade was financed through the medium of bills of exchange drawn on London, with Paris only playing a supporting, parallel role, primarily within Europe. London's huge discount market hardly had any equivalent in Paris. The London Stock Exchange was nearly twice as large as the Paris Bourse, with the nominal value of the securities quoted on the two markets being respectively £11.3bn. and £6.2bn. in 1913.

The largest French bank, the Crédit Lyonnais, was on a par with the leading three British clearing banks (London City & Midland Bank, Lloyds Bank, and London County & Westminster Bank), with deposits of *c.* £100m. in 1913. It had only been rivalled as the world's largest bank since the turn of the century. Although it had a network of foreign branches, including a powerful presence in the City, the Crédit Lyonnais's stature was a consequence of its domestic, rather than its international, affairs. In any case, British international banking was primarily conducted by merchant banks and corporate overseas banks, which numbered thirty-one in 1913 and had collectively 1,387 branches abroad.[3] There were fewer French overseas banks (a dozen), since the large deposit banks mostly undertook this type of business. Nonetheless, the Banque de l'Indochine, Banque de l'Algérie, and the Banque Impériale Ottomane were all major financial institutions.[4] In 1913, London was also host to some thirty foreign banks from twelve different countries, including the four largest French banks (Crédit Lyonnais, Société Générale, Comptoir National d'Escompte de Paris, Banque Nationale pour le Commerce et l'Industrie), three of the four 'D' German banks (Deutsche Bank, Dresdner Bank, and Disconto-Gesellschaft), and major American trust companies (Equitable Trust Company of New York, Guaranty Trust Company of New York, Farmers' Loan and Trust Company, International Banking Corporation).[5] There were some fifteen foreign banks in Paris in 1913, from seven countries, including five British (Lloyds Bank, London County & Westminster Bank, as well as the Anglo-Egyptian Bank, the London & River Plate Bank, and the Hong Kong & Shanghai Banking Corporation), but (for political reasons) no German banks.[6]

London was also more international, or truly global, as opposed to Paris's somewhat regional specialization. British capital flowed to nearly all parts of the world, though with a clear preference for the Americas (34 per cent for North America and 17 per cent for South America), the balance being more or less equally divided between Europe (13 per cent) Asia (14 per cent), Africa (11 per cent), and Australasia. French investors, on the other hand, favoured Europe (including Russia) and the Middle East (Ottoman Empire and Egypt), which together absorbed 60 per cent of their foreign investment. And, while the British Empire took up 40 per cent of the metropolis's overseas investment, the smaller and geographically more restricted French empire received a not insignificant 13 per cent.[7] These differences were largely reflected in the geographical distribution of the securities quoted on the London Stock Exchange and the Paris Bourse. However, both were highly internationalized markets, with foreign securities accounting for more than 50 per cent of stocks traded. As we have just seen, foreign banks established in London and the London-based multinational banks came from, and went to, a greater number of countries.

It should be emphasized that, on most if not all these counts, Paris was second only to London. The differences that have been highlighted must be considered alongside the intense vibrancy of Paris as an international financial centre during the *belle époque*, the French Edwardian Age, when its financial market is aptly described in this volume by Alain Plessis as a "noteworthy number two". Nevertheless, even during this era of broadly parallel developments, the gap between the first and second international financial centres was substantial, and this had more to do with London's exceptional position than with any failings on Paris's part.

The financial capacity of both centres was weakened by the impact of the First World War, though more so in the case of Paris, not least as a consequence of the Russian losses in 1917, than in that of London. While the pound struggled to return to gold at its pre-war parity, eventually accomplished in 1925, the franc suffered two severe crises in 1924 and 1926 before being officially stabilized in 1928 at a fifth of its pre-war value. French financial institutions were severely weakened by inflation and the depreciation of the franc. In real terms, the Crédit Lyonnais's total balance sheet did not regain its 1913 level before 1931.[8] In terms of size, the French big deposit banks were no longer in the same league as their English counterparts. In 1929, the total assets of Lloyds Bank, the largest British bank by this measure, reached £431m. and those of the National Provincial Bank, the smallest of the 'Big Five', £307m. as against £112m. for the Crédit Lyonnais and £108m. for the Société Générale.[9] A similar difference is observable in the two countries' long-term foreign investments. While Britain's total overseas investment reached $22.9bn. in 1938, France's had shrunk to $3.9bn., behind the United States ($11.5bn.) and even the Netherlands ($4.8bn.).[10]

It thus appears that during a period when both London and Paris lost some ground in terms of international status and influence, the gap between the two markets actually increased. The challenge to London's world leadership came from New York, not from Paris, and this contest over primacy only gradually developed because, if capital was henceforth more plentiful in New York, experience and expertise remained in London.[11] However, the role of Paris should not be overlooked, especially after 1926, once Poincaré had *de facto* stabilized the franc. Despite a conscious attempt at creating an acceptance market, Paris was never able to develop the range of financial services that would have enabled it seriously to challenge London. However, the Banque de France's gold reserves and sterling assets put Paris in a strong position vis-à-vis London and enhanced its international status, particularly during the immediate aftermath of Britain's departure from gold in 1931 (in many respects the real turning point in the City's history). This led the financial journalist Paul Einzig to write of a fight for financial supremacy between London, Paris, and New York during the early 1930s.[12] The depression of the

1930s and withdrawal into regional spheres of influence would put an end to this rivalry.

The divergent paths which London and Paris took during the second part of the twentieth century increased the gap separating these two centres with regard to their roles as providers of international financial services. Yet, the overall conditions prevailing within their two host countries were in many respects similar. For banks, the legacy of the war meant, as far as their business operations were concerned, a shift from commercial to government lending. Furthermore, state intervention took a further step after the war. In France, this led to the nationalization of the Banque de France and the four major deposit banks (though not the *banques d'affaires*), adding to a public sector that already included the Caisse des Dépôts et Consignations (the recipient of most of the assets of the savings banks). In Britain, only the Bank of England was nationalized, but the Big Five remained under strict official control, receiving precise instructions from the Treasury concerning not only their liquidity but their lending priorities; as Keynes had reflected, they hardly needed to be nationalized. In both countries, currency convertibility was only officially reintroduced at the close of 1958. And, since the 1930s, the two imperial powers had withdrawn into their colonial empire and zones of influence. The pound remained the world's second leading currency after the dollar thanks in large part to its role within the sterling area, while the franc remained the anchor of the smaller *zone franc*.

As is well known, the revival of the City of London during the 1960s was a result of the emergence of the Eurodollar market.[13] This is not the place to discuss the origins of these transactions in dollars outside the United States, which have to do with the United States' overseas investment and banking regulations, in particular the so-called Regulation Q (dating back to 1933 and enabling the Federal Reserve System to put a ceiling on the rate of interest that banks paid on domestic deposits). As foreign banks, initially British banks, were able to offer a higher rate, dollars were attracted to London. In the context of a comparison between London and Paris, it is of anecdotal interest to note that the first such dollar deposit is traditionally considered to have been made in Paris—at the Banque Commerciale pour l'Europe du Nord, a Russian bank whose telegraphic address was Eurobank, hence the appellation 'Eurodollar'. However, the Eurodollar market found its home in London, not in Paris, for reasons mainly connected with the amount of expertise existing in the City, its tradition as a global financial centre (which had not disappeared with the depression and the war), the English language, and the monetary authorities' relaxed attitude towards this new market.

Thereafter, the gap between the two centres grew much wider as London regained its position, alongside New York, as the world's leading financial centre. Indicators of size and performance are no more perfect for the late than for the early twentieth century, but those available are telling. International banking activity was far more intense in the United Kingdom than in France. The share of the former, measured by the foreign assets held by the country's deposit banks, was 17.1 per cent in 1965 and 25 per cent in 1970, as against 4.3 and 6.8 per cent for the latter.[14]

The number of branches of foreign banks in London rose from 54 in 1955 to 118 in 1970, as against 16 to 18 in Paris during the same period.[15] A wide array of figures is available for the very recent years in Richard Roberts's chapter in this volume, which compares London with other leading financial centres with regard to a number of key activities. The contrast between London and Paris is striking. There were 481 foreign banks in London in 2000 as against 187 in Paris. That same year, the United Kingdom's share of international cross-border lending was 19.5 per cent, as against 6 per cent for France. In 1998, London had a 32 per cent share of the average daily turnover in foreign exchange trading, as against 4 per cent for Paris. In 1999, 499 foreign companies were quoted on London Stock Exchange, as against 169 at the Paris Bourse.

These broad quantitative comparisons should assist to place the chapters that follow in an overall perspective. Throughout the twentieth century, there have always been substantial differences in both the scale and the scope of the operations of London and Paris as international financial centres. Moreover, these have been greater than those prevailing in most industrial sectors, which until the 1960s were far from insignificant.[16] And, unlike most sectors, and, indeed, the economy as a whole (whether measured by GDP or GDP per head), there has been no convergence between the size and overall influence of London and Paris as international financial centres since 1945. The two markets were in fact closer when the difference between the sizes of the British and the French economies was at its greatest (Britain's GDP was 69 per cent higher than France's in 1913), and further apart when this difference was at its narrowest (about 3 per cent in favour of France in 1989, and 8 per cent in favour of Britain in 2003).

This raises the question of the comparability of the two centres and, more generally, of the conditions under which comparative history can be undertaken. In a previous discussion of the matter, I had observed that comparative history would flourish when two alternative conditions were met: on the one hand, when the countries had a relative homogeneity—in terms of size, level of development, historical experience; and, on the other hand, when comparing a country with the leading power of the day, in order to measure the gap separating it from assumed best practice. As far as Britain and France are concerned, the first condition was met from the beginning of the seventeenth to the end of the nineteenth century. Thereafter, especially in the field of economic and business history, the motivation for Anglo-French comparisons weakens since the two countries were, in turn, overtaken by new competitors—the United States, Germany, and later Japan.[17]

From this perspective, London and Paris as international financial centres present some peculiarities in comparison with the two 'host' countries' general courses of economic and business development. It is, for example, significant that the discourse on the performance of the financial sector, whether by contemporaries or by historians, contains no reference to two popular though increasingly discarded concepts used to analyse the two countries' respective business and economic performance: French backwardness and British decline. This could be explained by the fact that both centres enjoyed what was undoubtedly their golden ages when Britain and France were no longer the world's two leading economic powers. Nonetheless, their standings were not identical. Before 1914, London's pre-eminence rested on Britain's position as a 'dominant economy', even though it had been overtaken as an industrial power by the United States during the 1880s and by Germany at the turn of the century. London's, and Britain's, position derived from strengths in foreign trade, services, and finance as well as discharging roles at the centre of the multilateral payments system.[18] Paris's rank as number two was possibly less in line with France's economic power and international influence. In both countries, there were discussions of a mature or *rentier* economy and concerns expressed about excessive capital exports to the detriment of domestic industrial investment, though they have been dispelled by historical research.[19] However, from a business history perspective, the emphasis has been on the dynamism and entrepreneurship of British and French bankers and financiers and, whatever doubts might have been raised, on the efficiency of their capital market.

The issue of decline has been discussed in connection with both centres, after the First and, especially, the Second World War, but in a context quite different from similar debates related to other fields of business activity or to the two countries' overall economic performance. Interestingly, the theme of entrepreneurial failure is rarely found in analyses of the performance of London and Paris as international financial centres. The concept, admittedly, has become less fashionable in business and economic history, though it has far from entirely disappeared and is still referred to in different guises, whether structural or cultural. As far as London and Paris are concerned, the causes of decline have been considered as primarily exogenous: war, inflation, the sale of foreign assets, constraints on the balance of payments, state intervention and regulation—which all played in favour of the new main contender in world finance: New York. Criticisms have been made of financial institutions, but they do not necessarily apply to financial centres taken as a whole. Paris's lacklustre role as an international market after the Second World War has not been attributed to any failure on the part of the French banks but rather to the constraints resulting from the 'overdraft economy' (financing through banks rather than capital markets) established by the authorities. Conversely, the fact that virtually all the merchant banks, once the flower of the City, have been taken over by foreign banks during the last fifteen years of the twentieth century could be considered as a case of entrepreneurial failure, though this does not affect the global success of the City, which is enjoying a position reminiscent of its pre-1914 'glory days'.

Whatever these common features, the experiences of London and Paris have also presented, as we have seen, a sharp contrast over the course of the twentieth century. This raises the question: why has there not been a greater convergence between the size, range of services, and international openness of the two centres since 1945? The question is relevant given, as we have noted above, the 'comparability' of Britain and France and the convergence that has taken place with regard to most other aspects of their economies. Moreover, financial activities have always played an important role in France's economic life, and repeated attempts have been made to promote the role of Paris as an international financial centre and challenge London's pre-eminence. The most serious contest was mounted during the 1860s, when France, spurred by the dynamism of the Pereire brothers and their rivalry with the Rothschilds, was exporting more capital than Britain, and Napoleon III seized the opportunity to launch the Latin Monetary Union and a proposal for a monetary unification.[20] Paris had no real possibility of supplanting London, but the ambition was there, as it was to be, as we have seen, in the 1920s and, again, in the 1960s. During the latter decade, a series of liberalizing measures intended to enhance the importance of Paris as an international financial centre, in particular within the context of the Common Market, were taken. However, as in the 1920s, they remained short lived and partially implemented, and any chance of success was thwarted by the events of May 1968.

The reasons for the diverging paths followed by London and Paris over the second half of the twentieth century are to be found in both the two markets' capabilities to rise to real global status and the strategic choices made by political and business leaders. As far as capabilities are concerned, although the two centres declined from 1914, London had fared better, being the much larger centre during the 1950s, supplying a far wider range of services and international connections. But it was somnolent. For Lord Franks, chairman of Lloyds Bank between 1954 and 1962 and a former academic and senior civil servant, 'it was like driving a powerful car at 20 miles an hour'.[21] Yet the power, inherited from more than a century of world dominance, was there and, certainly, in greater abundance than in Paris or any other European centre. Making it run at full capacity, however, could no longer be done on the British economy's dwindling strength. This could only be attained through internationalization, starting with the birth of the Eurodollar market and culminating in 'Big Bang' in 1986. The choice of opening up the City was in many respects deliberate, though it was taken in several steps extending over two decades and it is doubtful whether all its implications, ultimately leading to the 'Wimbledonization' of the City in the 1990s, had been foreseen.

Paris did not have the same opportunities for growth during the 1950s and 1960s. Convergence in the financial sector took place during the *Trente Glorieuses*, but mainly in domestic banking as measured, however imperfectly, by the size of the French big deposit banks. These institutions, by the early 1970s, caught up with their British counterparts and then overtook them a decade later. But not in international banking. The *dirigisme* of the French state certainly played a role in this, though liberalizing measures were taken from the late 1950s. However, the degree of control exerted by the British Treasury over the financial sector should not be underestimated. Nonetheless, a distinction was made between retail domestic banking, denominated in sterling, where exchange controls remained in place until 1979, and wholesale international banking, denominated in foreign currencies, above all in dollars, which the Bank of England, unlike other European central banks, including the Banque de France, was prepared to leave mainly unregulated. When deregulation took place in all major financial centres during the 1980s and

1990s, London had already asserted its position, with New York and Tokyo, as one of the world's three global centres.

Strategic choices were thus partly dictated by existing opportunities and, vice versa, in permanently changing conditions. But they are also the result of idiosyncratic economic and political cultures, which are different though not diametrically opposed—and thus comparable—in Britain and France. Be that as it may, French financial leaders have tended to favour institutions, whether publicly or privately owned, over markets. French banks have been more successful internationally than Paris as an international financial centre, despite the crisis experienced by Crédit Lyonnais in 1994. When faced with the same opportunities, it is doubtful whether the French authorities would have been prepared to open up the Paris markets to the extent that their British counterparts eventually did—no doubt a heritage of Britain's world role. In the same way, the global role traditionally played by the City can be contrasted with Paris's more European tradition, reflected in the leading French banks' European strategies. There is also a specific financial culture which, though present in France and within the Parisian business elite,[22] has been pervasive in Britain since the eighteenth century. This point arises whether one considers the 'weight' of finance in the British economy or the position of the financial elites in British society,[23] a peculiarity well described by the concept of 'gentlemanly capitalism' coined by Peter Cain and Tony Hopkins in the mid-1980s.[24]

In the end, Paris appears to have been more in the 'norm' than London, if the 'norm' is for a country to have an international financial centre more or less commensurate with its 'host' economy's size and international influence. In that respect, the City is far more an 'offshore' centre than Paris, bringing nonetheless enormous benefits to London and south-eastern England, and to the British economy as a whole. However, the risks associated with such a status remain to be properly assessed. On the other hand, the City has been increasingly contributing to the economy of the European Union, with a 55 per cent share of its wholesale financial services in 2000. It has been estimated that a fragmentation of this concentration would result in severe losses not only for London but also for the entire European economy.[25] There remains the question of why Paris, given the deeper international financial traditions existing in France than in Germany and the convergence between the French and German economies, has not managed to steal a march upon Frankfurt. The answer will have to be left for another volume, though Paris's ascendancy might have taken place by the time it is published.

In the meantime, this volume concentrates on London and Paris, and it should by now be clear that this bilateral comparison is a worthwhile undertaking. Multilateral comparisons or other bilateral comparisons could be equally or possibly even more interesting, but they would serve a different purpose. As much as a comparison between London and Paris as international financial centres, this book intends to be an Anglo-French comparison; in other words, to consider, through the prism of finance, several aspects of the two countries' economic, business, social, and political histories. This is undertaken in a 'parallel' rather than in a direct comparative way. The following chapters are not in essence comparative; each primarily deals with either London or Paris, or with an aspect of either centre's financial activities. The objective of this Introduction has been to give the reader a few comparative keys with which to link together the national studies rather than summarize them. In addition, a broad chronological and interpretative framework is provided in the first two chapters, by Ranald Michie and Alain Plessis, who offer an overview of the long-term development of each centre from the late nineteenth to the late twentieth century.

For the rest of the book, the comparison between London and Paris has been conceived as a contrast between two eras of globalization: the pre-1914 years (with four chapters) and the last four decades of the twentieth century (with six chapters), while two chapters deal with the intervening period of national and regional withdrawal. Throughout, each chapter on the City is matched by one concerned with Paris and, for the periods 1890–1914 and 1958–80 (which each comprise of four chapters), two primarily concerned with the functioning of the capital markets, and two with the networks of relationships and the strategies of the leading protagonists. Nevertheless, differences in both content and approach still remain between parallel chapters, with archive-based case studies—more frequent in the case of Paris—occasionally matching literature surveys. Such differences are unavoidable given the uneven state of historical research on the subject in the two countries and their idiosyncratic historical questioning, not to mention the authors' personalities. These should not deter from the capturing and comparing the nature of each centre and its market and institutional surroundings at a given period, and from better understanding the political economy of Britain and France in the twentieth century.

Notes

I should like to thank Eric Bussière and Philip Cottrell for their helpful comments on an earlier draft of this chapter.

1. On definitions of financial centres, see C. P. Kindleberger, 'The Formation of Financial Centers', *Princeton Studies in International Finance*, 36 (1974), 1–78; H. C. Reed, *The Preeminence of International Financial Centers* (New York, 1981); G. Jones, 'International Financial Centres in Asia, the Middle East and Australia', in Y. Cassis (ed.), *Finance and Financiers in European History* (Cambridge, 1992), 405–28; R. Roberts (ed.), *International Financial Centres: Concepts, Development and Dynamics* (Aldershot, 1994).
2. United Nations, *International Capital Movements during the Interwar Period* (New York, 1949).
3. G. Jones, *British Multinational Banking 1830–1990* (Oxford, 1993).
4. E. Kaufmann, *La Banque en France* (Paris, 1914), 181–201; H. Bonin, 'L'Outre-mer, marché pour la banque commerciale de 1875 à 1985?', in *La France et l'outre-mer. Un siècle de relations monétaires et financières* (Paris, 1998), 437–83.
5. Y. Cassis, *La City de Londres 1870–1914* (Paris, 1987), 40–2.
6. Kaufmann, *La Banque en France*; L. Dufourq-Lagelouse, *Les Banques étrangères en France* (Paris, 1922).

7. M. Simon, 'The Pattern of New British Portfolio Investment, 1865–1914', in A. R. Hall (ed.), *The Export of Capital from Britain 1870–1914* (London, 1968), 15–44; J. Bouvier, R. Girault, and J. Thobie, *La France impériale 1880–1914* (Paris, 1982), 99; J. Marseille, *Empire colonial et capitalisme français. Histoire d'un divorce* (Paris, 1984), 100–1.
8. O. Feiertag, 'Le Crédit Lyonnais et le Trésor Public dans l'entre-deux-guerres: les ressorts de l'économie d'endettement du XXe siècle', in B. Desjardins et al., *Le Crédit Lyonnais 1863–1986* (Geneva, 2003), 809.
9. *Banking Almanac* (1929).
10. C. H. Feinstein and K. Watson, 'Private International Capital Flows in Europe in the Inter-War Period', in C. H. Feinstein (ed.), *Banking, Currency, and Finance in Europe between the Wars* (Oxford, 1995), 97.
11. K. Burk, 'Money and Power: The Shift from Great Britain to the United States', in Cassis (ed.), *Finance and Financiers*, 359–69.
12. P. Einzig, *The Fight for Financial Supremacy* (London, 1931). See also P. Coste, *Les Grands Marchés financiers: Paris, Londres, New York* (Paris, 1932).
13. A recent discussion of the various aspects and implications of the phenomenon can be found in S. Battilossi and Y. Cassis (eds.), *European Banks and the American Challenge: Competition and Cooperation in International Banking under Bretton Woods* (Oxford, 2002).
14. IMF, *International Financial Statistics Yearbook* (1981, 1988).
15. C. Schenk, 'International Financial Centres, 1958–1971: Competitiveness and Complementarity', in Battilossi and Cassis (eds.), *European Banks and the American Challenge*, 75.
16. For comparative data, see Y. Cassis, 'Divergence and Convergence in British and French Business in the Nineteenth and Twentieth Centuries', in Y. Cassis, F. Crouzet, and T. Gourvish (eds.), *Management and Business in Britain and France: The Age of the Corporate Economy (Oxford, 1995),* 1–29.
17. Cassis, 'Divergence and Convergence in British and French Business', 1–2. See also Y. Cassis, *Big Business: The European Experience in the Twentieth Century* (Oxford, 1997).
18. See F. Crouzet, *L'Économie de la Grande-Bretagne victorienne* (Paris, 1978).
19. See S. Pollard, 'Capital Exports, 1870–1914: Harmful or Beneficial?', *Economic History Review*, 38 4 (1985); M. Lévy-Leboyer, 'La Balance des paiements et l'exportation des capitaux français' in M. Lévy-Leboyer (ed.), *La Position internationale de la France, XIXe–XXe* siècles (Paris, 1977).
20. See J. Autin, *Les Frères Pereire. Le Bonheur d'entreprendre* (Paris, 1984), B. Gille, *Histoire de la maison Rothschild*, 2 vols. (Geneva, 1965); L. Einaudi, *Money and Politics: European Monetary Unification and the International Gold Standard (1865–1873)* (Oxford, 2001).
21. Quoted in A. Sampson, *The Money Lenders* (London, 1981), 121.
22. See for example L. Bergeron, *Les Capitalistes en France 1780–1914* (Paris, 1978); A. Plessis, 'Bankers in French Society 1860s–1960s', in Cassis (ed.), *Finance and Financiers*, 147–60.
23. See Y. Cassis, 'Financial Elites Revisited', in R. Michie and P. Williamson (eds.), *The British Government and the City of London in the Twentieth Century* (Cambridge, 2004).
24. P. J. Cain and A. G. Hopkins, *British Imperialism: Innovation and Expansion 1688–1914* and *British Imperialism: Crisis and Deconstruction 1914–1990* (London, 1993). The concept of 'gentlemanly capitalism' first appeared in Cain and Hopkins's two articles: 'Gentlemanly Capitalism and British Expansion Overseas, I. The Old Colonial System, 1688–1850', *Economic History Review*, 39 4 (1986), 501–25 and 'Gentlemanly Capitalism

and British Expansion Overseas, II: New Imperialism, 1850–1945', *ibid.* 40 1 (1997), 1–26.

25. Centre for Economic and Business Research, *The City's Importance to the European Union Economy* (Nov. 2000), quoted in R. Roberts and D. Kynaston, *City State* (London, 2001), 189.

PART I

London and Paris in Long-Term Perspective, 1890–2000

2

A Financial Phoenix: The City of London in the Twentieth Century

Ranald Michie

The great advantage that historians possess is that they know the future of the past they are examining. As a result, there is a certain sense of inevitability to the process. It appears inevitable that London would emerge as the world's premier financial centre in the nineteenth century owing to the success of the British economy and the fact that Britain was at the centre of a vast empire. Equally inevitable appears the decline of London as a financial centre in the twentieth century, with the disappearance of the empire and the eclipse of Britain as an economic power. Consequently, extrapolating from general economic and political trends the rise and fall of London as a financial centre appears relatively easy to explain. However, on closer investigation, such general explanations of cause and effect appear both more complex and uncertain, especially for the period after 1900. In the twentieth century, the British economy was overtaken by that of Germany, which came to be the dominant force in Europe, but that was not accompanied by a similar status for either Berlin before 1939 or Frankfurt after 1945. Instead, London remained the most important financial centre in Europe, by a large margin, throughout the twentieth century. This was despite the process of European economic, political, and monetary union after 1945 that left Britain on the fringes. Similarly, in world terms, the United States' economy came to dwarf that of Britain, as did that of Japan, but London remained an international centre of, at least, equal importance to both New York and Tokyo. Clearly there is a paradox to be explained here which cannot be ascribed simply to inertia, because New York did appear to have displaced London as the dominant financial centre in the world as a result of the Second World War. The revival of London as a global financial centre after 1960 suggests that not only did the City of London possess underlying strengths, unrelated to general economic and political forces, but also that these strengths were sufficient to allow it to recover its position in the global hierarchy. Inertia alone could not have achieved that.[1]

Although it is by no means clear what criteria should be used to measure the relative importance of financial centres, there appears to be no doubt that the City of London was the most important financial centre in the world by the beginning of the twentieth century.[2] To contemporaries, it appeared obvious because London possessed more banks, issuing houses, investment companies, and brokerage firms than anywhere else, as well as larger and more active financial markets. After Charles Turner had toured the streets of the City of London in 1902 he was in no doubt that

> London is the chief abode of the great god money, whose throne, visible to all men, is the heart of the City.... From here the greatest and most numerous of his activities are conducted; for London, in spite of the rivalry of New York and the growing importance of Paris and Berlin as money centres, is still paramount as a headquarters of exchange and banking.[3]

On the eve of the First World War the City of London continued to occupy this position, possessing as it did the largest money, capital, and securities markets in the world and the only ones with a truly international role. In 1912/13 L. D. Wilgress, a Canadian banker with both New York and Paris open to him, noted that 'London is the word's financial centre, and is the clearing house for international payments.'[4] Similarly, in 1914/15 another Canadian banker, W. W. Swanson, observed that 'although New York, Berlin and Paris have become great money centres they have never been able, despite the adoption of every expedient they could think of, to seriously threaten the paramount position of London as a world market'.[5] These views of contemporaries have been endorsed by financial historians who also see the City of London as the dominant financial centre of the pre-First World War era, only disagreeing on the degree to which it was being challenged by others, most notably New York, Paris, and Berlin.[6]

Nevertheless, though the City of London was the most important financial centre in the world, finance did not completely dominate its activities. London remained a major port, and thus home to a host of commercial, marine, and related activities before 1914. The City of London as a financial centre was taking shape in addition to the City of London as a commercial centre, not instead of it. What were disappearing in the City were residential and manufacturing activities, as the space they had filled and the employment they had once provided could no longer compete with the rents and incomes generated by trade and finance. At the same time, the City of London had become an increasingly cosmopolitan centre as international rather than domestic activities dominated its activities. In London, for example, were to be found representatives of banks from every country in the world while activity on the money and other markets was both responsive to, and a major influence upon, international financial forces. Similarly, merchants, brokers, dealers, and others in the City provided an essential link in the matching of supply and demand worldwide, aided by the ability to communicate quickly and reliably around the globe using the telegraph. The development of international telegraphy had allowed the City to emerge as the central market for numerous commodities, permitting positions to be adjusted on a continuous basis and so avoid sudden shocks by the anticipation of problems and the sharing of risk. Furthermore the continuing importance of international commerce in London remained a major spur for the development of other activities in the City. The insurance market, Lloyd's, was principally engaged in the insurance of ships and the cargoes they carried, irrespective of nationality, while activity on the Baltic Exchange was concerned with the employment of ships internationally. Similarly, the growth of the City of London as a centre for the world mining industry was related both to the role it played in the international distribution of minerals and metals and to its importance as a financial centre. Generally, the City was one of the few centres, if not the only one, that possessed the range and depth of expertise, connections, and markets that was required to organize, evaluate, and finance major projects in such fields as transport and mining, considering the risks and uncertainties involved.[7]

Lying at the heart of the City of London as a financial centre in this period were the numerous individuals and firms that undertook an enormous variety of financial business. The composition of these was continually changing as some groups declined in importance or disappeared, like the private bankers, while others grew steadily in importance, such as joint-stock banks operating both domestically and overseas. Generally, what was driving the City forward as a financial centre was the continual turnover of personnel and firms as the new replaced the old, the foreign replaced the British, the public replaced the private, and the balance between enterprising and conservative waxed and waned. Most marked of all was the degree of functional specialization that existed in the City in this period compared to other financial centres, including long-established ones in Europe like Paris and Berlin. Only a financial centre of the size and connections of the City of London could support the degree of specialization evident by the late nineteenth/early twentieth century. By 1913 there were some 226 banks and quasi-banks with offices in London. These ranged from the merchant banks and discount houses to the major British joint-stock banks or the branches of large European banks. British banking, for instance, was increasingly dominated by a small number of banks run from City head offices but operating nationwide branch networks, while the City was also home to a number of banks that operated branch networks in Australia, New Zealand, South Africa, Latin America, and Asia. In contrast, there were also numerous small privately owned banks in the City that survived by focusing on specialist niches like trade credit and new issues. In turn, those banks with a presence in the City were linked to thousands of other banks and financial intermediaries all over the world not only through their own offices but also through agencies and correspondents. The result was to make London the payments centre of the world economy, for through these connections it was possible to settle almost any international transaction there. Hence the fact that the 'bill on London' was the near universal currency of international trade and finance, whether it involved transactions between China and the United States or France and Australia.[8]

The fact that London was the payments centre of the international economy had major implications for its money market. As payments were always being made or received in the City, the result was that it was home to money from around the world which was temporarily idle as it awaited employment. Thus it was not surprising that the London money market was both very large and internationally important. In addition, as the practice of banking spread around the world so did the need for banks to employ temporarily but profitably the huge sums of money that they had to keep idle in case of general demand, either in the form of withdrawals by depositors or borrowing by regular customers. British banks had long been accustomed to send such funds to the London money market. The very size and sophistication of that money market permitted banks to lend very large sums and recall them when otherwise required, as the reduction of supply by one bank would be matched by the increase of another because the overall level generally remained stable. This process was greatly aided by the Bank of England for, with its large reserve of cash, it acted as lender of last resort when a shortage did develop. Thus it was only to be expected that as banking systems developed elsewhere in the world they would avail themselves of such a facility. Also, the more use that was made of the London money market the better it became at employing money for short periods at positive rates of return, so attracting more money from around the world. In turn the City of London had to find uses for these funds that would permit interest to be paid to those that lent them, while being sufficiently flexible so that any amount could be employed or withdrawn whenever required. Consequently, the City was at the very hub of international trade finance, for there was a constant need to provide the short-term credit required in order for producers in one country to receive payment before their products were eventually delivered and sold in another. Before 1914, the exports and imports of countries like Australia, Argentina, South Africa, and Japan were largely financed in London, no matter the source or destination of the trade, while even countries such as Germany and the United States relied on the City for trade credit. Though other financial centres possessed large and active money markets before 1914, such as Paris, Berlin, Amsterdam, and New York, none was as large and important as London.[9]

However, even this dominant position in international trade finance was not sufficient to absorb all the short-term funds seeking employment in London and so they were increasingly used for long-term investment, but in such a way as to allow their easy recall. Railway companies, for example, had an enormous demand for funds in order to build and equip transport systems all over the world. For this purpose they issued securities such as shares, stocks, bonds, and debentures. Though not redeemable these were transferable, and with the development of stock exchanges they became easy to buy and sell, so allowing them to be held using short-term funds. By the First World War the London Stock Exchange was, by far, the largest and most international in the world, providing a market for securities with a paid-up value of £11.3bn., of which at least half was foreign.[10] This international commitment of the London capital market, however, has led to the charge that so successful was the City as a global financial centre before 1914 that it ignored the financial needs of the British economy. This view is part of a constant debate that sees not only benefits to Britain from hosting such an important international financial centre, through the employment and profits generated, but also costs in terms of the diversion of domestic funds abroad. Clearly, any investigation of the London capital market for this period does reveal it to be heavily orientated towards the issue of securities for foreign governments and railways rather than British business, for that was largely left to provincial centres. This has been seen not as some natural division within the capital market but as systematic bias against domestic finance within the City, leaving British industry short of the finance required to fund new enterprises, especially in such technologically important areas as the production of motor vehicles and chemicals and the provision of electricity and telecommunications. However, detailed investigations of City–industry relations over this period reveal strong and flexible links and an absence of any financing difficulties from either bank lending or new issues of securities. Consequently, there appears little evidence that the City of London's development as a financial centre before 1914 was, itself, directly detrimental to the growth of the British economy, including manufacturing industry.[11] Instead, what emerges is how wide-ranging and sophisticated was the capital market in London in those years. Arranging large loans for foreign governments and corporations was a complex business, requiring a great deal of expertise and effort and the acceptance of considerable risk. It also took place in a competitive environment both within the City, with new firms always ready to challenge the old, and internationally, as rival centres such as Paris and New York could exploit any reluctance or excessive profit-taking by London. Equally complex and risky was the tailoring of finance for smaller industrial concerns but that was also not neglected in the City at this time, even extending abroad when the opportunity arose. A growing demand from Canadian industrial companies for finance met a ready response in London, for example, with Canadian financiers migrating there to handle the business.[12]

Though there can be no doubt that the City of London flourished before 1914, offering a range and depth of financial services and markets—unrivalled anywhere else in the world—by focusing on particular areas of the City, there have also been suggestions that it was becoming less dynamic. Especially through a focus confined to the merchant banking houses the impression is gained that a closed elite increasingly dominated the City, and that this financial elite, through education and marriage, was being absorbed into the long-established landed elite of southern England, losing its dynamic drive in the process, though gaining sufficient political influence to ensure that government policy was in its exclusive interest.[13] Certainly, evidence of the fusion of wealthy families in the City with those from the landed aristocracy can be found to corroborate this trend. However, the City of London was a much larger and more varied place than one populated by merchant banking families with connections to the landed gentry, for very few were in that position.[14] Instead, it was both open and cosmopolitan with a continuous entry and exit of individuals and firms. As such, it is difficult to accept that a handful of families could so influence its structure or so direct its affairs for it to ignore the opportunities open to it. The evidence points otherwise. Similarly, evidence is lacking to support the view that those in the City were sufficiently powerful, or even interested, to have an effect on policy-making, for the conclusion that emerges is that all they wanted was to be left to get on with their business.[15] Generally, it is clear that on the eve of the First World War the City of London stood at the very pinnacle of its importance as a financial centre, even though commerce continued to be an important element within it, and competition existed for it from other financial centres in Britain and around the world. As Mira Wilkins has observed, 'There was something very special about London,' while a recent econometric study of one aspect of the City's activities noted, 'Britain had the largest and most liquid capital market in the world in the early 20th century.'[16]

On the eve of the First World War, the City of London was the leading financial centre in the world, with a quantitative and qualitative lead over all of its rivals. It was also the most important commercial centre in the world, being at the very centre of international trade and shipping. Thus, it was inevitable that an intense and prolonged war between the major economic powers of the world, and involving their far-flung empires, would have serious consequences for the City of London. The City was always vulnerable to financial crises anywhere in the globe, given its position as the international financial centre, but ways and means to avoid, diffuse, and minimize these had been devised over the years. What could not be devised was any simple means of preventing a crisis created by the outbreak of hostilities on the scale that began in late 1914. Such a conflict not only shattered the payment flows that took place continuously between the countries involved, in response to commercial and financial transactions, but also destroyed the trust upon which so much lending and borrowing, buying and selling, took place.[17] The result was a breakdown in the international payments mechanism, which had become essential if the world economy was to continue functioning successfully, and was the basis of the City of London's role as a global financial centre. With the collapse of both that mechanism, and trust generally, the First World War was a major blow to the City of London for it undermined one of the most important advantages it possessed. It was also not easy for the City to recover during the continuance of hostilities. In order to mobilize the savings of its population for the war effort the British government increasingly monopolized the London money and capital markets through a combination of appeals to patriotism and official/unofficial controls. Altogether, the National Debt, for instance, rose from £706.2m. in 1914 to £7,481.1m. in 1919. The result was to deny access to the London markets to those whose needs were not war related, so greatly reducing the City's ability to finance international trade and investment. As financial transactions between nations continued despite the war, the consequence was the development of alternative arrangements and the use of financial centres other than London. Financial transactions were re-routed, encouraging the use of local centres and direct links between economies once served by London intermediaries. Alternative financial centres were also favoured, as with Amsterdam in the neutral Netherlands or New York in the United States, which was far removed from hostilities and did not go to war until 1917. Foreign companies and governments ceased to borrow in London, unless permitted to do so because they were allies, while much international trade not involving Britain or the shipment of war supplies had to be financed elsewhere.[18]

Compounding the City of London's difficulties was the forced disposal of the huge holdings of American securities, which had been slowly built up by British investors, as the British government desperately needed dollars in order to complete its purchase of vital war materials in the United States. Around £850m. or $4.0bn. of these securities were sold during and immediately after the war. In addition, the British government also borrowed extensively in the United States during the war as a direct means of obtaining the currency required to make purchases there. Total such borrowing had reached £1.4bn. by the end of the war.[19] As the economy of the United States was booming at this time American investors were in a position both to buy back those securities held abroad and purchase those being issued by foreign governments, while US banks were able to provide the credit needed to finance the country's international trade. This greatly enhanced the position of New York as a financial centre compared to London as the City lost most of its American business. As New York was already a major financial centre before the First World War, dominating the money and capital markets of North America, it possessed the personnel, banks, brokerage houses, and markets that were able to replace the services once provided by London, not only in the United States itself but also in areas such as Latin America. It was the First World War that made New York into an international financial centre.[20]

The City of London was not destroyed during the First World War, having suffered little physical damage, while Britain both escaped invasion and emerged victorious. One informed contemporary, R. C. Wyse, writing in the *Economic Journal* in 1918, was of the opinion that the City of London remained the pre-eminent financial centre in the world, though accepting that its position had been considerably undermined.[21] Thus, the City emerged intact if diminished from the war, ready to rebuild its position, despite the increased importance of New York. The rapid growth of a foreign exchange market in the early 1920s, for example, indicated the City of London's continuing ability to exploit new opportunities and profit from adversity. In the face of post-war monetary turmoil the value of currencies was no longer stable against each other, as it had been under the pre-war gold standard, creating a need both to trade currencies and to minimize the risks of rapid depreciation/appreciation. The response in London was rapid with the development of the largest and most active market in currencies, utilizing the latest communications and information processing technology and attracting numerous brokers and dealers from among the City's financial community. 'As it exists today the London foreign exchange market is very largely an after-war development,' was the view in 1922 of one participant, Dudley Ward of the British Overseas Bank.[22] During the 1920s the City of London also tried hard to reassert its position in the financial activities and markets in which it had been so important before 1914. This was being gradually achieved in the money market, encompassing such activities as trade credit and foreign exchange, but London had lost its position as the centre of international finance to New York. During the 1920s it was to New York that most of those wishing to borrow resorted, as access to London for other than imperial borrowers remained restricted. American investors and financial institutions possessed a far greater capacity to meet demands than did those in Britain. Thus New York replaced London as the capital market of the world, with all that meant for the investment banks and the stock exchange. Even within Europe, though centres such as Berlin, Frankfurt, and Vienna had been crippled by the war and the immediate post-war political and economic difficulties, Amsterdam, Zurich, and Paris were serious rivals benefiting from the neutrality of the first two and the prosperity of France in the 1920s for the third.[23]

Nevertheless, London remained a financial centre of the first rank in the 1920s. It rivalled New York's money market, was more important in areas such as commerce, shipping, and marine insurance, and was only outclassed in terms of the capital market. Even then major traditional borrowers returned to the London capital market, such as Australia which had £525m. outstanding there by 1930, while new ones also appeared as in the case of German companies faced with the collapse of domestic savings due to hyperinflation. Generally, foreign financial institutions continued to see it as important to have a presence in London. The financial agent of the Russian communist government—the Moscow Narodny Bank—opened a London office in 1919, the Bank of China established its first overseas branch there in 1929, while four Japanese banks set up operations in London during the 1920s. No other centre could offer such a number and range of international connections as could London, and so it continued to act as a magnet for those needing direct access to the world's payments system. In turn, that continued to create a demand both for the traditional facilities of the money and capital markets and for new requirements like the foreign exchange market.[24] At this stage there was little substantial change in the structure and composition of the City, for it still remained both a commercial and financial centre, and one with a very pronounced international orientation. This was despite the growth in importance of domestic finance, whether in the form of the British government's greatly increased short- and long-term borrowing requirements, or the needs of British business to tap the London capital market because of the effects of low profitability and high taxation upon internal and informal sources of funds. In response to these needs there was a significant reorientation within the City towards domestic opportunities. Activity in the discount market, for example, was dominated by the government's borrowing requirements in the form of Treasury bills rather than international trade finance. Similarly, many finance houses in the City, whether new or old, became involved in the conversion of established British firms into public companies as well as the flotation of entirely new enterprises, especially in fields involving new technology and new products. Especially, in the late 1920s there was a flurry of such companies attracting the interest of numerous new investors who had first acquired securities during the war as a result of the War Loans issued on behalf of the government. As a result the London Stock Exchange became an increasingly important market for the shares of British companies, ranging from both established national concerns to small, speculative ones, bringing it into conflict with the provincial markets.[25]

However, the focus of the City remained international in the 1920s for there was the expectation that the global business on which it had thrived before the war would revive. At the same time London-based firms and markets faced strong competition in the field of domestic finance from provincial centres, for these had long-established expertise and connections in these areas. In the wake of the 1931 financial crisis, when Britain had to abandon the gold standard, the City of London was forced to accept that there was to be no rapid and general revival of international business. The events of 1931 dealt a damaging blow not only to the importance of sterling as an international currency but also to London as a global financial centre, because the pound was no longer freely exchangeable for gold at a fixed exchange rate and so its value in terms of other currencies was not guaranteed. For those foreign banks using London to employ their idle balances remuneratively there was no longer the certainty that the value of their money would remain the same, unless they were in the sterling area, and that it could be easily and quickly reclaimed when needed. As a consequence there was now a greater risk attached to employing spare funds in London, as well as lending and borrowing there, if the transaction might require the conversion into and out of sterling. The 1931 monetary crisis represented a turning point for the City of London as an international financial centre for it destroyed much of the confidence that had continued to be placed in it by the international community in the 1920s, despite the problems that beset the British economy at that time. Britain's leaving the gold standard in 1931 provoked a more serious financial crisis around the world than had the Wall Street Crash of 1929. The result was to usher in a period when the role of international financial centres, including London, was greatly diminished, for the movement of money from one country to another became circumscribed by government-imposed controls, and there was a wariness among banks and investors about placing money abroad because of the greater risks they now ran. A number of British merchant banks with strong connections with Germany almost collapsed, for instance, when that country's government declared a standstill on the repayment of foreign loans in the early 1930s, so illustrating the risks being run in international finance. Similarly, the French bank Société Générale ran down its operations in London during the 1930s, though still maintaining its branch there.[26]

In the face of the exchange controls, embargoes, preferential agreements, barter arrangements and cartels that became standard practice in the international economy in the 1930s the scope for the City of London to operate as a global commercial and financial centre was considerably reduced. As Richard Roberts has observed, 'Overall, the 1930s were little short of calamitous for most aspects of the City's international activities.'[27] However, as this was a general phenomenon that worked against all international financial centres in the 1930s it was not to the particular disadvantage of London. Otherwise, it would have further undermined the City of London's position. As it was, the operations of all financial centres were so circumscribed by internal and external controls that if became impossible for them to displace the City of London from its long-established position. Such was the severity of the crisis following the Wall Street Crash that the US government intervened to restrict the operations of both banks and the financial markets, while continuing turmoil in foreign exchanges forced the United States off the gold standard in 1933. As a result many financial observers, like Einzig writing in 1933, or Truptil in 1936, were of the opinion that London remained the financial centre of the world economy, despite the challenges from Paris in Europe and New York internationally. Similarly, those who have looked either at rival financial centres or at international finance generally in the 1930s have continued to stress the advantages that London possessed compared to all others, especially in terms of its money market. No other centre, for example, could yet match the extensive links that London possessed not only throughout the Empire, and with those countries that had tied their currencies to sterling, but generally in the world. One estimate for 1932/3 suggested that over two-thirds of the world's banks possessed a branch, an agent, or a correspondent in London, while in 1938 London was also the head office for twenty-four British overseas banks with 2,315 branches spread around the globe, and this placed it in a position far superior to any other financial centre in the world in terms of international connections.[28]

Nevertheless, despite these advantages the level of international business undertaken in the City of London was greatly reduced in the 1930s. One illustration of that was the issue of securities in London on behalf of overseas borrowers. These were running at £150m. per annum in 1927/8 but fell to £50m. in 1931 and then collapsed to £21m. by 1935 before recovering slightly to around £30m. in 1937/8. As this was echoed in other areas of the City there was no alternative but to try and generate more domestic business, and this is what took place in the 1930s. Issues of domestic securities, for example, held up much better than those on behalf of foreign borrowers during the collapse of the early 1930s, and then grew strongly thereafter, before declining as the Second World War approached. In 1935–7 such issues were averaging around £165m. per annum. Both established houses and new firms turned to the finance of British industrial firms as an alternative to the international business that now appeared permanently lost. Similarly, the money market was increasingly concerned with meeting the short-term financial needs of the British government rather than providing the credit required for international trade, which remained very depressed. In insurance the covering of risks for British motor car drivers flourished, as automobile ownership grew, while marine insurance languished because of the depression in world shipping due to the collapse of international trade. Throughout the 1930s the City of London appeared to grow as a major financial centre, judging from the increased numbers reported as working there, but that success masked a collapse in international business and a growth of domestic activities. This switch was achieved in competition with other financial centres in Britain and was to their disadvantage as they lost business, personnel, and firms to London during the 1930s.[29]

Throughout all these events the government had an increasing influence over the City, having become involved with the outbreak of the First World War and the financial crisis that accompanied it. What was established during the war was a close relationship between the government, the Treasury, and the Bank of England that was much more intimate than in the past, when the Bank acted as the government's financial agent. Now the government, through the Treasury, was using the Bank of England to influence or direct the City in line with changing policy requirements. Thus the government intervened in the City's money and capital markets to ensure than its own financing requirements were given priority. What this meant was that other borrowers, whether British or foreign, were either denied access completely, as with overseas companies, or faced major restrictions, especially when it involved the use of foreign exchange. The government even went so far as to requisition those dollar securities held by British investors, so that they could be sold in New York and the proceeds used to purchase vital war materials from the United States. Though control over the City was lessened after the end of hostilities, the pressure remained, being exerted through the influence the government possessed as the largest single player in the London money and capital markets. This was especially the case in the period leading up to the return of sterling to the gold standard in 1925, at the pre-war parity to the dollar, as it attempted to maintain the value of the pound. After 1925 the intervention of the government in the affairs of the City did decline, though indirect controls and influence remained through the Bank of England. The Bank of England was even drawn into assisting the reorganization of troubled sectors of British industry in the late 1920s as it sought to respond to the concerns of government. With the financial crisis of 1931 government intervention became more explicit again, with the introduction of exchange controls managed on its behalf by the Bank of England. The result of the role played by the government in the 1930s, especially the introduction of exchange controls, was to make the City of London much less responsive to needs outside Britain and much more aware of the requirements of the government itself.[30]

Perversely, the result of the City's growing involvement with both the British economy and the British government between the wars was to attract criticism as it was blamed by many for the economic difficulties experienced at that time. Much of this criticism stemmed from the unfavourable view reached by the government-appointed Committee into Finance and Industry.[31] This reached the conclusion that, despite the excellence of the London money market, there were noticeable weaknesses in the capital market with regard to the finance of smaller and medium-sized businesses. While criticism of this kind was restrained and technical there also built up a general view, especially on the left of the political spectrum, that those in the City cared little about the plight of the British economy, which was identified with northern manufacturing industry, and that the only remedy was even greater government control. One Labour politician, Douglas Jay, writing in 1938, went so far as to state that

> Few in the City care whether it is socially desirable that this or that industry should be enabled to develop. Any such motive our financiers would regard as 'political'. Instead, they stick to 'business'—which means the attempt to outwit one's neighbour by cunning, luck, inside information or the deliberate spreading of false rumours. Small wonder that scandals abound, savings are mis-invested, and the small investor continually robbed.[32]

The opinion was now widespread that Britain gained little from the City of London as an international financial centre, because the business that was done there appeared both irrelevant and harmful. However, subsequent detailed research into bank lending to industry between the wars has indicated a willingness to provide both short- and long-term funds as long as there was a prospect of the business surviving and prospering. Only when that was not the case was finance refused. Similarly, it is now clear that the London capital market was particularly active and innovative between the wars, with the entry of new firms employing new methods in response to the new business in domestic industrial and commercial securities.[33] The fact that many in the City were themselves suffering was hidden from public view because it was mainly small, private firms doing an international business that were experiencing the greatest difficulties, while the large banks and insurance companies focusing on the domestic market appeared to be prospering, in contrast to much of British manufacturing industry. There was also little public understanding of the causes of exchange rate fluctuations, stock exchange speculation, or the cautious lending policies adopted by bankers. Instead, the City was perceived as having failed, in both domestic and international terms, with the only solution being greatly increased state control. What this reflected was a general disenchantment with markets because they were blamed for the economic problems experienced by Britain between the wars, rather than the unstable conditions that existed at the end of the First World War. Consequently, there was widespread support for measures to curb the ability of the City of London to operate as it had in the past and, instead, to respond to some notion of national interest, though moves in that direction were limited before 1939. Exchange controls and trade barriers did affect the City's international financial and commercial activities but more radical suggestions, such as the nationalization of the banks and the establishment of a National Investment Board, were not pursued.[34]

Though still remaining a major international financial centre, the City of London became much more domestic in its focus before 1939, and this affected all its principal activities ranging through the money, securities, and capital markets to areas such as insurance. At the same time its power and influence was greatly reduced both at home and abroad. Internationally, the collapse of a relatively open world economy, particularly in the 1930s, reduced or destroyed the role played by many of the markets and financial intermediaries in the City of London, promoting in its stead national centres. Domestically, the enhanced power of the government, especially after the introduction of exchange controls in 1931, meant that the City no longer had the freedom to operate simply in response to the impersonal forces of supply and demand. Thus, even though the City could grow at the expense of other financial centres within Britain, all were now reduced in importance because of the power of the government, operating either directly or through the Bank of England. As it was, the Second World War appeared to mark the end of London's long reign as the financial centre of the world economy. During the Second World War the City was subjected to large-scale aerial bombing during which around one-third of the area was destroyed, especially those buildings along the Thames and around the railway stations. This alone made it almost impossible for the City to continue in its traditional role as a major commercial centre, distributing commodities and manufactures not only within Britain but also around the world. Even the ability to direct domestic and international trade was made very difficult as offices and markets were destroyed and communications disrupted. However, the physical destruction was only the most visible evidence of the severe effects that the Second World War had upon the City of London.[35] Unlike the First World War the outbreak of the Second did not come as a surprise, so both the government and those in the City had time to prepare, using the experience of the First as a guide. Though it was not possible to plan fully for the consequences of a new and different war, especially one involving much more civilian disruption, the government imposed from the outset a comprehensive and authoritarian regime of control. Money, commodity, and capital markets were either brought under government supervision or closed because their functions were now handled by an official agency. The experience of the First World War had made clear the necessity of mobilizing all resources as effectively as possible for the war effort and that meant the replacement of the constant interaction of supply and demand forces, which the City thrived upon, with a regime of government direction and control. Thus the role of the money market was to provide the government with the means of meeting its immediate financial requirements while the capital market existed to handle its longer-term borrowing, through which the costs of war would be borne by later generations. The National Debt, for example, rose from £7.9bn. in 1939 to £21.4bn. in 1945 as the government monopolized the savings of the British people in its quest for military victory. Inevitably, the result of these controls, and the diversion of skilled personnel into military or administrative posts, was to prevent the City fulfilling its traditional functions as a financial and commercial centre for the global economy.[36]

As New York had already overtaken London in certain areas and was the financial centre of the world's largest economy, it was best placed to profit from the restrictions under which the City operated during the war. New York already possessed the institutions, personnel, markets, connections, and infrastructure that a global financial centre required, and was far removed from the hostilities even after the United States was eventually drawn into the conflict. There can be no doubt that by the end of the Second World War New York had replaced London as the most important financial centre in the world, located as it was in the country whose economy was now dominant, considering the fate that had befallen the likes of not only Britain but also France, Germany, and Japan during the fighting. Switzerland was one of the few European countries to escape the direct effects of the war and this had beneficial consequences for Zurich as a financial centre.[37] All this did not mean that London was no longer of major importance as a financial centre, but rather that it had lost its international primacy to New York while in Europe Zurich was now of major significance. Conversely, potential rivals to London as a global financial centre, such as Paris, Berlin, Frankfurt, or Tokyo, had suffered even more during the war, in terms of either physical destruction, the impossibility of maintaining international connections, or both. There was also the question at the end of the Second World War of whether the world actually needed a global financial centre of the kind that had existed in the past, with open markets and private intermediaries, as it appeared that governments and international agencies would now fulfil many of these functions. In the monetary sphere, for example, there was to be no sudden abandonment of exchange controls for there was every expectation that central banks, operating individually and collectively, would now intervene to maintain stability. One of the first acts of the incoming Labour government in 1945 was to take direct control of the Bank of England, so ensuring that it was now an official arm of the state. From then on it is not possible to see the Bank of England in any other way for its role was to carry out the bidding of government, not that of the City of London, even if that could be expressed in any collective way.[38] Thus, at the end of the Second World War the City of London had to serve two masters successfully if it was to thrive as a financial centre, with one being the traditional users of the facilities for trade and finance it provided while the other was the British government and its desire to control and direct the economic affairs of the country. Never before in a time of peace did the location of the City within Britain matter as much as it did at the end of the Second World War, because the policies pursued by the British government now constrained its ability to compete with other financial centres.[39]

In contrast to the difficult years between the wars, especially the 1930s, the rapid recovery of the world economy from the effects of the Second World War, and then the enormous expansion in international trade and finance during the decades of the 1950s and 1960s, did present great opportunities for the skills and markets that the City of London possessed. Britain was still an important economy with extensive international connections through the Empire and sterling area, and thus the City was well placed to benefit from the need for international financial and commercial intermediation, even if New York was now dominant. However, it was no simple matter for the City to recapture its pre-war activities. During the war connections had been lost, skilled personnel had been killed or departed, and customers had found alternative ways of operating. In addition, the government not only maintained exchange controls but was reluctant to grant the markets for money, capital, securities, and commodities the freedom they required to operate successfully. That was only slowly permitted in the 1950s for many, while exchange controls remained in force until 1979. The climate under which the City of London operated during the 1940s, and long afterwards, was one in which the experience, long built up, of operating in relatively free and open world markets was of limited value, so undermining the advantages it possessed.[40]

Thus the Second World War was another watershed for the City of London. To an extent it also represented a new beginning because the wholesale destruction, followed by planning controls, forced businesses to consider what they gained from a presence in the City. The result was that many decided that the benefits did not outweigh the costs, especially those operating in such areas as commerce, shipping, and insurance. The City became, for the first time, a purely financial centre, with even the commodity markets operating largely to allow buyers and sellers to offset risk. Even as a financial centre there was an increasing concentration upon a particular group of closely related financial services that both contributed to and drew from each other. Helping to drive these post-war changes in the City of London was the role played by government. During the war the government became aware of the power it possessed to direct the economy through its control over business and markets. At the same time those in the City became accustomed to the intervention of government, and so adjusted their way of operating so as to accommodate policy requirements.

The effects could be seen in both the London money and capital markets. During and immediately after the war the money market largely operated to meet the government's need for short-term finance, and did so under conditions determined by the Bank of England. Similarly, the government maintained tight control over new issues so as to ensure that priority was given to its own long-term borrowing and that the external value of the pound was maintained by limiting capital exports. Thus, though the London capital market was keen to respond to new opportunities, government-imposed constraints limited its ability to do so. Generally, the immediate post-war years saw the ability of the City of London to try and rebuild lost business and exploit new opportunities greatly circumscribed by the continuation of government controls, especially internationally, so driving it to focus on whatever domestic opportunities there were.[41]

Nevertheless, by the late 1940s the City of London had both recovered from the destructive effects of the war and devised means of operating within the restrictive framework allowed by the government. The result was a financial centre that was much more domestically orientated than in the past, with bankers, brokers, and markets being attuned to meet the needs of the British government and British industry, rather than foreign governments and foreign business. Though the degree of control exerted by the government was gradually lessened in the 1950s, with the replacement of the post-war Labour government by a Conservative one in 1951, the pace of liberalization was a slow one. The foreign exchange market, for example, was reopened in 1951, involving merchant banks like Brown Shipley and foreign banks like Société Générale, but only under the strict control of the Bank of England.[42] Generally, either directly or indirectly the City now operated under government guidelines that prevented or discouraged it from doing more than a limited amount of international business. Instead, the domestic focus was progressively emphasized, such as the handling of the conversion of private British firms into public companies, the growing activity in mergers and acquisitions, and the need for accountancy and legal advice at a time of high taxation. London was not even competing with New York for the role of leading international financial centre, while Zurich was becoming increasingly important in Europe, with foreign banks opening branches there.[43] However, all was not lost for the City of London as an international financial centre in the late 1940s and 1950s, despite the growing weakness of Britain as an economy and sterling as an international currency.

The increased level of government intervention and regulations that the City experienced after the Second World War was common to all financial centres, including Paris and New York. This restricted the development of alternative financial centres to London because the need was simply not there. Exchange controls and trade barriers created segmented capital and money markets in which there was only a limited role for an international financial centre to play. Instead, financial flows were channelled through banks and multinational corporations, while central banks and governments undertook many of the activities and transactions that had once passed through and between financial centres. What was being fostered was the growth of financial institutions such as banks, not markets and the expertise and interconnections they provided. Thus, though New York had replaced London as the most important financial centre in the world, much of that rested upon its central role within the economy of the United States, as the world's largest, rather than its international importance.[44] The international money, capital, securities, and commodity markets were slow to recover in the more restrictive environment of the post-war years, leaving London in a relatively strong position because it already possessed them as a legacy of the past. Potential European rivals, like Amsterdam and Zurich, thus remained too small to mount a realistic challenge as they were not building up the range and depth of financial services, connections, and markets necessary to compete with London. The City of London still remained the most internationally orientated of any major financial centre even though it was less important than it had been, both in terms of its own past and in comparison with other financial centres around the world.[45] Consequently, not only did those foreign banks that still had offices in London after 1945 retain them but new ones were also opened, as with the Czech bank Zivnotenska Banka in 1948 and the Bank of Japan in 1951. London also continued to host a group of British overseas banks with extensive international connections. In 1955 there were eighteen of these banks and they operated 3,612 branches worldwide, especially in Australia, New Zealand, and Africa. One measure of the extent of the City's continuing international connections after 1945 was the fact that the largest UK commercial bank in 1948, the Midland, maintained a specialist branch in the City, employing around 1,000 staff, in order to conduct business on behalf of 16,000 banking and other correspondents from abroad.[46] No other European centre could yet match London in the markets for money, foreign exchange, securities, and commodities, even though the late 1940s and 1950s were rather lean years for such activities. Instead, at that time the importance of the City rested upon the services it provided, such as insurance and financial advice, rather than the markets it possessed and those who operated in them.[47]

From the early 1960s onwards the expertise, facilities, and markets that continued to exist in the City of London were in increasing demand, as the liberalization of the global economy gathered pace and New York became a less attractive location from which to transact international business. The restrictions and regulations imposed on the US financial system in the 1930s, especially the splitting of commercial and investment banking and the control over the stock exchange, had hampered the ability of New York to compete as a financial centre, encouraging a number of US banks and brokerage houses to maintain a London operation after 1945 because of the less restrictive environment prevailing there. Nevertheless, these disadvantages of New York as a financial centre were overcome by the strength of the American economy, the importance of the dollar in international trade and investment, and the lack of serious competition. However, new and more onerous restrictions were imposed by the US government from the late 1950s in an attempt to support the international value of the dollar by restricting its use by foreigners. Among the most important of these was the tax levied on the interest paid on deposits, the curtailing of short-term lending to foreigners, and the forcing of US multinational corporations to raise new funds abroad. All this would not have undermined New York as a financial centre if London had not responded by offering not only an alternative base from which to operate but also a means of doing so in dollars, for sterling was in serious decline as an international currency. In response to that decline, particularly after the 1957 sterling crisis, banks and others in the City had begun to switch to the dollar as the basis of their international operations, and so were ready to respond to those who wished to either borrow or lend at attractive rates but retain their money in dollars. Hence the development of the Eurodollar markets covering a wide range of financial instruments. As the merchant banker Sir Cyril Kleinwort noted in 1971, 'The whole structure of London's financial system and its techniques floated up on a surge of new money and new ideas.'[48] The result of this was that London attracted an increasing number of those banks from around the world who needed to conduct international operations, especially in the money, foreign exchange, securities, and capital markets. There was a rush of Japanese banks and other financial institutions opening offices in the City of London from 1960 onwards, for example, as they had large amounts of money to employ but no longer found New York as attractive a place in which to do it. Whereas only 82 foreign banks had branches in the City in 1961, the number had almost doubled to 159 by 1970, and virtually doubled again by 1978, to 280. It was in 1973 that the German Deutsche Bank re-established a presence in London after having been ejected during the First World War, and this was followed by the opening of a branch in 1976. Similarly, it was during the 1970s that London branch of the Paris bank Société Générale began to revive in importance.[49]

One of the few major drawbacks still attached to the City of London as an international financial centre in the 1970s was the continuance of exchange controls, for these hampered the free movement of money in and out. In 1979 these exchange controls were removed, so ending that disadvantage and giving a great boost to the City of London's continuing rehabilitation as an international financial centre. By 1989 the number of foreign banks with operations in the City of London was 521 and continued to grow slowly but steadily, reaching 550 by 1997, by which time they employed around 72,000 staff. The presence of these foreign banks reflected the fact that the City of London could provide all that they required in order to participate fully in international financial markets, through which financial transactions between nations were now organized and settled. The collapse of the government/central bank-managed international monetary system in the early 1970s gave a large boost to financial firms and markets and thus to the City of London, where so many were already located. Building upon its existing importance in many major areas of international financial activity, such as trading currencies, issuing bonds, bank lending, and securities dealing, the City of London acted as a magnet to those not already operating there. As had been the case before 1914 London was able to benefit from a virtuous cycle where its size and success made it essential for financial institutions from around the world to have a presence there, which in turn attracted others as they found in the City the one location in the world that gave them immediate access to the largest single concentration of financial intermediaries and markets. In turn, that meant the City possessed all the support services required for the successful operation of a financial business, such as corporate lawyers, accountants, and technical experts as well as the best pool of qualified staff in whatever field. As one survey of the City concluded in 1990, 'Access to this pool of specialised, expert financial services labour represents a powerful attraction both to firms already in London and for potential in-migrants.'[50] In comparisons of financial centres over the 1990s the City of London emerged as the most important when judged in terms of international business, such as the presence of foreign banks, turnover in the foreign exchange market, cross-border lending and securities trading, issuance of Eurobonds, and global equity management.[51] Thus the governor of the Bank of England could state in a speech in December 1999 that the City of London was the 'predominant international financial centre'.[52]

This revival of the City did not happen automatically, however, for it involved a considerable relearning of lost skills, a willingness to accept foreigners, and an ability to change. Though much in the way of personnel and expertise had been lost in the City during the more heavily regulated years of the 1940s and the 1950s, business had not come to a standstill and so continuity with the past had been preserved. There remained many who were acquainted with the ways and techniques of an era when money and capital markets had dominated international financial transactions, such as Sigmund Warburg and his partner Henry Grunfeld who were pioneers in the issue of Eurobonds. Similarly, the success of Warburg and Grunfeld indicates the continuing ability of outsiders to be successful in the City, for both had fled Germany in the 1930s and then prospered in London in the 1950s. In addition, there was a constant influx of other nationalities into the City in the post-war years, especially from the United States and the Empire from the 1960s onwards. Finally, though there was an inevitable resistance to change, particularly where vested groups saw their interests being threatened, the City was neither sufficiently closed nor sufficiently homogeneous to resist it indefinitely. It was not a single entity like a bank or a corporation, though often identified as such, but a series of independent firms and markets with both complementary and conflicting aims and objectives. The income of one group was often the expenditure of another. The eventual deregulation of the stock exchange in 1986, when fixed commissions and the restrictions on admission and activities of members were abandoned in one 'Big Bang', indicated that even an institution as powerful as that could not resist the forces for change. 'Big Bang' was much more a delayed City response to the new challenges and opportunities created by the abandonment of exchange controls in 1979 than a change masterminded by the government and forced through against universal opposition.[53] Therefore, the post-Second World War history of the City of London appears one of remarkable and continuing success, for it recovered from having been overtaken by New York to emerge, yet again, as the key financial centre of the global economy. In 1996, for example, London overtook New York as the international centre for credit derivatives even though they had been created there in 1992 and involved mainly US banks and Japanese brokerage houses.[54] Such a success has defied the predictions of expert observers throughout the period. As recently as the late 1980s American economists were prophesying a brighter future for New York as an international financial centre than London while a British economist, Coakley, noted in 1992 that 'It is not inconceivable that by the middle of the 1990s London will be struggling to compete with Paris and Frankfurt for financial hegemony in Europe.' Similarly, at various times throughout the 1990s the *Financial Times* has taken a gloomy view of the City's prospects, as in May 1998: 'For more than a century, London has been at the heart of the financial markets of Europe, but the City's position is looking vulnerable, particularly with the arrival of the single currency of which sterling is not a part.'[55] As yet none of the predictions or wishes has come true.

However, this remarkable story of the City's post-war renaissance as an international financial centre, achieved against a background of Britain's relative economic decline, did not result in universal praise for its achievement, rather the reverse. Both in popular and academic spheres the connection has been made between Britain's poor economic performance and the City's success, with the result that the former was blamed on the latter. In particular, there appeared to be a link between the level and nature of the funding available for manufacturing industry in Britain after 1945 and either the lack of interest from the banks and investment managers in the City of London or their desire for short-term gains and high returns. What continued to be seen as the main cause of Britain's economic problems was a City–industry divide that robbed manufacturing of the support that it received in other countries, especially Germany.[56] This perception of the City as at best simply neglecting the British economy or at worst actually harming it meant that criticism came from across the political spectrum, such as both the membership of the business organization the CBI and the left-wing pressure group the Fabian Society.[57] Such criticism has prompted detailed enquiries into the role played by the City in the finance of British business since 1945, ranging from comparisons between the actions of London-based banks and those in Germany, the operation of individual City investment houses, and specific studies of the financial requirements of major firms or sectors of the economy. The outcome of most of these investigations has been to reveal similar relationships between British banks and their customers as with German banks, a great deal of innovation in the City in trying to meet the needs of borrowers, and the continuing support given to British firms by City institutions even in face of poor performance. What they do not support are contentions of either neglect or short-termism.[58] As Bowden concluded from a recent study of one group of financial institutions in the City of London,

> The growth and role of the finance houses during the postwar decades provides an important counter to those critics who cite the absence of innovation in the provision of finance and the lack of constructive links between the City and industry as factors in the problems of British industry after 1945.[59]

Nevertheless, the City continues to be held responsible for Britain's economic problems, even though direct evidence of how this came about has been difficult to establish. One important area where evidence has been sought is through the City's influence on the economic policies followed by successive governments of different political persuasions. The argument is that without the influence of the City post-war governments would not have followed policies that maintained Britain as an open economy but would have provided the protection and intervention that manufacturing required. Whether Britain really was an open economy before the 1980s is itself to be doubted, as is the question of whether alternative policies would have had the required results. At the same time it is clear that the relationship between the government and the City was not one-way, for the evidence suggests that the power rested with the cabinet and Treasury not the City. Only if the Bank of England is considered an integral part of the City, rather than an arm of the government as it surely was after 1945, is it possible to see the City determining government policy.[60] Also, more recent research appears to indicate that the policies being followed by post-war governments were, themselves, directly responsible for many of the economic difficulties experienced by British industry, even when they were trying to assist. Similarly, the development of the City's successful Eurodollar operations in the 1960s, for example, was achieved not with the aid of British governments during the 1960s but in the face of the hostility of the Labour Party, which was in power from 1964 to 1970.[61] Indifference from Conservative administrations and hostility from Labour ones between 1945 and 1980 hardly constitutes the triumph of the City over government.

During the twentieth century the City of London survived the impact of two world wars, a worldwide economic collapse, the growing restrictions on international trade and finance imposed by governments, and the decline of Britain as an economic and imperial power. All these were major blows to its standing as a financial centre, and it did appear that it had finally lost its dominant position in the world to New York after 1945 while its role in Europe was threatened by Zurich. The fact that the City was able to both reclaim its international importance, and repel European competition, was testimony to the inherent strengths it possessed at the beginning of the century, its ability to transform itself in response to opportunities and challenges, and the failure of alternative centres to capitalize on London's weaknesses and so replace it. Without the operation of all these three elements it is most unlikely that the City of London would have remained an international financial centre of the first rank in the twentieth century, placed alongside only New York and Tokyo. The explanation of the City of London's success must therefore be sought not only in what it had achieved before 1900 but also in what it did during the twentieth century, and in what other financial centres failed to do, for whatever reason. Where the explanation cannot be sought is in some trade-off between the City's success and Britain's economic decline, for there was no direct causal connection between the two. Such a link can only be made if the changes undergone by London as a financial centre in the twentieth century are ignored along with the fundamentally altered relationship between it and the rest of the world. At the beginning of the twentieth century London was the leading financial centre in the world largely because of the continuing size and strength of the British economy. Britain remained the world's largest trading nation, being at the centre of a commercial network extending far beyond the confines of its own empire, and this was supported by a dominant position in both international shipping and international investment. In addition, the British people enjoyed the highest per capita incomes in Europe, making them among the richest in the world, and this was sufficient to generate both an enormous demand for goods and a vast supply of savings, so maintaining Britain's pre-eminent in the global economy. In turn, this provided a solid foundation for the activities of the City of London, even without the added demands of other countries. This position occupied by London was similar to, though greater than, that of the other major European financial centres, like Paris and Berlin, for their importance rested primarily on the wealth, success, and links of their domestic economies rather than the role they played as intermediaries in the commercial and financial currents of the global economy.

In contrast, by the end of the twentieth century the position of not only the British economy in the world, but also those of France and Germany, was greatly diminished, for the global economy was no longer a Eurocentric one and the European people were no longer the dominant international investors. Instead, the relative standing of the different European financial centres rested much more upon the services they were able to perform for the global economy, rather than their own domestic economies and their international links. Based simply on domestic requirements both New York and Tokyo were far more important financial centres than any European city, located as they were within separate national economies. What differentiated London from other European financial centres was the degree to which its activities were driven by, and dependent upon, global transactions as witnessed by its leading position in foreign exchange transactions. Despite the fact that the pound had long been replaced as an international currency by the US dollar, followed by the German mark, the Japanese yen, the Swiss franc, and latterly the euro, currency trading was dominated by London. The importance of a financial centre has to be seen in terms of both the offices, markets, and institutions it hosted—the hub—and the depth and breadth of the network of which it was the centre—the spokes. At the beginning of the twentieth century the City of London was a very large hub compared to the spokes because of the size and importance of the British economy and its domestic and international requirements. It was the most important financial centre in the world because of the economy within which it was located. This had been reversed by the end of the century because the British economy had shrunk relative to that of the world. As a result the spokes were now of far greater importance for along them flowed the business that maintained London as one of the premier financial centres of the world. Shorn of these spokes, and the transactions they transmitted from far-distant centres like New York and Tokyo, London would be on a par with Paris and Frankfurt, dependent upon the activity generated by the domestic economy and its interactions with other economies around the world. Whereas in London in 1900 the hub generated most of the activity that flowed out along the spokes, as the British people invested their wealth worldwide and drew a vast income from abroad, in 2000 it was the spokes that sustained the hub, for along the spokes came a never-ending stream of transactions as the City of London redistributed the world's currencies, savings, and risks. In the course of the twentieth century the City of London had been forced to replace a secure domestic base with a much more fickle international one in order to remain the leading financial centre in Europe and one of the most important in the world. Only by understanding this changed relationship between hub and spoke is it possible to appreciate both what the City of London had achieved in the twentieth century and the vulnerable position it now occupies as a financial centre compared to 100 years ago.

Notes

1. Inertia appears as a common explanation for the City of London's persistence as a major international financial centre in the twentieth century. See D. Porteus, 'The Development of Financial Centres: Location, Information, Externalities and Path Dependence', in R. Martin (ed.), *Money and the Space Economy* (Chichester, 1999), 95–6, 101.
2. J.-P. Abraham, N. Bervaes, and A. Guinotte, 'The Competitiveness of European International Financial Centres', in J. Revell (ed.), *The Changing Face of European Banks and Securities Markets* (London, 1994), 230–1, 239–40.
3. C. Turner, 'Money London', in C. Sims (ed.), *Living London* (London, 1902), 1.
4. L. D. Wilgress, 'The London Money Market', *Journal of the Canadian Bankers Association*, 20 (1912–13), 210.
5. W. W. Swanson, 'London and New York as Financial Centres', *Journal of the Canadian Bankers*, 22 (1914–15), 198.
6. See, for example, Y. Cassis, *City Bankers, 1890–1914* (Cambridge, 1994), 5–8: K. Burk, in Y. Cassis (ed.), *Finance and Financiers in European History, 1880–1960* (Cambridge, 1992); 360, and H. Bonin, *Société Générale in the United Kingdom* (Paris, 1996), 11, 16 for both statements on London's position and divergent views on whether it was becoming more or less important.
7. For these points see R. Michie, 'The City of London and International Trade, 1850–1914', in D. C. M. Platt (ed.), *Decline and Recovery in Britain's Overseas Trade, 1873–1914* (London, 1993) and C. Harvey and J. Press, 'The City and International Mining, 1870–1914', *Business History*, 32 (1990).

8. *The Banking Almanac* (London, 1913), 38–57; A. S. J. Baster, *The International Banks* (London, 1935), 4; S. Nishimura, in A. Teichova, G. Kurgan-Van Hentenryk, and D. Zeigler (eds.), *Banking, Trade and Industry: Europe, America and Asia from the 13th to the 20th Century* (Cambridge, 1997), 379–92; O. Checkland, S. Nishimura, and N. Tamaki (eds.), *Pacific Banking, 1859–1959: East meets West* (London, 1994), 17, 36, 47–8, 175. See also Cassis, *City Bankers*; G. Jones, *British Multinational Banking, 1830–1990* (Oxford, 1993); P. L. Cottrell, in Cassis (ed.), *Finance and Financiers*.
9. For a recent attempt to estimate this importance statistically see G. Tullio and J. Wotters, 'Was London the Conductor of the International Orchestra or Just the Triangle Player? An Empirical Analysis of Asymmetries in Interest Rate Behaviour during the Classical Gold Standard, 1896–1913', *Scottish Journal of Political Economy*, 43 (1996); for an Australian perspective on London's importance see D. T. Merrett, 'Global Reach by Australian Banks: Correspondent Banking Networks 1830–1960', *Business History*, 37 (1995). For a more general account of the money market see W. M. Scammell, *The London Discount Market* (London, 1968).
10. See R. C. Michie, *The London Stock Exchange: A History* (Oxford, 1999).
11. See A. Cairncross, *Home and Foreign Investment* (Cambridge, 1953); W. P. Kennedy, 'Institutional Response to Economic Growth: Capital Markets in Britain to 1914', in L. Hannah (ed.), *Management Strategy and Business Development* (London, 1976); K. Watson, 'Banks and Industrial Finance: The Experience of Brewers, 1880–1913', *Economic History Review*, 49 (1996); F. Capie and M. Collins, *Have the Banks Failed British Industry? An Historical Survey of Bank/Industry Relations in Britain, 1870–1990* (London, 1992); J. F. Wilson, 'The Finance of Municipal Capital Expenditure in England and Wales, 1870–1914', *Financial History Review*, 4 (1997).
12. See T. Suzuki, *Japanese Government Loan Issues in the London Capital Market 1870–1913* (London, 1994), G. P. Marchildon, 'British Investment Banking and Industrial Decline before the Great War: A Case Study of Capital Outflow to Canadian Industry', *Business History*, 33 (1991), and 'Hands across the Water: Canadian Industrial Financiers in the City of London 1905–20', *Business History*, 34 (1992).
13. For the most comprehensive statement of this view see P. J. Cain and A. G. Hopkins, *British Imperialism: Innovation and Expansion, 1688–1914* (London, 1993), 141–60, and a critique of it in M. Daunton, in Cassis (ed.), *Finance and Financiers*, 21–46.
14. E. A. Wasson, 'The Penetration of New Wealth into the English Governing Class from the Middle Ages to the First World War', *Economic History Review*, 51 (1998), 39, 43.
15. See R. C. Michie, 'Insiders, Outsiders and the Dynamics of Change in the City of London since 1900', *Journal of Contemporary History*, 15 (1998).
16. M. Wilkins, in Cassis (ed.), *Finance and Financiers*, 433–4; D. W. Elmendorf, M. L. Hircheld, and G. D. N. Well, 'The Effect of News on Bond Prices: Evidence from the UK 1900–1920', *Review of Economics and Statistics*, 78 (1996), 341.
17. E. V. Morgan, *Studies in British Financial Policy, 1914–25* (London, 1952), 74–8; T. Balogh, *Studies in Financial Organization* (London, 1947), 231. See J. Peters, 'The British Government and the City–Industry Divide: The Case of the 1914 Financial Crisis', *Twentieth Century British History*, 4 (1993).
18. D. T. Merrett, 'Capital Markets and Capital Formation in Australia, 1890–1945', *Australian Economic History Review*, 37 (1997), 192–3; A. Turner, 'British Holdings of French War Bonds: An Aspect of Anglo-French Relations during the 1920s', *Financial History Review*, 3 (1996), 154–5; Morgan, *British Financial Policy*, 332.

19. See R. C. Michie, 'The London Stock Exchange and the First World War', *Arbeitskreis für Bankgeschichte*, 2 (1999).
20. Burk, in Cassis (ed.), *Finance and Financiers*, 360–2; C. R. Geisst, *Wall Street: A History* (Oxford, 1997), 152; Morgan, *British Financial Policy*, 332.
21. R. C. Wyse, 'The Future of London as the World's Money Market', *Economic Journal*, 28 (1918), 386.
22. D. Ward, 'A Description of the Foreign Exchange Market in London', *Manchester Guardian Commercial*, 20 Apr. 1922.
23. Burk, in Cassis (ed.), *Finance and Financiers*, 364–5; H. van B. Cleveland and T. F. Huertas, *Citibank 1812–1970* (Cambridge, Mass., 1985), 114; Geisst, *Wall Street*, 161; Y. Cassis, 'Financial Elites in Three European Centres: London, Paris, Berlin, 1880s–1930s', *Business History*, 33 (1991), 56; A. Roberts, *Schroders: Merchants and Bankers* (London, 1992), 154, 174, 213–14. See J. M. Atkin, *British Overseas Investment, 1918–1931* (New York, 1977).
24. FT/Banker, *International Banking in London*, FBSA 50th anniversary (7 Nov. 1997), 30–9; Sir Paul Newall, *Japan and the City of London* (London, 1996), 19; Bonin, *Société Générale*, 34; B. Attard, 'The Bank of England and the Origins of the Niemeyer Mission. 1921–1930', *Australian Economic History Review*, 32 (1992), 67–8.
25. See Michie, *London Stock Exchange*.
26. C. Armstrong, *Blue Skies and Boiler Rooms: Buying and Selling Securities in Canada, 1870–1940* (Toronto, 1997), 172–211; Roberts, *Schroders*, 249; Balogh, *Financial Organization*, 231; Bonin, *Société Générale*, 34. See D. Williams, 'London and the 1931 Financial Crisis', *Economic History Review*, 15 (1962/3).
27. R. Roberts, 'The City of London as a Financial Centre in the Era of Depression, the Second World War and Post-war Official Controls', in A. Gorst, L. Johnman, and W. S. Lucas (eds.), *Contemporary British History, 1931–61* (London, 1991), 68.
28. P. Einzig, 'London as the World's Banking Centre', *The Banker*, 28 (1933), 182–4; R. J. Truptil, *British Banks and the Money Market* (London, 1936), 274; Royal Institute of International Affairs, *The Problem of International Investment* (Oxford, 1937), 11; Cleveland and Huertas, *Citibank*, 161–2, 169; Geisst, *Wall Street*, 230–3; M. D. Bordo and R. Sylla (eds.), *Anglo-American Financial System: Institutions and Markets in the Twentieth Century* (New York, 1995), 199; M. G. Myers, *Paris as a Financial Centre* (London, 1936), 163–77; Merrett, 'Global Reach', 81–2; Jones, *Multinational Banking*, 414–15.
29. See R. C. Michie, 'The International Trade in Food and the City of London since 1850', *Journal of European Economic History*, 25 (1996); R. C. Michie, 'The London Stock Exchange and the British Economy, 1870–1939', in Y. Cassis (ed.), *Capitalism in a Mature Economy* (London, 1989); R. C. Michie, 'The London and Provincial Stock Exchanges, 1799–1973', in D. H. Aldcroft and A. Slaven (eds.), *Enterprise and Management* (Aldershot, 1995); S. Diaper, 'Merchant Banking in the Inter-war-Period: The Case of Kleinwort, Sons and Company', *Business History*, 27/8 (1985/6); C. Trebilcock, 'Phoenix: Financial Services, Insurance and Economic Revival between the Wars', in P. Clark and C. Trebilcock (eds.), *Understanding Decline* (Cambridge, 1997).
30. G. Toniolo (ed.), *Central Banks' Independence in Historical Perspective* (Berlin, 1988) A. Cairncross, in 42–6; E. Hennessy, *A Domestic History of the Bank of England, 1930–1960* (Cambridge, 1992), 83; W. R. Garside and J. I. Greaves, 'The Bank of England and Industrial Intervention in Interwar Britain', *Financial History Review*, 3 (1996), 71–3, 75, 79, 81–3; Balogh, *Financial Organization*, 268. See also J. R. Garrett, 'Monetary Policy

and Expectations: Market Control Techniques and the Bank of England, 1925–1931', *Journal of Economic History*, 55 (1995).

31. *Committee on Finance and Industry: Report* (London, 1931).
32. Douglas Jay, *The Nation's Wealth at the Nation's Service* (Labour Party pamphlet, 1938), 38. Quoted in R. Coopey and D. Clarke, *3I: Fifty Years Investing in Industry* (Oxford, 1995), 14. For a sustained attack on the City at this time see A Citizen, *The City Today* (Fabian Society, 1936).
33. F. Capie and M. Collins, P. Ziegler, and D. M. Ross, in P. L. Cottrell, A. Teichova, and T. Yuzowa (eds.), *Finance in the Age of the Corporate Economy* (Aldershot, 1997), 176–8, 201, 218; D. M. Ross, 'The Clearing Banks and the Finance of British Industry, 1930–1959', *Business and Economic History*, 20 (1991), 24–5; D. M. Ross, 'The Unsatisfied Fringe in Britain, 1930s–80s', *Business History*, 38 (1996), 18–23; J. Tomlinson, 'Atlee's Inheritance and the Financial System: Whatever Happened to the National Investment Board', *Financial History Review*, 1 (1994), 140–5, 155. See Capie and Collins, *Have the Banks Failed British Industry*.
34. See Tomlinson, 'Atlee's Inheritance', 140–4.
35. See C. H. Holden and W. G. Holford, *The City of London: A Record of Destruction and Survival* (London, 1951).
36. Roberts, 'City of London', 69–70. See Rudolf Wolff and Company, *Wolff's Guide to the London Metal Exchange* (London, 1991), 16.
37. Burk, in Cassis (ed.), *Finance and Financiers*, 364–5; Cleveland and Huertas, *Citibank*, 225–5; Y. Cassis, in Y. Cassis, G. D. Feldman, and U. Olsson, *The Evolution of Financial Institutions and Markets in Twentieth Century Europe* (Aldershot, 1995), 67–71
38. Bordo and Sylla (eds.), *Anglo-American Financial System*, 45; Cairncross, in Toniolo (ed.), *Central Banks*, 42–6; J. Fforde, *The Bank of England and Public Policy, 1941–1958* (Cambridge, 1992), 695–7.
39. See D. Sachs, 'Survey of the Financial Institutions of the City of London', in Institute of Bankers, *Current Financial Problems of the City of London* (London, 1949).
40. See J. H. Dunning and E. V. Morgan, *An Economic Study of the City of London* (London, 1971); F. W. Paish, 'The London New Issue Market', *Economica*, 18 (1951).
41. Fforde, *Bank of England*, 695–7; Roberts, *Schroders*, 313; Roberts, 'City of London', 69–72; *Wolff's Guide*, 16–17, 53–63; Tomlinson, 'Atlee's Inheritance', 143–54; Ross, 'Clearing Banks', 24–5.
42. P. Einzig, *A Textbook on Foreign Exchange* (London, 1966), 17; A. Ellis, *Heir to Adventure: The Story of Brown Shipley and Company* (London, 1960), 148–54, Bonin, *Société Générale*, 29–30.
43. Cassis et al., *Evolution of Financial Institutions*, 67–71; M. Ikle, *Switzerland: An International Banking and Finance Center* (Stroudsburg, Pa., 1972), 30; Cassis (ed.), *Finance and Financiers*, 364–5; Cleveland and Huertas, *Citibank*, 224–5; Geisst, *Wall Street*, 276.
44. R. M. Stulz, in M. Feldstein (ed.), *International Capital Flows* (Chicago, 1999), 260.
45. See Central Office of Information, *UK Financial Institutions* (London, 1957); P. Bareau, 'The Financial Institutions of the City of London', in Institute of Bankers, *The City of London as a Centre of International Trade and Finance* (London, 1961).
46. H. H. Thackstone, 'Work of the Foreign Branch of a Commercial Bank', in Institute of Bankers, *Current Financial Problems and the City of London* (London, 1949), 122; *International Banking in London*, 30; Newall, *Japan and the City*, 21–2. Jones, *Multinational Banking*, 414–15.

47. See H. Cockerell, *Lloyds of London: A Portrait* (London, 1984); R. L. Carter and P. Falush, *The London Insurance Market* (London, 1996).
48. Sir Cyril Kleinwort, 'The City in Britain's Invisible Earnings', *The Banker*, 121 (1971), 171.
49. S. Bell and B. Kettell, *Foreign Exchange Handbook* (London, 1983), 75–6; P. Einzig, *The Euro-bond Market* (London, 1969), 65, 147, 195; E. W. Clendenning, *The Euro-dollar Market* (Oxford, 1970), 7, 22–3, 186; P. Einzig, *The History of Foreign Exchange* (London, 1962), 241; *International Banking*, 53; Newall, *Japan and the City*, 24–5, 32, 50; Cleveland and Huertas, *Citibank*, 253–5; Geisst, *Wall Street*, 311, 331, 356–7; Roberts, *Schroders*, 418; L. Gall et al., *The Deutsche Bank, 1870–1995* (London, 1995), 754; Bonin, *Société Générale*, 60. See C. R. Schenk, 'The Origins of the Euro-dollar Market in London, 1955–1963', *Explorations in Economic History*, 35 (1998); W. M. Clarke, *The City and the World Economy* (London, 1965); R. Fry (ed.), *A Banker's World: The Revival of the City, 1957–1970* (London, 1970); Inter-bank Research Organisation, *The Future of London as an International Financial Centre* (London, 1973); R. Shaw, in S. F. Frowen (ed.), *A Framework of International Banking* (London, 1979).
50. A. Rajan, *Capital People: Skills Strategies for Survival in the Nineties* (London, 1990), 29–30.
51. *International Banking*, 6, 20, 50–3; Bonin, *Société Générale*, 108; Rajan, *Capital People*, 14–16, 153, 180; P. Bancroft et al., *London's Size and Diversity: The Advantages in a Competitive World* (London, 1996), 2, 31; A. D. Smith, *International Financial Markets: The Performance of Britain and its Rivals* (Cambridge, 1992), 130, 146–8, 154, 159. For recent assessments of London's relative position see Bank of England, 'London as an International Financial Centre', *Bank of England Quarterly Bulletin*, 29 (1989); City Research Project, *The Competitive Position of London's Financial Services: Final Report* (London, 1995); Bank of England, *Practical Issues Arising from the Euro* (London, Dec. 1999 and Nov. 2000).
52. Speech by Eddie George, 7 Dec. 1999 (www.bankofengland.co.uk/speeches/speech65.htm).
53. R. O'Brien, *Global Financial Integration: The End of Geography* (London, 1992), 19–20, 33, 74; P. Thompson, 'The Pyrrhic Victory of Gentlemanly Capitalism: The Financial Elite of the City of London, 1945–90', *Journal of Contemporary History*, 32 (1997), 295–6, 437. See Michie, *London Stock Exchange*, Michie, 'Insiders, Outsiders', and R. C. Michie, 'Friend or Foe: Information Technology and the London Stock Exchange since 1700', *Journal of Historical Geography*, 23 (1997).
54. *Financial Times*, 20 Nov. 1996.
55. T. Noyelle (ed.), *New York's Financial Markets: The Challenges of Globalization* (Boulder, Colo., 1989), 28; J. Coakley, in L. Budd and S. Whimster (eds.), *Global Finance and Urban Living* (London, 1992) 70. *Financial Times* 14 May 1998.
56. For a sample of these views see D. Coates, *The Question of UK Decline: State, Society and Economy* (London, 1994), 261; B. Fine and N. Harris, J. Zysman, and H. Radice, in D. Coates and J. Hillard (eds.), *UK Economic Decline: Key Texts* (London, 1995), 220, 223–4, 243; W. Hutton, *The State We're In* (London, 1995), 5, 123, *National Westminister Bank Quarterly Review* (Aug. 1991)—debate on short-termism
57. See CBI, *Investing for Britain's Future: Report of the CBI/Industry Task Force* (London, 1987), and D. Goodhart and C. Grant, *Making the City Work* (London, 1988).
58. See N. Dimsdale and M. Prevezer (eds.), *Capital Markets and Corporate Governance* (Oxford, 1994); S. Bowden and J. Maltby, 'Under-performance, Short-Termism and

Corporate Governance: The City and the British Motor Corporation, 1952–1967', *Financial History Review*, 5 (1998); Capie and Collins, *Have the Banks Failed.*

59. S. Bowden, 'Competition and Collusion in the Finance Sector in the Post-war Period', *Financial History Review*, 4 (1997), 164.

60. See the contrasting view of a government economic adviser in A. Cairncross, 'The Bank of England: Relationships with the Government, the Civil Service and Parliament', in Toniolo, *Central Banks' Independence in Historical Perspective*, who sees the power in the hands of government, and a political historian, E. H. Green, in Cassis (ed.), *Finance and Financiers*, who sees the power in the City.

61. Two recent examples relating to industrial finance are F. Carnevali and P. Scott, 'The Treasury as a Venture Capitalist: DATAC Industrial Finance and the Macmillan Gap, 1945–60', *Financial History Review*, 6 (1999) and L. Johnman and H. Murphy, 'A Very British Institution: A Study of Undercapitalisation: The Role of the Ship Mortage Finance Company in Post-delivery Credit Financing within shipbuilding, 1951–67', *Financial History Review*, 6 (1999). For the Eurodollar market see Einzig, *Euro-bond Market*, 15, 50.

3
When Paris Dreamed of Competing with the City...

Alain Plessis

An international financial centre is a market carrying out large-scale financial activities within the monetary system governing trade between countries and operating well beyond the boundaries of its home base. It covers money markets (short-term markets such as monetary and discount markets and those dealing with shares and precious metals and so on) of interest to undertakings in many countries.

'Indices' for measuring the growth of a financial centre are often not very reliable and always need to be interpreted with care.[1] The first of these might well be the total capital exported from countries with generally a metropolitan financial market. But an outflow of capital seeking a safe haven abroad is not a sign of international expansion. The number of agencies set up abroad by the banks of a particular market place is also used, yet the number of foreign agencies setting up on the market in question is also a sign that it is attractive. An international financial centre is like a revolving table capable of simultaneously exporting and importing capital, opening up further banking headquarters on other financial markets, and welcoming branches of foreign banks. It plays an active part in international movements of capital and the decisions taken by the chief actors in the market (banks and other financial intermediaries) to some degree sway nationals of other countries. That is the reason for its influence abroad.

During the nineteenth and twentieth centuries all financial markets seemed very hierarchical in nature. For a long time the outstanding one was London. In the history of financial centres the Paris market was assessed in various ways, seen by some writers as competing with London for first place 'since the Napoleonic wars'[2] and by others as not really a financial centre.

During the nineteenth century, and particularly under the Second Empire, Paris was already aiming to be the pre-eminent financial centre, and had several advantages. First, it was alone in having an adverse balance of trade with the other European countries and a favourable one with the United Kingdom, which for its part had an unfavourable one with the continent. That situation 'imposed the franc as the continental reserve and settlement currency',[3] which meant that Paris could play an important part as a clearing centre, be the leading exchange market in Europe[4], and 'play a key part in world payments' (Kindleberger). During the same period, the Banque de France, which had just been converted to having a variable discount rate, sought to attract floating capital. Whenever there was an economic crisis, it reacted immediately to each rise in the Bank of England's discount rate by raising its own. The two issuing banks engaged in what their contemporaries called 'the war of the banks'. As Bagehot notes, Paris at the time was acting as a European settling house, or at least as a European monetary centre, and its pre-eminence was partly linked to political power,[5] specifically to the desire for power of Napoleon III, who actively contributed to the launching of the Latin Union. For France, the Second Empire was also a time of great Europe-wide capital exports, their combined total amounting to 13m. francs in 1870.[6] The old *haute banque* houses and the Pereire brothers' Crédit Mobilier, often in competition, played an essential part in these capital exports. In the reign of Napoleon III, therefore, the Paris financial market really did acquire international status, and it could even be said that although a huge number of shares were traded on the London Stock Market and foreign state funds were mostly quoted in London, they were chiefly negotiated in Paris.[7]

France's defeat by the Germans in 1870–1 brought the first phase of the Paris market place's period of expansion to an abrupt end. A period of political withdrawal ensued for France, and in 1870 the Banque de France was obliged to suspend convertibility and this lasted for eight years. As Bagehot stresses, 'since the suspension of specie payments by the Bank of France, its use as a reservoir of specie is at an end. No one can draw a cheque on it and be sure of getting gold or silver for that cheque. Accordingly the whole liability for such international payments in cash is thrown on the Bank of England . . . all exchange operations are centring more and more in London.'[8] Paris could no longer serve as a discount market, all the more so as France's favourable balance of trade had decreased considerably. In addition a part of the French portfolio of foreign securities had been cashed to pay the 5bn. francs of 'war indemnity' demanded by Bismarck, and until 1895 the net export of French capital, which during the Empire had peaked at 1,351m. francs in 1865, was a great deal lower, with an annual average of 307m. for the years 1871–94.[9] All this meant that the influence of the Paris market (which was also affected by violent collapses) beyond France's national boundaries waned to some degree.

And yet the period in the Second Empire when France had been seen as a dynamic financial market at the international level had left a considerable legacy, including major institutions which were subsequently to last and grow significantly. The principal one was the Paris Bourse, which henceforth was to function thanks to two sets of competing intermediaries in the field of stocks and shares. On the one hand there were the sixty state-appointed ministerial officers or *agents de change*, forming the Floor and claiming the monopoly of negotiating large share deals, and on the other the unofficial brokers from around two hundred respectable firms alongside what Dupont-Ferrier calls 'a horde of dealers' providing a free market for countless shares, including a large number of foreign securities. In addition, most of the French insurance companies came into being at that time, although their rise was restricted as a result of government constraints obliging them to specialize by field in separate companies for each type of risk.

It was during the Second Empire that the big new banks appeared on the scene as competitors of the *haute banque*. Although the Crédit Mobilier, which the Pereire brothers had been obliged to cease managing, could no longer claim to play a major part internationally, the new credit establishments set up as limited companies, such as the Comptoir d'Escompte de Paris (1848–1952), the Crédit Lyonnais (1863), and the Société Générale, began to develop. From the start, they were interested in international financial transactions, and began to set up branches abroad, particularly in the City, and the Comptoir d'Escompte de Paris, which already had a number of agencies in Asia (Shanghai and Calcutta (1860), Hong Kong and Bombay (1862), Yokohama (1867), as well as Alexandria (1869)), opened one in the City in 1869. The Crédit Lyonnais followed suit in 1870 and the Société Générale in the following year.

There are still further lasting legacies of the Second Empire. During that period, the Paris market enjoyed real influence abroad and left behind it a culture encouraging interest in major international deals abroad, leaving a lasting impression on the collective memory of the capital's financial circles, where there was still a latent desire to compete with London once the circumstances were right.

1. The heyday of the Paris market place

Circumstance *was* right at the end of the nineteenth century and during the years before the First World War. As far as trade was concerned, of course, France was in no position to compete with the United Kingdom (British exports of manufactured goods were 30 per cent of the world total, as against France's barely 12 per cent)[10], and there was nothing like the Port of London in France. In addition, the British Empire was much more heavily populated and a great deal richer than France's colonial possessions. Britain's outstanding role in world trade was one of the reasons for the growth of the credits the City could offer to traders throughout the world, which accounts for the exceptional growth of the London acceptances market. The greater part of international trade was financed by means of letters of credit drawn on London and accepted by merchant bankers. For their part, French banks financed only certain French trading operations by means of French trading securities, and, as from that point of view Paris was not an international banking market, 'French banks commonly asked specialized London credit houses to take them on for them!'[11]

On the other hand, France did enjoy a regular considerable and favourable current balance of payments, largely due to its invisible exports surplus (tourism, profits from freight, insurance and other services, income from capital) making it possible for the country both to import large amounts of gold and to keep up a sustained outward flow of capital, which were the main factors enabling Paris to become an international financial centre once again.

A large proportion of the gold coming into France was stored in the vaults of the Banque de France, which at the time was practising, at the instigation of the governor, Pallain, a hoarding policy, for both political and economic reasons.

The holdings, which were far bigger than those of any other issuing institution in other European countries except Russia, were meant both to provide war funding in the event of a new conflict with Germany and to help to maintain the lowest and most stable discount rate possible.[12] The gold meant that notes issued by the Banque de France were convertible. The franc was thus a stable and reliable currency, inspiring confidence abroad. In addition, although sterling was the outstanding currency for international settlements and the Bank of England could attract large sums of foreign capital should the need arise, the Banque de France was an important factor in the working of the monetary system of the time, the gold standard, ensuring its regulation and stability. At a time of crisis or tight money, it could, as a major gold-holding institution, delay raising its discount rate and let some of its yellow metal flow towards England, or even cushion France against the effects of the crisis, make some of its gold available to the Bank of England, and cooperate with it as it did in 1907. London may have been the world monetary centre and the deciding factor in the movement of capital, but the Banque de France, given its gold reserves, was the bedrock of the international monetary system, and in 1907 was 'the true centre', regulating liquidity.[13]

The very high rate of saving in France, which was not absorbed by domestic investment and state requirements, and the growing balance of current payments surplus, enabled the country to export increasing amounts of capital. It was in fact the foreign creditor for an estimated total amount of 38.5bn. francs on the eve of the 1914 war and thus a creditor country second only to Great Britain with its foreign assets of probably 100bn. francs.[14]

The Paris Bourse, which became the leading continental financial market, was of international stature. Between 1892 and 1913 issues of foreign securities were on average almost half of all issues and in 1904 even two-thirds.[15] An examination of the capitalization of securities officially quoted on the Bourse shows that from the beginning of the nineteenth century, more foreign than French ones were involved, although foreign shares can of course be quoted on more than one stock exchange at a time.[16] It should also be noted that Russia was the main destination for the flow of capital exports (with Russian loans totalling over 10bn. francs, and almost a third of the capital exported), followed by other continental European countries and the Ottoman Empire and to a far lesser extent by distant countries of the Americas, Asia, Oceania, and South Africa. The Paris financial market was thus more European and less international than the London Stock Exchange.

French banks also developed their international activities to a large extent. The houses of the *haute banque*, which were still growing, were traditionally on the lookout for financial transactions abroad. The new banks set up as limited companies, however, and the great deposit banks in particular, made large short-term credit available to foreign states, loans on contango to foreign stock exchanges, particularly Berlin, and played a large part in the issuing of foreign securities in France. Their names frequently appeared in investment and guarantee syndicates for such issues, along with those of the merchant and foreign banks they were collaborating with; they opened up their counters for subscribers to such foreign securities, which they actively advertised, subsequently issuing the relevant coupons to their clients. Their commission on such transactions laid them open to violent attacks, often inspired by nationalistic feelings, and they were accused of depriving French industry, which was threatened by competition from Germany, of the use of French savings. Such was the polemic launched in 1906 by a journalist using the pseudonym Lysis, and subsequently published in a work entitled *Contre l'oligarchie financière* (*Against Financial Oligarchy*).

The major banks also expanded abroad, as did the Comptoir National d'Escompte de Paris, which had always had been very active internationally, the Société Générale, and the Crédit Lyonnais. The last-named, in fact, was a world leader, with its total resources equalling those of the biggest German or English banks. Yet the major French banks' breakthrough onto the international scene needs to be put into some kind of context: around 1913, they had at very most 500 agencies abroad, as against the British banks' at least 1,300, which reflect the ratio at the time between the capital exports of the two countries.

At the end of the *belle époque*, Paris can perhaps be seen as the second international financial centre, a good way behind London. At a time when the two neighbours finally concluded the Entente Cordiale, financial rivalry with London was less keen than it had been under the Second Empire: there were several examples of collaboration between the Banque de France and the Bank of England, the merchant banks often took part in joint syndicates with foreign, and particularly English, banks, the destination of French was markedly different from that of English capital, and a *de facto* demarcation of priority investment zones tended to establish itself.

Even if at the time Paris could not really claim to be the financial centre of the world and had to resign itself to being a noteworthy second to London, the age saw the Paris Bourse acquire considerable prestige and the major French banks make large profits from their participation in international financial transactions. Its institutions grew in size, prosperity, and solidity, which were to enable them to survive subsequent major trials and encourage them, in a hostile environment, to claim that they still had a part to play on the international scene and to try to keep at least a toehold on it.

2. Withdrawal, 1914–1926

The Great War strengthened London's financial preponderance in Europe. It was the only payments centre for the Entnente Cordiale countries through which they could borrow and settle their purchase worldwide. At the same time, and until 1926, the capital of a country that had been partly occupied saw the very basis of its influence disappearing. To finance unprecedented expenditure, France had to commit some of the gold held by the Banque de France and sell off a fair proportion of its foreign assets. To a much greater extent than the Anglo-Saxon countries, it had recourse to printing money, and there was high inflation until 1926. The franc weakened and, under attack on the exchange markets, collapsed in 1924 and again in 1926 when the lack of confidence in it caused an outflow of speculative capital. In addition, the moratorium given to the banks at the beginning of hostilities and the closure of the Bourse for many weeks robbed both institutions of their credit for a long time.

The share portfolio held by French investors shrank considerably following the resale of the best securities abroad and the collapse of loans to Russia and the Ottoman Empire, and from being a creditor France became a debtor nation. There could be no question of setting up the portfolio again. During the whole of the war, and until 1920, the current balance of payments was heavily in deficit. The nation's savings, which had fallen very significantly, had to be used solely for the needs of the state and for financing reconstruction. Opinion was therefore very hostile to any return to issuing foreign securities on the Paris market, and a 1916 law prohibited all such issues not having ministerial approval, which drove foreign investors away and amounted to a *de facto* ban on the export of capital. This meant that the level of such activities was negligible, with the sole exception of the loan negotiated in Paris by the Belgian government following an agreement with its French counterpart.

Foreign securities quoted on the Paris Bourse still amounted to a quarter of French securities, however, but it is true that the falling value of the franc on the exchange market increased their relative value. In addition, from 1921 onwards, there was once again a current balance of payments surplus, and to take steps to protect themselves against the falling franc or to avoid new taxes or other fiscal threats, French nationals bought foreign securities either in Paris or elsewhere (in the latter case, usually when they were not quoted on the Paris Bourse). This often 'invisible' flight of capital led to an increase in the French portfolio of foreign securities, assessed at 25bn. Poincaré or 5bn. gold standard francs for the period 1921–6. In the latter year, French holdings abroad probably amounted to a hundred million Poincaré francs or 20m. gold francs, roughly half of what it had been in 1913.[17]

The years from 1914 to 1926 were also a time of relative decline for the great deposit banks, which had suffered from inflation and the depreciation of the franc. In constant francs, their resources had declined, with those of the Crédit Lyonnais amounting to only one-third of the Westminster Bank's at the end of the period. At the time, the biggest five French banks' resources were a fifth of those of the big five English banks. Their market value also fell, to such an extent that in autumn 1926 the directors of the Crédit Lyonnais were afraid that the control of their bank might pass to a foreign—American or German—bank, and to secure their position they issued 100,000 shares carrying a plural vote. Despite some weakness, France's financial and monetary difficulties hampering their activities on the international scene, and their efforts to support French government loans and French companies' securities, these banks still tried to keep up their position and even expand abroad. Thus, in 1919 the Comptoir National d'Escompte de Paris, with its very long-standing international activities, provided an example, adding to its many agencies abroad (London, Liverpool, Manchester, Sydney, Melbourne, Bombay,

Alexandria, Cairo, Port Said, Brussels, San Sebastian . . .) an American branch in New York, the French American Banking Corporation. Its board of directors justified this action in its report for the financial year 1920: 'on the world affairs market, which reflects the activities of our foreign business, the Comptoir has long kept its place in the first rank of French banks. Following its time-hallowed paths, it has sought, by developing its foreign department, to maintain the many contacts which enable it to attract the greatest possible number of commercial transactions towards our country.'[18]

Between 1914 and 1926, the Paris financial market did not really play an active international part, but the relations with foreign countries maintained by the banks and certain French investors were able to support renewed activity abroad.

3. The great hope, 1928–1930

The situation improved radically once Poincaré had stabilized the franc *de facto* in 1926 and then *de jure* in 1928. Once inflation had been halted, the franc, after having lost four-fifths of its value, became once more a credible currency, capital that had deserted the country flowed back to it, and from 1929–30 a great deal of foreign capital in countries with threatened currencies sought a haven in France. As the Banque de France required a certain proportion of the foreign currency coming into the country to be converted into gold, its holdings of gold reached unprecedented levels, and Paris became a gold centre in a position to attract gold from abroad, which gave rise to acute tension with London. Thus, in the early 1930s, Paris built up holdings of gold exceeded only by the Federal Reserve System in the United States.

The new strength of the franc and flow of capital from or back from abroad helped the Parisian market to function again at the international level. On the one hand, thanks to a solid current account surplus (in part primarily due to German reparations) issues of non-Bourse foreign securities managed to achieve some importance from 1927, representing in 1930 12 per cent and in 1931 17 per cent of total issues, but still far less then the pre-war figures. Such foreign loans, which were still quite small, mainly involved the governments of Poland and Hungary (1927), Turkey and Romania (1928), Romania and Bulgaria (1929), Chile, Hungary, and the Young plan for German reparations (1930), and Romania, Yugoslavia, and Great Britain (2.5bn. francs' worth of Treasury notes) (1931). It can be seen that amongst the states benefiting from French capital at the time were several central European and Balkan countries in which, for political reasons, the French government had encouraged the major French merchant banks (the Banque de Paris et des Pays-Bas and the Banque de l'Union Parisienne) to invest.

At the same time, the inflow of capital (amounting probably to 35bn. Poincaré francs) caused a certain increase in deposits in the great deposit banks which, in terms of constant francs, had never risen to their pre-war levels. For the chief players on the Paris market place to regain the really strong position they had reached before 1914, the influx of floating capital would have had to persist for a long time.

Very soon, however, there was an ambitious plan in certain financial and political quarters to exploit the extraordinary affluence created by the inflow of capital to organize a huge international acceptances market in Paris and challenge London's traditional pre-eminence in the field.[19] The acceptance market, which was financed in the British capital by a score of merchant bankers, encouraged the use of the bill on London for financing foreign trade. Until 1927 the Paris acceptances market 'scattered among deposit banks, was so to speak non-existent when compared with that of London'. Whilst English, essentially London, acceptances amounted to over 8bn. gold francs in 1913, the French total was around 1.2bn. including 619m. in the portfolio of the six major credit establishments. 'The war and the post-war years had practically wiped out the use of acceptance in France for as long as monetary depreciation lasted.' The opposite was the case across the Channel, where the pound returned to its pre-war gold parity, making London once more the international accepting centre, which could only be financed on the basis of a stable currency. In 1927, French acceptances totalled a mere 500m. francs, or the equivalent of 100m. gold francs.

Once the franc was stabilized, the plethora of foreign currencies encouraged the organization of an acceptances market in Paris, which tended to push French capital back abroad and make Paris a real bill negotiating centre, since bills of exchange were naturally negotiated in the market where they had been accepted.

In order to encourage the market to develop, there were several favourable modifications in the French tax system, aimed at encouraging the discounting of foreign bills in France, and the Banque de France helped in rediscounting acceptances. In particular, a French accepting bank was founded on 20 December 1929, with the support of the Banque de France, by the main French *banques d'affaires* (Banque de l'Union Parisienne, Banque de Paris et des Pays-Bas, Crédit Mobilier Français, Banque de l'Indochine) and most of the major French deposit banks (Crédit Lyonnais, Société Générale, Banque Nationale de Crédit, Crédit Commercial de France) associated with two Belgian establishments. Its special purpose was 'acceptances, especially in the field of commercial transactions involving France and foreign countries, or two foreign countries'. The founding banks were represented on its board of directors and had to spread out major credits amongst themselves, thus sharing the risks involved in transactions.

As Henri Laufenburger has pointed out, the French accepting bank was unable 'to produce a volume of business even remotely approaching that of London'. In 1930, the major French banks' acceptances amounted to 1.3m. Poincaré francs, and those of the Banque Française d'Acceptation 563m, with the latter falling to 323m. in 1931 and 88m. in 1935, as against 700m. for the other French banks in the same year. At the end of 1936, the total amount of credits granted by the Banque d'Acceptation was no more than 31m.

There are many reasons for the rapid failure of the specialized accepting bank, and more widely for the ambitious project of setting up a Paris market capable of vying with London for the status of the European or world acceptances leader. Some arise from the outstanding importance of the Port of London, others from what Laufenberger calls 'the technical inferiority of the Paris market, declaring that its failings can be summed up as 'a lack of flexibility, arising from the direct participation of the Banque de France in the accepting organism, a lack of technical know-how, of experience and tradition'[20].

In addition, the 1931 world slump which 'put even the very technique of acceptance in jeopardy' hit a new organization like the Banque Française d'Acceptation hard at a time when it was faced with a very unfavourable economic situation. More generally, every attempt to recreate an international role for the Paris marketplace was essentially based on the return of capital that had moved abroad, and re-establishing it depended essentially on a temporary inflow of short-term capital. Any progress made was wiped out the moment it was France's turn to feel the effects of the crisis and its concomitant further outflow of such capital.

4. An enduring eclipse, 1931–1958

The then managing director of the Crédit Lyonnais, Maurice Schlogel, who was at the centre of French financial affairs during this period, emphasizes in a few lines the negative impact of the events affecting the Paris market for about twenty years. 'For a very brief period from 1928 to 1931, Paris seemed to be on the way to regaining its earlier position... Two wars and an economic crisis were unfortunately to test France to the limit, undermining its economy, destabilizing its currency, paralyzing its foreign trade and blocking the flow of its external investments. For several decades, the country's place on the international financial chess board was a very modest one.'

The 1930s saw an increased exodus and hoarding of capital, which reduced the assets of French banks. The successive crises on the franc exchange markets, which suffered three consecutive devaluations between 1936 and 1938, bear witness to a marked monetary instability, which discouraged savings. At the end of the period, the Paris Bourse and the banks were essentially financing the French state and prioritizing its rearmament policy.

The immediate consequence of the Second World War was the introduction of exchange control, organized by a series of decrees in September 1939 (and soon controlled by the German Occupation), which was to last until 1967. During the Occupation, the only financial transactions were with Nazi Germany, conducted within a very unequal Franco-German clearing system, and the major French banks were mostly cut off from their foreign branches. Vichy's *dirigiste* policy affected both banks, with the first banking law of 1941, and the Bourse, with the creation in 1942 of a chamber of brokers replacing free-market off-floor trading.

Between the Liberation and the end of the Fourth Republic, France had a severe balance of payments deficit and the franc was weak and often under attack on the currency market. The country's growth rate was higher than that of the UK, but that did not make Paris an international financial centre, and it could even be said that first reconstruction and then the modernization of the economy were to some degree carried out at the expense of international financial relations, as capital was primarily used for the benefit of the state and large (and often nationalized) firms. The flow of finance abroad was hindered by strict regulations. The expansion of the now-nationalized great deposit banks within France itself was tightly controlled, and they had primarily to invest in state funds. As for the Paris Bourse, its role was essentially reduced to investing state loans and nationalized firms' bonds. The issues of foreign securities, which still required government authorization, remained virtually nil until 1964.

And yet, surprisingly in such an unfavourable economic environment, financial relations with the rest of the world were undertaken, re-established, and even developed. Thus, a marginal current of international activity was maintained on the Bourse. The banking sector too did its best to expand abroad. The *haute banque* houses, and above all Rothschilds and Lazards, which had both shown a more dynamic approach, and the major *banques d'affaires* that had avoided nationalization, were particularly involved. Even the nationalized banks themselves tried to use their foreign branches in new types of transactions and to extend their foreign connections. The Société Générale, for example, thanks to its presence in New York, participated strongly in the business created by the Marshall Plan. As for the Crédit Lyonnais, it intensified its relations with its correspondents in Germany, opening an agency in Frankfurt in 1948, and also in Italy, and set up branches in South America, the Lebanon (1951), and Iran (1958).[21]

Thus, although the Paris marketplace could not claim during the whole of the period to have an international part to play (apart from a limited one in the franc zone, where Paris was the financial centre), there were financial actors in the French capital maintaining and even developing relations with foreign countries, and particularly with London and New York. These were the people who were subsequently to attempt, when circumstances were more favourable and politicians more supportive, to increase the influence of Paris abroad.

5. Towards a new international role for Paris as a financial centre

After a further crisis for the franc at the end of the Fourth Republic, the 1958 recovery plan made it possible to balance the budget. At the time, France's participation in the European Common Market meant re-establishing the external convertibility of the currency, which was done in late 1958. The implementation of the Treaty of Rome in 1959 was, as Maurice Schlogel says, 'an event of wide-reaching scope that was to mark the beginning of a totally new era'.[22] Finally, in 1967, a law regulating France's financial relations with foreign countries made free exchange the rule and controls the exception. Banks benefited from the Debré decree-laws of 1966–7, which gave them greater freedom of activity. In a still rather *dirigiste* framework, liberal provisions were made from 1966 to encourage the growth of Paris as an international financial centre. In its report for 1966 the board of directors of Crédit Lyonnais noted that the year had been 'marked by the various measures taken by the public authorities to develop relationships abroad, in particular the abolition of the compulsory deposit of foreign securities in a bank and the repeal of regulations forbidding the remuneration of foreign accounts in francs'. In 1967, the same body noted with satisfaction 'a tax provision abolishing, with effect from 1 January 1968, the obligation to deduct one third from income from foreign securities, a measure which should increase the international importance of the Paris financial market'. In the new climate, foreign securities transactions increased on the Bourse, and a start was made on some issues of foreign securities, initially the European Coal and Steel Community loans in 1964. The major banks extended their networks abroad with a new vigour. The crisis of May 1968, which closed the Bourse for twelve sessions, and very shortly thereafter a new crisis for the franc halted the progress.

Soon after, however, the idea of internationalizing the Paris market came into the foreground once more. In 1971 it was at the centre of the reflections of the Baumgartner Commission, which proposed opening up markets, with the suggestions being drawn up in the perspective of the opening-up of capital within the European Economic Community. It was also clearly what François Bloch-Lainé, the then president of the Crédit Lyonnais, had in mind in a document he wrote in 1974.[23]

> If a financial market such as Paris is to move from the national to the international sphere, several conditions must be met. Over the last few years, the financial authorities have expressed support for that aim. Rather curiously, they have stressed the importance of the role of the Bourse. If an active and well-organized securities market is of prime importance from that point of view, many other elements and conditions also have to come together. Some of them, concerned with the organization of efficient and attractive welcoming structures, are essentially a matter for the public authorities: taxation, exchange control, the regulation of financial markets and credit, town planning, transport and telecommunications.

But the Crédit Lyonnais could also contribute to the move towards internationalization, for which three conditions were necessary:

- the existence of large establishments directed from Paris and capable of organizing financing in any country with or without transfers of capital;
- the presence within such establishment of teams with a strong liking for and a recognized competence in international transaction;
- the attraction to Paris of both firms seeking finance and capital-holders seeking investment.

The contribution the Crédit Lyonnais could make to the process could be summarized under a few headings:

- Developing its own international network of agencies, subsidiaries, and representatives;
- Giving a concrete content to the policy of European cooperation;

- Bringing foreign firms and investors to the Bourse;
- Playing an active part on international capital markets;
- Setting up, from Paris, new international geographical (Union of French and Arab Banks) or functional (lend-lease portfolio management, networks).

Completing such a project as internationalizing the Paris market, which monetary and political instability had for so long made merely a utopian dream, was still the aim of a policy subsequently and recurrently pursued, despite many temporary setbacks, through the active collaboration of the public authorities, the heads of great banks, and the chief financial intermediaries of the market place.

Notes

1. Michel Fior, *Les Banques suisses, le franc et l'Allemagne. Contributions à une histoire de la place financière suisse (1924–1945)* (Genèva, 2002), 19–20.
2. Charles P. Kindleberger, *Histoire financière de l'Europe occidentale* (Paris, 1986), 182, 311.
3. Maurice Lévy-Leboyer, *La Position internationale de la France. Aspects économiques et financiers, XIXe et XXe siècles* (Paris, 1977), 27.
4. Jean-Louis Billoret, 'Systèmes bancaires et dynamique économique dans un pays à monnaie stable en France, 1816–1914' (Nancy, economic sciences thesis, 1969), 227–38.
5. Walter Bagehot, *Lombard Street: A Description of the Money Market* (1873; repr. London, 1917), 32–4.
6. Rondo Cameron, *La France et le développement économique de l'Europe, 1800–1914* (Paris, 1971), 86.
7. Pierre Dupont-Ferrier, *Le Marché financier de Paris sous le second Empire* (Paris, [*c.* 1926]), 225.
8. Bagehot, *Lombard Street.*
9. Calculation based on the balance of payments reconstituted by Lévy-Leboyer, *La Position internationale*, 120.
10. Paul Bairoch, 'La Place de la France sur les marchés internationaux', in Lévy-Leboyer, *La Position internationale*, 47.
11. Alfred Pose, *La Monnaie et ses institutions* (Paris, 1942), i. 320.
12. Regine Vignat, 'La Banque de France et l'État (1897–1920): la politique du gouverneur Pallain' (University of Paris X -Nanterre, doctoral thesis, 2001).
13. Oskar Morgenstern, *International Financial Transactions and Business Cycles* (Princeton, 1959), 128–37.
14. Franco Bonelli, *La crisi del 1907: una tappa dello sviluppo industriale in Italia* (Turin, 1971), 42.
15. In the view of Lévy-Leboyer, *La Position internationale*, 15, 121.
16. According to Françoise Marnata, *La Bourse et le financement des investissements* (Paris, 1973), 80.
17. See Pierre-Cyrille Hautcœur, 'Le Marché boursier et le financement des entreprises françaises (1890–1939)' (University of Paris 1, doctoral thesis, 1994), 10.
18. Alfred Sauvy, *Histoire économique de la France entre les deux guerres* (Paris, 1984), ii. 173.
19. R. J. Truptil, *Le Système bancaire anglais et la place de Londres* (Paris, 1934), 65.
20. Quoted from Pose, *La Mannaie*, 540–1.
21. See the contributions of Roger Nougaret, Georges Smolarski, and Eric Bussiere in *Le Crédit Lyonnais, 1863–1986* (Geneva, 2003), 485 ff.

22. M. Schlogel, ibid.
23. Francois Bloch-Lainé's unpublished typescript 'Contribution du crédit Lyonnais à l'internationalisation de la place financière de Paris', with a mass of manuscript annotations, is part of his private papers.

PART II

'Golden Age', 1890–1914

4

The City of London and British Imperialism: New Light on an Old Question

NIALL FERGUSON

Capitalists prefer peace and 3 per cent to 10 per cent with the drawback of bullets in the breakfast room.

(Lord Salisbury)[1]

1. The City: 'governor of the imperial engine'?

The idea that the City of London played a decisive and malign role in late nineteenth- and early twentieth-century imperialism is hardly new. A century ago, radical critics of British imperialism made the case in often emotive language. In *Imperialism: An Essay* (1902), J. A. Hobson fired an intemperate broadside against the City, singling out one firm in particular for special mention:

If the special interest of the investor is liable to clash with the public interest and to induce a wrecking policy, still more dangerous is the special interest of the financier.... These great businesses—banking, broking, bill discounting, loan floating, company promoting—form the central ganglion of international capitalism. United by the strongest bonds of organisation, always in the closest and quickest touch with one another, situated in the very heart of the business capital of every State, controlled, so far as Europe is concerned, chiefly by men of a single and peculiar race, who have behind them many centuries of financial experience, they are in a unique position to manipulate the policy of nations... Does anyone seriously suppose that a great war could be undertaken by any European State, or a great State loan subscribed, if the house of Rothschild and its connexions set their face against it?

Every great political act involving a new flow of capital, or a large fluctuation in the values of existing investments, must receive the sanction and the practical aid of this little group of financial kings... As speculators or financial dealers they constitute ... the gravest single factor in the economics of Imperialism... Each condition ... of their profitable business ... throws them on the side of Imperialism... There is not a war, or a revolution, an anarchist assassination or any other public shock, which is not gainful to these men; they are harpies who suck their gains from every sudden disturbance of public credit... The wealth of these houses, the scale of their operations, and their cosmopolitan organisation make them the prime determinants of economic policy. They have the largest definite stake in the business of Imperialism, and the amplest means of forcing their will upon the policy of nations . . . [F]inance is . . . the governor of the imperial engine, directing the energy and determining the work.[2]

Twelve years later, in *The War of Steel and Gold* (1914), Henry Noel Brailsford went still further:

In the heroic age Helen's was the face that launched a thousand ships. In our golden age the face wears more often the shrewd features of some Hebrew financier. To defend the interests of Lord Rothschild and his fellow bondholders, Egypt was first occupied, and then practically annexed by Great Britain. . . .

It is . . . a perversion of the objects for which the State exists, that the power and prestige, for which all of us pay, should be used to win profits for private adventurers. The hunting of concessions abroad and the exploitation of the potential riches of weak states and dying empires is fast becoming an official enterprise, a national business. We are engaged in imperial trading, with the flag as its indispensable asset, but the profits go exclusively into private pockets.[3]

Claims like these were widely believed, and not only in Britain. The complaint that British overseas expansion was the work of sinister financial interests and in no way benefited the colonized was echoed throughout the world: by populists and Progressives in the United States and by Bolsheviks in Russia; by anti-Dreyfusards in Paris and anti-Semites in Vienna; and by pro-independence movements from Cairo to Calcutta. Of course, there had always been critics of Britain's empire, at home as well as abroad. But the decisive transformation of 'empire'—something about which the British could feel proud—into 'imperialism'—something of which they should feel ashamed—can be traced back to the generation of Hobson and Brailsford.

It is easy to see why Hobson and others inferred a causal link between the growth of London as a financial centre and the expansion of Britain's overseas empire. The boom in overseas lending from London closely coincided with a dramatic expansion of British colonial rule. Between 1865 and 1914 more than £4bn. worth of capital flowed from Britain to the rest of the world, giving the country a historically unprecedented and since unequalled position as a global net creditor—'the world's banker' indeed; or, to be exact, the world's bond market. More or less simultaneously, the territorial extent of the British Empire grew from 9.5 million square miles in 1860 to 12.7 million square miles. Some 444 million people lived under some form of British rule on the eve of the First World War: at least a fifth of the world's population, inhabiting roughly the same proportion of the world's land surface.[4] Throughout this period of economic and territorial expansion, relations, both political and social, between the financiers of the City and the government ministers at Westminster were manifestly close. In Brailsford's words, 'Liberalism became an Imperialist party . . . Lord Rosebery [the Liberal Foreign Secretary and Prime Minister] belonged by marriage to the Rothschild family, and it was the Rothschild influence which brought about the occupation of Egypt.'[5] It was but a short step to conclude that 'finance' was the 'true governor of the imperial engine'.

Yet much of the modern literature on the subject has cast serious doubt on such judgements. It is now more than forty years since Robinson and Gallagher made their case that strategic considerations were more important than economic ones in extending the imperial frontier in the late nineteenth century, and it has lost little of its original persuasiveness.[6] Research by financial historians has also cast doubt on the Hobson–Brailsford view. Davis and Huttenback pointed out that only around a quarter of total British investment went to the Empire between 1865 and 1914, whereas 45 per cent went to other foreign economies (in particular, the United States).[7] Moreover, they argued that overall rates of return on investments in the Empire fell below returns on domestic investments in the period after 1884—by as much two-fifths—casting doubt on the economic incentives to empire-build.[8] More recently, it has been argued by Bordo and his collaborators that adherence to the gold standard was, by itself, sufficient proof of creditworthiness and bona fides to give a country access to the London market.[9] Clemens and Williamson have argued that capital was attracted to peripheral economies with scarce labour and rising wages, regardless of their political status; poor, populous Asian economies proved unattractive to investors, regardless of whether or not they were colonies.[10] A recent paper by Obstfeld and Taylor finds no evidence of an investor preference for imperial possessions before the First World War.[11] Such quantitative studies seem to bear out the argument of Cain and Hopkins that the 'gentlemanly capitalists' of the City of London did not make a fundamental distinction in practice between formal imperial possessions and countries under Britain's informal financial influence.[12]

This chapter seeks to reassert the importance of formal empire in the 'unofficial mind' of the late nineteenth-century City, suggesting that even if they did not *initially* see independent gold standard countries as more risky than colonies, investors learned through experience that they were. The reality was that membership of the British Empire was a more reliable 'no default' guarantee than adherence to the gold standard by itself. The political upheavals of the period before, during, and after the First World War revealed the limits of commitments to gold in the face of war and revolution. By the 1920s, bitter experience combined with a new regulatory environment to increase substantially the proportion of overseas investment going to the Empire.

2. Gold as a commitment mechanism

A prima facie case for this argument can be found in the theoretical literature on foreign lending. As is well known, there are three fundamental difficulties with cross-border investment – though they are also part of its allure. In the first place, lending across borders can involve an additional risk quite distinct from default risk; namely the danger that the exchange rate of the currencies of lender and borrower may unexpectedly diverge, to the disadvantage of one of the parties (depending on the terms of the loan contract). Secondly, it is harder to ensure that a foreign borrower honours his obligations than to ensure payment of interest and capital from a borrower living under the same national jurisdiction as the lender. Defaults present more serious problems for foreign than for domestic bondholders, because the former generally have no 'voice' in representative institutions and may be less able to use the legal system to press their claims on the government.[13] Finally, it is harder to be sure that a foreign borrower will put overseas funds to good use: informational asymmetries are generally greater, the further the lender is from the borrower. As C. K. Hobson put it in 1914:

> It is often difficult to judge the quality of a possible investment in a distant land, especially when that land is inhabited by a different race of men, possessing different institutions, and speaking a strange tongue. Barriers to intercourse impede the flow of capital to those parts of the world where it would yield the highest return.[14]

One obvious way of overcoming these difficulties from the point of view of investors is to place the monetary and fiscal policies of the borrowing country under some form of constraint. The most straightforward such constraint is an exchange rate peg, and the most widely adopted form of peg in the late nineteenth century was the gold standard. In 1868 only Britain and a number of its economic dependencies—Portugal, Egypt, Canada, Chile, and Australia—had currencies that were convertible into gold on demand. France and the other members of the Latin Monetary Union, as well as Russia, Persia, and some Latin American states were on the bimetallic system, while most of the rest of the world was on the silver standard. By 1908, however, only China, Persia, and a handful of Central American countries were still on silver. The gold standard had become, in effect, the global monetary system, though in practice a number of Asian economies had a gold exchange standard (with local currencies convertible into sterling rather than actual gold) and a number of 'Latin' economies in Europe and America did not technically maintain convertibility of notes into gold.[15] According to Bordo and Rockoff, adherence to the gold standard was a signal of fiscal rectitude, a 'good housekeeping seal of approval' which 'facilitated access by peripheral countries to capital from the core countries of Western Europe'. Gold standard membership indicated that 'a country followed prudent fiscal and monetary policies and would only temporarily run large fiscal deficits in well-understood emergencies'. It was a 'commitment mechanism': a way of affirming that a government would eschew time-inconsistent fiscal and monetary policies such as printing money to collect seigniorage or defaulting on debt.[16] A commitment to gold, they argue, reduced the yield on government gold-denominated bonds by around 40 basis points.[17]

As a *contingent* commitment, however, membership of the gold standard was nothing more than a promise of self-restraint—a pledge on the part of a government to peg its currency in terms of gold, and therefore (by implication) to subordinate its economic policy to the maintenance of that peg. Countries on gold reserved the right to suspend convertibility in the event of what Bordo has called 'well-understood emergencies'. Such emergencies—wars, revolutions, balance of payments crises—were in fact quite common before 1914. Argentina, Brazil, and Chile all experienced substantial financial and monetary crises between 1880 and 1914. By 1895 the currencies of all three had depreciated by around 60 per cent against sterling. This had serious implications for their ability to service their external debt, which was denominated in hard currency (usually sterling) rather than domestic currency. Argentina defaulted in 1888–93, and Brazil in both 1898 and 1914.

Altogether different was the kind of commitment which came with the imposition of direct British rule. This amounted to an unconditional 'no default' guarantee; the only uncertainty investors had to face concerned the expected duration of British rule. Before 1914, despite the growth of nationalist movements in colonies from Ireland to India, political independence still seemed a distinctly remote 'emergency'; even the major colonies of white settlement had been granted only a limited political autonomy. Moreover, the British imposed a distinctive set of institutions on their colonies which, at least on paper, was likely to enhance their appeal to investors: not only economic openness (free trade as well as free capital movements), but also public order, the rule of law (specifically, British-style property rights), balanced budgets, and 'sound' specie-based currency, as well as relatively non-corrupt administration.[18] A modern survey of forty-nine countries concluded that 'common-law countries have the strongest legal protections of investors'. The fact that eighteen of the sample countries have the common law system is, of course, almost entirely due to their having been at one time or another under British rule.[19] In other words, while investors who put their money in independent gold standard countries got little more than a promise not to print money, investors who put their cash in colonies could count not just on sound money, but on the full range of Victorian 'public goods'. It would therefore be rather puzzling if investors had regarded Australia as no more creditworthy than Argentina, or Canada as no more creditworthy than Chile.

At least some contemporary testimony supports the intuition that being a colony offered better assurances to investors than simply being on gold. For most of the nineteenth century and the decades before the Great War, the Rothschild family collectively disposed of the largest private portfolio of financial assets in the world; they also ran one of the best-informed financial institutions in the world and exercised, as underwriters and traders, unrivalled influence over the principal European bond markets. Yet their attitude towards the gold standard—on the rare occasions when they expressed themselves on the subject—was far from consistently positive. When Gladstone and his Chancellor of the Exchequer sent Alfred de Rothschild to represent Britain at the International Monetary Conference held at Brussels in 1892—on the assumption that he must be a 'good staunch monometallist'—he dismayed them by proposing a scheme to prevent or at least slow the international demonetization of silver. Five years later his brother Nathaniel, the first Lord Rothschild, declined to sign a City memorandum against bimetallism.[20] On the other hand, the Rothschilds became committed (though not uncritical) supporters of British imperial expansion, notably in Egypt, the Sudan, Burma, and South Africa. As one member of the family said half-jokingly in 1885, he wished to see the Union Jack planted 'on every island of the Polynees, on every crag of the Himalayas, on every minaret of the East'. The British flag had, as he put it, 'magic powers'.[21]

3. The direction of British capital flows

As is well known, there were two great waves of British capital export between the 1870s and the First World War. From 1861 until 1872, net British foreign investment rose from just 1.4 per cent of GNP to 7.7 per cent, falling back to 0.8 per cent in 1877. It then climbed back to 7.3 per cent in 1890, before once again dipping below 1 per cent in 1901. In the second upswing, foreign investment reached an all-time peak of 9.1 per cent in 1913—a level not subsequently surpassed until the 1990s.[22] In absolute terms, this led to a huge accumulation of foreign assets, rising more than tenfold to somewhere between £3.1bn. and £4.5bn. compared with a British gross domestic product of around £2.5bn.[23] Put differently, the share of British wealth invested abroad rose from 17 per cent in 1870 to 33 per cent in 1913.[24] Davis and Huttenback estimate that, between 1865 and 1914, as much British capital raised on the stock market went to Africa, Asia, and Latin America (29.6 per cent) as to the UK itself (31.8 per cent).[25]

No other country came close to this level of foreign investment: the closest, France, had foreign assets worth less than half the British total, Germany just over a quarter. Britain accounted for something like 44 per cent of all foreign investment on the eve of the First World War.[26] Far from 'starving' British industry of investment, as used to be alleged, this capital outflow effectively paid for itself. In the

Fig. 4.1. British overseas investment earnings as a percentage of GDP, 1850–1913
Source: B. R. Mitchell and P. Deane, *Abstract of British Historical Statistics* (Cambridge, 1971), 333 f. Figures for GNP from C. H. Feinstein, *National Income, Expenditure and Outputs of the United Kingdom, 1855–1965* (Cambridge, 1972).

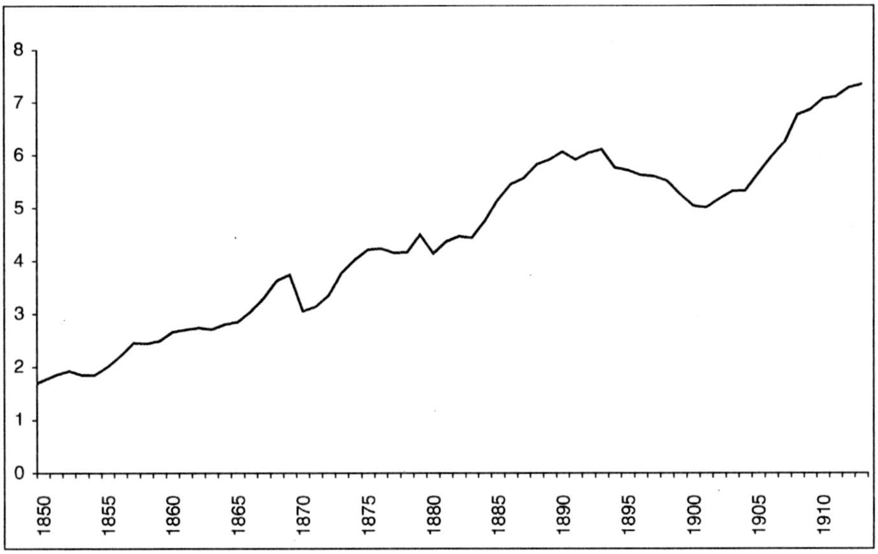

Fig. 4.2. Overseas investment as a percentage of British GNP, 1856–1913
Source: Michael Edelstein, *Overseas Investment in the Age of High Imperialism: The United Kingdom, 1850–1914* (New York, 1982).

1890s net foreign investment amounted to 3.3 per cent of gross national product, compared with net property income from abroad of 5.6 per cent. For the next decade, the figures were 5.1 and 5.9 respectively (Fig. 4.1).[27]

A large proportion of this capital export took the form of portfolio investment in the bonds of foreign governments and government-owned utilities. Between 1865 and 1914 around 35 per cent of all British overseas investments in quoted securities were in public sector bonds; while most of the rest was concentrated in sectors generally characterized by a high level of government interest, if not intervention, such as railways, mines, and public utilities. Only 4 per cent was in manufacturing.[28] In 1862 it was calculated that the aggregate capital of national debts in the world was £2.6bn., of which more than a quarter were quoted on the London Stock Exchange. Ten years later, the total had risen to £4.6bn. and the proportion quoted in London to 53 per cent.[29] Foreign or colonial government issues rose from around 6 per cent of the total value of securities quoted on the London Stock Exchange in 1853 to 26 per cent in 1883.[30] As Fig. 4.3 shows, by 1913 the face value of total foreign securities quoted on the London Stock Exchange exceeded total UK output.[31]

Just how much exported British capital went to countries the British themselves ruled? According to the best available estimates, something like 42 per cent of the cumulative flows of portfolio investment from Britain to the rest of the world went to British possessions (see Table 4.1). The imperial proportion of

Fig. 4.3. Value of colonial and foreign government bonds quoted on the London Stock Exchange as a percentage of GDP, 1853–1913.
Source: Ranald Michie, *The London Stock Exchange: A History* (Oxford, 1999), 88 f., 175, 184, 320, 322, 360 f., 419. Calculated using GDP figures in Feinstein, *National Income*.

stocks of overseas investment on the eve of the First World War was even higher: 46 per cent.

Were imperial possessions able to borrow at lower rates of interest than independent countries (or the colonies of other powers)? The available data on bond yields would appear to suggest that they were. Fig. 4.4 shows that Britain and its principal possessions had among the lowest average bond yields for the period 1870 to 1914. By comparison, bonds issued by the Latin American economies—which also attracted substantial inflows of British capital without actually coming under British rule—were significantly higher. Argentine yields, to give just one example, were more than 200 basis points higher than those on Indian bonds.

Attempts to explain such differentials in terms of fiscal policy tend to rely on anachronistic measures of fiscal balance (such as ratios of debt to gross domestic product). When one looks at the fiscal indicators to which contemporary investors had access, however, a different picture emerges. Late nineteenth-century handbooks like *Fenn's Compendium* provided a variety of different measures: principally the ratio of debt to tax revenue, but also the ratio of debt to exports (relevant for most borrower countries since their external debts nearly always had to be serviced in hard currency, regardless of whether they were on or off gold). One typical snapshot—from the mid-1880s—reveals no very obvious difference between the

Table 4.1. *Cumulated flows and stocks of British overseas capital (millions of 1913 pounds sterling)*

	Cumulated flows 1865–1914 (publicly issued capital only)	% of total	Stocks in 1913/14 (includes FDI)	% of total
Europe	*478*	*11.7*	*224*	*5.6*
Austria-Hungary	41	1.0	8	0.2
Denmark	10	0.3	11	0.3
France	60	1.5	8	0.2
Germany	26	0.6	6	0.2
Italy	46	1.1	12	0.3
Portugal	11	0.3	8	0.2
Russia	145	3.6	110	2.8
Spain	36	0.9	19	0.5
Turkey	44	1.1	24	0.6
North America	*1,334*	*32.8*	*1,448*	*36.4*
USA	898	22.0	873	22.0
Canada	**436**	**10.7**	**575**	**14.5**
Latin America	*829*	*20.3*	*731*	*18.4*
Argentina	380	9.3	320	8.0
Brazil	185	4.5	148	3.7
Chile	67	1.7	61	1.5
Cuba	28	0.7	33	0.8
Mexico	89	2.2	99	2.5
Peru	38	0.9	34	0.9
Uruguay	34	0.8	36	0.9
Oceania	*467*	*11.5*	*416*	*10.5*
Australia	**376**	**9.2**	**349**	**8.8**
New Zealand	**91**	**2.2**	**67**	**1.7**
Asia	*555*	*13.6*	*672*	*16.9*
China	80	2.0	123	3.1
India and Ceylon	**347**	**8.5**	**379**	**9.5**
Indonesia/Dutch East Indies	7	0.2	41	1.0
Japan	85	2.1	102	2.6
Malaysia/Straits-Settlements			**27.3**	**0.7**
Africa	*410*	*10.1*	*483*	*12.2*
Egypt	**71**	**1.7**	**45**	**1.1**
Rhodesia	**51**	**1.3**		
South Africa	**288**	**7.1**	**370**	**9.3**
Br. East and Central Africa			**31**	**0.8**
Br. West Africa			**37**	**0.9**
Total Empire	**1,698**	**42.0**	**1,880**	**46.0**
World	4,073	100.0	3,974	100.0

Source: Moritz Schularick, 'Development Finance in Two Eras of Financial Globalization, (1890–1914 vs. 1990–2000)', draft chapter, Free University Berlin (2003). I am grateful to Mr Schularick for permission to reproduce this table.

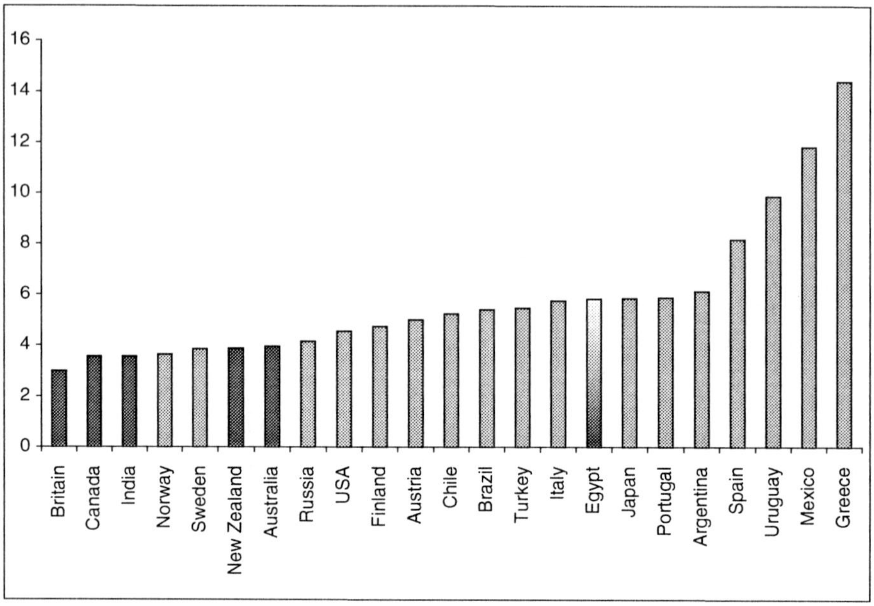

Fig. 4.4. Average bond yields, 1870–1914
Source: Data kindly provided by Alan Taylor.

fiscal position of imperial and non-imperial economies. As Table 4.2 shows, Australia and Canada had quite high debt–revenue ratios in the mid-1880s—not much lower than those of Argentina, Brazil, and Mexico.

The reason that British colonies could attract more capital and at lower rates than economies at comparable stages of economic development cannot be captured by such crude measures of fiscal balance, for the significance of British rule was broader than that. It conferred more than just a 'seal of approval'. It was itself a system of good housekeeping—a guarantee not only of time-consistent fiscal and monetary policies but also of law and order over the lifespan of a long-term bond. As Salisbury said, it promised more than 'good housekeeping'. It guaranteed against 'bullets in the breakfast room'.

4. Egypt: a case study in imperial finance

In order to understand how a country's policies and therefore its credit rating could be transformed as a result of its coming under British rule, it may be helpful to consider a specific case—Egypt—and to contrast it with the experience of its neighbour and former imperial master, Turkey.

In the aftermath of the Crimean War, both the Sultan in Constantinople and his vassal the Viceroy (or 'Khedive') in Cairo had begun to accumulate huge and ultimately unsustainable domestic and foreign debts. Between 1855 and 1875, the

Table 4.2. *Measures of indebtedness in* Fenn's Compendium, *1887*

Country	Nominal debt/revenue	Nominal debt/exports
United Kingdom	7.9	2.5
British Asia	2.3	1.7
British Australasia	6.3	3.4
British N. America	7.2	2.7
Austria-Hungary	6.7	6.9
Denmark	3.7	1.2
Greece	7.4	8.2
Italy	6.3	10.3
Portugal	16.0	21.5
Serbia	4.6	5.2
Spain	7.4	9.1
Sweden	2.9	1.0
Norway	2.4	1.0
Russia	6.9	7.3
Turkey	8.7	12.6
Egypt	11.6	10.5
Japan	4.0	6.2
Argentina	7.6	5.1
Brazil	7.5	5.2
Chile	2.5	1.7
Mexico	7.0	4.6
United States	3.1	2.0

Source: Robert Lucas Nash, *Fenn's Compendium of the English and Foreign Funds . . .*, 14th edn. (London, 1889).

Ottoman debt increased from around 9m. Turkish lire to around 251m. In relation to the financial resources of the Ottoman government, this was a colossal sum: as a percentage of current revenue, the burden rose from 130 per cent to around 1,500 per cent; as a percentage of expenditure, interest payments and amortization rose from 15 per cent in 1860 to a peak of 50 per cent in 1875.[32] By 1877 the Turkish debt had reached 251m. lire, of which, after commissions and discounts, the Treasury in Constantinople had received just 135m. The Egyptian case was similar: between 1862, the date of the first Egyptian foreign loan, and 1876, the total public debt rose from 3.3m. Egyptian pounds to 76m., roughly ten times total tax revenue; in addition, the Khedive Ismail owed around 11m. pounds on his own private account. In the 1876 budget debt charges amounted to more than half (55.5 per cent) of all expenditure.[33] Compared with other major borrowers on the international market, Turkey and Egypt were out of control.

The transformation of Egypt from an Ottoman fiefdom into a British dependency began with the declaration of Turkey's bankruptcy in October 1874. It was this that forced the Khedive to offer his shares in the Suez Canal to the British government for £4m.—an enormous sum, equivalent to more than 8 per cent of the entire British budget net of debt charges, but not enough to end Egypt's financial plight.[34] In the wake of this asset sale, a new Caisse de la Dette Publique was established to place Egyptian finances under the supervision of representatives of Britain, France, Italy, and Austria, the principal creditor countries. It fixed the consolidated debt at £76m. (a figure which did not include £15m. of private debts secured on the Khedive's lands and a substantial floating debt which may have been as much as £6m.).[35] In 1878 the Caisse recommended that an 'international' government be appointed with an Englishman as Finance Minister and a Frenchman as Minister of Public Works.[36] In April 1879, however, the Khedive dismissed the 'international' government, which had made itself unpopular with Egyptian taxpayers. The powers duly reimposed their authority by replacing the Khedive with his son Tewfiq, but a nationalist military revolt led by an army officer named Said Ahmed Arabi finally drove the British government to direct military intervention. In July 1882 Alexandria was shelled, and by September Arabi had been overthrown. Thereafter, Britain ruled Egypt directly or indirectly until the Second World War, with a military presence there until the 1950s.

It is important to remember that the British did not set out to take over Egypt. Indeed, the Prime Minister responsible for the occupation, Gladstone, had previously condemned his arch-rival Benjamin Disraeli for meddling in Egyptian affairs. 'Our first site in Egypt,' Gladstone had warned while in opposition, 'be it by larceny or be it by emption, will be the almost certain egg of a North African Empire, that will grow and grow until . . . we finally join hands across the Equator with Natal and Cape Town . . . '[37] In the third of his famous speeches to the voters of Midlothian, Gladstone had set out his six principles of Liberal foreign policy. The second was the preservation of peace, the third was good relations with the other European powers, the fourth was the avoidance of needless overseas entanglements, the fifth was the equal rights of all nations and the sixth was that the British foreign policy should always be inspired by 'the love of freedom'. This was hardly a manifesto for unilateral annexation. Indeed, as late as January 1882, Gladstone was still arguing that 'Egypt for the Egyptians' would be 'the best, the only solution of the "Egyptian question"'.[38] Even after the occupation, he continued to hope for 'real movement towards institutions & local self-government' in Egypt,[39] insisting to all who would listen that Britain's military presence was a temporary expedient. 'Should the Khedive desire it,' declared Gladstone, 'a small British force may remain in Egypt, at the charge of that country, until his authority is solidly established & placed beyond risk.'[40] By August 1883, Gladstone himself had already made no fewer than five public pledges to leave Egypt.[41] All told, there would be sixty-six such declarations of intent between 1883 and 1922.[42] Nevertheless, all attempts to agree a departure date with the other powers foundered. Egypt remained formally self-governing under a vestigial Ottoman suzerainty; in practice it became a British colony, though the British sought to be (in the words of Lord Salisbury) 'wire-pullers' rather than 'ostensible rulers'.[43]

British wire-pulling turned out to mean root and branch fiscal reform; perhaps not surprisingly, given the Prime Minister's substantial personal stake in the Ottoman Egyptian Tribute loan of 1871 and 1854 Ottoman loan, both of which were secured on the country's annual tribute to the Porte.[44] In 1884 the First Lord at the Admiralty, Lord Northbrook—himself a member of the Baring banking family—was dispatched to Egypt to enquire into the country's situation; his cousin Evelyn Baring (later Lord Cromer) was already in Cairo. It was the latter Baring who did most of the work of stabilizing Egyptian finances in his capacity as British agent and consul-general from 1883 to 1907.[45] Cromer's philosophy was uncompromisingly autocratic: 'We need not always enquire too closely what these people . . . themselves think is in their own interests . . . It is essential that each special issue should be decided mainly with reference to what, by the light of Western knowledge and experience . . . we conscientiously think is best for the subject race.'[46] Gladstone used similar language in his diary: the challenge, he wrote, was 'to plant solidly western & beneficent institutions in the soil of a Mohamedan community'.[47] What this turned out to mean was budget surpluses and retrenchment. The absolute debt burden was reduced from a peak of £106m. in 1891 to just £94m. in 1913; simultaneous increases in taxation meant that the debt-to-revenue ratio halved, from ten to five times current tax income. Once reform was well under way, Cromer was able to bring Egypt back to the London capital market, borrowing at far lower rates than had been possible before.[48] The Rothschilds were happy to manage the new issues: between 1885 and 1893 they underwrote four major Egyptian bond issues worth nearly £50m. The loans of 1890 and 1893 were conversion loans, refinancing existing debt at lower interest rates. Thereafter Cromer felt able to raise new funds for investment in infrastructure, building railways and the first Aswan dam.[49]

By comparison, there was never any serious possibility of a British takeover of Ottoman finances; the other great powers, particularly Russia, would never have countenanced it. As a result, Turkish finances remained under the kind of great power supervision that had previously failed in Egypt. From the point of view of investors, this was clearly preferable to complete independence. However, the Administration de la Dette Publique exercised a markedly less stringent control over the Sultan than Cromer was able to exercise over the Khedive. In 1889, after a major debt rescheduling in 1881, the Turkish debt-to-revenue ratio was 8.7 to 1; by 1909 it was back above 10, as it had been in 1879. As a percentage of expenditure, debt service rose from 12 per cent in 1890 to 33 per cent in 1910, the year of the Young Turks' revolt.[50] Fig. 4.5 shows the diverging paths of Egyptian and Turkish fiscal policy.

This was not without its effect in London. Fig. 4.6 shows that, having been sharply negative prior to the British occupation, the Turkish–Egyptian yield spread became positive from then until the end of the period, averaging around 30 basis points. The average yield on Egyptian bonds between 1890 and 1914 was 3.85 per cent, not only lower than Turkish yields, but also lower than Russian, Austrian, Japanese, and all Latin American yields. Having been one of the world's 'basket case' economies in the 1870s, by 1900 Egypt had joined the elite of 'A-rated' emerging markets. Even more striking are the figures for new issues in Fig. 4.7,

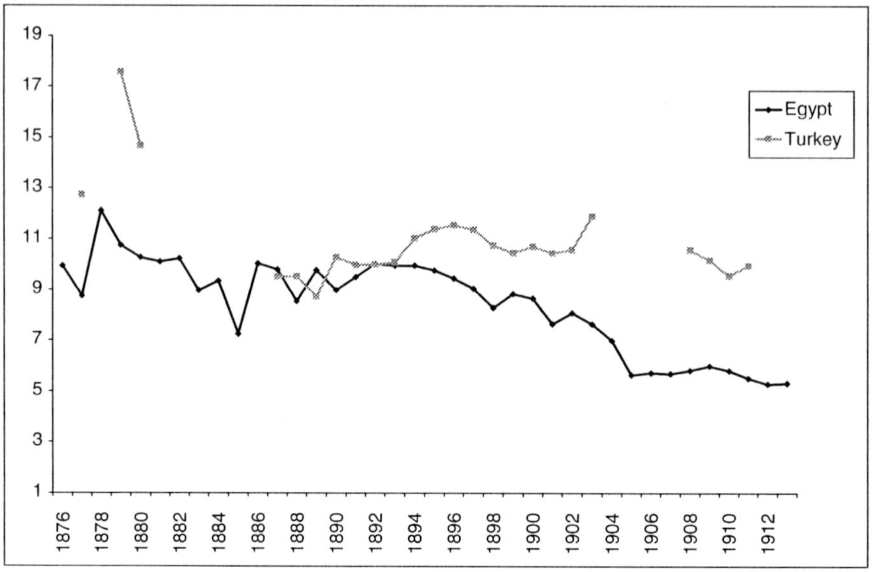

Fig. 4.5. Debt–revenue ratios for Egypt and Turkey, 1876–1913
Source: A. E. Crouchley, *The Economic Development of Modern Egypt* (London, 1938), 274 ff.; C. Issawi, *Economic History of the Middle East, 1800–1914* (Chicago, 1966), 100 f., 104 ff.; S. J. Shaw, 'Ottoman Expenditures and Budgets in the Late Nineteenth and Twentieth Centuries', *International Journal of Middle East Studies*, 10 (1978), 374 ff.

Fig. 4.6. Turkish–Egyptian yield spread, 1870–1914 (bps)
Source: Own calculations from data kindly provided by Alan Taylor.

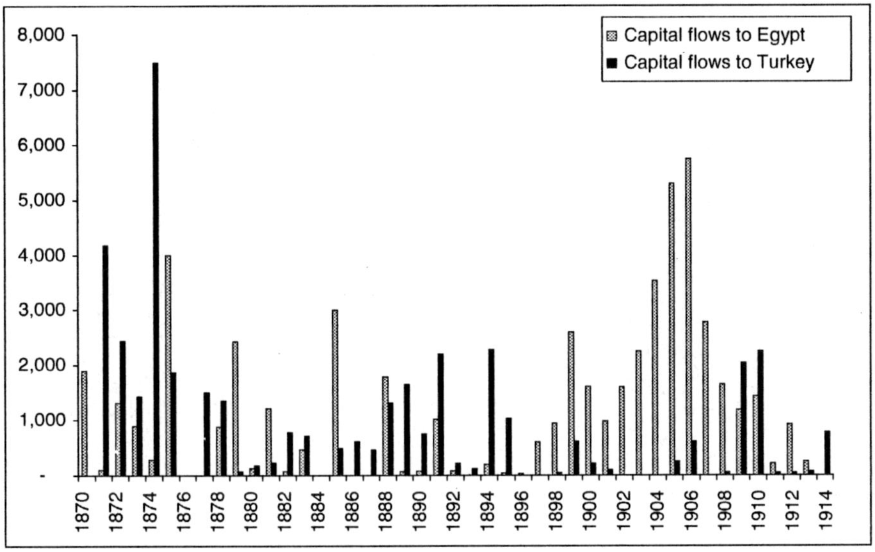

Fig. 4.7. Capital flows from Britain to Egypt and Turkey, 1865–1914
Source: Irving Stone, *The Global Export of Capital from Great Britain, 1865–1914* (London, 1999).

which show that Egypt was able to raise substantially more funds than Turkey after Cromer's fiscal overhaul.

5. Anticipated and actual returns

Did it pay to invest in British possessions? To answer this question, it is necessary to distinguish between anticipated and actual holding period returns on overseas investments. Taking the rather longer period from 1850 to 1914, anticipated (*ex ante*) returns were in fact not significantly lower on colonial bonds than they were on other foreign bonds. (Note that Egypt only came under British rule halfway through the period, hence its relatively high *ex ante* figure.) But the same cannot be said of the actual (*ex post*) returns. If one takes an average of the three colonial countries in the sample the anticipated yield was 5.3 per cent, compared with 4.7 per cent for the three South American countries. But the actual returns were significantly different: 4.7 per cent as against 2.9 per cent.

This helps to explain why, when the same countries returned to the bond market in the inter-war years, they paid significantly different risk premiums. On average, the *ex ante* returns Latin American borrowers had to offer investors were 270 basis points higher than those on new colonial issues. Even so, actual returns on Latin American bonds were once again worse than expected and worse than those on colonial bonds (see Figs. 4.8 and 4.9).

Table 4.3. *Anticipated and actual returns on a selection of international bonds, 1850–1945*

	1850–1914		1915–1945	
	Ex ante	*Ex post*	*Ex ante*	*Ex post*
UK	2.2	1.31	3.11	2.23
Australia	4.35	3.02	5.16	4.18
Canada	4.47	4.77	4.51	3.41
Egypt	7.18	6.41	3.75	4.41
Argentina	5.07	3.52	5.81	3.34
Brazil	4.86	2.26	7.85	4.71
Chile	5.39	2.79	7.86	0.54
Mexico	5.78	−0.74		
Japan	4.36	1.85	7.71	5.89
Russia	4.94	1.31		
Turkey	7.39	1.61	4.3	−3.16
Total sample	5.32	2.12	5.82	3.85

Note: Definitions: *ex ante*—internal rate of return implied by the bond issue price and repayment terms; *ex post*—real realized rate of return deflated by consumer price index of lending country.
Source: Peter H. Lindert and Peter J. Morton, 'How Sovereign Debt has Worked', University of California—Davis Institute of Governmental Affairs Working Paper 45 (Aug. 1997).

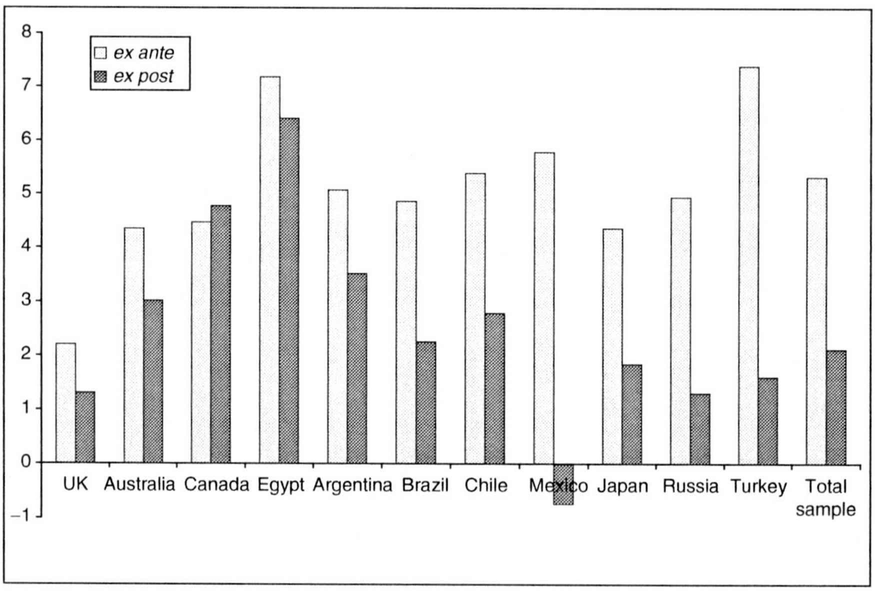

Fig. 4.8. Anticipated and actual returns on eleven governments' bonds, 1850–1914

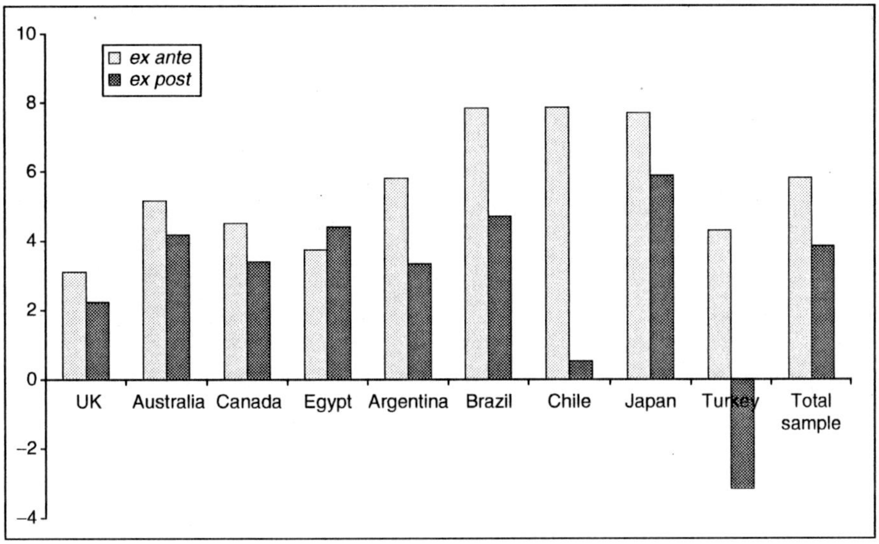

Fig. 4.9. Anticipated and actual returns on nine governments' bonds, 1915–1945
Source: As for Figure 4.4.

In short, experience showed that money invested in a *de jure* British colony such as India, or in a colony in all but name like Egypt, was more secure than money invested in an independent, albeit informally 'colonized' country such as Argentina. Gold standard members who were otherwise sovereign states could not only suspend gold convertibility of their currencies; they could also default on their debts. To varying degrees and at various times, Argentina, Brazil, Chile, Mexico, Japan, Russia, and Turkey all did precisely that.[51] Membership of the Empire was different. British colonies were not much more likely to suspend convertibility and no more likely to default than Britain herself. Certainly by the 1920s, if not before, membership of the Empire was therefore confirmed as a better 'good housekeeping seal of approval' than gold.[52] In the words of Ranald Michie: 'The Empire found it easier and less expensive to borrow in Britain than foreign countries, as the British investor was more inclined to trust those who belonged to the wider British community, though the actual security offered might be identical.'[53]

That imperial membership offered better security to investors than mere adoption of the gold anchor should not surprise us. At the turn of the century, legislation was introduced, in the form of the Colonial Loans Act (1899) and the Colonial Stock Act (1900), which gave colonial bonds the same 'trustee status' as the benchmark British government perpetual bond, the 'consol'.[54] At a time when a rising proportion of the National Debt was being held by Trustee Savings Banks, this was an important boost to the market for colonial securities.[55] Moreover, after the First World War, it was agreed between the Treasury and the Bank of England that new bond issues by British possessions should be given preference over new issues by independent foreign states.[56]

Over and above that, there was the cast-iron commitment of colonial governors and administrators to the principles of Gladstonian finance. Even colonial constitutions had been drafted with at least one eye on creditor preferences. Writing in the 1950s, the Canadian historian Harold Innis declared: 'The constitution of Canada, as it appears on the statute book of the British Parliament, has been designed to secure capital for the improvement of navigation and transport.'[57] It was inconceivable, declared the governor of the Gold Coast in 1933, that the interest due on Gold Coast bonds should be compulsorily reduced: why should British investors 'accept yet another burden for the relief of persons in another country who have enjoyed all the benefits but will not accept their obligation'?[58] When the self-governing dominion of Newfoundland came to the brink of default in the early 1930s, a royal commission under Lord Amulree recommended that its parliament be dissolved, its government entrusted to a six-man commission, and a royal governor appointed from London. Amulree's report made it clear that he and his committee regarded the end of representative government as a lesser evil than default:

> No part of the British Empire has ever yet defaulted on its loan obligations; in the absence of any precedent, the consequences which would follow from a default by Newfoundland must remain to some extent a matter for speculation. But if no precedent can be drawn from the history of the Empire, instruction may be derived from the experiences of other countries, and it is clear from these that any plan of default such as that outlined above could be approved [only] with the greatest apprehension.
>
> The fulfilment of a private money contract depends, of course, in the last resort on the capacity of the debtor to pay, and the law provides accordingly for the bankruptcy of an insolvent debtor. But bankruptcy is at best an ugly word and carries a stigma which a nation even more than an individual would do well to avoid. Directly or indirectly, national bankruptcy is liable to affect the fortunes of every citizen.[59]

Small wonder an increasing share of British overseas investment ended up going to the empire after the First World War. In the period from 1856 to 1914, around two-fifths (39 per cent) of British overseas capital went to the Empire, compared with three-fifths (61 per cent) to the rest of the world. But after the First World War, the balance shifted. Between 1919 and 1938, the Empire got two-thirds, the rest a third.[60]

6. Conclusion

Writing in 1924, John Maynard Keynes observed caustically that it was 'remarkable that Southern Rhodesia—a place in the middle of Africa with a few thousand white inhabitants and less than a million black ones—can place an unguaranteed loan on terms not very different from our own War Loan'.[61] Keynes's point was that this state of affairs was not in the economic interests of Britain itself. With unemployment stubbornly stuck above pre-war levels and mounting evidence of industrial stagnation, capital export seemed a misallocation of resources and Keynes believed British savings would be better employed at home in creating jobs and modernizing the capital stock of the British economy.[62] But from the point of view of colonies like Southern Rhodesia, the British system of 'financial imperial preference', had obvious advantages, giving them significantly easier access to the London capital market than they would otherwise have enjoyed. This conclusion is very different from the view of imperialism formed by Hobson a century ago. Quite apart from its historical interest, the implications of this finding for contemporary debates on economic development are worth pondering.

Notes

1. Andrew Roberts, *Salisbury: Victorian Titan* (London, 1999), 53.
2. J. A. Hobson, *Imperialism: A Study* (London, 1988; 1st edn. 1902), 56 ff., chapter entitled 'Economic Parasites of Imperialism'.
3. Henry Noel Brailsford, *The War of Steel and Gold: A Study of the Armed Peace*, 10th edn. (London, 1917; 1st pub. 1914), ch. 2, entitled 'Real Politics a) Finance and Diplomacy'.
4. Mary Evelyn Townsend, *European Colonial Expansion since 1871* (Chicago, 1941), 19.
5. Brailsford, *War of Steel and Gold*, ch. 3, 'The Egyptian Model'.
6. Ronald Robinson and John Gallagher, *Africa and the Victorians: The Official Mind of Imperialism* (London, 1961).
7. Lance E. Davis and R. A. Huttenback, *Mammon and the Pursuit of Empire: The Political Economy of British Imperialism, 1860–1912* (Cambridge, 1986). See also Michael Edelstein, *Overseas Investment in the Age of High Imperialism: The United Kingdom, 1850–1914* (New York, 1982).
8. Davis and Huttenback, *Mammon*, 107.
9. Michael Bordo and Hugh Rockoff, 'The Gold Standard as a "Good Housekeeping Seal of Approval"', *Journal of Economic History*, 56/2 (June 1996), 389–428.
10. Michael A. Clemens and Jeffrey G. Williamson, 'Where did British Capital Go? Fundamentals, Failures and the Lucas Paradox: 1870–1913', NBER Working Paper No. 8028 (Dec. 2000).
11. Maurice Obstfeld and Alan M. Taylor, 'Sovereign Risk, Credibility and the Gold Standard: 1870–1913 versus 1925–31', NBER Working Paper No. 9345 (Nov. 2002).
12. P. J. Cain and A. G. Hopkins, *British Imperialism, 1688–2000*, 2nd edn. (Harlow, 2001).
13. Allan Drazen, 'Towards a Political-Economic Theory of Domestic Debt', in G. Calvo and M. King (eds.), *The Debt Burden and its Consequences for Monetary Policy* (London, 1998), 159 ff.
14. C. K. Hobson, *The Export of Capital* (London, 1914), p. xii.
15. Barry Eichengreen and Marc Flandreau, 'The Geography of the Gold Standard', *International Macroeconomics*, 1050 (Oct. 1994), table 2.
16. Michael D. Bordo and Finn E. Kydland, 'The Gold Standard as a Commitment Mechanism', in Tamim Bayoumi, Barry Eichengreen, and Mark P. Taylor (eds.), *Modern Perspectives on the Gold Standard* (Cambridge, 1996), 56; Michael D. Bordo and Anna J. Schwartz, 'Monetary Policy Regimes and Economic Performance: The Historical Record', NBER Working Paper No. 6201 (Sept. 1997), 10.

17. Bordo and Rockoff, 'Good Housekeeping', 327, 347 f.
18. Niall Ferguson, *Empire: How Britain Made the Modern World* (London, 2003), esp. ch. 4.
19. Rafael La Porta, Florencio Lopez-de-Silanes, Andrei Shleifer, and Robert W. Vishny, 'Law and Finance', *Journal of Political Economy*, 106/6 (Dec. 1998), 1113–55.
20. Niall Ferguson, *The World's Banker: The History of the House of Rothschild* (London, 1998), 874 f.
21. Ibid. 849.
22. Edelstein, *Overseas Investment*, 24 ff., 48, 313 ff. Cf. *Financial Times*, 6 May 1997: gross direct plus portfolio investment in the period 1990–5 was just under 12% of GDP.
23. Cain and Hopkins, *British Imperialism*, 161–3.
24. Kevin H. O'Rourke and Jeffrey G. Williamson, *Globalization and History: The Evolution of a Nineteenth-Century Atlantic Economy* (Cambridge, Mass., 1999), 208.
25. Davis and Huttenback, *Mammon*, 46.
26. Sidney Pollard, 'Capital Exports, 1870–1914: Harmful or Beneficial?', *Economic History Review*, 2nd ser. 38/4 (1985), 491 f.
27. Edelstein, *Overseas Investment*, 24 ff., 48, 313 ff.
28. Nicholas Crafts, 'Globalisation and Growth in the Twentieth Century', International Monetary Fund Working Paper No. 00/44 (Mar. 2000), 28. Cf. Michael D. Bordo, Barry Eichengreen, and Douglas A. Irwin, 'Is Globalization Today Really Different Than Globalization a Hundred Years Ago', NBER Working Paper No. 7195 (June 1999), 30.
29. Robert Lucas Nash, *Fenn's Compendium of the English and Foreign Funds, Debts and Revenue of All Nations, Together with Statistics Relating to National Resources & Liabilities, Imports, Exports, Population, Area, Railway Guarantees, Municipal Finance & Indebtedness, Banks of All Nations and All Descriptions of Government, Provincial, and Corporate Securities held and dealt in by Investors at Home and Abroad; The Laws and Regulations of the Stock Exchange, &c.*, 14th edn. (London, 1889), 5.
30. Ranald Michie, *The London Stock Exchange: A History* (Oxford, 1999), 88 f., 175, 184, 320, 322, 360 f. Notes: From 1883, figures include foreign government bonds payable abroad but quoted on the London Stock Exchange.
31. This is of course to compare a stock with a flow, but the point is merely to show that market capitalization grew substantially faster than the economy as a whole.
32. See S. J. Shaw, 'Ottoman Expenditures and Budgets in the Late Nineteenth and Twentieth Centuries', *International Journal of Middle East Studies*, 10 (1978), 374 ff.; C. Issawi, *Economic History of the Middle East, 1800–1914* (Chicago, 1966), 94–106; Z. Y. Hershlas, *Introduction to the Modern Economic History of the Middle East* (Leiden, 1964), 53–66; R. Owen, *The Middle East and the World Economy, 1800–1914* (London, 1981), 106.
33. See A. E. Crouchley, *The Economic Development of Modern Egypt* (London, 1938), 274–8; Issawi, *Economic History*, 439–45; Hershlas, *Introduction*, 99–122.
34. For details see Ferguson, *World's Banker*, ch. 25.
35. Crouchley, *Economic Development*, 276.
36. Hershlas, *Introduction*, 104 f.
37. H. C. G. Matthew, *Gladstone*, ii: *1875–1898* (Oxford, 1995), 24.
38. Ibid., 131.
39. Richard Shannon, *Gladstone: Heroic Minister, 1865–1898* (London, 1999), 301.
40. Ibid., 305.
41. Ibid., 318.

42. Matthew, *Gladstone*, ii. 139.
43. Roberts, *Salisbury*, 229.
44. At the time Gladstone ordered the British army into Egypt, these bonds accounted for no less than 37% of his entire portfolio (£51,500 nominal): Matthew, *Gladstone*, ii. 14 n., 135 f., 375 f.
45. Issawi, *Economic History*, 439–45; Hershlas, *Introduction*, 113–22.
46. Denis Judd, *Empire: The British Imperial Experience from 1765 to the Present* (London, 1996), 97.
47. Shannon, *Heroic Minister*, 318.
48. Crouchley, *Economic Development*, 274 ff.
49. Ferguson, *World's Banker*, 839.
50. Shaw, 'Ottoman Expenditures', 374 ff.
51. Details in Peter H. Lindert and Peter J. Morton, 'How Sovereign Debt has Worked', University of California–Davis Institute of Governmental Affairs Working Paper No. 45 (Aug. 1997).
52. As demonstrated by Obstfeld and Taylor, 'Sovereign Risk'. For a contrary argument see Michael D. Bordo and Hugh Rockoff, 'Was Adherence to the Gold Standard a "Good Housekeeping Seal of Approval" during the Interwar Period?', NBER Working Paper No. 7186 (June 1999).
53. R. C. Michie, 'The Social Web of Investment in the Nineteenth Century', *Revue internationale d'histoire de la banque*, 18–19 (1979), 164–8.
54. Cain and Hopkins, *British Imperialism*, 439, 570.
55. James MacDonald, *A Free Nation Deep in Debt: The Financial Roots of Democracy* (New York, 2003), 380.
56. John Atkin, 'Official Regulation of British Overseas Investment, 1914–1931', *Economic History Review*, 2nd ser. 23/2 (Aug. 1970), 324–35.
57. Cain and Hopkins, *British Imperialism*, 233.
58. Ibid. 584 f.
59. David Hale, 'The British Empire In Default: Should Newfoundland Be a Role Model for Argentina?', mimeo, 28 Jan. 2003.
60. Cain and Hopkins, *British Imperialism*, 439.
61. D. E. Moggridge, *Maynard Keynes: An Economist's Biography* (London, 1992), 422.
62. Ibid. 421.

5

Paris, London, and the International Money Market: Lessons from Paribas, 1885–1913

Marc Flandreau and François Gallice

International short-term lending still awaits its historian.

(Jacob Viner, *Studies in the Theory of International Trade* (London, 1937), 407)

Increased global financial integration and the speculation and crises associated with it have led to a renewal of interest in short-term international capital movements and their potential for destabilization. The subject has a certain *déjà vu* feel to it. It was lengthily debated during the twentieth century and is commonly associated with the Nurkse–Von Haberler controversy. While Nurkse emphasized the destabilizing nature of speculation and short-term capital flows, Haberler saw them as mostly stabilizing. The debate had its roots in the historical experience of the gold standard during the *belle époque*. Haberler followed the teachings of his Viennese master von Mises and saw the system as a well-oiled mechanism automatically regulated by the impact of interest rates on capital flows.[1] But Nurkse had doubts. Speculation, he argued, was destabilizing. More recently, some analysts such as Marcello de Cecco described the pre-1914 gold standard as rife with speculation and kept stable only by the central banks' visible hands.[2]

This chapter deals with one aspect of short-term capital movements over the period 1885–1913. It studies the role of the French *haute banque* in the operation of the international monetary system. We adopt a monographic approach, examining the international balances of the Banque de Paris et des Pays-Bas (henceforth referred to as Paribas, its nickname), in an attempt to reinterpret what is known of the pre-1914 international money market's structure.

The novelty of this methodology is that it uses microeconomics as a financial probe to reveal a number of more general problems. This is in contrast with macroeconomic studies of statistical interrelations among national interest rates which treat markets as black boxes. This is also in contrast with the historians' investigations of the minutiae of market situations, which generally tend to elude the question of economic organization, ignore how given set-ups emerge, and treat structures as given.

Why choose Paribas? The first reason is that, like any other member of the so-called *haute banque* (which might perhaps translate into either 'merchant banks' or 'investment banks'), Paribas could rely on a vast network of correspondents, was at par with the best signatures, and as a result had a pre-eminent position on the international money market. The second reason is that, unlike what is typically the case for other members of the *haute banque*, the accounting records of Paribas, which was a joint-stock concern, rather than a private bank, have now been made available to scholars. The last, but perhaps most important reason, is that Paribas stands as an example. The bank was founded in 1872 at the instigation of the French government in order to weaken the grip of the House of Rothschild on the Franco-Prussian War Indemnity loan. It resulted from the merger of French, Dutch, and Belgian bank concerns, and was thus immediately endowed with international contacts for purchasing the exchange France needed to hand over to the Reich: Bismarck, it will be recalled, had insisted on being paid in sterling, mark, Belgian franc, or Dutch florin. On the bank's staff was one gifted clerk, Ottomar Haupt. Haupt was appointed to the bank's Paris headquarters to oversee exchange operations. He later reached senior positions and joined the board of directors. His celebrated handbook, *Arbitrages et parités*, was printed and translated many times over. According to Paul Einzig, he was 'one of the late 19th century's top international financial authorities'.[3] A bank with this kind of firepower could be expected to be active in every sector of the market where profits were to be made.

Using the example of Paribas, we shall therefore try to dissect the structure of the global money market at the time of the gold standard, and expect to gain some insights. The chapter is laid out as follows. Section 1 presents an overview of the existing literature on the subject. Section 2 explains the methodology, based on a description of the *haute banque*'s accounting practices, and sets out the findings. Section 3 reinterprets, from the study's conclusions, the main debates concerning the monetary architecture of the international gold standard era.

1. International Balances and the International Gold Standard: a Survey

This section presents an account of the material written on the pre-1914 international money market, putting the Paribas example into perspective. Given the incomplete nature of the literature, the result cannot be very neat and tidy; it is more like a walk in a wilderness park.

Measurement problems: money market and international balances

Noblesse oblige, our starting point is A. I. Bloomfield's monograph on short-term capital movements.[4] Although this was the first attempt at gathering raw materials for serious study, it is not his most-quoted work—almost surely because his main conclusion is the one that one detests, namely that international monetary flows are almost impossible to track. The shortage of hard evidence is not due to statistical 'benign neglect' motivated by the fact that the global monetary system virtually 'ran itself'.[5] The subject, in effect, cropped up regularly in the press and records of the time.[6] But in those days the state did not meddle much in the secrets of financial affairs, with the result that we do not have any composite source: it is necessary, therefore, to investigate bank by bank.

Bloomfield focused his research on the main central banks as well as some commercial ones in a 'large number of West European countries'. In the case of the central banks, the information was fairly plentiful. Some used their specie reserves as practically their only instrument of action, whereas others used them as a part only of their panoply.[7] Foreign exchange was a common substitute for reserves and the documentation for this was quite good—providing not too much is demanded as to the exact composition of currency holdings.[8] The private banks, however (except in the Nordic countries and Canada where they performed certain central-bank tasks), provided much more meagre pickings. A set of very rough figures, relating solely to foreign asset holdings, was arrived at for France. Bloomfield, relying essentially on published balance sheets, managed to compile a portfolio of 'international bills' covering the four major French commercial banks (Crédit Lyonnais, Crédit Industriel et Commercial, Société Générale, Comptoir National d'Escompte) along with one merchant bank—Paribas, as it happened.

The pitfalls in this kind of approach were obvious to Bloomfield himself. It is notoriously risky to place faith in published accounts. A number of scholars have held that such 'official' statements are apt, so as to protect the secrecy of certain operations or to give the impression of being more 'liquid', to lump various items together.[9] 'Bills', on the other hand, are only one aspect of international balances, possibly a secondary one, as will be seen. Bloomfield noticed, for example, that until 1905 the Paribas official accounts displayed a separate 'foreign correspondents' item on both the assets and liabilities side of the ledger listing large amounts of international balances. Since, for reasons that will be discussed below, the item disappeared from published statements following 1905, Bloomfield had to make the best of what he found and the international deposits were dropped from the entire series.

In this highly confused background, Bloomfield nonetheless came to a few certain conclusions:

- He first noted a sharp rise in the international assets of the *official* institutions (central banks and treasuries), especially after 1900. This he explained as resulting from the spread of the 'gold exchange standard', which rested, not on specie convertibility, too expensive on account of its 'sterile' immobilization of bullion, but on convertibility into a currency itself pegged to gold: in practice, these gold exchange standard regimes implied that the domestic circulation would be secured by interest-bearing international assets (deposits) held in one or several of the big financial centres.
- Where the *private banks* were concerned, Bloomfield surmised, although he could not really prove, that something along the same lines ought to

have taken place as a minor image of official deposits. He also remarked upon the existence of a high degree of 'volatility' in private international balances, which he ascribed, among other things, to interest rate differentials and exchange rate fluctuations.

- As to short-term capital movements, he balanced between seeing them as sometimes stabilizing (Scandinavia), sometimes destabilizing (other countries). All told, however, he concluded that short-term flows were more often 'erratic, perverse, and disequilibrating'.[10]

Market mechanics: key currencies, pulling power, and central banks

Bloomfield's spadework formed the basis for Lindert's classic on official balances in which he popularized the concept of *key currency*.[11] Key currencies, he argued, rose up out of the gold standard system, as central banks and governments began to turn to international currency holdings as substitutes for gold.

What mattered to Lindert (he was writing in the 1960s, when de Gaulle was threatening to get his dollar holdings converted into gold as Bretton Woods rules normally permitted) was to compare the key currency balances of the gold exchange standard countries with the gold reserves backing the same key currencies. This comparison provided a test of the system's ability to survive a doomsday scenario of a scramble for gold.

Lindert's first, but often overlooked, observation was that the pound was not the only key currency: francs and marks also mattered.[12] A second observation was the very large amount of liabilities that key currency countries faced, compared with their gold reserves. Sterling balances considerably exceeded the Bank of England's gold reserves. The situation in Germany was much the same. Only France showed signs of being less 'under threat'.

The survival of the system despite such obvious flaws calls for an explanation. Lindert argued that the force that stabilized the key currencies was the 'pulling power' of their central bank. A dip in the reserves produced by a weakening of the exchange rate could be offset by an interest rate increase which would 'pull in' foreign balances. For all to be well, the key currency countries ought to have exerted a strong pulling power. While Lindert's econometrics accorded pride of place to London interest rates, authors like Goodhart, Sommariva and Tullio, Tullio and Wolters, or Contamin and Denise have later stressed other influences, in particular those of America and Germany.[13]

The debate over relative pulling powers is tightly related to the question of whether central banks, under the gold standard, cooperated or instead competed.[14] We can measure, for example, what impact a change in the Bank of England's interest rate had on the other central banks. But interpreting the nature of these 'chain reactions' is more complex. Direct archival evidence suggests that over time many different patterns have been obtained, as illustrated by the couple between France and Britain. Before 1848 for instance, cooperation was the rule, and central banks swapped reserves to avoid interest rate rises. This was followed, during the

1850s and 1860s, by a period of conflict with Paris and London competing for gold output.[15] Finally after 1890, the Banque de France adopted a policy of systematic support to its British counterpart providing it with gold (Baring crisis) or, after 1905 and until the war, buying sterling bills in Paris to support London.

This discussion shows how important it is to study not only how markets were connected but also how private concerns behaved, since it was they which were supposed to react to interest rate differentials and move their capital accordingly. This returns us to the problem of international money balances statistics. On this account, Lindert argued that we were bound to remain on shaky ground, and saw no other way out except to measure the positions of the main financial centres indirectly, by looking at the key currencies holdings of other nations.[16]

The City's pivotal role: London as international financial centre

London's reputation for soundness, sophistication, and liquidity is commonly pointed out as the main reason for its growing ascendancy, dating back to the early nineteenth century. As one Rozenraad declared in 1902:

> Owing to her well-organized banking and currency system, to the absolute certainty that claims on Great Britain will always be paid in gold, from all parts of the globe one can draw on London, in every part of the world sterling bills are readily taken, and are always negotiable.[17]

Another factor that helped London's rise was the improvement in communications between the continent and the City dating from the 1850s and 1860s.[18] This era marked a break with the days when, according to King,[19] monetary relations among the major financial centres were comparatively weak. Up till that time,[20] British portfolios apparently had not contained much in the way of continental bills, just as British paper was probably rare in continental portfolios.[21] In the early 1860s, however, Goschen was able to write of the 'solidarity' among the financial centres.[22] Recent calculations show that, during the 1860s, there was indeed already a high degree of interest rate correlation across the main European financial market places.[23]

According to King, who adopts a thesis developed by Walter Bagehot in *Lombard Street*,[24] the progress of London as a global money centre was aided after 1870 by France's transition to 'limping bimetallism', which left London with an open field, for the City became the only place where private claims could be changed into gold. As a result, most continental bankers 'of any importance' were wont to hold English paper 'as their gold reserve'.[25]

London's transformation into an international money market was in this view a self-sustaining phenomenon that led the main continental banks to open branches in and around Lombard Street. French and German banks were among the first to do so: the Comptoir d'Escompte in 1867, the Crédit Lyonnais in December 1870; the Société Générale in 1871;[26] the International Bank of Hamburg in 1871, the

German Bank of London in 1871, the Englisches Bank und Wechsler Geschäft in 1873, and the Deutsche Bank in 1873.[27] Although these banks were junior in the acceptances market (foreign banks being considered as 'agencies', and commanding a lower-ranked signature), they acted as channels of communication which made London and the continent more dependent on one another.

Again according to King, the Boer War brought about a significant change at the turn of the century by swelling the supply of Treasury bills.[28] Like bills of exchange, they were keenly sought after by continental investors, for the same reason, namely liquidity. The banker Felix Schuster estimated in 1901 that French claims on London (in bills of exchange, Treasury bills, and securities) amounted to £50–70 m. (1.25–1.5 bn. francs). Before the First World War, foreign-held sterling claims on City institutions had become the leading item on the London money market, well ahead of the 'inland trade bills' that had contributed to its early prosperity.[29] As King concludes, 'Lombard street... is no longer a purely English, or even British institution; it belongs to all nations.'[30]

Economics and politics: Paris and the Alliance banks[31]

Whereas there is an abundant supply of literature dealing with the City's central position with regard to Europe's markets, very much less is known concerning the relations among these markets. We find some references to the 'support' offered to the German banks by the French banks in the form of short-term credits, especially in 1898.[32] Eichengreen uses the same example: 'The French money market [was not] closely linked to foreign markets, although French banks invested some short-term funds in neighbouring countries, notably Germany.'[33] As Alain Plessis remarks, one of the major difficulties here is that the political implications shrouded the issue with a considerable amount of secrecy.[34]

From the scattered information available, it would appear that financial links did exist between Paris and Berlin, and, on several occasions, the French monetary (and therefore political) authorities chose to prop up the German banks in the interests of global monetary and financial stability, even if that meant interrupting the official policy of mutual isolation practised by the two rival countries. It is difficult to tell whether these episodes were routine or exceptional. According to Patron, support for the 'Berlin banks' in 1898 came in the shape of a syndicated loan, principally advanced by the Crédit Lyonnais, amounting to 750 m. francs.[35] Plessis indicates that 'according to Aupetit' there were other operations 'at the beginning of the twentieth century'.[36] Poidevin is more specific, telling of another agreement at the end of the first half of 1908, under which American banks provided the refinancing.[37]

Relations between French banks and Austrian and Hungarian institutions, as recounted in the few sources which deal with the subject, followed the same pattern of interaction between monetary and diplomatic factors. Michel, for example, says that money market links existed, despite the political ban on any large-scale financial dealings with the Austro-Hungarian monarchy.[38] France, he states, held large balances in Vienna, which moved in response to rate changes and political events. Foreign capital, 'almost exclusively French', showed up in Vienna in 1908, attracted by high interest rates. It departed when Bosnia-Herzegovina was annexed, returned in 1910, flowed out again at the time of the Agadir crisis in July 1911, and came back once more after October 1911 because of the large 'profits' that banks could make in Vienna.[39] Little is known, however, about the exact pattern of this see-saw of short-term loans, or even its real scope.[40] What we do know, thanks to Bernard Michel, is that Paribas was an important player in these operations.[41] All in all, the dominant impression is one of confusion, or rather a problem in mapping and explaining the linkages that seem to have existed, politics notwithstanding, between French banking houses and German or Austro-Hungarian ones. One is left with the suspicion that international monetary ties on the continent, on the eve of the First World War, were much more significant than is usually thought.

2. The business of moving money: Paribas 1885–1913

Methodology: nostri accounts, lori accounts, and portfolios

The previous section has underlined the numerous problems (of data, of measurement, of interpretation) that pave the study of international money balances. In this section, we take a completely different angle of attack to produce new insights. Specifically, our source consists of Paribas's Great Ledgers (*Grands Livres*), a handwritten and unpublished half-yearly (June and December) set of accounts listing the particulars used by the bank to draw up its published balance sheets. We systematically perused the Great Ledgers for the period 1885–1913. These hefty quarto volumes enclose accountancy items detailing the bank's different 'portfolios' (commercial paper, securities, carryovers or 'repos', etc.) as well as the position of the different deposit accounts held with correspondents 'in France' and 'abroad'. They are, we found, incredibly detailed and well organized.

With all this material, it is possible to overcome some of the hurdles traditionally associated with reliance on official financial statements. We therefore seek to reconstruct, from an account-by-account analysis of the Great Ledgers material, the path of international monetary assets and liabilities.[42]

The international monetary items break down under two main headings:

- The first is the commercial paper portfolio whose details (type of instrument, maturity, currency) are contained in a folder called '*Position du portefeuille*'. This folder gives the make-up and value of the portfolio at ledger-closing day.
- The second, entitled '*Correspondants étrangers*' ('Foreign Correspondents'), gives the international deposit position. The book sets out the net position, correspondent by correspondent, using the traditional merchant bank classification of *nostri* and *lori* accounts. This separation is explained by the need to deal adequately with the exchange risk problems posed by the use of different

units of currency. An assets side *nostri* 'foreign correspondent' entry denotes a Paribas deposit asset abroad, denominated in the currency of the country concerned. An assets side *lori* 'foreign correspondent' entry records an overdraft in francs granted abroad by Paribas. A *nostri* 'foreign correspondent' liability entry signals an overdraft in foreign currency granted to Paribas by an institution abroad. Lastly, a *lori* 'foreign correspondent' liability entry signifies a deposit with Paribas by a foreign correspondent in francs.

Table 5.1 outlines the distribution in the ledger of the items analysed, including the domestic currency 'liquid' items (Portfolio France, assets and commitments with French correspondents) whose aggregate amounts will be used as a yardstick since these measure 'French' monetary assets, as opposed to foreign ones. The following paragraphs review the various items in the balance sheet. Let us begin with the bills portfolio.

International paper

The portfolio is divided into two categories: 'Paris or the provinces' and 'foreign countries'. In principle, the '*portefeuille*' of foreign bills is supposed to consist of bills with two or three signatures at least, representing either a commercial transaction or bankers' drafts (other terms used included 'finance bills' or 'bank paper'). These instruments were traded on large liquid money markets, where they could be sold according to the terms of discount prevailing at the time of their negotiation on the financial centre where they were payable—and to the exchange rate. The French portfolio is much the same, but only includes instruments payable in France.

Table 5.1. *Stylized 'monetary' sub-balance of Paribas*

Assets	Liabilities
1. Cash and deposit accounts	
1.1 In France (Banque de France and cash in hand): limited amounts.	
1.2 Abroad (cash in London): limited amounts	
2. Bills portfolio	
2.1. Bills on Paris and provinces	
2.2. Foreign bills	
3. Correspondents Paris and provinces (Claims by Paribas)	7. Correspondents Paris and provinces (Claims on Paribas)
4. *Nostri* accounts Paribas deposits abroad (foreign currency)	8. *Nostri* accounts Overdrafts granted to Paribas by foreign sources (foreign currency)
5. *Lori* accounts Overdrafts granted abroad by Paribas (francs)	9. *Lori* accounts Foreign deposits with Paribas (francs)

Note: It is obvious that the assets and liabilities in this sub-balance need not cancel each other.
Source: See above.

Therefore, the French and foreign portfolios showing in the final balance sheet express primarily a division in currencies (francs vs. foreign currencies).

In effect, as anticipated by earlier research, we found, under the portfolio heading—and for amounts that are far from trifling—large packets of government drafts and private short-term bonds, those issued by foreign railway companies in particular. These 'bills' do not show up from 1885 to 1895, and start to increase in frequency from 1895. They take off in 1903–4 (see Fig. 5.1). For instance, mixed with the portfolio of London bills, we find Argentinian (June 1897) and Portuguese (December 1898, June–December 1899) government drafts. At the turn of the century, there are also entries for Chilean, Cape of Good Hope, and Quebec Treasury bonds, followed after 1908 by São Paulo Treasury bonds. We find also a good sprinkling of English municipal authorities, such as the Birmingham Corporation or the City of London in 1904, for very substantial amounts. At that date, they accounted for half of the sterling portfolio (20m. out of a total of about 40m. francs).[43]

More surprisingly perhaps, we observe an increase in official bills issues in francs, evidence that the franc was being used as a currency of denomination for international short-term debt. Initially, this was 'colonial' paper, like the 1896 Protectorate of Annam and Tonkin drafts; but in December 1899, alongside the sterling drafts on the Portuguese government, we start seeing drafts in francs. From 1908, Canadian bonds, then, in 1910, a large bunch of franc-denominated Lake Shore Michigan bonds, find their way into the 'claims on France'. To end with, in 1913, the amount of franc-denominated bonds skyrockets: more than a quarter (28m.) of the portfolio 'France' consists of foreign government bills, many of which were issued by the Balkan States (Serbia, Greece, etc.).

The surge in these sterling or franc instruments is observable also for the other currencies included in the portfolio. A cursory glance may give the impression that the Paribas portfolio after 1905 contains lire, crowns, or roubles. A closer look shows that this truly consists of government bills issued by the Italian, Austro-Hungarian, or Russian authorities. Moreover, all these bills had gold clauses that fixed the exchange rate of these currencies in terms of franc and sterling. This is unlike what happens for US dollar bills, which also increase substantially around that period. The surge of dollar-denominated assets in Paribas's portfolio after 1903 corresponds to a mixture of 'New York City', 'Dominion of Canada', or 'Mexican Central Line' short-term bonds, to name just a few. No gold parity is stated: a clear indication that, by 1913, the dollar had reached a key currency status, being at the same time used as an instrument of denomination by a number of issuers and free from gold clauses.[44]

In order to discuss the variations of the portfolio of French and foreign bills, it is essential therefore to sort out the bookkeeping for these different instruments, which are highly dissimilar in reality. In liquidity terms, the packets of foreign short-term bonds cannot be likened to commercial paper. Argentinian Treasury bonds and City of London instruments are securities that are very different from true 'London bills'. Furthermore, the maturity of these securities, some of which can be traded only over the counter, is usually longer (six months) than that of commercial paper, which in most cases may not exceed three months. Fig. 5.1 shows the detail of the Paribas portfolio structure after 'cleaning up'.

As can be seen, Paribas's foreign bills portfolio amounts to about one-fifth of its full bills portfolio. Claims on France thus make up a sizeable fraction of the merchant bank's paper holdings. Evidence for the early years of Paribas, however, shows that, on the other hand, the bank can nevertheless muster up large volumes of foreign assets when the need arises.[45] The second salient feature is the high proportion of bills on London in the foreign bills total (Fig. 5.2*a*).

Claims on the City outweigh every other item, with the possible exception of claims on Germany, which in some years can add up to a considerable amount: quite large quantities of marks are entered in December 1897, June 1898, 1904, June 1906 and 1911.[46] The 1911 figures are also something of a surprise, given the international diplomatic tension that was reigning.

The leading place occupied by claims on the City was subject nevertheless to quite wide variations. The period before 1893 was marked by relatively large holdings of London bills (Fig. 5.2*b*). Their share in the total portfolio then declined, before another sharp rise occurred from June 1904 to June 1905. They then subsided again and stayed low thereafter except in June 1907 and December 1911–December 1913.

These gyrations in the London assets portfolio are not easy to explain. Table 5.2 tests various possible explanations of the reasons for changes in the portfolio's composition. A priori, interest rate differentials (either bank rates or market rates) should have mattered, along with the exchange rate. Other things being equal, higher interest rates in London than in Paris should have caused the share of sterling

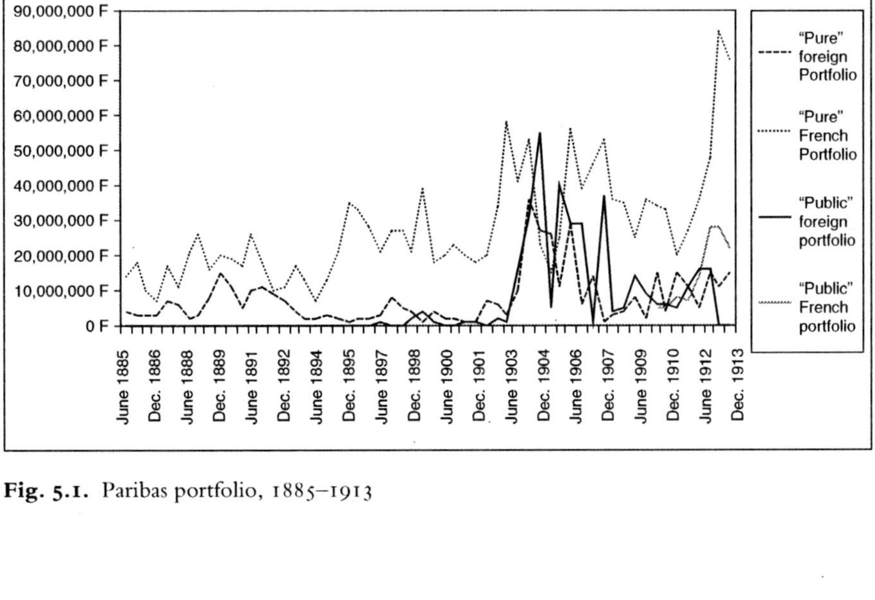

Fig. 5.1. Paribas portfolio, 1885–1913

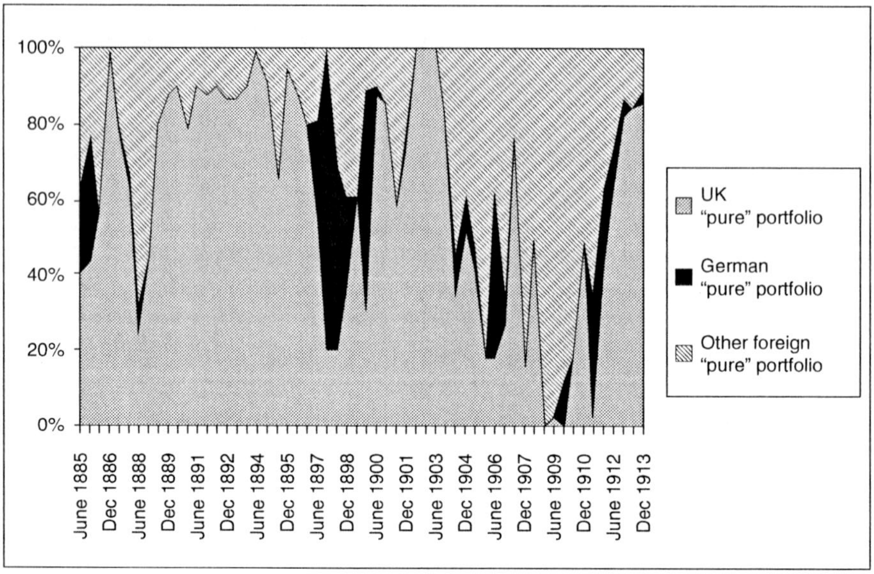

Fig. 5.2*a*. Paribas 'pure' foreign portfolio, 1885–1913

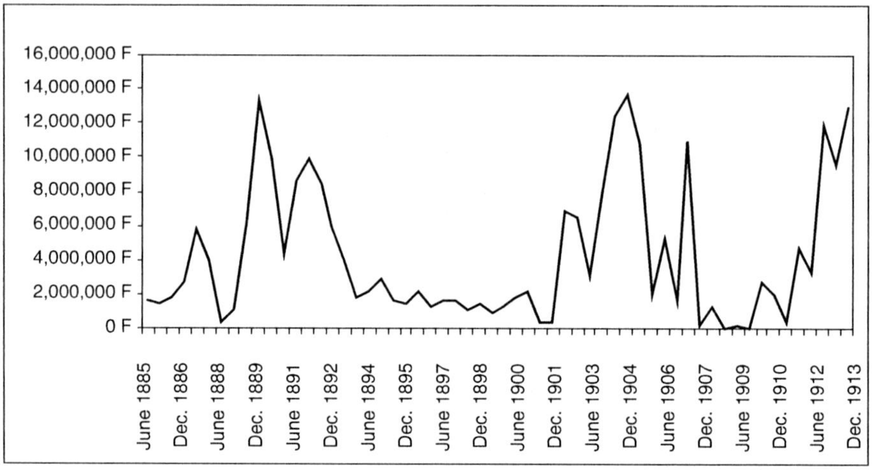

Fig. 5.2*b*. Paribas 'pure' London bills

bills to increase. On the other hand, a depreciated franc (a higher exchange rate) should have reduced the share of sterling, since investors would have expected an eventual recovery and worried about correspondent capital losses on their sterling holdings. While the influence of exchange rates is correctly signed but not significant, the effect of interest rate differentials between London and Paris has the wrong sign in general (negative, when it should be positive),

Table 5.2. *Explaining sterling holdings*

Explained variable	Share of £ in bills portfolio		Share of £ in bills portfolio		Variation in £'s share	
Econometric model	OLS (i)		AR1 (ii)		OLS (iii)	
Interest rate differentials						
Bank rates[a]	−0.0046		−0.006		−0.008	
(t-stat)	(−0.26)		(−0.42)		(−0.73)	
Open Market Rates[b]		0.0067		−0.017		−0.003
(t-stat)		(0.36)		(−0.99)		(−0.25)
Exchange Rate[c]	−0.93	−0.34	−0.10	−0.10	−0.09	−0.13
(t-stat)	(−0.42)	(−1.31)	(− 0.45)	(−0.45)	(−0.44)	(−0.56)
Time Trend	−0.003*	−0.003*	—	—	—	—
(t-stat)	(−3.07)	(−3.01)				
Constant	7.5	8.8	2.85	2.85	−0.0004	−0.0004
(t-stat)	(1.16)	(1.35)	(0.47)	(0.47)	(−0.03)	(−0.03)
Check statistics						
DW	0.9	0.9	1.84	1.86	2.18	2.2
R^2	0.16	0.16	0.02	0.012	0.02	0.015

Note: * = significant at 5%.

Source: *Archives Paribas*, Grand Livres (portfolio), *The Economist* (interest rates and exchange rates). Authors' elaborations (data presented in the appendix). (i): straight ordinary least squares estimates. DW suggests presence of autocorrelation in residuals motivating (ii). (iii) is similar to (i) but dependent variable is changes in portfolio's structure.

[a] London rate minus Paris rate, end of month data.

[b] London open market minus Paris open market, end of month data.

[c] Francs per £.

and is never significant. These conclusions are obtained regardless of the type of equation and estimation technique considered. The conclusion is that the 'standard' variables do not explain at all variations in Paribas portfolio of sterling bills.

Briefly put, our study of the international bills portfolio confirms some popular conclusions in the literature, namely that claims on London lorded it over international bills in general and that other currencies such as the mark or the franc played a role. On the other hand, it provides some more troubling conclusions: interest differentials were not, at least from a microeconomic standpoint, the primary engine of fluctuations in sterling portfolios. Finally, the study also reveals fresh facts. First, there was the rise after 1900 of a new breed of claim: debt instruments denominated mostly in pounds and francs, but distinct from traditional commercial paper. The choice by different borrowers of British, French, or American money for this type of instrument suggests that those currencies were liquid enough to support the emergence of new international financial instruments. Concerning the pound, this is hardly a scoop, but, for the franc and dollar, it is a finding that deserves attention.

International deposits

Correspondents' accounts: assets. The correspondents' deposit accounts feature in both the assets and liabilities columns of the ledgers. Generally speaking, they involve deposits or interest-bearing lines of credit (overdrafts), repayable on demand subject to prior notice. A thorough analysis of the year 1905 reveals that their distribution is very uneven.[47] On the asset side (both *nostri* and *lori*), 25 per cent of the accounts comprised about 97 per cent of the total amount for each item. On the liabilities side, they comprised 99 per cent.[48] The conclusion is that the major share of business was done with a comparatively small number of correspondents, about sixty in round figures.[49]

Random sampling in these circumstances is not a good idea. We therefore decided to focus on the more limited target of the biggest accounts, with the aim of covering at least 95 per cent of the sums deposited, thereby reducing the task to manageable proportions. The data gathering involved collecting, for each individual account, the name of the correspondent, the national origin, and the type of client (a distinction was further made between place of origin and place of operation). We divided business into four broad institutional categories: 'governments', 'central banks', 'private banks' (banks and syndicates), and 'companies' (railways, insurance, mines, steel, chemical industries, etc.). On the other hand, thirty-one countries were identified, an indication of Paribas's vast network of international connections.[50] We created an imaginary thirty-second country, 'Syndicatia', for holding accounts of banking operations carried out by several institutions from various countries and not otherwise detailed. For convenience, countries were further regrouped in broad areas: north-west Europe comprises the Old World's 'creditor' or 'core' countries: Belgium, the Netherlands, Germany, Switzerland, the United Kingdom.[51] The European 'periphery' is divided into three groups: 'Central Europe' (Russia, Romania, Bulgaria, Serbia, Austria, Hungary), 'Mediterranean' (Italy, Greece, Ottoman Empire, Egypt, Morocco, Spain, and Portugal), and 'Scandinavia' (Norway, Sweden, and Denmark). America is divided into 'North America' (United States and Canada) and 'Latin America' (Argentina, Brazil, Mexico, Peru, Uruguay, and Guatemala). A final group ('Other') covers the deposits in Asia (China) and Africa (e.g. Johannesburg). So for instance, the Deutsche Bank's London branch was assigned the residence code 'England', the origin code 'Germany', and the business code 'private banks'. Finally, while it is technically possible to analyse the portfolio on a biannual basis over the whole period, we decided, given the substantial effort that data collection involves, to limit our investigation to yearly intervals ending each June.[52]

As said, deposit accounts are arranged on the assets side in two broad groups: Paribas holdings with foreign institutions in foreign currency (*nostri* accounts) and overdrafts granted in francs to other institutions (*lori* accounts).[53] Trends are shown in Fig. 5.3.

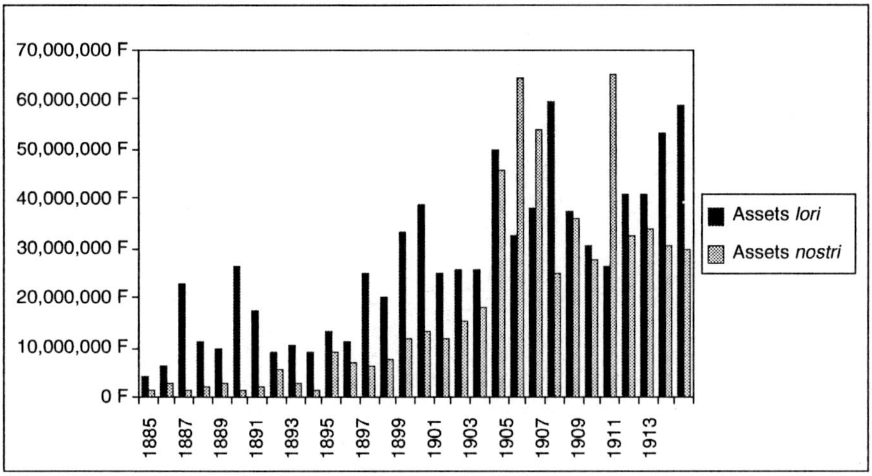

Fig. 5.3. Assets, foreign correspondents *nostri–lori*

Deposits abroad keep growing steadily. They shoot up after 1903, dwindle in 1907, recoup in 1910, then fall again. At their peak, the amounts deposited abroad exceed 60m. francs, well above the amounts held in the bills portfolio. On the other hand, overdrafts are on average (except in 1905, 1906, and 1910) higher than deposits, implying that foreign institutions constantly ran up heavy debts in francs.

To gain a sense of the kinds of transaction underlying changes in the bank's international asset structure, it is useful to break these assets down into their institutional components. As it appears (Fig. 5.4*a*) deposits with foreign banks (*nostri*) predominate.

In the *lori* column, things are less clear (Fig. 5.4*b*). Until 1900, overdrafts to central banks (1887, 1890–1, 1895) and, on occasion, to governments (1897) outweigh overdrafts granted to private banks. Beginning in 1898, however, the latter overdrafts soared and remained well ahead of the rest until the end of the period. When the overdrafts granted by Paribas to industry are included, private overdrafts constantly exceed public ones after the turn of the century.

The geographical distribution of Paribas's international balances also deserves careful attention. Figure 5.5*a* sorts foreign deposits (*nostri*) into major geographical areas.

We observe a rising tide, as from 1903, of West European deposits. They are the driving force behind the very distinct rise in the *nostri* accounts. It is also worth noting the regular increase of deposits with North American institutions; they involve large amounts, particularly in June 1908, i.e. in the months following the 1907 US financial crisis. The breakdown of north-west European deposits, on the other hand, does confirm very clearly London's position as a nexus. The post-1900

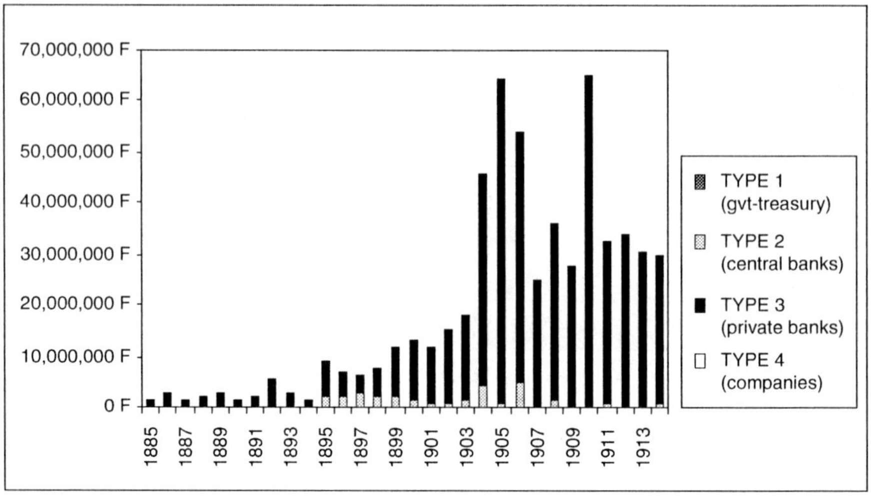

Fig. 5.4*a*. Assets *nostri* by type

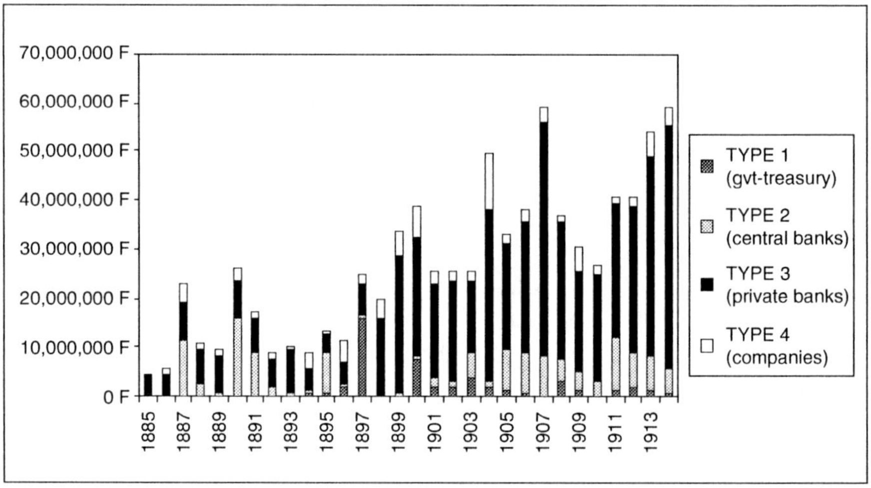

Fig. 5.4*b*. Assets *lori* by type

rise in London deposits dwarfs any other evolution. Obviously, at some time in the early 1900s, something induced Paribas to step up its sterling assets.

Finally, it is worth analysing claims on London by correspondents' nationality. The result is striking (Fig. 5.5*b*). Over the whole period, balances held in London were not primarily held with British banks. On the contrary, German, Austro-Hungarian, and Anglo-Austrian houses were the leading counterparts. The upsurge in deposits in London in 1903 was indeed a consequence of the increase in the

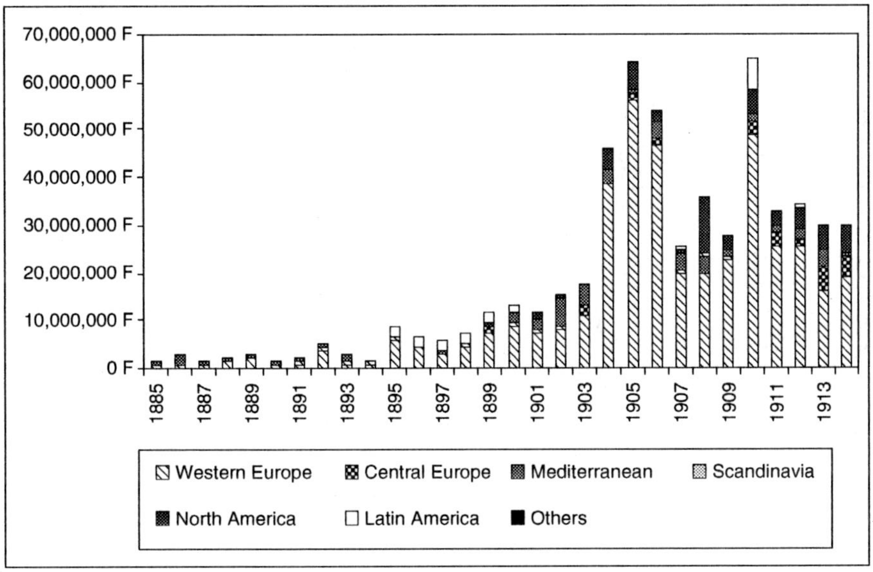

Fig. 5.5*a*. Assets *nostri*: geographical distribution

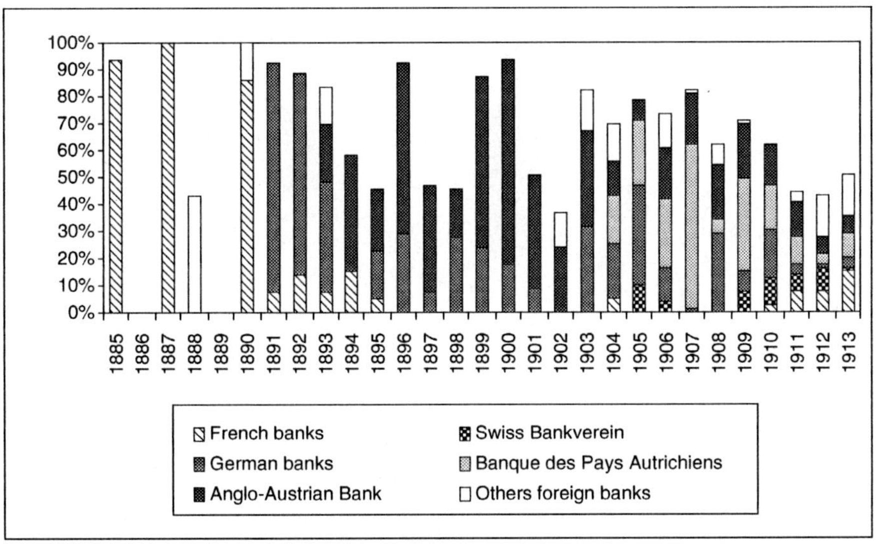

Fig. 5.5*b*. Assets *nostri*: share of foreign and Anglo-foreign banks in Paribas' *nostri* in London

balances held by Paribas with these institutions. When we add direct deposits in Germany to those made via London, we reach the extraordinary conclusion that, right at the time of the run-up to the First World War, most of Paribas's international deposits were going to the Triple Alliance. London, we find, acted less as an English centre than as a cosmopolitan money market where banks in search of liquidities and others with money to spare found themselves on common ground.

The geography of the *lori* accounts on the asset side of the Paribas ledgers reveals several interesting features which contrast with the trends noted in the case of deposits (Fig. 5.6). The difference here is that the 'peripheral' countries, rather than the developed Western European countries, account for the major part of the sums in question. When we seek to trace the origin of the surge of franc overdrafts to the periphery, we often find operations that were intended to support official establishments, such as the Bank of Spain.[54] At the beginning of the period the 'Mediterranean' group dominates (1885–95, and especially in 1887 and 1890–1). Beginning in 1893–4, the Central European group followed in their stead.[55] The 'Mediterranean' overdrafts returned to the fore from 1899, at the same time as overdrafts granted to Latin America began to grow. When credit in francs was being extended, the periphery clearly received more than the European north-west. This, most probably, is because north-west European countries were able to finance themselves in their own currency (except perhaps in times of crisis as happened in 1907, when we see franc overdrafts for Germany playing a significant role). One test of this interpretation is that we should find limited amounts

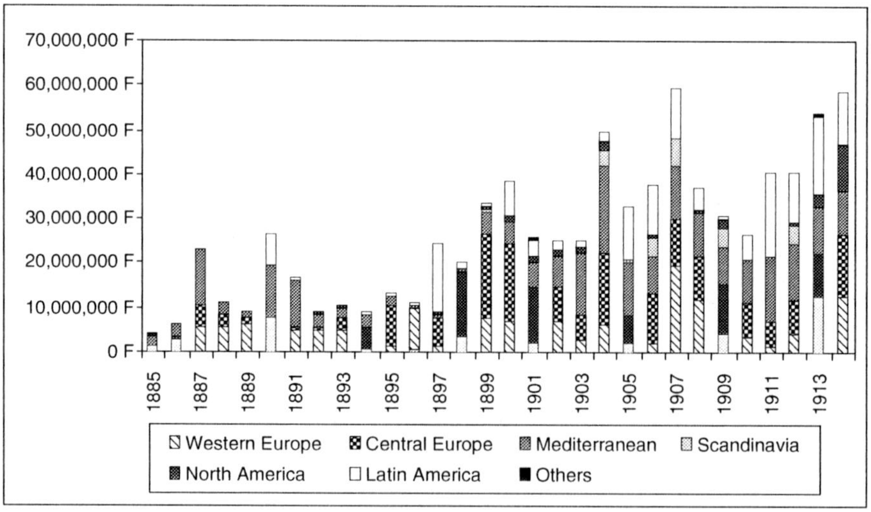

Fig. 5.6. Assets *lori*: geographical distribution

of foreign currency overdrafts in the liability side of Paribas—France being a north-west European country—and such is indeed the case, confirming the hypothesis.

In the end, it appears that while borrowers in the developed countries were able to attract deposits denominated in their own currency (arguably by bidding up for foreign funds), the peripheral countries were more likely to contract debts in the currency of the lending financial centre. In this way, the franc became a short-term finance instrument both for public institutions seeking the backing of French financiers to manage their exchange reserves and for private institutions seeking to balance their books. By contrast, overdrafts in francs were only marginally used by private institutions in the major financial centres (i.e. precisely when domestic liquidity disappeared). Finally, the role of key currencies as instruments for international deposits is illustrated by the spectacular, if temporary, upswing in Paribas's north-west European balances after 1903, of which most were held in London if not deposited with British banks. To conclude: a key currency country attracts deposits, others get overdrafts.

Correspondents and current accounts: liabilities. On the liability side of the Paribas ledgers, the nostri accounts record overdrafts in foreign currencies obtained by Paribas: as argued they should be, and indeed are, negligible. *Lori* accounts on the other hand record deposits in francs placed with the bank by foreign correspondents. They are the place to look for evidence of international debt. The result is up to expectations for, as Fig. 5.7*a* shows, the volume of these foreign funds is really substantial. Until 1900 or thereabouts, the sums did not exceed 50m. francs.

Deposits came mostly from the same regions as the ones to which the bank granted overdrafts, namely Central Europe and the Mediterranean zone. There are also deposits from the north-west Europe countries but the amounts are smaller. After 1892–3, following a spell of fragility that was the natural aftermath of the 1890 crisis, Spanish[56] and Central European deposits began mounting in the Paribas ledgers. As from 1903—which, as we saw, was precisely when the London deposits began their rise—Paribas's foreign intake leapt upwards. In 1906, foreign deposits totalled close to 460m. francs, which was more than two-thirds of the bank's entire balance. Alongside the Central European deposits, those from North America grew also. After 1906, however, these deposits evaporated. Some return after 1907. It may be noted also that, after 1910, the mean volume of the Central European deposits shrank drastically.

The institutional source of these foreign funds is the expansion of official deposits (see Fig. 5.7*b*). The 1903 surge in foreign deposits was due primarily to an increase in deposits by the Russian, Bulgarian, and Romanian official institutions (Treasury or state banks). In fact, the subsequent ballooning of Russia's deposits (which totalled 200m. francs in June 1906) was the reason for the disappearance of a separate heading for foreign funds in Paribas's published balance sheet. The rationale for this change which had worried Bloomfield so much is now understood: most probably, Paribas had been embarrassed at letting the public know that a goodly part of its ressources consisted in deposits by a state whose finances it helped to manage in the midst of the serious political crisis of 1904–6, by underwriting its

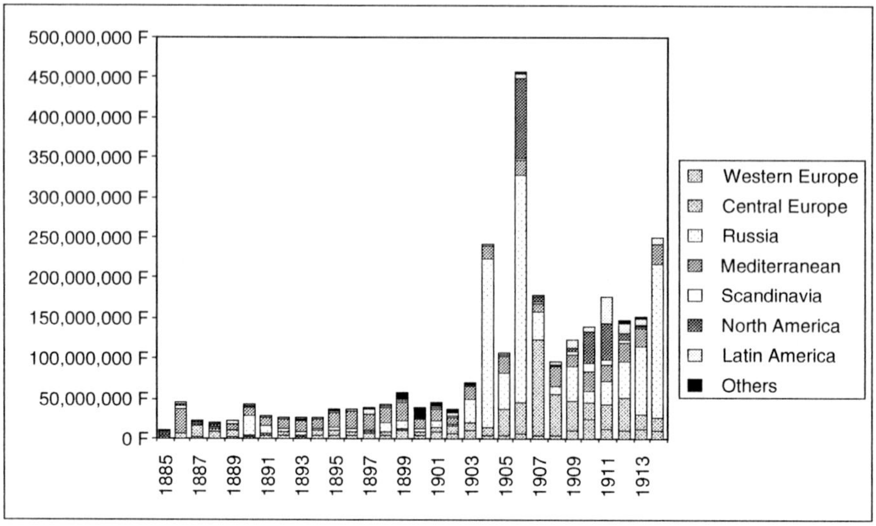

Fig. 5.7*a*. Liabilities *lori*: geographical distribution, 1885–1913

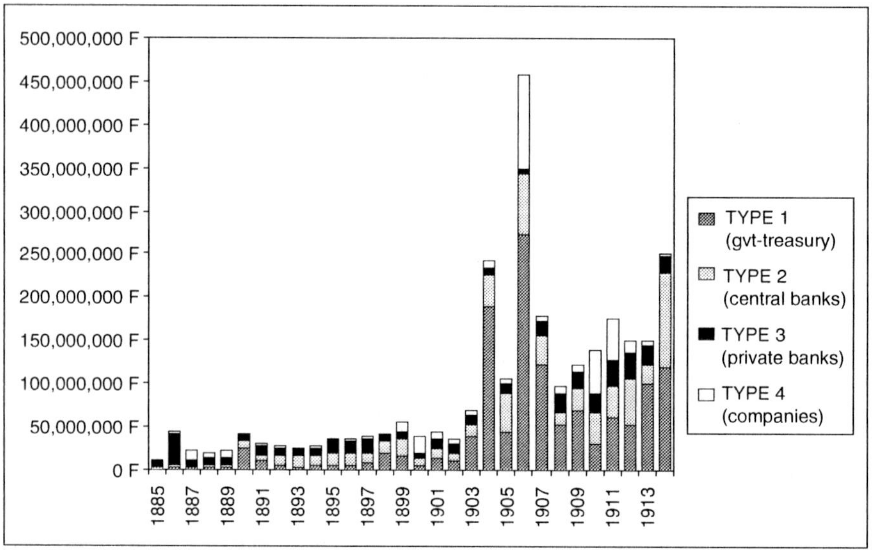

Fig. 5.7*b*. Liabilities *lori* by type

loans with other French banks. As can be seen, these deposits receded fairly abruptly afterwards, suggesting a potential risk of liquidity mismatch. It was better not to let the market place know that one of Paribas's depositors held close to half of the bank's total resources, and that this depositor was Russia.

3. Conclusion: interpretations and speculations

It is now time to tie together the various threads investigated so far. Our examination of Paribas's international monetary balances brought to light a number of facts concerning not only the monetary aspects of the *haute banque*'s activity but also the workings of the international monetary system of the time. Let's review them in turn.

This chapter has dealt a lot with monetary geography. As a matter of fact, we identified a geographic structure in the books of Paribas. This structure was found to rest on two interconnected circles or networks, one public and the other private. Traditionally regarded as distinct by Bloomfield and Lindert, these networks were the two sides of a single reality. On the one hand, the public sector's presence in the books of Paribas was associated with sovereign lending, as already emphasized: Spain in the early years, Russia, and Bulgaria a little later, were typical recipients. The franc was used to denominate loans precisely because it was needed to pay coupons to French investors. For the same reason, it became an international deposit currency. Official institutions, as a result, featured on both the assets side, through the overdrafts granted to them as part of exchange support operations, and the liabilities side, through the funds they deposited, which in some years could amount to huge sums. Treasuries and central banks were obviously the *haute banque*'s top-drawer customers. Their selection of such or such market to issue their debt, while it was obviously determined *ex ante* by the liquidity services that alternative markets provided, influenced, *ex post*, the very liquidity of the chosen market.

A private financing network coexisted with this public activity. As argued we found that only agents located in a money centre could bank deposits in their own currency: London, Paris, and Berlin were all qualified in this regard. As a result, private concerns in these centres could be found receiving foreign funds originating from private institutions. Some centres were more equal than others: the system's heart was undoubtedly London. From the mid-1900s, London was *the* great market for European bank deposits. It was international finance's neutral ground where French and German banks could hobnob in a political no man's land. The information we have unearthed tends to confirm the hunches already expressed by others. Despite the politicians, or perhaps with their tacit consent, finance in the years leading up to the First World War was 'European', at least for the short-term capital market, and its headquarters was London. There is no call in any case to exaggerate the political aspect of the situation. Paribas was capable on occasion of placing money directly in Germany or Austro-Hungary. The fact of going through London to lend to the Deutsche Bank did not imply that the operation was illicit; it was at most a question of discretion at a time when nationalist sentiment brought the spotlight to bear on capital movements. It was even more probably a matter of taking advantage of the City's remarkable financial technology. Given these facts, London quite logically plunged into a severe crisis when the Great War broke out.

Much has been written about the key currencies and their ranking, but no full explanation of their emergence has ever been given. Our study, which underlines the position of sterling in the 'private' circuit described earlier, confirms this ranking order and sheds more light on its nature. As argued, states in the periphery managed their finances with the north-western European bankers' help, with the consequence that government accounts and private bank balance sheets became intertwined. The improvement in the 'peripheral' treasuries situation after 1896 noted in Flandreau, Le Cacheux, and Zumer's 'Stability without a Pact' was reflected in a dramatic increase in the 'official' liabilities of the international merchant banks.[57] This plenty could also become a source of worry for them. In any case higher 'official' liabilities disclosed the critical vulnerability of their books: this is, we found, the reason why Paribas began cooking its published accounts after 1905.

In this background, the distinct character of the 1900s is clearly apparent. As we have noted, there was a surge in resources connected with the increase in international deposits, particularly Central European deposits within which Russian funds played a dominant role. There was also an offsetting surge in international entries (not overdrafts, which at bottom are partially related to the financial position of the recipient correspondents and thus exogenous—but deposits), which were found to be made either in London or in German banks or both. Put otherwise, the improved official balances of the periphery after 1900 generated a recycling problem: what to do with all this public money? The need for security and liquidity (these large deposits might have to be paid on short notice) restricted the choice to monetary options. The preferred solution appears to have been to re-export at least part of the incoming capital to the world's largest and most liquid market, which was the City. The jump in resources consequent upon the increase in public deposits then translated into a proliferation of London entries. It was as though Paribas was trying to transfer part of its foreign deposits, unstable by nature, to the City. This explanation tells us why, despite the fact that the pound had already become an international instrument in the 1860s, a spectacular rise in deposits with London occurred in the period following 1900. In short, the triumph of the key currencies after 1900 was engendered by new macroeconomic conditions in the borrowing countries.

The process did not stop there, however, and we may be forgiven for some final speculation. The gyrations in claims on London in Paribas's monetary assets portfolio remind us of Bloomfield's remarks on the growing volatility of London balances, the mechanism of which we should now better understand. What was at work in these changes was, we suggested, the counterpart of the variations in the continent's merchant banks' liabilities, themselves driven by changes in the short-term creditor position of long-term debtor states. This cannot be unrelated to the growing sense of monetary instability in the years preceding the First World War, and to the paradox that this creates: this sense must have been ultimately related to a deep trust in sterling, which must have motivated the accumulation of London balances to begin with. Stability feeds fragility.

Seen in this perspective, the Banque de France's policies for shoring up the London market, which as we argued intensified after 1906, become more intelligible. London's use as a market for recycling the continental banks' liabilities implies that the changing volume of deposits in the City was only partly related to discount rate fluctuations. In the case of Paribas at least, we have seen that the interest rate differential between Paris and London only poorly explains the bank's portfolio choices. And yet the Bank of England's sole available weapon against fund withdrawals was to raise its interest rate. The Banque de France policy of routinely buying up English bills in Paris may be understood as follows. The Bank of England, confronted with unwelcome cashings of London bills by the continental banks who had to meet the demands of their sovereign depositors, was obliged to respond by hiking its rates. The Banque de France, in order to prevent the Bank of England from pushing them too high, went out buying in Paris whenever the French banks started selling their sterling bills portfolios. This is well illustrated in Fig. 5.8, which shows the negative correlation existing from 1906 to 1913 between variations in the Paribas bills portfolio and the portfolio of the Banque de France—when Paribas sold, the Banque de France bought. As is apparent, changes in Banque de France sterling holdings reacted to changes in the Bank of England discount rate as if the Bank of France had sought to maximize profits.

Thus, paradoxically, the variations in the French bank of issue's bills stock were much more consistent with British interest rate changes than were those in our private bank's bills portfolio. This is because, we argue, private banks mostly bought London bills for liquidity purposes and were thus irresponsive to interest rate differentials.

The conclusion to be drawn from our research is more than a little disconcerting. We found private banks, described in the conventional literature as guardians of the system's self-adjustment by reason of their 'automatic' behaviour, acting as bankers for 'emerging' nations, a role today performed by international financial institutions. This led their balance sheet to reflect international financial trends. When borrowers plunged into financial trouble, private banks extended overdrafts

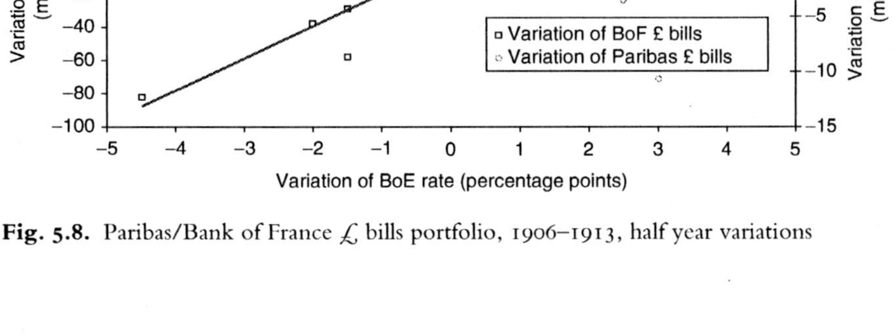

Fig. 5.8. Paribas/Bank of France £ bills portfolio, 1906–1913, half year variations

to them to help them out, and this drained the liquid resources of the international financial system. When the situation of borrowers improved, they accumulated balances (denominated in key currencies) in the books of international banks and this increased the global supply of funds. Today, the IMF's resources, and hence its stabilizing power, are closely tied to developments in the world macroeconomic situation, just like what happened to international banks one century ago. Today, periods of global prosperity make support for a particular debtor country more probable and its financing easier, whereas periods of recurrent crisis drain the international financial institutions' accounts and make their intervention less likely. The lesson, obviously, is that global stability is pro-cyclical.

Symmetrically, we found a central bank (the Banque de France), portrayed by some authors as a guarantor of world order by reason of its cooperative attitude, reacting to interest rate hikes in London in quasi-merchant fashion, buying at attractive prices bills which private banks dumped on the market to meet their official depositors' withdrawals. Thus while private institutions did not behave automatically, public ones did what the private sector ought to have done.

As the gold standard loses more and more of its mystique, studying it becomes more and more fascinating and, we are inclined to hope, more and more instructive.

Notes

1. For an intellectual genealogy of the Nurkse–Haberler debate, see M. Bordo and H. James, 'Adam Klug Memorial Lecture: The Case for Floating Exchange Rates as an Alternate for Bretton Woods', in A. Arnon and W. L. Young (eds.), *The Open Economy Macro-model: Past, Present, Future* (Boston, 2002), 161–82. As to its historical roots, see M. Flandreau and J. Komlos, 'How to Run a Target Zone? Age Old Lessons from an Austro-Hungarian Experiment', Working Papers 556 (2001).
2. M. De Cecco, 'Short Term Capital Movements under the Gold Standard', in J. Braga de Macedo et al. (eds.), *Currency Convertibility* (London, 1996), 111.
3. *The Theory of Forward Exchange* (London, 1937). For one thing, *The Economist* relied on Haupt for its published estimates of gold points among leading financial centres.
4. *Short Term Capital Movements under the Pre-1914 Gold Standard* (Princeton, 1963).
5. We are reminded of Callaghan's famous quip, quoted by Lindert: 'Why do you have balance of payment problems now, when you didn't have them fifty years ago?' 'There were no balance of payments problems fifty years ago because there were no balance of payments statistics.' George Dixon, 'Let's Abolish Statisticians', *Washington Post*, 4 Oct. 1965.
6. See, for example, Quai d'Orsay Archives, New Series, Carton NS 45, on French capital assets in London. Similarly, Plessis quotes a 1909 memo in which Robineau, an inspector at the Bank of France, states that 'paper created abroad forms a large part of the big Paris banks' portfolios', in A. Plessis, *Histoires de la Banque de France* (Paris, 1998), 157.
7. On Belgium, see P. Kauch, *La Banque Nationale de Belgique, 1850–1918* (Brussels, 1950); on Portugal see J. Reis, 'An Art, not a Science: Central Bank Management in Portugal under the Gold Standard' (mimeo, Instituto de Ciências Sociais da Universidade de Lisboa, 2003); on Austria-Hungary, see C. Jobst, 'Micro-Managing the Gold Standard: The Austro-Hungarian *Devisenpolitik*', *European Historical Economics Society* (5th Conference,

Madrid, July 2003); on France see M. Flandreau, *The Glitter of Gold: France, Bimetallism and the Emergence of the International Gold Standard* (Oxford, 2004).

8. As reported by R. H. I. Palgrave, *Bank Rate and the Money Market in England, France, Germany, Holland and Belgium, 1844–1900* (London, 1903), some central banks, such as the Reichsbank, did give the currency breakdown of their foreign assets by nationality. Some other institutions were more secretive: the Banque Nationale de Belgique, for instance, a pioneer in the holding of foreign bills, reported totals only.
9. See Plessis: 'Commercial portfolios are . . . composite. They lump together bills liable to be rediscounted by the institute of issue, lots of foreign bills . . . and one suspects from time to time that they contain bundles of securities.' The case in point was made in the pamphlet *Lysis*, which claimed that the balance sheets of the main large banks included, under the heading '*portefeuille*' (portfolio), very heterogeneous instruments, Plessis, *Histoires de la Banque de France*, 146.
10. A. I. Bloomfield, 'Short Term Capital Movements under the Pre-1914 Gold Standard', Princeton Studies in International Finance, No. 11 (Princeton, 1963), 90.
11. As regards public holdings, Lindert fills in Bloomfield's estimates to what he claims to be 'ninety percent' complete. As to private balances, he adopts Bloomfield's figures, with the remark that his total probably represents 'much less than one half [of the actual overall balances], and . . . progressively lower for earlier years' (!) in 'Key Currencies and Gold, 1900–1913', Princeton Studies in International Finance No. 24 (Princeton, 1969), 8.
12. In Lindert's words, 'While greater balances were held in London than in any other international financial center, a larger size was held in France and Germany than has been generally realized. By 1913, Germany in particular had begun to challenge London's position, the mark having become a more popular official reserve asset on the Continent than sterling,' 'Key Currencies', 76–7. This conclusion, Lindert emphasized, had been anticipated by Bloomfield, 'Short Term Capital Movements', 93.
13. C. Goodhart, *The Business of Banking, 1891–1914* (London, 1972); A. Sommariva and G. Tullio, *German Macroeconomic History, 1880–1979* (London, 1987); G. Tullio and J. Wolters, 'The Determinants of the Bank of France's Discount Rate and its Liquidity Ratio during the Classical Gold Standard: An Econometric Analysis, 1876–1913', unpublished working paper, Universities of Brescia and Berlin (1998); R. Contamin and C. Denise, 'Quelle autonomie pour les politiques monétaires sous l'étalon-or, 1880–1913?', *Économie internationale*, 78 (1999), 59–84.
14. B. Eichengreen, *Golden Fetters: The Gold Standard and the Great Depression, 1919–1939* (Oxford, 1992); M. Flandreau, 'Central Bank Cooperation in Historical Perspective: A Skeptical View', *Review of Economic History* (1997).
15. Flandreau, 'Central Bank Cooperation'; M. Flandreau, *The Glitter of Gold*.
16. As he wrote, 'No British figures on short-term external claims have been released by any of the larger banks . . . and the apparent inability of the Cunliffe and Macmillan Committees to discern Britain's prewar short-term position suggests that the appropriate aggregates will never be forthcoming from the British side. The same pessimistic appraisal seems unavoidable regarding German and French data. The smaller countries, on the other hand, were more willing to scrutinize and publicize their foreign exchange positions.' Lindert, 'Key Currencies', 6. His conclusion echoes Bloomfield's rueful remarks: 'Very little can be said with assurance about the currency proportions prevailing in private portfolios. Certain a priori arguments and descriptions by financial observers would lead one to suspect that the private supremacy of London over Paris and the

German centers was greater than is revealed by the proportions for official holdings, but these same considerations have led to an exaggeration of London's uniqueness as an official reserve center... As long as quantitative evidence is lacking, it is better to avoid guesses about currency proportions .... One can make the usual assumption that sterling was the world's chief currency... and presume that its share was not rising after the turn of the century.' Ibid. 21.

17. C. Rozenraad, 'The International Money Market', *Journal of the Institute of Bankers*, 23/4 (1902), 197–8.
18. See R. Michie, *The London Stock Exchange: A History* (Oxford, 1999), 74. The London-to-Paris cable was laid in 1851, and the one from London to New York in 1866.
19. See W. T. C. King *History of the London Discount Market*, (London, 1936) ch. VIII.
20. King might have added, as another contributing factor, the change in monetary regulations that followed the crisis of 1857, which led to a removal of the ceilings on central-bank interest-setting in France, Belgium, Germany (Hamburg), Denmark, and other countries.
21. King, *History*, 266, draws on the work of Newmarch for the 1840s: 'Moreover, it is clear that at this period foreign bills formed only a small proportion of the total outstanding at any one time—for the middle forties the proportion had been estimated (by Newmarch) at under 14 per cent.' This latter claim is more implicit than explicit in King's work. King, relying on contemporary opinion, according to which interest differentials did not stimulate any substantial international flows of capital, concluded that 'A noteworthy fall in the London market rate below the Hamburg rate would lead a Hamburg banker to remit his English acceptances for immediate discount, instead of holding them to maturity, as was customary.' Thus London paper did enter the portfolios of continental bankers, but not to the extent required to provoke immediate flows of capital.
22. G. J. Goschen, *The Theory of Foreign Exchanges* (London, 1860).
23. See M. Flandreau, 'Was the Latin Union a Franc Zone?', in J. Reis (ed.), *International Monetary Systems in Historical Perspective* (London, 1995), 71–90.
24. (London, 1873).
25. Luke Hansard, quoted by King, *History*, 278.
26. On the Crédit Lyonnais branch in London, see François Gallice, 'Le Crédit Lyonnais à Londres 1870–1939', in B. Desjardins, M. Lescure, R. Nougaret, P. Plessis, and A. Straus, *Le Crédit Lyonnais 1863–1986*, (Geneva, 2003).
27. Recent essays have examined the chronology of the German banks' establishment in the City: M. Pohl and K. Burk, *Deutsche Bank in London 1873–1998* (Münich, 1998); G. F. Feldman, L. Gall, et al., *The Deutsche Bank 1870–1995* (London, 1995).
28. 'The legal framework providing for the development of Treasury bills was set up in 1877. Bagehot had recommended that these bills should resemble as much as possible the "commercial bills of exchange", issued under a known interest and with stated date of redemption.', King, *History*, 276. In 1902, Treasury bills became a legitimate 'ways and means' instrument, providing short-term finance in a routine way.
29. Nishimura mentions the net decline in the supply of 'inland bills'. S. Nishimura, *The Decline of Inland Bills of Exchange in the London Money Market, 1855–1913* (Cambridge, 1971).
30. King, *History*, 282.
31. Financial ties with Italy are not dealt with here. Although very strong at the time of the *Risorgimento*, they weakened gradually. When Italy fell into Germany's orbit in the

1890s, the divorce could be said to be complete. The reasons for this were, however, certainly more than 'merely' political.

32. See C. P. Kindleberger, *Manias, Panics and Crashes: A History of Financial Crises*, 4th edn. (New York, 2000).
33. Eichengreen, *Golden Fetters*, 53.
34. Plessis, *Histoires*. The most often quoted reference is M. Patron, *The Bank of France and its Relation to National and International Credit*, Senate Doc. No. 494 (Washington, 1910), although the primary source is R. Poidevin, *Les Relations économiques et financières entre la France et l'Allemagne de 1898 à 1914* (Paris, 1969), 181–2.
35. Patron, *The Bank of France* 142. Plessis claims that the package had the Banque de France's blessing.
36. Plessis, *Histoires* 132. Plessis does not give a specific reference to Aupetit. The likelihood is that he refers to A. Aupetit et al., *Les Grands Marchés financiers, France (Paris et Province), Londres, Berlin, New York* (Paris, 1912).
37. Poidevin, *Les Relations économiques*, 655.
38. B. Michel, *Banques et banquiers en Autriche au début du 20ème siècle* (Paris, 1976): 'We need to banish the idea that political antagonisms created a rift between the Paris and Vienna markets. Short-term capital movements took place almost every day.' 'At first sight, French capital is completely absent from Austrian banking history; but if you know where to look, it is everywhere,' concludes Michel, ibid. 255.
39. Michel, ibid.; G. Köver, 'The Austro-Hungarian Banking System', in R. Cameron and V. I. Bovikyn (eds.), *International Banking 1870–1914* (New York, 1991), 319–45, drawing on Bartsch's study of the Austro-Hungarian balance of payments, F. Bartsch, *Statistische Daten über die Zahlungsbilanz Oesterreich-Ungarns vor Ausbruch des Krieges*, (Vienna, 1917), 45, agrees with Michel's thesis. As Köver puts it, 'Before the Moroccan crisis of 1911, however, Belgian and especially French short-term credits played big roles in the Vienna and Budapest money markets.' The exact amounts withdrawn by French banks from Vienna and Budapest are a matter of dispute. Michel quotes Hollo, a Hungarian MP, who claimed that 'France has taken back between 300 and 400 million francs in floating capital which in favourable times are available to us', but adds that Bartsch was probably 'closer to the truth when he estimates that from 60 to 80 million francs' worth of French deposits in Vienna and Budapest were repatriated in 1911'. See also S. Chapman, *The Rise of Merchant Banking* (London, 1984), 121.
40. As Von Mises writes, the Austrian banks' needs were much more modest than those of their Berlin counterparts. 'There are times on the money market, i.e. the market for short loans, when the greatest Austrian foreign assets are met with but a trifling set-off on the part of foreigners.' L. Von Mises, 'The Foreign Exchange Policy of the Austro-Hungarian Bank', *Economic Journal* (1909), 208–9.
41. '[Paribas], along with the Wiener Bankverein and the Deutschebank, was one vertex of a potent triangle of financial operations in Central Europe.' Michel, *Banques*, 248.
42. The approach led us to concentrate on the ledger items dealing with short-term assets, for the most part deposits and paper. Naturally, the distinction between short and long term is arbitrary. Securities quoted abroad could equally well have acted as a medium for short-term transactions. The capital-loss risk posed by daily fluctuations meant, however, that securities lay a few notches further down the liquidity scale than monetary instruments properly speaking.

43. We may also note in 1904 large sums in Great Northern Pacific Line and Ontario Railway bonds.
44. On these issues see M. Flandreau and N. Sussman, 'Old Sins: Exchange Clauses and European Foreign Lending in the 19th Century', in B. Eichengreen and Ricardo Hausman (eds.), *Others People's Money* (Chicago, forthcoming, 2004).
45. The data available on the first years of the Banque de Paris et des Pays-Bas's existence show the impact of paying the war indemnity, although these traces fade with time. In June 1873, only 5 m. in claims on France stand against 20 m. in claims abroad.
46. 1906 stands out: the 12 m. francs in claims on Germany exceed claims on the City.
47. See Appendix Table 5.A1.
48. Figure for the *lori* accounts. There are virtually no *nostri* balances (overdrafts granted to Paribas by foreign institutions) for reasons that will appear later. This item will be neglected for the rest of the analysis.
49. Jobst, 'Micromanaging the Gold Standard', lists about 40 international houses engaged in exchange transactions with the Austro-Hungarian bank. Here too a few houses do most of the business.
50. Argentina, Austria-Hungary, Belgium, Brazil, Bulgaria, Canada, China, Denmark, Egypt, Finland, Germany, Greece, Guatemala, Italy, Mexico, Morocco, the Netherlands, Norway, Ottoman Empire, Peru, Portugal, Romania, Russia, Serbia, South Africa, Spain, Sweden, Switzerland, United Kingdom, United States, and Uruguay.
51. Holland, curiously in view of the bank's name, did not receive any deposits from Paribas.
52. That half-year being probably less open to 'fiddling' than the December balance sheet.
53. It sometimes happened that overdrafts were granted in a foreign currency (especially sterling overdrafts for South American debtors) but it was not common practice.
54. This evidence from the creditor's vantage point confirms the analyses of Jaime Reis on the Bank of Portugal 1854–91 which purchased foreign exchange to shore up the exchange rate by running down foreign overdrafts in London and Paris. Reis, 'An Art'.
55. This could have been an effect of the monetary stabilizations attempted in Russia and Austro-Hungary.
56. By the Bank of Spain in particular, the Paribas management having succeeded in winning over this traditional client of the Rothschilds.
57. M. Flandreau, J. Le Cacheux, and F. Zumer, 'Stability Without a Pact: Lessons from the European Gold Standard, 1880–1913', *Economic Policy* (1998), 117–62.

APPENDIX 5.A1.

Table 5.A1. *Concentration of Paribas deposits, 1905*

Type of account	Total number of accounts	10% largest balances		25% largest balances	
		Threshold (FF)	% of total deposits	Threshold (FF)	% of total deposits
Nostri (asset side)	103	1,000,000	82	150,000	97
Lori (asset side)	84	750,000	82	200,000	97
Lori (liab. side)	266	200,000	95	50,000	99

Source: Authors' computations from *Archives Paribas, Grand Livre 1905*. *Nostri* liabilities are omitted because in 1905, as explained in the text, they were always negligible.

Table 5.A2. *Data for regressions in Table 5.2*

Semester	Franc bills	£ bills	Paris open market	London open market	Bank of France	Bank of England	Exchange rate
1885:1	14,325,212	1,698,279	2.5	0.75	3	2	25.19
1885:2	17,804,279	1,419,430	2.5	3	3	4	25.23
1886:1	9,538,597	1,761,829	1.375	1	3	2.5	25.245
1886:2	6,571,921	2,747,381	2.625	4.125	3	5	25.38
1887:1	17,386,375	5,728,286	2.125	1.25	3	2	25.235
1887:2	10,876,882	4,027,628	3	2.75	3	4	25.325
1888:1	21,411,707	443,877	2.375	1.125	2.5	2.5	25.265
1888:2	26,076,455	1,165,856	4.125	4	4.5	5	25.34
1889:1	15,694,926	6,154,263	2.75	1.375	3	2.5	25.18
1889:2	19,744,411	13,329,600	3	3.875	3	5	25.185
1890:1	18,805,852	9,937,851	3	3.5	3	4	25.16
1890:2	17,177,637	4,237,382	3	4.125	3	5	25.215
1891:1	26,460,494	8,575,183	2.625	1.5	3	3	25.26
1891:2	18,496,740	9,975,155	2.625	2.275	3	3.5	25.195
1892:1	9,728,593	8,405,465	1.625	0.875	2.5	2	25.175
1892:2	10,993,714	5,977,955	2.375	1.75	2.5	3	25.12
1893:1	16,763,765	3,887,350	2.5	1.75	2.5	2.5	25.17
1893:2	13,007,152	1,745,859	2.5	2.375	2.5	3	25.185
1894:1	7,460,209	2,068,770	2	0.75	2.5	2	25.155
1894:2	12,626,050	2,860,734	2	0.9375	2.5	2	25.185
1895:1	21,419,721	1,595,485	1.75	0.5625	2	2	25.205
1895:2	35,033,882	1,363,958	1.875	1.125	2	2	25.225
1896:1	33,085,472	2,083,376	1.75	0.8125	2	2	25.155
1896:2	27,530,895	1,262,943	2	3	2	4	25.23
1897:1	21,294,086	1,529,337	1.875	1	2	2	25.1
1897:2	27,265,659	1,663,341	2	2.9375	2	3	25.24

continues

Table 5.A2. *Data for regressions in Table 5.2 (Continued)*

Semester	Franc bills	£ bills	Paris open market	London open market	Bank of France	Bank of England	Exchange rate
1898:1	26,902,726	994,235	1.875	1	2	3	25.225
1898:2	21,353,616	1,359,557	3	3.125	3	4	25.235
1899:1	39,049,701	810,799	2.875	2	3	3	25.18
1899:2	17,961,903	1,283,983	4.5	6	4.5	6	25.315
1900:1	19,593,206	1,810,305	2.875	2.5	3	3	25.125
1900:2	22,613,166	2,109,273	3	4	3	4	25.08
1901:1	20,051,610	379,100	2	2.6875	3	3	25.2
1901:2	18,158.655	433.323	2.75	3.375	3	4	25.15
1902:1	20,434,071	6,820,479	2.5625	2.5625	3	3	25.18
1902:2	33,972,011	6,411,295	2.8125	3.5	3	4	25.14
1903:1	57,973,837	3,000,057	2.75	2.3125	3	3	25.135
1903:2	40,780,970	7,943,171	2.875	3.25	3	4	25.165
1904:1	52,798,301	12,490,013	1.5625	1.875	3	3	25.19
1904:2	23,399,691	13,578,546	2.75	2.5625	3	3	25.145
1905:1	14,716,009	10,793,634	2	2	3	2.5	25.155
1905:2	24,647,259	1,976,588	3.125	3.875	3	4	25.085
1906:1	56,273,233	5,287,280	2.625	3.25	3	3.5	25.145
1906:2	39,173,465	1,637,785	3	5.75	3	6	25.25
1907:1	45,882,052	10,903,902	3.5	3.6875	3.5	4	25.16
1907:2	52,666,157	186,021	3.875	6	4	7	25.195
1908:1	36,283,273	1,267,983	1.75	1.3125	3	2.5	25.125
1908:2	34,976,198	0	2.75	2.0625	3	2.5	25.12
1909:1	25,320,511	165,701	1.5	1.6875	3	2.5	25.205
1909:2	35,716,379	0	2.75	3.75	3	4.5	25.2075
1910:1	34,395,833	2,645,682	2.25	2.125	3	3	25.185
1910:2	33,005,614	2,060,230	2.125	3.5	3	4.5	25.265
1911:1	20,145,499	431,979	2.125	2.25	3	3	25.31
1911:2	26,851,564	4,712,255	3.5	3.75	3.5	4	25.2
1912:1	35,772,231	3,209,650	2.875	2.8125	3	3	25.23
1912:2	48,144,862	11,920,256	4	4.8125	4	5	25.14
1913:1	83,707,520	9,601,886	3.75	4.25	4	4.5	25.245
1913:2	89,988,421	12,967,649	3.75	4.75	4	5	25.3
1914:1	69,443,379	5,691,771	2.75	2.375	3.5	3	25.185

6

London Banks and International Finance, 1890–1914

Youssef Cassis

The period from 1890 to 1914 is usually considered to constitute the City of London's 'Golden Age'.[1] Why should these years, rather than the last two decades of the twentieth century that brought enormous wealth to the City, have received this epithet from historians? The reasons are twofold. There is, first, the position of the City as the world's financial centre, then unchallenged. From the end of the First World War, its primacy was to be contested and eventually attained by New York. Even after the City reasserted its world role in the 1960s, this regained status had to be shared with other global centres (New York, Tokyo), and meet the rivalry of continental European centres, in particular Frankfurt and also Paris. The second is that the City's standing before 1914 was, in turn, the result of Britain's dominant position within the world economy[2] rather than stemming from its own circumstances, including deep-rooted financial traditions that were to lead to its resurgence during the 1960s. Quite apart from a century-long development of financial activities, in particular their much greater complexity and sophistication, the differences between the City's world position in 2000 and in 1900 can be clearly perceived by considering the actors who occupied centre stage during the late nineteenth century. British institutions were in a far more dominant position than they were to be, although foreign banks had become strongly established in the City over the fifty years before the First World War.

These actors, more precisely, those involved in the City's international financial operations, will form the subject of this short chapter. Their development, of course, has already been studied in great depth. The growth of London's major banking institutions, especially its merchant banks, has given rise to more quality historical monographs than any other similar group elsewhere in the world.[3] This chapter will thus be limited to a few reflections upon these actors' experiences in the light of the changes that were to be brought about within the City by the late twentieth century's further phase of globalization. After establishing who were the main actors in international banking, these reflections are concerned with three broad themes: first, the question of entry and exit; second, the level of competition; and, third, strategic options.

1. Who were the actors?

Leaving aside members of the London Stock Exchange (around 5,000 during the decade preceding the war),[4] investment trusts, which channelled a part of British savings overseas,[5] together with those who could be called 'independent financiers' (whose number is impossible to estimate, but included the City's leading light during the period, Sir Ernest Cassel (1853–1919)),[6] four main functional groups of banking institutions were involved in international finance before 1914. The firms and institutions of each varied considerably in terms of size, specialization, forms of ownership, and control.

The first comprised the clearing banks, which at the beginning of the period under review included both private banks and joint-stock banks, the latter operating either solely in London or in both London and the provinces. As a result of the amalgamation movement,[7] which reached its height after the Baring crisis of November 1890, there was only one private deposit bank remaining within the City in 1913—Glyn, Mills, Currie & Co. Glyns had been a leading private bank since the mid-nineteenth century through its atypical combination of railway finance, industrial finance, and international and merchant banking activities.[8] Though not entirely a spent force, this banking house was increasingly overshadowed by a group of eleven London-based joint-stock banks, each with a countrywide network of branches. By the eve of the First World War, their managements controlled about two-thirds of the nation's banking deposits. Three giant banks, each with deposits of around £100m., headed this group (Lloyds, London City & Midland, and London County & Westminster), followed by two with deposits of some £60m. (Barclay & Co. and National Provincial Bank of England). Furthermore, there were six other lesser, but by no means insignificant, banks, including Parr's, Union of London & Smiths, London Joint Stock, and Capital & Counties, each with deposits ranging between £50m. and £40m. In terms of size, the clearers constituted by far the largest of the four banking groups.

The merchant banks constituted the second. According to some estimates, there were as many as 105 in the City in 1914, up from 45 in 1885; more conservative censuses put the figures at 74 in 1914, up from 66 in 1900.[9] The inner circle comprised the twenty-one members of the Accepting Houses Committee, formed in August 1914 to meet the liquidity crisis caused by outbreak of war.[10] The leading houses were N. M. Rothschild & Sons (probably still retaining its foremost position secured seventy-five years earlier, mainly because of its partners' enormous wealth and financial interests); Baring Brothers & Co. (which had staged a remarkable recovery after the crisis of 1890 due to its impeccable socio-political credentials and the entrepreneurial drive of its leader John Baring (1863-1929), the second Lord Revelstoke); Morgan, Grenfell & Co. (the up-and-coming house, increasingly present at the interface between finance and politics thanks, in no small part, to its close connection with J. P. Morgan & Co. in New York); J. Henry Schröder & Co. (which combined a substantial acceptance business with a growing involvement in issuing securities); and Kleinwort, Sons, & Co. (the leading acceptor during the early twentieth century).

As is well known, merchant banks remained private partnerships *de facto* if not, for a few of them, *de jure*, until well after the First World War. Remarkably, they were able to retain this status despite being dwarfed, in terms of size, by the joint-stock banks. The balance-sheet totals of the largest did not exceed £20m., in other words hardly a fifth of those of the biggest clearing banks. The reasons are to be found primarily in the English banking system's functional specialization, which enabled these houses to retain significant market shares in the City's two main international financial activities—the acceptance of bills of exchange (some 70 per cent in 1914),[11] and the issue of foreign loans and securities (some 35 per cent).[12] Furthermore, merchant bankers were personally able to exert overall control over some of London's major financial institutions (joint-stock banks, insurance companies, investment trusts) through their considerable presence on their boards of directors.[13]

The third group were the overseas banks, or the 'British multinational banks', to borrow the terminology coined by Geoffrey Jones. They were 'British' in the senses that their head offices were, for virtually all of them, located in London,[14] and their ownerships and managements were mostly British, although they operated primarily abroad, with a significant number within the Empire. They numbered thirty-one in 1913, when they had collectively 1,387 branches.[15] The overseas banks varied in size, but even the largest (Hong Kong & Shanghai Banking Corporation throughout the period) was, with deposits approaching £30m. in 1913, some way behind the leading clearing banks. Other significant institutions amongst this group included: London & River Plate Bank, Chartered Bank of India, Australia and China, Standard Bank of South Africa, Bank of Australasia, and Union Bank of Australia, with deposits ranging from £17m. to £22m. Although operating mainly abroad, overseas banks made ample use of London's money and financial markets.

Finally, there were some thirty foreign banks of twelve different host nationalities in London in 1913, operating through one or several City branches. They had come to take advantage of the innumerable business opportunities offered by the world's financial centre. The most active were French (in the first place Crédit Lyonnais, but also Comptoir National d'Escompte de Paris, the first to establish a London branch in 1869, and Société Générale) and German (Deutsche Bank, Dresdner Bank, Disconto-Gesellschaft). The United States' 'national banks' were prohibited, until the Federal Banking Act of 1913, from opening branches abroad. However, American trust companies, which were growing rapidly during this period, were not subjected to this legislation, and some of the most important (Equitable Trust Company of New York, Guaranty Trust Company of New York, Farmers' Loan and Trust Company, American Express Company, and others) opened a branch in the City.[16]

These were the main types of banks, which ensured London's functioning as the world's financial centre, primarily through two major activities: the financing of international trade and the export of capital. As is well known, each bank type tended to specialize in one financial activity: the clearers in deposit banking, the merchant banking houses in accepting and issuing, the overseas and foreign banks in foreign exchange and accepting. And, yet, they competed, to a certain extent, against each other—group against group, bank against bank.

2. Entry and Exit

There has been much discussion about the openness of the City's upper strata and the renewal of its elite during the three decades preceding the First World War.[17] The extent varied according to the type of bank. There was a high degree of continuity at the apex of the merchant banking hierarchy throughout the nineteenth and twentieth centuries. The 'prime movers', to use Alfred Chandler's terminology, established during the first half of the nineteenth century, proved able to maintain their competitive advantage. This was certainly the case with respect to Rothschilds and Barings, and also Schröders, Morgan Grenfell, and Hambros. Latecomers were relatively few: Kleinworts in the 1850s, Lazards in the 1870s, whereas steep decline and extinction was relatively rare, with Stern Brothers, one of the leading issuing houses in the 1860s and 1870s, being probably the most notable case. This does not mean that there was no change; some firms proved more dynamic at particular stages in their development, but the leading group of merchant banks was able to maintain long-term market dominance.[18]

More change occurred within commercial banking. The main exit was that of the private banks, the leading houses being members of the London Clearing House. Their number decreased somewhat between 1870 and 1890—from thirteen to ten—but then fell sharply to five in 1891 and one in 1914, as they were, one after the other, acquired by joint-stock banks.[19] Amongst the joint-stock banks, the 'prime movers' (London & County, London & Westminster, National Provincial) maintained their dominance until the 1880s. Thereafter, the rise of the 'challengers', especially Lloyds and London City & Midland, but also Parr's and Barclays, was far more spectacular than the changes that occurred within merchant banking. Lloyds and Midland became the country's two largest banks at the beginning of the twentieth century through aggressive amalgamation policies. Lloyds took over thirty-three banks between 1890 and 1914, increasing its deposits more than fivefold, from £23.3m. to £117.7m. The growth of Midland Bank was even more impressive; with a fifteenfold increase in its deposits (from £8.1m. to £125.7m.) over the same period, in part the result of the acquisition of over twenty-three banks. Barclays & Co. Ltd. was founded in 1896 through the simultaneous amalgamation of twenty private banks, so becoming immediately a major City institution, and was to absorb over seventeen more banks during the ensuing eight years. The long-established London joint-stock banks reacted by staging the first merger between major banks: in 1909, London & County and the London & Westminster joined forces to form London County & Westminster Bank.[20]

There was more stability in the upper levels of the overseas banking, with each main geographical area (Australasia, East Asia, Africa, and Latin America) dominated by a handful of banks and hardly any merger amongst them occurring during this period. A number of Australian banks disappeared after the 1893 crisis, though this episode did not affect the leading banks. The only significant amalgamations were those that led in 1912 to the formation of the Anglo-South American Bank, to bring it to the forefront amongst 'British Latin American' banks, thanks to the dynamic policy of its management.[21] However, apart from their size, always an indicator of financial weight, there is little ready evidence of the overseas banks' financial 'clout' within the City, though Hong Kong & Shanghai Bank was the most active in the issuing business.

The same is true of the foreign banks. Despite their 'entry and exit' being decided by head offices located abroad, and with such decisions not necessarily determined by performance criteria, we know that their individual positions within the City were not directly related to the respective market dominance each could enjoy in their home country. Foreign banks had to establish their reputations in the City. The Crédit Lyonnais is a case in point; it took the French bank more than twenty years to become London's 'number one' foreign bank, and it had to comply with the City's requirements in terms of the volume of business and the liquidity of its assets.[22]

3. Competition

This raises the question of the extent of competition prevailing within the City's international sector. There was competition in all fields of financial activity. However, from this chapter's perspective, it might be useful to distinguish between two broad levels: competition amongst banks within the same group (clearing banks, merchant banks, overseas banks, and foreign banks) on the one hand, and competition between different types of bank on the other.

With regard to the situations within the four functional groups, there was intense competition—in terms of market presence and, therefore, size—between the clearers. At the height of the amalgamation movement, clearing banks often targeted the same bank for takeover to compete for its acquisition. General managers played a decisive role in amalgamations, and were offered personal enticements to convince them to sell their institutions However, by and large, the clearers did not compete on price. In the same town, they offered as a rule the same rate of interest on deposits (1.5 per cent below Bank rate), though infractions did take place.[23] Yet, despite agreements between these banks, there were innumerable breaches *of them* by their zealous managers. There was a never-ending struggle to open accounts by more or less 'fair' means, such as offering a lower interest rate for a loan, in the hope of snatching an account away from another bank. However, such competition was limited to domestic banking and there are, so far, few known instances of competition between clearing banks in the provision of acceptances and undertaking security issues.

Competition was also fierce amongst merchant banks. In the case of floating loans and companies, the early dominance of Rothschilds and Barings over foreign government loan contracts was challenged by a succession of houses: Hambros in 1850s, Morgans in the 1870s, Schröders in the 1900s, to name but the most prominent, with many others also involved in both government and corporate issues.[24] From the 1870s, seven houses came to dominate American railway bond issues: Barings, J. S. Morgan, Morton Rose, Brown Shipley, Rothschilds, Seligman Brothers, and Speyer Brothers.[25] In the provision of acceptances, some firms, in the first place Kleinworts and Schröders, were prepared to take greater risks, operating with higher ratios of capital to acceptances than other houses (1 : 4 for Schröders and 1 : 5 for Kleinworts as against a commonly agreed practice of 1 : 3 to 4),[26] to overtake their rivals during the period. Nevertheless, the acceptance houses and merchant banks tended to specialize in certain geographical areas. Alliances and friendships, especially in underwriting syndicates, tended to be fairly stable, and encroachments into a leading firm's territory, although occurring, were the exception rather than the rule. Some houses could be at one and the same time allies and rivals; by the turn of the century, Barings had regained their former prominence in Argentina, yet they were increasingly forced to share this resumed supremacy with their 'friends' J. S. Morgan, who could guarantee direct access to the New York market.[27]

Finally, foreign banks competed with one another, especially in stock exchange dealings. Competition was probably more cut-throat amongst this group than any other. German banks were particularly aggressive within the City. In 1906, for example, the brokerage charged by Dresdner Bank for British railway debentures was half that of Crédit Lyonnais; and Deutsche Bank was between twice and four times cheaper on industrial debentures, British railways, and some American railways.[28] This competition was reflected on the London Stock Exchange to threaten the maintenance of the dual capacity. Foreign banks tended to deal directly with jobbers to buy and sell securities, so bypassing brokers and, thus, avoiding their commission charges. Brokers, for their part, were tempted to deal directly with foreign banks on behalf of their customers, and offered a lower commission to large foreign institutions. The imposition of a minimum commission in 1912 eventually restored the old order, though exceptions were made for international arbitrage operations.[29]

Competition between different types of banks was probably stronger than that amongst functional groups of banks. In international banking, it mainly took place within the merchant banks' prime fields of activity, in other words, accepting and security flotations. In 1913, the largest accepting house was not Kleinworts, but Dresdner Bank, and, from 1900, only four of the leading ten houses were British merchant banks (Kleinworts, Schroders, Barings, and Brown Shipley). The others were not only foreign banks (Dresdner, Deutsche, Disconto-Gesellschaft, and Crédit Lyonnais), but also domestic clearing banks (Westminster, Lloyds, Midland, Union Bank of London).[30] Furthermore, there was a host of smaller players, whether merchant banks, clearing banks, foreign banks, or overseas banks.

This was undoubtedly the most contested field of international banking, and it is all the more remarkable that the leading merchant banks were able to maintain dominant positions in the City. This was due to the fact that, however fierce, competition was nonetheless constrained. In the first place, there was some restraint on the part of the clearing banks which, given their huge size, could have been far more active in the accepting business. The reasons for their relative passivity have to do with the English banking system's specialization, and a division of labour, at both a business and a socio-professional level, within the City of London.[31] In any case, the inroads made by the joint-stock banks in the acceptance business were not considered tolerable by the City's establishment, in other words, the leading merchant banks. 'Considerable pressure' was apparently put on the clearers during the early 1900s to reduce their involvement,[32] although this did not prevent their market share from growing to reach 24 per cent by the eve of the First World War. Second, a significant component of the joint-stock banks' acceptances comprised finance bills, in other words, bills drawn for the purpose of borrowing money rather than supporting a trade transaction, or which were related to short-term capital movements under the gold standard. And, third, the domestic market had a degree of protection since foreign banks' acceptances were not eligible at the Bank of England, whether for discount or as security for a loan, unless endorsed by two English firms. In any case, their acceptances were mostly used to finance the trade of their home country through employing sterling-denominated bills and the London discount market. And, as in the case of the clearing banks (and possibly in a higher proportion, though this is difficult to estimate), they mainly consisted of finance bills.

The issue of loans and equities on the London capital market was restricted by custom and practice to British firms. Foreign banks were involved in those issues simultaneously floated across several financial centres, but they did not compete with British banks on their home turf. Here, competition was mainly between merchant banks, joint-stock banks, and overseas banks, which together controlled around two-thirds of the market during the period under review. Other overseas issues were shared amongst a number of other institutions, including: investment trusts, stockbrokers, company promoters, as well as foreign governments and corporations via their London bankers or as their own issuers,[33] which have not been included in this study.

Rather than competition, there were encroachments in this field of business by the joint-stock banks and, to a lesser extent, the overseas banks. One should not underestimate the position and the prestige of a bank such as the London & Westminster and its pioneering role in connection with colonial, especially Australian, loans. Furthermore, Parr's, initially a provincial bank but which rose to prominence within the City during the 1890s, was particularly active in the issue of several Japanese loans during the fifteen years preceding the war, including leading a consortium that brought out a £10m. loan in 1899. The managements of Lloyds and Midland, the two most dynamic during the period, inevitably turned their ambitions to international finance, though their achievements remained modest. The former undertook a £2m. bond issue at 4 per cent on behalf of the municipality of Budapest in 1910, and the latter was charged in 1909 with the issue of the £3.4m. 4 1/2 bonds of the Aramavir-Touapsé Railway, guaranteed by the Russian government.[34] The share of the clearing banks over the period 1870–1914 was a mere 10 per cent, but this 'era average' masks their increasing penetration that by 1914 had achieved a 17.4 per cent share of overseas flotations.[35]

The overseas banks' involvement was also limited, despite their close connection with countries regularly raising funds on the London capital market. London & River Plate, for example, only issued two loans on behalf of Argentina, in the early 1890s. Merchant bankers, such as Barings with regard to Argentina and Rothschilds for Brazil, remained better placed through their expertise and links with both the borrowing countries and the City to undertake this business. The exception was the Hong Kong & Shanghai Banking Corporation, which played a leading role in Chinese government loans, worth at least £60m. between 1895 and 1914, as well as in Japanese loans issued in London. The bank enjoyed a unique competitive advantage in this particular field, derived from its management's knowledge of the Far East, its powerful connections in the City, particularly with the Rothschilds, and the support of the Foreign Office (because of several of these loans' political character).[36] In any case, whatever the competition between merchant banks, clearers, and overseas banks, it was further tempered by their collaborations in issuing and underwriting syndicates.

Finally, much has been made of the competition between the foreign banks and the clearing banks, with alarming articles in the *Bankers' Magazine* about the 'invasion' of Lombard Street by foreign banks and the insularity of the British clearing banks.[37] Competition certainly existed, but its real extent is not well documented beyond the provision of foreign exchanges, where the clearing banks were at first at a clear disadvantage. Their managements had long neglected this area of activity. Rather, foreign exchange dealings had been the preserve of the merchant bankers, but they increasingly left it to foreign bankers during the second half of the nineteenth century as they turned their attention to what were considered more prestigious tasks. Competition was partial elsewhere since foreign banks' London branches did not really seek deposits, mostly relying on the resources of their respective 'mother bank'. In any case, the clearing banks were not prepared to concede anything in this field to their foreign rivals. Indeed, some were prepared to take the offensive. In 1905, for example, the Midland Bank poached a clerk from the Crédit Lyonnais's London branch in order to set up a shipping department, and subsequently successfully captured the ship owners' accounts that the French bank had managed to win over the years.[38] On the other hand, the foreign banks' increasing presence was seen by commentators and practitioners alike as a sign of the strength of the City of London. As the *Bankers' Magazine* put it: 'In all probability, no other city in the world has such a cosmopolitan collection of banking institutions, and this fact in itself is a tribute to the standing of London in international business'. However, it added that 'whilst these foreign banks were steadily increasing in number, the hold of London financial firms upon the exchange market was steadily waning'.[39]

4. Strategy

It is of course impossible to discuss in any detail the strategies of the City's main actors in international finance before 1914. Three points, however, can be briefly made. A first, general consideration is that the period 1890–1914, despite the internationalization of capital, was not an era of major financial innovations. Consequently, firms, houses, and institutions were not being forced by a rapidly changing environment to adapt their respective strategies.

Second, strategies varied considerably, and not only between types of banks but also between individual banks. Consolidation was undoubtedly the joint-stock banks' main objective, and the amalgamation movement was the most important aspect of their development during this period. On the other hand, hardly any merger took place between merchant banks. At the level of individual banks, to take but two examples, the managements of Lloyds and Midland were far more expansionary minded than those of National Provincial and the London & Westminster among the clearing banks, while among merchant banks the partners of J. S. Morgan gave priority to foreign issues and those of Kleinworts sought to expand their house's acceptances.

If one common feature amongst the banks' various strategies should be isolated, it is diversification, which came to be pursued by all the managements of the different types of banks, albeit within the limits of the English banking system's specialization. Merchant banks tended to become more akin to banks, in the English sense of the words, i.e. deposit takers. At Schröders, for example, the share of 'balances and deposits' on the liabilities' side increased from 30 per cent at the turn of the century to 65 per cent by the eve of the First World War.[40] The joint-stock banks were increasingly attracted to international operations. They took part in underwriting syndicates, and some ventured into making foreign issues. Their managements also started to open foreign exchange departments. The first was London City & Midland Bank, in 1905, under its historic leader Edward Holden, who transformed a small provincial bank into the world's largest bank in less than thirty years. Several of the major clearers also opened branches abroad, initially in France. Lloyds opened in Paris in 1911, followed by the Westminster in 1913.[41]

However, the international business area that attained the fastest growth during this period was acting as London agent for a foreign bank. In 1913, Midland Bank was the London correspondent for 156 foreign banks as against only six in 1892. Its merger with City Bank in 1898 had increased significantly that number since the position of this absorbed bank had been much stronger in this particular field, with some forty agencies—and this was not the least of its attractions for London & Midland. This also indicates that the amalgamation movement was not solely motivated by domestic banking factors. London County & Westminster was the agent for more than 200 foreign banks in 1913, as against seven for the London & County in 1892 and, apparently, none for the Westminster. This development also led to new forms of foreign exchange dealing, based on foreign balances held with correspondents, and to the growth of a network of inter-bank relationships[42] (though there is no evidence concerning the importance of this activity within the businesses of the joint-stock banks).

Concluding remarks

Despite its openness and cosmopolitanism, fitting for the world's financial centre in an era of globalized capital, international business remained fragmented in the City of London before the First World War. There was competition but it was tempered by a number of institutional factors. Market leaders could be challenged, albeit within the limits of an established order. In this context, the role of the joint-stock banks deserves particular mention. They have usually been described as sleeping giants, with their role mainly consisting in making the entire system work through the employment of their huge resources. The clearers were thus at the very heart of the system, but not only in that respect. Despite the merchant banks' leadership in international finance and their prestige, glamour, and, for some, entrepreneurship, the main force for change in the City before 1914 was the major joint-stock banks. Their managements' strategies of diversification were the most extensive among all the four types of banks. Interestingly, this was more in the direction of international finance than domestic industrial finance, a business shift that has not been paid sufficient attention by the City's historians, although some have clearly acknowledged their role in the overseas capital market.[43]

And, yet, in the long run, the major clearing banks were not to be the winners in the City's reorganization during the late twentieth century caused by the break-up of its traditional structures following 'Big Bang' in 1986. Interestingly, two of the major protagonists of the pre-1914 years have all but disappeared: the merchant banks and the overseas banks. The merchant banks were to be taken over, one after the other, during the closing fifteen years of the twentieth century,[44] though by American and European banks rather than British banks. As a result, investment banking in the City mostly passed into the hands of foreign-owned institutions. In the case of the overseas banks, their number has shrunk to two, following waves of mergers, including with clearing banks, so that they are now grouped with the British clearing banks. At the end of the twentieth century, the dominant force, however, is a former overseas bank—HSBC. Its management, now fully London based, have turned their institution into a formidable international group, to become the world's second largest bank (behind Citigroup) following, among others, their acquisition of Midland Bank in 1992. This is not the place to discuss whether the clearing banks, or the merchant banks, could have done better over the course of the last century. However, events and developments from 1914 meant that there was little opportunity for their managements to have retained the dominant positions that these banks and houses had once enjoyed in a City which regained from the late 1950s its global and supranational status.

Notes

I should like to thank Philip Cottrell for his helpful comments on an earlier draft of this chapter.

1. This is for example the subtitle given by David Kynaston to the second volume of his history of London, *The City of London*, ii: *Golden Age, 1890–1914* (London, 1995).
2. See F. Crouzet, *L'Économie de la Grande-Bretagne victorienne* (Paris, 1977).
3. See in particular N. Ferguson, *The World's Banker: The History of the House of Rothschild* (London, 1998); J. Wake, *Kleinwort Benson: The History of Two Families in Banking* (Oxford, 1997); R. Roberts, *Schroders: Merchants & Bankers* (Basingstoke, 1992); K. Burk, *Morgan Grenfell, 1838–1988: The Biography of a Merchant Bank* (Oxford, 1989); P. Ziegler, *The Sixth Great Power: Barings, 1762–1929* (London, 1988).
4. R. Michie, *The London Stock Exchange: A History* (Oxford, 1999), 86.
5. See Y. Cassis, 'The Emergence of a New Financial Institution: Investment Trusts in Britain, 1870–1939', in J.-J. Van Helten and Y. Cassis, *Capitalism in a Mature Economy: Financial Institutions, Capital Exports and British Industry, 1870–1939* (Aldershot, 1990), 139–58.
6. See P. Thane, 'Cassel, Sir Ernest Joseph (1852–1921), Merchant Banker and International Financier', in D. J. Jeremy (ed.), *Dictionary of Business Biography*, (London, 1984), 604–14.
7. See J. Sykes, *The Amalgamation Movement in English Banking* (London, 1926), F. Capie and G. Rodrik-Bali, 'Concentration in British Banking, 1870–1929', *Business History*, 29/3 (1982).
8. See R. Fulford, *Glyn's 1753–1953: Six Generations in Lombard Street* (London, 1953); P. L. Cottrell, 'The Coalescence of a Cluster of Corporate International Banks, 1855–75', *Business History*, 33/3 (1991).
9. S. Chapman, *The Rise of Merchant Banking* (London, 1994), 58; R. Roberts, 'What's in a Name? Merchants, Merchant Bankers, Accepting Houses, Issuing Houses, Industrial Bankers and Investment Bankers', *Business History*, 35/3 (1993).
10. Y. Cassis, *City Bankers 1890–1914* (Cambridge, 1994), 29–31.
11. Chapman, *Merchant Banking*, 107.
12. P. L. Cottrell, *British Overseas Investment in the Nineteenth Century* (London, 1975), 31.
13. See Y. Cassis, 'Management and Strategy in the English Joint Stock Banks', *Business History*, 27/3 (1985).
14. The most notable exception was the Hong Kong and Shanghai Banking Corporation, whose head office was in Hong Kong.
15. G. Jones, *British Multinational Banking, 1830–1990* (Oxford, 1993) 396–7.
16. For a list of the foreign banks established in the City in 1913, see Y. Cassis, *La City de Londres, 1870–1914* (Paris, 1987), 40–2.
17. See S. D. Chapman, 'Aristocracy and Meritocracy in the City of London', *British Journal of Sociology*, 37/2 (1986); Y. Cassis, 'Merchant Bankers and City Aristocracy' and S. D. Chapman, 'Reply to Youssef Cassis', *British Journal of Sociology*, 39/1 (1988); M. Daunton, 'Gentlemanly Capitalism and British Industry 1820–1914', *Past and Present*, 122 (1989).

18. See company histories listed in n. 3.
19. See Cassis, *City Bankers*, 15–28.
20. R. S. Sayers, *Lloyds Bank in the History of English Banking* (Oxford, 1957); A. R. Holmes and E. Green, *Midland: 150 Years of Banking Business* (London, 1986); M. Ackrill and L. Hannah, *Barclays: The Business of Banking 1690–1996* (Cambridge, 2001); Cassis, *City Bankers*.
21. In 1902, the Bank of Tarapaca and London amalgamated with the Anglo-Argentine Bank under the name of Bank of Tarapaca and Argentine. In 1912, the new bank took the name of Anglo-South American Bank and absorbed the London Bank of Mexico and South America. See D. Joslin, *A Century of Banking in Latin America* (London, 1963) 109; Jones, *Multinational Banking*, 80.
22. F. Gallice, 'Le Crédit Lyonnais à Londres, 1870–1939', in B. Desjardins et al. (eds.), *Le Crédit Lyonnais 1863–1986* (Geneva, 2003), 506–7.
23. Cassis, *City Bankers*, 50–1; C. A. E. Goodhart, *The Business of Banking, 1891–1914* (London, 1971), 156–7, 178–88.
24. Chapman, *Merchant Banking*, 39–56.
25. D. Adler, *British Investment in American Railways* (Charlottesville, Va., 1970), 143–4.
26. Roberts, *Schroders*, 130–2; Wake, *Kleinwort Benson*, 125–6, Chapman, *Merchant Banking*, 74–6.
27. Ziegler, *Sixth Great Power*, 307–8.
28. Gallice, 'Crédit Lyonnais à Londres', 512–13.
29. Michie, *London Stock Exchange*, 123–31.
30. See Chapman, *Merchant Banking*, 121; Roberts, *Schroders*, 131.
31. See Cassis, 'Management and Strategy'.
32. According to J. S. Morgan, in Dec. 1906, quoted in Kynaston, *City of London*, ii. 293.
33. Cottrell, *British Overseas Investment*, 31.
34. Kynaston, *City of London*, ii. 188–9, 503–4; Holmes and Green, *Midland*, 135–6.
35. Cottrell, *British Overseas Investment*, 31.
36. Jones, *Multinational Banking*, 119–30.
37. See for example W. R. Lawson, 'Lombard Street under Foreign Control', *Bankers' Magazine* (Mar 1901).
38. Gallice, 'Crédit Lyonnais à Londres', 512–13.
39. *Bankers' Magazine*, 80 (1905), 19.
40. Roberts, *Schroders*, 132–5.
41. G. Jones, 'Lombard Street on the Riviera: The British Clearing Banks and Europe, 1900–1960', *Business History*, 24 (1982).
42. S. Battilossi, 'Financial Innovation in the Golden Age of International Banking: 1890–1931 and 1958–81', *Financial History Review*, 7/2 (2000), 145–57.
43. See in particular P. L. Cottrell, 'Great Britain', in R. Cameron and V. I. Bovykin (eds.), *International Banking 1870–1914* (Oxford, 1991), 25–47.
44. The only two houses of some significance which have remained independent are N. M. Rothschild & Sons and Lazard Brothers and they are both part of international partnerships.

7

Banking Alliances and International Issues on the Paris Capital Market, 1890–1914

SAMIR SAUL

Paris was an international financial centre throughout the nineteenth century. Since the 1820s, it had represented a source of capital for foreign states and railway companies, as well as a venue for clearing settlements in national currencies between continental Europe, Great Britain, and the Americas. Although it was less important than the City of London, Paris's financial market remained the world's second until 1914. They outstripped all others as pivotal hubs of international capital transfers.

As intermediaries between suppliers and users of capital, Parisian banks and bankers were the primary agents of the city's financial activity. They played a key role in the raising of capital for equity and loans. Until the 1870s, international finance was the domain of the *haute banque*, especially its leading exemplars, the Rothschilds. By the end of the century, joint-stock companies had supplanted even the most powerful private houses and become pre-eminent. Sometimes called investment banks, the *banques d'affaires* were in fact distinguished by the considerable resources of a small but wealthy group of associates relative to deposits. As for deposit (commercial) banks, they drew enormous amounts of hitherto unmobilized savings. Wielding until then unheard-of means, the combination of the two types of banks transformed and dominated the financial scene. While private banks and bankers hardly disappeared, they now had simultaneously to compete with the newcomers—this was especially the case for the Rothschilds—and to enter into arrangements with them in order to continue to play a part in international financial operations.

On the eve of the first World War Paris was at the heart of a grid of financial relationships based on the immense, apparently inexhaustible, reservoir of French savings and radiating to practically every corner of the earth. The flotation of foreign—that is, non-French—securities on its market is a notable aspect of Paris's role as an international financial centre. The scale of issues of shares, debentures and bonds by foreign companies, governments, and municipalities became such that only coalitions of sponsors could venture to undertake them and accept the attendant risk. The result was a web of alliances on the Paris market, sometimes extending to partners in other countries. Joint action usually meant the formation of syndicates, on the one hand to guarantee the underwriting of issues, on the other hand to ensure the selling of the securities to purchasers and investors outside the syndicates. Next to interlocking directorships or the setting-up of joint affiliates, syndicates represented a well-known form of alliance, sometimes ephemeral, often durable when associates reunited in what were described as 'groups'.

This study focuses on syndicates as a particular type of alliance between banks from 1890 and 1914. It is an overview aiming to establish the identity of the managers and participants in underwriting and issue consortia, to highlight patterns of participation, and to draw a portrait of the Paris financial market from the angle of the associations between its agents. Such an approach does not appear to have been attempted previously. Underwriting and issue syndicates will be examined according to the identity of the manager, that is, the bank which contracted the operation with the issuer and the one most likely to bring its network into the syndicate.

Three themes or problems will be addressed. It is intended to throw light on the nature of the relationship that representatives of private banking houses, especially the *haute banque*, and the new joint-stock banks established within syndicates. Each personified different stages in the methods of assembling capital for transfers abroad. While joint-stock banks were sometimes created specifically to compete with and supersede private banking houses, the latter often had members on the boards of the former. Rivalry was sometimes intense to win contracts for foreign loans, but cooperation was not unusual. The second matter deserving notice is the relationship between *banques d'affaires* and deposit banks within syndicates. Three of the five sections in the study are devoted to this, the dominant form of partnership in the period considered. How was the function of management distributed among them? Were there recurring combinations of investment and commercial banks? Did their collaboration conform to unwritten rules, such as reciprocity in the apportionment of participations in successive operations? Third, due attention needs to be paid to international banking connections. What place, if any, did foreign banks have in French-led syndicates on the Paris market? If joint action occurred between Parisian and foreign banks, did the membership of syndicates reveal underlying regularities?

This enquiry is concerned only with international operations, to wit, on behalf of non-French issuers. It may serve as a preliminary and exploratory step towards a wider investigation of syndicates for this period, a daunting enterprise requiring scrutiny of the records of each issue in the archives of several banks. Such studies have been conducted by historians for some issues; reference will be made to them.

1. The data base

An estimate of the sums handled by syndicates included in the data base to be examined relative to the total value of issues on the Paris financial market is called for. The issue of securities comprises several stages, to wit the contract between issuer and manager of the syndicate, subdivision of the operation among underwriters, transfers (*rétrocessions*) to partners of the underwriters, and placement of the securities in the hands of the investing public. The 'firm' price the underwriters agree to pay the issuer is lower than the price of issue asked from the public, and the latter is normally lower than the 'nominal' value assigned to bonds, debentures, and shares. Securities are usually retailed to investors at a discount; they may be sold at par, and occasionally above face value when a premium is levied on particularly attractive stock. As different questions are asked and distinct methods of collecting data are used, the resulting statistics vary from one compilation to the next. Calculating aggregate amounts of issues is not an exact science. Data are gathered to gauge the absorptive capacity of a market, to analyse capital demands of various sectors of an economy, to compare the weight of national and foreign issues on a market, or to measure amounts of capital exported from a country, rarely to identify underwriting consortia. Three sets of statistics are available, all based on the price of issue. Table 7.1 concerns sums effectively paid out by the public, rather than the higher totals representing face value of securities.

Over 47 per cent of the sums raised went to foreign issuers, testimony to the popularity of international investing among French banks and the French public. The reasons for this attraction have been a matter for considerable, sometimes polemical,[1] debate since the end of the nineteenth century. Weak demand for capital and low rates of return in France have been adduced as explanations of the phenomenon. More of the capital raised went abroad than stayed in France eight years out of twenty-two. Foreign state authorities borrowed in France five times as much as their French counterparts; their portion of total foreign issues is 62 per cent, as against 11 per cent for the French authorities' share of French issues. Capital raised by foreign companies is a little over a third of that which went to French companies.

In order to dispel any impression that a unique set of figures is available, or even possible to establish, two additional computations are provided. One is also based on the price of issue, but it includes conversions of original bonds and debentures to ones with lower rates of interest, and informal introductions without public issues. While posted prices furnish a readily accessible source of information, fresh capital raised during conversions is more difficult to assess and only rough estimations can be made of introductions *en coulisse* or over the counters of banks. As well as being incomplete, the figures in Table 7.2 are at variance with those in Table 7.1; they are considerably higher for foreign issues but lower for French operations.

According to these estimates, foreign issuers accounted for 72 per cent of the capital raised on the Paris market between 1898 and 1913. More capital was destined to be used outside France for fourteen out of the sixteen years. Foreign state authorities borrowed over nine times as much as their French counterparts, but their portion of total foreign issues was only 41 per cent from 1900 to 1913 whereas the French authorities' share of French issues stood at 12 per cent. Table 7.2 is at odds with Table 7.1 in the category of capital raised by foreign companies;

Table 7.1. *Stock publicly issued in France (million francs)*

	French issuers				Foreign issuers				Total
	Government bonds	Companies		Total	Government bonds	Companies		Total	
		Shares	Debentures			Shares	Debentures		
1892	19	139	409	567	275	29	27	331	898
1893	19	114	444	577	245	8	50	303	880
1894	72	126	378	576	668	62	79	809	1,385
1895	54	229	269	552	605	86	108	799	1,351
1896	195	262	326	783	410	116	36	562	1,345
1897	76	270	271	617	135	158	24	317	934
1898	99	441	426	966	355	293	55	703	1,669
1899	193	619	504	1,316	742	243	32	1,017	2,333
1900	34	645	564	1,243	258	185	86	529	1,772
1901	60	368	591	1,019	518	117	82	717	1,736
1902	393	246	315	954	522	265	72	859	1,813
1903	107	275	316	698	271	74	142	487	1,185
1904	67	258	267	592	1,023	100	36	1,159	1,751
1905	288	511	248	1,047	1,022	347	221	1,590	2,637
1906	78	552	563	1,193	1,141	204	256	1,601	2,794
1907	65	651	566	1,282	617	232	155	1,004	2,286
1908	49	393	943	1,385	674	57	364	1,095	2,480
1909	103	587	498	1,188	977	339	187	1,503	2,691
1910	122	741	953	1,816	1,551	539	490	2,580	4,396
1911	146	709	881	1,736	982	484	541	2,007	3,743
1912	308	1,117	1,197	2,622	417	645	448	1,510	4,132
1913	246	1,136	1,298	2,680	752	277	409	1,438	4,118
Total	**2,793**	**10,389**	**12,227**	**25,409**	**14,160**	**4,860**	**3,900**	**22,920**	**48,329**

Source: Emmanuel Chadeau, *L'Économie nationale aux XIXe et XXe siècles* (Paris, 1989), 254–5. Figures are based on the *Annuaire statistique*, 1951, 1961, 1966, published by the Institut National de la Statistique et des Études Économiques. See also Françoise Marnata, *La Bourse et le financement des investissements* (Paris, 1973), 58–9.

the latter received 1.8 times as much capital as went to French companies. If these estimates are correct, unsyndicated issues, sold privately or over the counter, must have been a more common practice than was previously thought.

A third calculus is provided by the *Moniteur des intérêts matériels*, a contemporary Brussels financial periodical. The *Bulletin de statistique et de législation comparée*, published in Paris from 1876, reproduced it annually. The intent was to present the amounts effectively raised in public issues of stock on European markets according to the identity of end-users of capital rather than from the perspective of the source of the capital. The *Moniteur* was interested in listing the countries where European capital was invested or headed, and in how much each country absorbed, not in the sums collected in one country or another for a variety of destinations, national and international[2]. Figures for France, when available, are culled from the user-country breakdown in the *Moniteur* and presented in Table

Table 7.2 *Stock issues in France (million francs)*

	French issuers				Foreign issuers				Total
	Government bonds	Companies		Total	Government bonds	Companies		Total	
		Shares	Debentures			Shares	Debentures		
1890									2,512
1891									2,293
1892									602
1893									301
1894									11,449
1895									1,608
1896									1,005
1897									452
1898				950				383	1,333
1899				740				951	1,691
1900		547	722	1,269	233	751	275	1,259	2,518
1901	272	230	140	642	1,565	373	113	2,051	2,693
1902	157	62	69	288	779	533	117	1,429	1,717
1903	92	171	515	778	1,625	329	402	2,356	3,134
1904	66	294	81	441	1,696	1,068	121	2,885	3,326
1905	229	527	130	886	1,077	1,380	544	3,001	3,887
1906	22	447	402	871	2,375	1,170	661	4,206	5,077
1907	59	479	430	968	981	504	394	1,879	2,847
1908	98	386	248	732	1,040	697	1,012	2,749	3,481
1909	155	893	738	1,786	809	1,103	597	2,509	4,295
1910	106	487	292	885	1,628	1,787	1,311	4,726	5,611
1911	7	518	289	814	989	1,137	1,756	3,882	4,496
1912	312	1,080	568	1,960	430	1,768	884	3,082	5,042
1913	151	1,211	808	2,170	754	1,103	901	2,758	4,928
Total	**1,726**	**7,332**	**5,432**	**16,180**	**15,981**	**13,703**	**9,088**	**40,106**	**76,298**

Source: Statistics are drawn from *L'Économiste européen* and compiled by Paul Cheminais, *Les Placements français à l'étranger. Des sociétés de gestion des valeurs mobilières étrangères* (Paris, 1929), 15. Additional figures in *L'Économiste européen* (15 Feb. 1896), 205; (5 Jan. 1900), 13; (12 Jan. 1900), 45; and (27 Dec. 1901), 814.

7.3. Experience points to the fact that capital used in France was raised in France. The sums in Table 7.3 should have corresponded to those of French issuers in Table 7.1. The fact that they do not is testimony to the tentative nature of the exercise aimed at tracking down the movement and destination of capital.

Alliances and networks formed for international issues may be studied at the source by perusal of correspondence between companies and individuals, or down the line at the final outcome of negotiations for collaboration. Information about the underwriting syndicates' managers, their composition, and, in particular, the proportion of the operation allotted to each participant is confidential. Publicity and prospectuses disclose the names of the banks in charge of the selling of the bonds, debentures, or shares to the public, not those of the underwriters, although

Table 7.3. *Stock issues for capital to be used in France (million francs)*

	State, local, and municipal bonds	Banks	Railways and industry	Conversions	Total
1890	117	21	207	—	345
1891	872	400	306	—	1,578
1892	15	—	223	66	304
1893	41	3	211	13	268
1894	244	—	257	7,546	8,047
1895	6	278	403	241	928
1896	330	78	370	188	966
1897	15	18	362	428	823
1898	n.a.	n.a.	n.a.	n.a.	1,134
1899	258	335	891	—	1,484
1900	n.a.	n.a.	n.a.	n.a.	1,521
1901	276	44	981	—	1,301
1902	548	20	482	6,801	7,851
1903	85	327	302	—	714
1904	213	22	353	4	592
1905	178	104	563	—	845
1906	n.a.	n.a.	n.a.	n.a.	1,297
1907	242	84	796	—	1,122
1908	388	109	924	—	1,421
1909	172	633	922	—	1,727
1910	n.a.	n.a.	n.a.	n.a.	1,753
1911	85	214	1,033	—	1,332
Total	**4,085**	**2,690**	**9,586**	**15,287**	**37,353**

Source: Moniteur des intérêts matériels.

most underwriters were retailers and most retailers figured among the underwriters. In view of the impressive number of issues, it is quite illusory to aspire to exhaustiveness in a brief enquiry.

Fortunately, one major deposit bank, the Crédit Lyonnais (CL), kept an important, if not complete, series of synoptic files on its participation in various syndicates. Each operation was summarized in standard form, providing essential data about each issue. This source is particularly valuable because the Lyonnais was the premier deposit bank in France, one whose size, reputation, and network of branches made it a sought-after partner when the object was to put a considerable amount of securities in the hands of the investing public. In fact, measured by the volume of assets, the Lyonnais was the leading bank in the world in 1913. Moreover, other major financial institutions in France such as the Banque de Paris et des Pays-Bas (BPPB, also known as Paribas), the Société Générale (SG), and the Comptoir National d'Escompte de Paris (CNEP) did not constitute similar collections. Of course, the CL was not a member of every syndicate formed on the Paris market from 1890 to 1914 but it figured in so many that its files offer a comprehensive picture of the financial scene.

In keeping with the theme of the present study, only stock issued in Paris for the benefit of foreign governments or companies is entered into the working data base. A total of 311 such issues were found; they make up the data base. The most important or the most representative operations will be referred to individually. Sources used are CL files,[3] Edmond Théry's *L'Économiste européen*, Alfred Neymarck's *Le Rentier*, and specialized area-orientated monographs.[4] Amounts are calculated on the basis of the price of issue to the public, not face value; conversions are included. As with the financial periodicals, the method is empirical; for each issue found, the price paid by the public is worked out and added to the total amount of the year. For stock issued in predetermined proportions in Paris and on foreign markets, only the portion sold in Paris is retained.

Not unexpectedly, the amounts tabulated in the data base (Table 7.4) are always lower than those given in Table 7.2, the margins sometimes being very wide. They are much narrower with reference to Table 7.1. Surprisingly the data base yields higher amounts for the years 1894, 1903, 1906, 1907, 1908, and 1909. The difference for 1894 is particularly striking; the explanation lies in the fact that a 3,000,000,000-franc conversion of Russian government funds was undoubtedly left out of the total in Table 7.1. As for the year 1903, a 744m.-franc Ottoman loan might not have been accounted for in Table 7.1. Otherwise, for the years showing lower totals in the data base than in Table 7.1, the average amount in the base is 73 per cent that in Table 7.1; the range is between 48 per cent in 1898 and 93 per cent in 1895. Bearing in mind the approximate and untidy method of aggregating amounts of stock issues, the body of information compiled provides a fairly accurate data base.

2. Private banks and their allies in international syndicates

Private banks and the *haute banque*—the latter being private bankers with greater resources, higher social standing, or international connections—were overtaken, in many cases dwarfed, by the joint-stock banks launched in the second half of the nineteenth century. The Rothschilds remained present on the international front, but they appeared to be alone. The barren 1890s left little opportunity for banking activity. By the time the economy recovered at the end of the decade, private banks were marginalized by the *banques d'affaires* and deposit banks which alone seemed able to raise the unprecedented sums required by governments and companies.

Of the roster of French private banks involved in international operations from the 1850s and 1860s, only the Rothschilds played a leading role between the end of the nineteenth century and 1914. Nevertheless, neither French nor non-French private banks surrendered the field of international finance. They continued to figure in underwriting syndicates, even issue syndicates, active on financial markets in Paris and other European centres.

Table 7.4. Foreign stock issued by the syndicates studied

	Million Francs
1891	2,773
1892	244
1893	230
1894	4,172
1895	745
1896	480
1897	205
1898	339
1899	671
1900	318
1901	557
1902	718
1903	1,538
1904	1,063
1905	1,460
1906	2,187
1907	1,277
1908	1,172
1909	1,932
1910	1,951
1911	1,008
1912	841
1913	976
1914	1,135

Issues of French or international stock on the Paris market plummeted following the 1882 Union Générale crash and the onset of a long-term slowdown of the European economy. No more than three international issues were found in 1891 for inclusion in the data base of syndicates. The number rose to four in 1892, only to return to three in 1893.

In 1892, the Compagnie du Gaz et des Eaux de Tunis, a small privately owned municipal utility, converted its 5 per cent debentures by creating 4 per cent stock issued at 490 francs. The operation was modest; no more than 1,420,020 francs were to be paid out by investors. Two entities, a private bank and a *banque d'affaires*, were entrusted with the issue to the public as well as, manifestly, the underwriting.[5] S. Propper et Cie was a relatively obscure Parisian private banking house which, by the turn of the century, became a regular minor member of the SG group whenever it entered into syndicates.[6] The other underwriter and retailer was the Banque Internationale de Paris, an entity in search of a mission. Born in 1870 as the Banque Franco-Égyptienne, its object then was to lend to the Egyptian government at the prevailing high, arguably usurious, rates.[7] Following Egypt's bankruptcy in 1876, banks and ad hoc financial outfits set up specifically for the purpose of extending lucrative loans to the state folded. The BFE was among them. However, after its liquidation in 1892, it continued to operate under its new name as a *banque d'affaires* interested in issues of French and foreign stock, particularly in the promising recently opened Russian market.[8] The BIP was wound up in 1901 upon merging with the Banque Française pour le Commerce et l'Industrie (BFCI), a new *banque d'affaires*. Tunisia's recourse to new underwriters did not sever its ties with its usual intermediary on the Paris market for larger loans, the Comptoir d'Escompte de Paris (CEP). The relationship was unaffected by the latter's debacle in 1889; Tunisia worked with the rejuvenated CNEP, then with the Crédit Algérien, and did not again resort to the services of substitute underwriters.

With the exception of the Rothschilds, of whom more below, no private banks in the data base led syndicates until 1909. Four loans were issued that year by Argentinian borrowers.[9] The 4.5 per cent bonds, payable in currency pegged on gold, created by the Province of Buenos Aires for a total amount of 60m. francs to finance railway construction, could be subscribed in pesos, francs, or sterling. The portion reserved for the French market was worth 42m. francs; it was guaranteed by two Parisian private banks, Bénard & Jarislowsky and Louis Dreyfus et Cie, and a *banque d'affaires*, the Crédit Mobilier Français (CMF). The London underwriters are unknown.[10] In turn, the provinces of Tucuman, Mendoza, and Santa Fe issued 5 per cent and 4.5 per cent loans the same year, respectively for 25m., 30m., and 8m. francs. Bénard & Jarislowsky, lead underwriters in the Tucuman loan, were seconded by the Banco Espanôl del Rio de la Plata and Louis Dreyfus; they appear to have been alone in the Mendoza loan. The Santa Fe loan was contracted by the Deutsche Uberseeische Bank, an affiliate of the Deutsche Bank, which only kept a fraction of it and relinquished the rest to Bénard & Jarislowsky and the CMF.[11] In 1910, Bénard & Jarislowsky headed another syndicate for a 48m. franc 5 per cent gold loan by Santa Fe. The BPPB was the other underwriter.

Argentina's buoyant economy explains in part the exertions of foreign underwriters, particularly German banks. Bénard & Jarislowsky first appeared on the Argentinian scene in 1903. It ranked first of three banks listed after the Paris head office of the Société du Port de Rosario, a French-registered company, for the placement of a 17m. franc gold loan bearing 5 per cent interest. The others were the CMF and the Crédit Foncier et Agricole d'Algérie.[12] Later Bénard & Jarislowsky apparently vied to be the Paris partner of the Dresdner Bank in its quest for South American business.[13] The CMF was also associated with a German bank. It hardly had the stature of its famous ancestor of 1852–67. Reborn in 1902, it sought expansion in Egypt,[14] in the Ottoman Empire,[15] in Russia,[16] and wherever business could be found. In 1909, it raised its capital from 25m. to 45m. francs with the help of the Nationalbank für Deutschland; representatives of the German bank henceforth sat on its board of directors.[17] In the context of its South American drive, the CMF underwrote, seemingly alone, a 5 per cent 45m. franc gold loan by the Brazilian state of Bahia in 1910. As for Louis Dreyfus, it was still primarily a trader in cereals and not unnaturally attracted by a big wheat exporter like Argentina. It should be noted that the leading deposit bank, the CL, with its large customer base, the well-frequented counters of its head office in Paris, and its extensive web of branches, was involved in placing the six state loans on the Paris market to the extent of 22 per cent for Buenos Aires, 53 per cent for Tucuman, 22 per cent for Mendoza, 47 per cent and 21 per cent for the two Santa Fe loans, and 13 per cent for Bahia.[18]

Another Parisian private banking house managed a syndicate in 1909. N. (Noël) J. (Jules) et S. (Simon) Bardac was the lead underwriter for a 4.5 per cent 52m.-franc loan by the South-East Railways Company of Russia. Bardac's activity was centred in the Ottoman Empire and in Russia. It had a predilection for railways. In 1894 it was instrumental in the flotation of the Smyrna–Cassaba Railway Co.'s shares.[19] In this as in subsequent operations, it became the ally of the powerful Imperial Ottoman Bank and a regular participant in syndicates it managed, especially in connection with railway concessions.[20] Following an unsuccessful attempt in 1894 to launch a Franco-Russian industrial company, Bardac seemed to be uninvolved in Russian affairs. It re-emerged in 1907 in the context of a project which set the stage for laying rail lines in the south-east. Another Franco-Russian company, known as the Consortium, was to be set up, ostensibly to promote railway construction, in fact to benefit from the confidence railway profits would generate in Russian securities in order to unload excess stock held by French and Russian promoters. Bardac, the IOB, and the *haute banque* connected with it formed one of the two competing French groups. It was pitted against Paribas and its partner the SG. The former combination carried the day but the Russian government opposed the Consortium's ambition to control Russia's economy and the scheme came to naught in 1908..[21]

Paribas's rebuff explains why Bardac could manage the South-East Railways syndicate, why Paribas and the SG came to terms with this reversal of fortune to the point of joining the combination in a relatively minor position, and why the CL, which had held aloof from the Consortium, entered the syndicate in a big way. Nevertheless, despite Bardac's leadership, the commanding presence of the Paris joint-stock banks in the South-East Railways syndicate was indicative of the location of the centre of gravity within the group. Three-quarters of the loan was underwritten by joint-stock banks, two-thirds going to deposit banks; the latter sold three-quarters of the loan to the public. Bardac is the sole private bank among the guarantors and the only underwriter to have had no role in placing stock in the hands of investors (Table 7.5).

In a class of their own stood Rothschild Frères of Paris and the Rothschild houses in general. The Paris entity was the quintessential *haute banque* and by far the most powerful French private bank. The scale of its operations set it apart from other private houses. The *haute banque* faced a rival in 1848 when the CEP emerged; designed as a commercial bank, it was soon involved in financial operations. Some joint-stock banks were formed specifically to draw business away from Rothschild Frères. Combinations of banks and bankers appeared as the only way to face the enormous resources the Paris branch of the Rothschild family could mobilize single-handedly.

Its supremacy was first challenged by Émile and Isaac Pereire's Crédit Mobilier; founded in 1852, it came to grief in 1867, not without a push from Rothschild. A second, more successful attempt was made in 1872 with the arrival on the financial scene of the BPPB as a result of the merger of the Banque de Paris (1869) and the Banque de Crédits et de Dépôts des Pays-Bas (1863). Paribas was more than the sum of its original parts. It was, in fact, a relatively stable federation of private bankers whose representatives formed its board of directors and 'Table' of close allies. Such a coalition wielded considerable means originating from the purse of its individual members. The outcome was serious competition for the Rothschilds on all fronts, national and international.

Contenders notwithstanding, Rothschild Frères remained a force to be reckoned with at all times, and more than ever when foreign states called on the Paris market for large amounts. Whether the loans were Russian, Italian, or Japanese, Rothschild managed underwriting syndicates throughout the period 1890 to 1914. Their advantages were either their seniority in the borrower country, as in Russia and Italy, or their prestige and reputation, as in Japan. In Russia, the Rothschild houses were practically on home turf, having been the promoters of the 1862, 1870, 1872, 1873, and 1875 loans on the London market. Because of Anglo-Russian tension during the Russo-Turkish War, they had to be content with participation in the 1877 5 per cent Russian loan managed by its one of their German allies, the Berlin banking house of Mendelssohn.

From the end of the 1880s to 1901, Russian loans gave rise to a see-saw rivalry between Rothschild and the newcomer Paribas, each bringing in tow its long-standing or occasional 'friends'. The BPPB quickly made its presence felt in 1889 by carrying the conversion of the 1877 5 per cent loan to a new 4 per cent stock. The international syndicate it put together for the 500m.-franc operation is interesting in several respects. First, it was made up of French, German,

Table 7.5. South-East Railways syndicate (%)

	Underwriters	*Retailers*
CL	44	53.55
Bardac	26.66	
BPPB	9.17	11
SG	9.17	11
CNEP	9.17	11
Crédit Industriel et Commercial (CIC)	1.83	2.2
International Bank of St Petersburg		6
Stockbrokers		5.25

Source: AHCL, 158AH 1.

Anglo-Dutch, and Russian banks, in the proportion of 55, 15, 10 and 10 per cent. The French group comprised, behind Paribas, the four main deposit banks underwriting jointly more than twice the amount covered by the leader. The only private French bank was E. Hoskier & Cie. Of Danish origin and settled in Paris under the Second Empire, Edmond Hoskier often acted as scout and facilitator for Paribas in Russia. The German and Anglo-Dutch groups had three participants each, familiar names in the BPPB constellation—Mendelssohn & Co., Berliner Handelsgesellschaft, Robert Warschauer & Co., Baring Bros., C. J. Hambro & Sons, Hope & Co. The Russian participants were two of the group of national banks which normally associated with their French counterparts in their country's borrowing—the Discount Bank of St Petersburg (DBSP) and the International Bank of Commerce of St Pertersburg (IBCSP). Tellingly absent from the consortium were Rothschild and its allies. As would be the case from 1889 on, irrespective of the proportions underwritten, the 1889 loan ended up largely in French investors' portfolios.[22]

The Hoskier–Paribas duo scored a 360m.-franc success in 1890, but Rothschild was back the following year to undertake the 378m.-franc conversion of the 1862 5 per cent loan originally piloted by itself, and then again for the conversion of 1.8bn. francs of 4.5 per cent short-term loans to 3 per cent paper. Hoskier–Paribas and the deposit banks associated with them responded by obtaining a 3 per cent 500m.-franc loan at the end of 1891. But the operation turned sour; Mendelssohn and Warschauer refused to join and, despite patriotic fervour generated by the Franco-Russian rapprochement, the public proved to be less enthusiastic than anticipated in the context of a famine in Russia.[23]

Paribas had to enlist the services of deposit banks and to increase Russian participation in 1893 for the conversion of the 178m.-franc 6 per cent loan of 1883 to 3 per cent bonds. The CL and CNEP were accompanied by the IBCSP, the DBST, the Bank of Volga-Kama (BVK), and the Russian Bank for Foreign Trade (RBFT). In Amsterdam, responsibility fell to Lippmann, Rosenthal & Co., and the BPPB branch.[24] The operation may not have been a resounding success because Rothschild Frères was in charge of the next, the 379m.-franc 3.5 per cent loan of 1894 sold to the public in Paris, London, Berlin, and Frankfurt. Its network was brought into play. N. M. Rothschild of London, Rothschild of Frankfurt, and three Berlin banks—Bleichröder, a house closely associated with the Rothschilds, Mendelssohn, and the Disconto-Gesellschaft—acted as other underwriters and retailers.[25]

Success bred success, as Rothschild Frères picked up the subsequent Russian operation in 1896, a 400m.-franc 3 per cent loan. It underwrote 72 per cent of the issue, leaving 6 per cent to each of the Berlin banks and bringing in the IBCSP and the CL. The CL sold 6 per cent of the issue. The inclusion of a large deposit bank like the CL was something of a precaution because suspicion about the state of Russian public finances slowed placement of the stock.[26] The services of the CL became more requisite. In 1899, it handled by itself the placement of the whole of three 4 per cent loans amounting to 287m. francs. It did likewise the following year for a 3.5 per cent 149m.-franc loan to the Imperial Land Bank of the Nobility.[27]

Rothschild was not yet counted out. It managed a 415m.-franc 4 per cent Russian loan in 1901, underwriting 50 per cent and distributing the rest in small amounts to a number of banks. Hottinguers was the only private banking house, but it guaranteed 9.43 per cent, more than any of the joint-stock banks. The CL, the BPPB the CNEP, the SG, and the CIC contracted for 8.87, 8.87, 4.35, 4.35, and 2.28 per cent respectively. Rothschild ceded 2.36 per cent to each of the IBCSP, the BVK, the DBST, and the RBFT. *Rétrocessions* of 1 per cent or less went to a French group made up of the BFCI, the Banque Parisienne, the Banque Suisse, the Crédit Algérien, the Banque Russo-Chinoise, the Société des Mines d'Or & d'Exportation, the Banque Transatlantique, the Société Lyonnaise de Dépôts, and the Société Marseillaise. Established in 1865 and 1863, the last two were among the 'provincial' deposit banks which often aided Rothschilds in placing securities in the heart of France while limiting the sway of the 'national' deposit banks. Nevertheless, Rothschild had to make room for the big Paris banks and for many smaller French banks. It had to replace its German allies with Russian banks. In the end, 36 per cent of the loan was placed by the CL.[28] The 1901 loan may be seen as Rothschild's swan song in Russia. However grand, it was an exit. Subsequent operations showed that Rothschild no longer had control of the Russian market. The new contenders were joint-stock banks, mainly the CL and the BPPB,[29] notwithstanding the 1909 one-time thrust of a private bank like Bardac. They had no need of Rothschild or its Berlin partners in their syndicates.

Rothschild was hardly reduced to idleness. It piloted a 45m.-franc 4 per cent issue to the Southern Austrian Railways (Südbahn) in 1900[30] and a Hungarian state loan conversion in 1902.[31] No sooner had it lost Russia than it found a sort of substitute in Japan. It contracted the 1905 4 per cent, the 1907 5 per cent, the 1910 4 per cent, and the 1913 5 per cent loans. The amounts were respectively 270m.,[32] 289m.,[33] 430m.,[34] and 196m. francs. Significantly, perhaps due to its Russian experience, its syndicates now included all the major Parisian joint-stock banks, as well as Paribas and the BFCI. Indeed, they collectively underwrote and sold most of the securities. Another fixture was Hottinguer & Cie., a *haute banque* possibly instrumental as an intermediary with Japan. Rothschild underwrote at most a third of each loan and placed from 13 to 33 per cent. Even if allotted amounts vary from one loan to another, the 1907 operation (see Table 7.6) gives an accurate picture of the breakdown of Rothschild's Japanese syndicates.

Harking back to the 1850s and 1860s when it had the Italian market all to itself, Rothschild led the 400m.-franc conversion of Italy's 5 per cent bonds to 3.75 per cent in 1907. The underwriters of the Japanese loans were again in the syndicate, but the percentages of all were reduced because 25 per cent of the amount guaranteed went to a German group and 15 per cent to a British group.[35]

Table 7.6. Syndicate for the 1907 Japanese loan (%)

	Underwriters	*Retailers*
Rothschild	33.33	12.79
CL	13.33	44.31
BPPB	24.68	13.15
Hottinguer	10	4
CNEP	6.66	10.71
SG	6.66	10.71
CIC	3.34	2.2
BFCI	2	1.38

Source: AHCL, 158AH 1. The figures were originally presented according to different criteria; they were reworked in the table above.

3. Banques d'affaires, deposit banks, and their international allies: Paribas and the Crédit Lyonnais

The instances presented, however noteworthy, do not detract from the fact that management of syndicates by private banks was not a common occurrence. Leadership was taken mostly by joint-stock banks, with private banks playing only an accessory role either as contractors or as simple beneficiaries of cessions by contractors of a portion of the amount guaranteed. This was a reflection of the reality that, by the second half of the nineteenth century, joint-stock banks had grown much larger than private banks. Rothschild did not fit the pattern. It was a banking house too important to be integrated as a simple member of a syndicate led by others or too proud to accept the leadership of the upstart banks. There are two exceptions in the data base. One is the 1906 loan by a US railway, the Pennsylvania Co., co-managed by the CL and the BPPB. The latter guaranteed about 23.5 per cent each, Rothschild 20 per cent, the SG 10 per cent, Kuhn Loeb & Co. of New York 10 per cent, Warburg & Co. of Hamburg 10 per cent, and Paris stockbrokers 3 per cent. The CL sold 56 per cent of the loan, the BPPB and the SG together 38 per cent, and the stockbrokers 6 per cent. Rothschild may have been needed because of the amount of the loan, 238m. francs.[36] Another was a 50 per cent participation in the 1911 underwriting syndicate led by the CL for a 59m.-franc 4.5 per cent loan to the Royal Dutch Co. for oil in the Dutch Indies. The CL guaranteed 25 per cent, Deterding 13 per cent, the BPPB 9 per cent, and the Banque de l'Union Parisienne (BUP) 3 per cent. The CL was responsible for 57 per cent of the reselling, Rothschild 26 per cent, Deterding 3 per cent; cessions were made to various others who then resold.[37] In this instance, it was Rothschild which needed the placement capacity of the CL.

The predominance of the new joint-stock banks was unmistakable. In the case of the *banques d'affaires*, they could mobilize more resources for underwriting than the *haute banque*. As for the deposit banks, not only did they possess the means to guarantee issues, but, with their ramified network of branches, they were the best equipped for retailing them to a wide new public of investors previously untouched by private banks.

The pre-eminent *banque d'affaires* and deposit bank were respectively the BPPB and the CL. Two banks could hardly be more different. Although their equity base was about the same, the structure of their asset and liabilities was a fair indication of their nature and activities. Crossover of upper-level personnel from one to the other was rare; Charles Sautter's passage from the CL to Paribas in 1872 was more the exception than the rule.[38] The CL and the BPPB were regulars in most syndicates, and, more than any other banks, managed consortia. Theirs was a complex and ambiguous relationship. They were drawn together by contradictory motives. Either one could probably mount a national or international operation by itself, with the assistance of smaller allies. But there was obvious advantage to spreading risk and great interest in avoiding the cost of acute rivalry. Not being competitors in their normal activity, they could more easily cooperate on international issues, the only important ground on which they came face to face.

Although unspectacular, loans to the Scandinavian countries were significant sources of business for banks. Between 1891 and 1914, thirty-four loans were issued by Sweden, Norway, Denmark, and Finland. No other region in the world called more frequently on the Paris market. The loans provided an opportunity for forming syndicates in which CL and Paribas interests intermeshed throughout the period. The CL was first on the scene. In 1891, it took charge of a 10m.-franc Swedish 4 per cent issue, keeping for itself 45 per cent of the amount underwritten. The balance went to two categories of partners—25 per cent to the smaller but older deposit bank, the Crédit Commercial et Industriel (CIC), and 30 per cent to two Swedish banks, Marcus Wallenberg's Stockholms Enskilda Bank (SEB) (5 per cent) and the Hernosands Enskilda Bank (HEB) (5 per cent) from the northern town of Härnösand. As in Russia and elsewhere, banks from the issuing country were almost ex officio members of syndicates, provided they were important enough. The SEB and HEB became regulars on all Scandinavian syndicates. The placement of the loan tells a familiar story; the CL was responsible for 81.5 per cent and the CIC for 18.5 per cent of the retailing.[39]

The CL followed up in June 1894 with another Swedish issue, this time for 15m. francs to convert 4 per cent bonds to 3 per cent. The syndicate it led had more members, resulting in the reduction of the CL's participation to 25 per cent. The Swedish share remained at 30 per cent. The SEB settled for 22 per cent in order to make way for the Sveriges Ricksbank (8 per cent), the country's bank of issue. Room had also to be found for foreign associates. Denmark's Landmandsbank came in at 10 per cent; London's Hambros was involved for up to 25 per cent; L. Behrens & Söhne of Hamburg covered 10 per cent. The CL in turn passed on (*rétrocessions*) part of its portion to smaller Parisian private banks. In the end, it underwrote 18 per cent of the loan, leaving 5 per cent to Goudchaux & Cie, 1.2 per cent to Hoskier & Cie, and 0.4 per cent to Dreyfus & Cie of Basle. Edmond Hoskier's Danish background made his banking house an obvious and frequent participant in Scandinavian operations. As for the CL, it recovered some of the concessions it made in the underwriting by placing 64 per cent of the loan and converting 36 per cent.[40]

Why did the syndicate have more members? The CL clearly felt the need to widen its circle of associates in the face of Paribas's bid to enter the Scandinavian market. Paribas first joined a group which competed with the CL for the Swedish loan. Within six months of the Swedish operation, Denmark issued a 34m.-franc 3 per cent loan managed by the BPPB and its local and foreign associates. Coming upon the heels of a 55m.-franc Norwegian loan, the Danish loan may have worried potential underwriters. The CL and its partners were therefore brought into a mixed syndicate. In the final group of guarantors, BPPB kept 21 per cent of the amount and gave the CL 21 per cent. Along with the SEB (4 per cent), new Scandinavian banks were also guarantors—the Privatbanken (21 per cent), Skandinaviska Kreditaktiebolaget (3 per cent), and Rivesbank (3 per cent). Hambros underwrote 21 per cent, Hamburg's Norddeutsche Bank 4 per cent, and Amsterdam's Lippmann Rosenthal 2 per cent. Again the CL ceded to Goudchaux and Hoskier about 1.5 per cent of the issue. In the end, Paribas sold 15 per cent of the securities, the CL 58 per cent, the Privatbanken 2 per cent. Hambros placed 25 per cent of the loan in London, a sign of concern about success on the Paris market.[41]

This turned out to be the only loan Paribas managed single-handedly for Scandinavian governments. It was the leader for two issues by the Société de l'Azote et des Forces Hydro-Électriques (Norsk-Hydro), but the Lyonnais placed 21 per cent of the 40m.-franc loan of 1910, and 29 per cent of the 39m.-franc loan of 1911.[42] The CL and the BPPB co-managed four operations—a 43m.-franc Danish 3.5 per cent loan in 1901, two Swedish 3.5 per cent loans in 1911 each worth 98m. francs, and an 86m.-franc 3.5 per cent loan issued by the Mortgage Bank of the Cities of Sweden in 1911. The CL itself co-managed three operations with Scandinavian banks—a 28m.-franc 3.5 per cent City of Copenhagen loan shared with the Privatbanken in 1902, and two Finnish 3.5 per cent loans for 25m. and 10m. francs steered jointly with the SEB and the Bank of Finland. Apart from these cases, all syndicates for state loans by northern countries on the Paris market were under CL management, but included Paribas among the underwriters. They needed each other to face German competition in the area, as the CL discovered when it lost a 150m.-franc Swedish conversion in 1895 to the Dresdner Bank and a 50m.-franc Swedish loan in 1900 to a German-Swedish combination headed by Warburgs.[43] Except for loans by Norway in 1895 and 1905, and by the City of Christiania in 1897, the CL and the BPPB guaranteed an equal proportion in each issue.

Two groups of underwriters took part in the CL's syndicates. The first was made up of Scandinavian banks, chief among them being the SEB. Others were the Stockholm Handelsbank, the Landmandsbank, and the Privatbanken of Denmark, the Christiania (Oslo) Handelsbank and the Centralenbanken for Norge. Their individual share of the amount guaranteed varied from loan to loan but it was always smaller than the SEB's. They underwrote issues in all Scandinavian countries, not exclusively those of their home country. The SEB alone was a member of all syndicates. The second group comprised the German banks. Behrens, Deutsche Bank, Nationalbank, and Norddeutsche Bank were frequent participants. Hambros participated occasionally, but not beyond 1899. The CL and the BPPB together normally guaranteed a greater portion of each loan than the Scandinavian group, although at times the SEB had a share equal to that of either of the French banks. The German group had the lowest percentage of each operation. It ceased to be in syndicates in 1907; Warburgs was added, but remained alone. The share of the Scandinavian banks rose to 60 per cent in 1908. From 1910 to 1914, it was reduced to 30 per cent, due mainly to the entry of the SG and the CNEP in the French group. Tension with Germany probably had repercussions on the CL's Scandinavian syndicates. Three operations illustrate the transition (see Table 7.7). The CL and the BPPB remained the main underwriters throughout, with the CL most often handling 100 per cent of the placement.

In Russia, as the Rothschild–BPPB rivalry subsided, a small *banque d'affaires* like the Banque Internationale de Paris conducted a 17m.-franc issue of 4 per cent debentures for the Société Métallurgique de l'Oural-Volga in 1899.[44] The securities were made available to the public in seven cities, an indication of the composition of the syndicate. The members were not of the first rank. The IBCST and the DBST represented the Russian component. While the BIP handled the issue in Paris, the BPPB branch and the Caisse Générale de Reports et de Dépôts tapped into the Brussels market. Lippmann Rosenthal sold stock in Amsterdam. In France, the BIP called on regional banks—the Crédit du Nord in Lille, the Société Marseillaise, the Société Nancéienne, and the Crédit Havrais.[45]

Past 1901, Russian loans belonged to the BPPB and the CL, backed by their Russian partners and a variety of minor participants. The SG, the CNEP, and the BUP emerged on the scene after 1908. In fact, the SG participated in a small way through the Banque du Nord, a St Petersburg bank whose establishment it sponsored in 1901. As they did for Scandinavia, the BPPB and the CL collaborated in syndicates, but leadership went sometimes to one, sometimes to the other. Once, in 1912, they co-managed a 4.5 per cent loan of 257m. francs to the Peasants' Land Bank of Russia. Each normally included the other in syndicates it led; their percentages as underwriters were close if not always equal. The SG, the CNEP, the CIC, and the BFCI participated regularly. Hoskier faded but Hottinguer was a frequent member, and a unique one because small private banking houses were rarely involved in retailing loans. Hottinguer placed portions of loans, up to 13 per cent in the 1903 4 per cent Railway loan led by Paribas.[46] The CL was always the foremost retailer, often placing 100 per cent of the debentures on the Paris market. Some operations were multinational in scope. Up to 47 per cent of the 2bn.-franc 6 per cent loan directed by Paribas in 1906 was reserved for resale on the Russian, British, Dutch, and Austrian markets. The group of Russian banks, Barings,[47] Hambro of Amsterdam, and, among other Austrian banks, the Wiener Bank Verein took care of the retailing outside of France.[48]

Table 7.7. *Underwriting syndicates for Scandinavian loans*

	1901 Denmark 3.5% 43 m. francs	1909 Mortgage Bank of Norway 3.5% 37 m. francs	1914 Sweden 4.5% 65 m. francs
CL	29	20	21.35
BPPB	29	20	21.35
SG			14.00
CNEP			13.30
Scandinavian group		60	30.00
Christiania Handelsbank	5		
Landmandsbank	5		
Privatbanken	5		
SEB	10		
German group			
Behrens	4		
Deutsche Bank	8		
Nationalbank	5		

Source: AHCL, 158AH 1.

No clear pattern emerges in the data base from the twenty-two Russian operations mounted from 1902 to 1914.[49] Two or more of the familiar Russian banks were usually present but their number, their identity, and the amounts they guaranteed changed from loan to loan. In general, they underwrote less than their French counterparts, but there were exceptions. In 1903, the CL managed a 27m.-franc 4.5 per cent loan for the City of Odessa. Its share was 30 per cent, while the RBFT, the BVK, the DBST, and the Discount Bank of Odessa guaranteed 55 per cent. The consortium was unusual in another respect; Warburg underwrote 15 per cent of the issue. It was the last time a German bank guaranteed a Russian loan managed by French banks following the waning of Rothschild, their traditional associates. In 1908 and 1909, Barings was part of CL underwriting syndicates for two loans to the City of Moscow with a share equal to the leader's. An occasional guarantor was the Banque Russo-Chinoise, a *banque d'affaires* set up jointly in 1896 by the BPPB, the CL, the CNEP, the SG, Parisian private banks, the IBCST, and the DBSP to promote business, such as railway construction, in China. In 1911, it merged with the Banque du Nord of St Petersburg to form the Banque Russo-Asiatique.

Practically all issues from 1912 to 1914 were for the laying of rail lines. The most active French bank in railway issues was Paribas. In two years, it directed the following 4.5 per cent loans on the Paris market:

1912–149m. francs for the Altaï Railway Co.;
1912–88m. francs for the West Ural Railway Co.;
1913–96m. francs for the Black Sea Railway Co.;
1913–62m. francs for the Black Sea Railway Co.;
1913–115m. francs for the Semiretchinsk Railway.

The BPPB and the CL participated at the same level in the underwriting syndicates, the percentages of the SG and the CNEP being slightly lower. Hottinguer, the BUP, the BFCI, the CIC, and the Crédit Algérien had to settle for cessions ranging from 0.15 to 3.5 per cent. To the DBSP, the BVK, the RBFT, and the IBCSP were added the Bank of the Azov-Don, the Bank of Commerce of Siberia, the Private Commercial Bank of St Petersburg, and the Banque Russo-Asiatique.[50] The CL's share in the resale to the public hovered around 40 per cent of the total. If harmony and collaboration seemed to prevail among banks active in Russian affairs, it was probably due to the availability and recurrence of business, not necessarily to the scale of individual operations.

Syndicates for Swiss issues brought together the BPPB, the CL, and their allies.[51] There were sixteen operations from 1892 to 1909. The first was a failure. In 1892, the Crédit Algérien, the SG, and several Swiss banks offered 3 per cent bonds of the Canton of Fribourg. But the issue price was too high in light of the fact that the credit of the borrower was tainted by high indebtedness.[52] The Canton of Berne inspired more confidence and borrowed 49m. francs in 1895,[53] 50m. in 1897, and 20m. in 1900. The BPPB managed the syndicates which drew the CL, at par with Paribas for the amount underwritten, and the Banque Cantonale de Berne, with less. The CL placed from 64 to 100 per cent of Swiss loans in Paris.

In 1897, when the BPPB co-managed the 8m.-franc 3 per cent issue of the City of Lausanne with the Union Financière de Genève, and the 15m.-franc conversion of the City of Berne with the Banque Cantonale de Berne, it had to lower the total underwritten by it and the CL from 36 per cent each to 25 and 22 per cent in order to make way for several Swiss banks. In the first instance, the Banque d'Escompte & de Dépôts, Ch. Masson & Cie, the Swiss Bankverein (Basle), and the Société de Crédit Suisse; in the second, the Syndicat de Banques Bernoises, the Basler et Zürcher Bankverein, the Société de Crédit Suisse (Zurich), and the Union Financière de Genève.

Operations with the Canton of Fribourg resumed in 1903 with a 40m.-franc loan; the BPPB co-managed it with the CL and the Union Financière de Genève. Six Swiss banks were underwriters but the percentage of the BPPB and the CL was raised to 35 per cent. Co-managing a railway loan and a federal loan in 1903 with the Banque Cantonale de Berne, the CL and the BPPB guaranteed 32 and 37 per cent of the issues, despite the presence of a group of Swiss banks in the syndicates. From 1905 on, the CL was sole manager and Paribas an underwriter with a share equal to the CL's.

Forgoing a Swiss manager probably contributed to reducing the number of Swiss underwriters and maintaining the amount the French banks could guarantee. The share of the Swiss banks was lower, except for the railway loan of 1907 when the Bankverein alone guaranteed 40 per cent of the operation. The French banks recouped their loss in the same year's Canton of Zurich loan, where they raised their share to 45 per cent each, leaving only 10 per cent to the Crédit Suisse. The last loan, that of the Federal Railways, in 1909 was co-managed by the CL and the BPPB. Their share in the guarantee was lower because of the entry of the

SG and the CNEP in the syndicate. The Banque Cantonale de Berne, the Banque Nationale Suisse, and the Banque Suisse et Française only underwrote 21.25 per cent of the issue. Paris market conditions could explain why the SG and the CNEP had to place 19 per cent of the bonds, while the CL did no better than 56 per cent.

In the Habsburg Empire, the Rothschilds were no longer alone. Combinations concerning Austro-Hungarian operations on the Paris market revolved around two poles, the SG[54] and the CL.[55] In 1899, the SG conducted the 19m.-franc 3.5 per cent loan sought by the Mortgage Bank of Hungary. Its director general, Louis Dorizon, sat on the board of the issuer bank.[56] Through the CL, the Austrian-Hungarian State Railways borrowed 63m. francs at 4 per cent in 1900. The syndicate comprised the Austrian Mortgage Bank with a share of 50 per cent, the BPPB with 25 per cent, and Count Germiny with 1.5 per cent. The CL guaranteed only 23.5 per cent of the issue but, as expected, placed 100 per cent.[57] It did so again in 1908 for an 18m.-franc operation.

The City of Vienna 4 per cent loan of 1902 was a 300m.-franc operation, of which 125m. were reserved for the Paris market. The CL and Paribas co-managed the syndicate for the French portion, guaranteeing each 42 per cent and giving 16 per cent to the Deutsche Bank. The CL resold to the public 94 per cent of the bonds, the BPPB 6 per cent. In 1910, it managed a 24m.-franc 4 per cent loan to the First National Savings Bank of Pest. The CL underwrote 88 per cent of the operation, the Société Belge de Crédit Industriel et Commercial 9 per cent, the Bank of the Homeland (Budapest) 1.5 per cent, and Wertheim and Gompertz 1.5 per cent. The Brussels bank placed 9 per cent of the bonds, stockbrokers 1 per cent, the CL 90 per cent. The Brussels link recalls the role Belgian banks played in the introduction of the Hungarian borrower's securities on the Paris market in 1903 and 1905.[58] But the rationale was probably political—the possible offence to sensitivities made lending to a potential enemy a risky business proposition.

The recourse to foreign markets was again evident in the CL-managed 50m.-franc 4 per cent loan by the Hungarian Commercial Bank of Pest in 1911. The CL branch in Geneva underwrote 70 per cent and sold 50 per cent of the bonds. The CNEP branch in Brussels underwrote 23 per cent and sold 15 per cent. In Paris, the CL sold 25 per cent and the CNEP 10 per cent of the loan. The borrower bank guaranteed 8 per cent of its own issue. In the City of Budapest 100m.-franc 4 per cent loan of the same year, co-managed by the CL and the BPPB, the CL underwrote 22 per cent, the BPPB 22 per cent, the SG 14 per cent, the CNEP 13 per cent, and four Hungarian banks in the syndicate[59] a full 29 per cent. The Geneva and Brussels branches of the Paris banks participated in the guarantee, and part of the bonds—maximum 43 per cent—were sold on those markets. A second loan of 35m.-francs by the First National Savings Bank of Pest in 1912 produced the same consortium as in 1910, save for the fact that the CL branch in Geneva underwrote 48 per cent and placed 51 per cent of the bonds. In the 5m.-franc 4 per cent loan of the Mortgage Bank of Austria of the same year, Paribas and its Brussels branch guaranteed 32 per cent of the issue, the same as the CL, the Wiener

Bankverein 25 per cent, and the Société Suisse de Banque et de Dépôts (Lausanne) 11 per cent. The latter resold to the public 19 per cent of the issue.

No foreign markets were needed to retail bonds of two first-time borrowers in Paris.[60] In 1903, the CL managed the issue of the City of Warsaw 88m.-franc 4.5 per cent loan and placed it entirely by itself. However, it underwrote less than 25 per cent itself and had to structure a carefully balanced syndicate from various interested parties. The Deutsche Bank guaranteed 27 per cent, and 29 per cent went to five Polish participants—the Bank of Commerce of Warsaw (15.2 per cent), the Discount Bank of Warsaw (6 per cent), the Bank of Commerce of Lodz (2.4 per cent), S. Natanson and Synowie of Warsaw (3.6 per cent), and Wawelberg of Warsaw (1.8 per cent). Nineteen per cent of the total was ceded to the BIP (4.2 per cent), the BPPB (2.2 per cent), and three Russian banks—the BVK (4.2 per cent), the DBSP (4.2 per cent), and the RBFT (4.2 per cent). The Chicago, Milwaukee & St Paul Railway Co. turned to the Paris market in 1910 with a 243m.-franc 4 per cent issue. Paribas, the manager, underwrote 20 per cent, the same as the CL and the SG. It gave 13.3 per cent to the CNEP, 3 per cent to Arthur Spitzer, an SG partner, 2.5 per cent to H. Schroeder, and 2 per cent to Édouard Noetzlin, a Paribas director. Kuhn Loeb & Co., the American component in the syndicate, guaranteed 15 per cent. The manager ceded 4.2 per cent to many French private, joint-stock, and provincial banks. As befits operations directed by a *banque d'affaires*, 82 per cent of the placement was the work of the three deposit banks.

The Crédit Foncier Franco-Canadien's intermediary on the Paris market was the BPPB, its main founder in 1880.[61] In the 1906, 1908, and 1909 loans, the CL, the only other underwriter, guaranteed one-third of the issues and retailed 100 per cent. When the Belgian and Swiss markets were called upon, a change occurred in the syndicate, henceforth managed by the CL. The leader's head office in Paris underwrote 15 per cent and its Geneva branch 25 per cent; Paribas guaranteed 15 per cent, its Geneva branch 25 per cent, and its 'Table' 20 per cent. Nearly all the debentures were retailed by the CL—45 per cent in Paris, 22 per cent in Geneva, and, for reasons difficult to fathom, 28 per cent by its Brussels branch. The rest was sold by stockbrokers. Two 4 per cent loans in 1911, amounting to 15m. francs, were underwritten by the two head offices for 15 per cent each and by their Geneva branches for 25 per cent each, 20 per cent going to Paribas's 'Table'. Half of the bonds were placed by the CL branch in Geneva, most of the rest by its head office on the Paris market. The arrangement for the two 4 per cent loans of 1912 amounting to 52m. francs continued that of 1911, except that in the second, the Geneva branches were replaced by correspondents, the Union Financière de Genève for the BPPB, Von Ernst & Co. for the CL. The CL head office and its Geneva branch placed 100 per cent of the loans, with a slightly higher amount being marketed in Geneva. Switzerland's contribution was not sought for the two 24m.-franc 5 per cent loans of 1913. Each head office guaranteed 40 per cent and the Paribas 'Table' 20 per cent. The CL placed over nine-tenths of the debentures on the Paris market; stockbrokers resold the rest.[62]

Apart from the previously mentioned operations managed by private banks, Latin American loans were largely BPPB undertakings. Paribas was in charge of several Brazilian operations. The 15m.-franc 5 per cent loan of 1894 to the State of Espirito Santo was managed in conjunction with the Brazilian National Bank.[63] A 29m.-franc conversion of the bonds of the Compagnie Française des Chemins de Fer Brésiliens in 1895 also involved the SG and the CIC.[64] The BPPB was probably the manager of the 1895 20m.-franc São Paolo Railway loan.[65] It also conducted the 63m.-franc loan to the State of Minaes Geraes in 1896.[66] It associated with the Dresdner Bank for the 94m.-franc 5 per cent loan of the São Paolo State Railways Co. in 1905, and with the SG for the São Paolo State loans of 1907, 1908, and 1913.[67] The BPPB returned in 1910 with the SG for a 80m.-franc 4.5 per cent loan to the Brazilian Railway Co.,[68] and again in 1911 with the latter for a 35m.-franc 5 per cent loan to the Compagnie Française du Port de Rio Grande do Sul.[69]

Through its ties with Jacob Schiff of Kuhn Loeb, Paribas took an interest in Mexican affairs; it participated in the founding of the National Bank of Mexico[70] and the issue of its shares, amounting to 53m. francs in 1905.[71] Along with the BUP, the CNEP, and the SG, it conducted a 136m.-franc 4 per cent loan to the Mexican National Railways in 1907.[72] The 1910 4 per cent Mexican State 274m.-franc loan was important; German, US, and Mexican interests had to be assuaged. The manager, the BPPB, underwrote 12 per cent, the CL 10 per cent, the SG 10 per cent, and the CNEP 9 per cent. Seventeen per cent went to the National Bank of Mexico, and 42 per cent to Bleichöder, the Deutsche Bank, the Dresdner Bank, J. P. Morgan, and S. Morgan Grenfell. Cessions to various intermediaries were made. The bonds were sold entirely on the Paris market by the CL (39 per cent), the SG (28 per cent), the CNEP (21 per cent), the BPPB (10 per cent), and by stockbrokers and intermediaries (2 per cent).[73]

Next to attract Paribas's attention was Argentina. The 1909 5 per cent loan was for 252m. francs, with 84m. reserved for the Paris market, 75m. for the British, 51m. for the US, and 42m. for the German markets. Paribas underwrote 40 per cent, while the SG, the CL, and the CNEP covered 20 per cent each. Placement on the Paris market was reasonably well distributed—14, 31.5, 28, 26.5 per cent respectively.[74] In 1911 and 1912, the CL contracted four Banque Hypothécaire Franco-Argentine[75] 4.5 per cent loans for a total of 96m. francs. The only other underwriter was the BUP, on a 50–50 basis. The fifth was led by the BUP in 1914, the same proportions being kept. The CL placed from 88 to 100 per cent of the bonds. Paribas led a syndicate the same year for a 70m.-franc 4.5 per cent issue by the Compagnie Française des Chemins de Fer de la Province de Santa Fe; the CL was an underwriter for over 21 per cent and placed 36 per cent of the issue.[76]

China was compelled to become a loan-seeker following its defeat in the war of 1894–5. Although the manager is not always known, the BPPB is the only bank belonging to all consortia. It took part with the CL and Hottinguer in the syndicate for the guarantee of the 392m.-franc 4 per cent issue of 1895.[77] Its partners in the 1899 64m.-franc 5 per cent loan were the SG, the CNEP, the Banque Parisienne, the BIP, and the Banque Française de l'Afrique du Sud. The last two members were replaced by the BFCI in the 44m.-franc 5 per cent operation of 1902. In 1903, the BFCI itself gave way to the Banque Russo-Chinoise in the 39m.-franc 5 per cent loan.[78] Subsequent issues were managed by the Banque de l'Indochine.[79]

In one respect, Morocco was similar to China. Its loans were international operations setting in motion banks as well as their national governments. In 1910, the 99m.-franc 5 per cent loan was attributed two-thirds to a French group of eleven banks led by the BPPB, one-third to four German banks headed by Mendelssohn and sixteen Spanish banks represented by the Banco de España. French participants made room for Sir Ernest Cassel in the portion of the amount they underwrote. All important French joint-stock banks were in the consortium and took part in resales to the public.[80]

4. Other banques d'affaires, deposit banks, and their international allies

Even if the BPPB and the CL dominated the Paris financial market and managed the most syndicates, they were not alone. The BUP, a *banque d'affaires* second only to Paribas, led three syndicates in the data base. One was for the 65m.-franc 3 per cent Haitian loan of 1911. A newcomer in Russia, the BUP participated in the issue of shares of the Factories of Briansk in 1906 with, among others, the SG.[81] In 1913, it managed a 69m.-franc 4.5 per cent loan to the Company for Branch Lines; the make-up of the syndicate holds no surprise—the four prime Paris joint-stock banks and seven Russian banks. As a *banque d'affaires*, it had great need of a retailer; the CL, with 15 per cent of the amount guaranteed, sold 49 per cent of the bonds on the Paris market. As was stated, it led a syndicate for the Banque Hypothécaire Franco-Argentine in 1914. The BFCI was in charge of a 40m.-franc 5 per cent loan by Brazil in 1909 and a 30m.-franc 4.5 per cent loan to the Mortgage Bank of Serbia in 1910. A lesser *banque d'affaires*, the Crédit Mobilier Français, conducted a 45m.-franc 5 per cent issue for the Brazilian State of Bahia in 1910, a 25m.-franc 4.5 per cent operation for the Caisse Hypothécaire Argentine in 1911, and, the same year, a 25m.-franc 5 per cent loan for the Victoria-Minas Railway in Uruguay.[82]

The largest deposit bank after the CL was the SG. It was active in Egypt in the early 1900s. Borrowing by Egypt began in earnest at the end of the nineteenth century after a period of recovery from the after effects of the bankruptcy of 1876. The Crédit Foncier Égyptien and the sugar-refining company were the main applicants. The SG sponsored five loans and three increases of capital for the CFE between 1897 and 1907, in all 377m. francs. It also sponsored the Société Générale des Sucreries et de la Raffinerie d'Égypte in its bid to expand rapidly. Three loans and three increases of capital were conducted by the SG from 1902 to 1904 for a total of 49m. francs. Syndicates included regular SG partners—joint-stock banks such as the BPPB, the CNEP, the CIC, the BFCI, and others; banking houses like Heine, Hirschler, Hottinguer, Verne, Propper, Kirchheim, and others. Chastened by the bankruptcy of the sugar company in 1905,[83] the SG saw the CL pilot later CFE loans. There were seven from 1908 to 1914, amounting to 466m.

francs. CL-led syndicates were limited to the SG, the BPPB, the CNEP, Paribas's British ally Cassel,[84] and the SG's ally Spitzer.[85]

The SG was deeply involved in Russia. After a lull attributable to the 1904 and 1905 revolution, borrowing for railway construction picked up. Caution by the larger French banks opened the way for regional institutions, members of the Syndicat des Banques de Province, who found an opportunity to venture into Russia by themselves. In 1908, the Banque Privée Lyon-Marseille, Adam et Cie, the Banque de Bordeaux, the Crédit du Nord, and the SM handled the issue of a 31m.-franc 4.5 per cent loan railway loan.[86] Larger banks soon re-entered the field. The SG co-managed with the CL a 223m.-franc loan in 1908 for the North-Donetz Railway Co.; it was also the main underwriter with 18 per cent of the operation. The major French joint-stock banks and the IBCSP took part in the syndicate. The SG brought with it the Banque du Nord (St Petersburg), the Société Française d'Entreprises Industrielles Russes, the Société Générale de Belgique, as well as Spitzer, Hirschler, and Thalmann, its close allies among Parisian private banks. Along with the CNEP, it co-managed a 7m.-franc loan to the Donetz Iron and Steel Mills in 1911 and another one for 5m. francs in 1913. The SG managed alone a new loan to the North-Donetz in 1912; the structure of the syndicate was the same as that of 1908.

However present it may have been in syndicates managed by others, the CNEP itself led few. A rare case was the 4 per cent Romanian loan of 1910, for 128m. francs, to be placed, according to the wish of the issuer, on the Paris and Berlin markets. The syndicate had among its members the BPPB, the SG and the Disconto-Gesellschaft. Another was the 175m.-franc Greek 5 per cent loan of 1914. Ranking as the third Parisian deposit bank, the CNEP lacked the stature and the connections needed to control the market. The same held true for the CIC and the Société Marseillaise. The SM was no longer a regional bank, but neither had it become a national deposit bank no syndicate could afford to be without. It did sponsor the Land Bank of Egypt and the Union Foncière d'Égypte—total equity and debentures worth 232m. francs—in 1905 in association with three Alexandria and two London commercial and banking houses.[87]

5. Banques d'affaires, deposit banks, and their international allies: specialized overseas institutions

The last group of joint-stock banks active in syndicates is that of specialized overseas institutions. The one most tied to a single country was the Banque d'État du Maroc. Established in 1906 as an international entity, it was at the same time a central bank, a *banque d'affaires*, and the institution entitled to conduct borrowing by Morocco.[88] In fact, it was closely linked to the French banks. The BEM became their surrogate in Morocco, *inter alia* managing syndicates in the place of the BPPB. A case in point was the 169m.-franc 4 per cent loan of 1914 placed entirely in France.[89] The BEM underwrote 22 per cent, but the other ten guarantors, all French, were to all intents and purposes those of the syndicate of 1910. The amount covered gave an indication of the importance of the participant—12 per cent to each of the BPPB, the CL, the SG, and the CNEP; 8 per cent to the SM, 5 per cent to the BFCI, etc. All took part in the retailing, the CL, the SG, and the CNEP handling 27, 21, and 16 per cent of the reselling to the public.

Three other specialized regional banks did not limit their activities to a single country. The International Ottoman Bank was the oldest. An Anglo-French central bank and *banque d'affaires* founded in 1863, it was dominant in the Ottoman Empire and extended its influence to the Balkans. Syndicates for Ottoman operations were managed by the IOB. In 1894–5, it conducted the 35m.-franc 4 per cent loan of the Smyrna-Cassaba Railway Co.; Bénard & Jarislowsky placed the loan in Paris.[90] It did likewise in 1901 for the 32m.-franc 4 per cent loan of the Damascus–Hamah Railway. The syndicate comprised the usual Parisian associates—the BPPB, the SG, and the CNEP—the local rail specialist N. J. et S. Bardac, and two German banks, Bethmann of Frankfurt and the Deutsche Bank, a sign of German interest in Ottoman railways.[91]

The 168m.-franc 4 per cent Ottoman loan of 1902 followed a similar pattern. It was underwritten 52.1 per cent by the IOB, 22.1 per cent by the Deutsche Bank, 15.44 per cent by the BPPB, 5.12 per cent by the SG, and 5.12 per cent by the BFCI. The BPPB and the SG ceded parts of their shares to their usual associates.[92] Placement was distributed between the IOB (33.3 per cent), the SG (21 per cent), the BFCI (10 per cent), the BPPB (9.2 per cent), and two non-members of the syndicate, the CNEP (18.4 per cent) and the CIC (8.1 per cent). In 1903, the IOB managed the 744m.-franc unification of the Ottoman debt.[93] The 1905 Ottoman 4 per cent loan for 105m.-francs was under its patronage. The IOB guaranteed only 13 per cent; the rest went to the BPPB, the SG, the CNEP, the CIC, the BFCI, and the BUP.[94] In the 217m.-franc 4 per cent loan of 1905, the IOB guaranteed 23 per cent, but placed only 12 per cent, with the three major deposit banks reselling 24 per cent each.[95]

The Paris market absorbed all the securities offered. However, the Young Turk revolution of 1908 shook its hegemony in Ottoman borrowing. In the 4 per cent loan of June 1909, 27.4m. francs were reserved for each of the French, British, and German markets. Another 4 per cent operation was mounted in October 1909 for 143m. francs. Thirty-one per cent of the amount was attributed to the London market. But the issue there failed and the bonds had to be redirected to Paris. The Deutsche Bank was an underwriter twice but took no part in placing the first loan.[96] The 35m.-franc issue of 1911 by the Smyrna–Cassaba Railway Co. was a purely French affair. The IOB and its partners underwrote 56 per cent, the SG and the CNEP 22 per cent each. The debentures were sold to the public by the SG (46 per cent), the CNEP (35 per cent), and a deposit bank until then inconspicuous in Ottoman financial ventures on the Paris market, the CL (13 per cent).[97] German interests were back, along with Belgian, Swiss, and Russian participants, in 1914. In fact, non-French underwriters covered 32 per cent of the first segment of a 409m.-franc loan issued in two portions that year.[98] Intense rivalry among European powers and Turkish desire to loosen the financial grip of France explain the presence or the absence of non-French participants.

In the Balkans, the IOB was regularly involved in Serbian transactions. It contracted the 44m.-franc loan of 1893 with the CL and the Berliner Handelsgesellschaft.[99] In the 54m.-franc 5 per cent issue of 1903, it called on the SG, the CNEP, the BFCI, Hoskier, the Société Financière d'Orient, and the Austrian Länderbank.[100] It was not involved in the 1907 syndicate for a 89m.-franc loan.[101] The 1910 loan was international—112.5m. francs to the French market, 37.5m. to the German. Joining the IOB and its affiliates, like the Société Financière d'Orient and the Banque Franco-Serbe, were the BPPB, the SG, the CNEP, Bardac, Bethmann, and the Berliner Handelsgesellschaft. The SG, the CNEP, the CL, and the BPPB placed 74 per cent of the French portion. In 1914, the IOB left the 175m.-franc 5 per cent loan to its affiliate founded in 1910, the Banque Franco-Serbe, which led a syndicate composed mainly of the IOB's usual Parisian confrères.[102]

In Bulgaria, the IOB did not always act as an intermediary for that country's loans. The 1896 30m.-franc issue was contracted by the BPPB, the BIP, the SG, the CNEP, and the Länderbank.[103] The IOB was listed among the issuers in Paris in the 95m.-franc 5 per cent of 1902, but not in that of 1907 for 131m. francs.[104] The Romanian 4 per cent loans of 1898, 1905, and 1910 were guaranteed by the BPPB, the CNEP, and the SG. The 128m.-franc operation of 1910 was intended for the French, German, and Romanian markets.[105] For obvious reasons, the IOB was absent from Greek issues. Greece usually reserved parts of its loans for the London market and for wealthy Alexandrian expatriates. The Paris share of the 15m.-franc loan of 1898 was 33 per cent; no French bank guaranteed more than 10 per cent. By 1914, the French market took 70 per cent of the 250m.-franc 5 per cent issue; London absorbed 17 per cent; the rest went to Egypt, Greece, and New York.[106]

The specialist in African loans was the Crédit Algérien. In 1899, the Société Générale de Mines d'Algérie-Tunisie issued a 4.5 per cent loan of 7m. francs through the SG and the Compagnie Algérienne.[107] There were loans to the Gouvernement Général de l'Afrique Occidentale Française in 1903 (38m. francs), 1905 (4m. and 27m.), 1907 (40m.), 1909 (31m.), and 1910 (31m.). Tunisia borrowed in 1904 (10m. francs), 1906 (21m.), 1908 (57m.), and 1911 (36m.). The Gouvernement Général de la Colonie de Madagascar called on the Paris market in 1903 (50m. francs) and in 1906 (15m.). In 1906, Algeria did likewise for 19m. francs.

Consortia comprised the large Paris joint-stock banks and had no non-French members. The CNEP was the main underwriter for the Tunisian loan of 1904 with 40 per cent of the total, probably in deference to its seniority in the country. By 1905, the pattern of Crédit Algérien-led syndicates was set. The CA, the CL, the CNEP, the SG, and the BPPB had equal portions. Lesser amounts were attributed to the CIC, the BFCI, the SM, and the Banque Française de l'Afrique Occidentale. The CL was the leading reseller to the public with 30 to 62 per cent.

The Banque de l'Indochine had priority whenever the Gouvernement Général de l'Indochine turned to financial markets. Like the Crédit Algérien, it had in its syndicates the major Paris joint-stock banks and no non-French institutions.[108] In the 55m. franc loan of 1899, it guaranteed 37 per cent of the issue, a percentage well above the 18 per cent of the next underwriter, the BPPB. The CL obtained a slightly higher amount than the BIC's in the 78m.-franc 3 per cent loan of 1902, a situation reversed in the 83m.-franc loan of 1905. In the next loan, the 53m.-franc issue of 1909, the BIC, the CL, the CNEP, the SG, and the BPPB were each at 15 per cent, the CIC had 10 per cent, the BFCI, the BUP, and the Crédit Algérien 5 per cent each. In the last operation, the 55m. franc loan of 1913, the three leading deposit banks had 17 per cent each, the BPPB 15 per cent, the BIC and the CIC 10 per cent each, the BUP, the BFCI, the Crédit Algérien, the CMF, and the Société Centrale des Banques de Province 3 per cent each. The BIC made forays outside Indo-China, leading a syndicate for a 3.5 per cent loan of 52m. francs to the Franco-Ethiopian Djibouti–Addis Ababa Railway Company in 1910. The BIC, the CL, the SG, the CNEP, the BPPB, the CIC, the BUP, and the BFCI divided the guarantee equally among them. In 1913, the BIC also managed the French portion of a 5 per cent international Chinese loan—170m. francs out of a total of 574m. The share of the three largest deposit banks and of Paribas in the syndicate for the French issue were the highest at 16.5 per cent; the BIC had 8 per cent, the same as the BUP and the CIC; the BFCI and the CMF had 6 per cent each. The leading reseller to the public, the CL, placed from 20 per cent to 37 per cent of the issues on the Paris market.

6. Conclusion

The enquiry provides answers to the questions formulated at the outset and raises doubts about the importance of international networks and alliances in the framework of underwriting and issue syndicates on the Paris financial market for the period considered.

Private banks were clearly marginalized by joint-stock banks. The enquiry confirms impressions on that score. The amounts to be raised and the repeated nature of demands on the financial market went beyond the capacity of banking houses to respond. They ceased to be indispensable either as underwriters or as retailers. Their role in syndicates dwindled considerably from the mid-nineteenth century, so much so that consortia which included them were in a distinct minority.

Bénard & Jarislowsky, Bardac, Hoskier might be first to seize a business opportunity. They might lead syndicates, but only on condition of rallying powerful partners. Even then the examples are few. As members of syndicates, private bankers were anything but prominent. Of course, private bankers were part of the process of draining, mobilizing, and tranferring capital, but mainly in an indirect fashion. As directors of joint-stock banks, private bankers exerted considerable influence. The archetype of a species of collective *haute banque* was the BPPB, later the BUP. As associates of the large deposit banks, private banking houses often earned a place in syndicates by way of *rétrocessions* from managers. Otherwise they were dependent on the understanding and enlightened self-interest of members of syndicates.

The Rothschilds were in a different category. Using a combination of prestige, connections in government circles in various countries, and a large capital base, they held their own. But even they had to give way to the joint-stock banks in Russia. When that happened, they moved elsewhere. The Rothschild name could attract governments unwilling to use the services of joint-stock banks too clearly identified with a big European power. Nevertheless, Rothschild's defensive position in the face of the Paris joint-stock banks induced it to widen its syndicates to some of these banks and to provincial banks and private bankers like Hottinguer.

As for relations between joint-stock banks in syndicates, the enquiry permits several conclusions. Any assumption to the effect that the *banques d'affaires* were more likely to lead syndicates than deposit banks is belied by the number of times a bank like the CL was at the head of a group of underwriters. The BPPB was the only important *banque d'affaires* for over three decades until the creation of the BUP. Yet, although it succeeded in directing many consortia, it held no monopoly on the position of leader. Management of syndicates was the result of a subtle interplay of priority in initiating an operation, capacity to put up at times enormous amounts quickly, and credibility from the point of view of the potential issuer.

Collaboration tended to be between *banques d'affaires* and deposit banks. No syndicate was made up exclusively of one type or the other. It was sensible to associate banks whose asset was immediately available resources and others who could easily reach the buying public through their branches. However, banks of the same type did coexist in the same syndicates. Big institutions collaborated, thus reducing risk and fostering goodwill for future business. Permanent coalitions of banks contending to win contracts and systematically seeking to exclude rivals were more the exception than the rule. There were perceptible patterns of distribution of shares in underwriting syndicates. The identity of members and the percentages allotted often changed little in some syndicates, generally those in charge of repeated issues for the same borrower. In such cases, the lead bank had arrived at an equilibrium which it strove to maintain.

The enquiry is revealing of the enormous power wielded by the big joint-stock banks, whether *banques d'affaires* or deposit banks, on the Paris financial market. They were in every respect dominant, and more so than was suspected. Such a conclusion is reinforced by the examination of the general composition of syndicates formed in Paris. The CL and Paribas were ubiquitous and usually in commanding positions. It is unlikely CL files are weighted in favour of the CL since they do indicate the names of banks, other than the CL, which led syndicates. Besides, other sources were used to establish the data base. Participation in consortia and, more so, leadership of consortia were governed by tangible criteria in terms of achieving the desired results. Placing maximum quantities of securities at the highest possible price and in the shortest possible time required agents possessing means and credibility. Large banks benefited immensely from their natural advantage. The Paris financial market was governed by discernible hierarchical relations.

A surprising finding is the rarity of ties between Parisian and foreign banks in the process of putting in touch foreign borrowers and French lenders. Issuing international stock on the Paris market did not necessarily imply that foreign banks would be part of syndicates, although this was at times so. Most banks on the syndicates examined were Parisian. International alliances and networks were no doubt a reality but not one reflected in underwriting or, even less, in issue syndicates. A contingent of local banks was co-opted or forced its way into consortia for loans to their countries. Some German banks might occasionally be included in French syndicates to forestall competition in a contested area. Nevertheless, syndicates on the Paris market were generally French affairs.

Some operations were international, with issues taking place on several markets simultaneously. This did not occur at the behest of banks; it was due to international political considerations—for example, rivalry between European nations for the control of a debtor state–or the reluctance of foreign governments to be dependent on a single foreign market. Separate national syndicates then underwrote and resold their portion of securities on their national markets. The incentive to share with foreign banks the commissions generated by the lucrative business of guaranteeing and selling stock can only be that of lowering the level of risk. The abundance of capital on the Paris market and the readiness of investors to buy made operations relatively risk free. There was little need to share commissions with foreign banks; concessions to French competitors were enough. Paradoxical as it seems, business considerations may have been less operative than political motives in making banks work in tandem with foreign vis-à-vis. Markets and agents on these markets appear to have continued to function within a national framework and with a national outlook, at least in the formation of syndicates until 1914.

Notes

1. The Lysis–Testis controversy was widely publicized. A populist critique of high finance and banks can be found in *Les Documents politiques, diplomatiques et financiers* (Paris, 1920–5), and in Financial [Raoul Mennevée], *La Politique économique et financière de la haute banque française* (Paris, 1920). See also wartime publications of J. E. Favre for chauvinist diatribes directed at the 'plutocracy' and at managers of French banks born outside of France, especially in Central Europe.
2. Administration de l'Enregistrement, des Domaines et du Timbre, *Bulletin de statistique et de législation comparée* (Jan. 1892), 85; (Feb. 1893), 171; (1897), 298; (1900), 299; (1905), 241; (1906), 264.
3. Archives Historiques du Crédit Lyonnais, 158AH 1 and *Résumés* (unnumbered file).
4. Jean-Claude Allain, *Agadir 1911* (Paris, 1976); Marc Autheman, *La Banque Impériale Ottomane* (Paris, 1996); Henry Collas, *La Banque de Paris et des Pays-Bas et les émissions d'emprunts publics et privés* (Dijon, 1908); René Girault, *Emprunts russes et investissements français en Russie, 1887–1914* (Paris, 1973); Yasuo Gonjo, *Banque coloniale ou banque*

d'affaires. La Banque de l'Indochine sous la IIIe République (Paris, 1993); Maurice Lewandowski, 'Le Marché de Paris'. *Revue économique internationale*, 2/2 (May 1906), 223–54; Raymond Poidevin, *Les Relations économiques et financières entre la France et l'Allemagne de 1898 à 1914* (Paris, 1998; 1st pub. 1969); Samir Saul, *La France et l'Égypte de 1882 à 1914. Intérêts économiques et implications politiques* (Paris, 1997); Jacques Thobie, *Intérêts et impérialisme français dans l'Empire Ottoman (1895–1914)* (Paris, 1977).

5. *L'Économiste européen* (7 Aug. 1892), 170–1.
6. Saul, *La France*, 322, 397; AHCL 158AH 1.
7. Saul, *La France*, 43–50.
8. *L'Économiste européen* (31 Dec. 1893), 845–6.
9. AHCL, 158AH 1.
10. Poidevin, *Les Relations économiques*, 561, cites Erlanger in London and the Nationalbank für Deutschland, but refers to a 1908 5% loan.
11. Ibid.
12. *Le Rentier* (7 June 1903), 216.
13. Poidevin, *Les Relations économiques*, 561.
14. Saul, *La France*, 110–11.
15. Thobie, *Intérêts* 281.
16. Girault, *Emprunts russes*, 505–13.
17. Poidevin, *Les Relations économiques*, 491. The CMF was acquired by the Banque de l'Union Parisienne (BUP) in 1932.
18. AHCL, 158AH 1.
19. Thobie, *Intérêts*, 337; Autheman, *La Banque Impériale*, 130.
20. Thobie, *Intérêts*, and Autheman, *La Banque Impériale, passim.*
21. Girault, *Emprunts russes*, 301, 470–6.
22. Ibid. 165, 167.
23. Ibid. 182–4, 188, 195, 226–8.
24. *L'Économiste européen* (10 Sept. 1893), Supplement.
25. Ibid. (8 Dec. 1894), 723.
26. AHCL, 158AH 1; Poidevin, *Les Relations économiques*, 50; Girault, *Emprunts russes*, 73, 314–20.
27. AHCL, 158AH 1. The CL sold all of an additional 40m.-franc loan to this bank in 1903.
28. Ibid.
29. See next section.
30. *Le Rentier* (17 June 1900), 13652.
31. Ibid. (7 May 1902), 168.
32. Bonds for a further 292m. francs were also issued in London (146m.), New York (73m.), and Germany (73m.). See Toshio Suzuki, *Japanese Government Loan Issues on the London Capital Market, 1870–1913* (London, 1994), 123–5.
33. A similar amount was intended for the London market. Ibid. 136–9.
34. An additional 261m. francs were issued on the London market. Ibid. 142–3.
35. The German and British banks are not identified.
36. Ibid.
37. Ibid. The BUP was a *banque d'affaires* founded in 1904 to succeed the Banque Parisienne.
38. On Sautter's life, see *L'Économiste européen* (1 May 1892), 489.
39. AHCL, 158AH 1.
40. Ibid.; *L'Économiste européen* (16 June 1894), 755.

41. AHCL, 158AH 1.
42. Ibid.; Éric Bussière, *Paribas, l'Europe et le monde, 1872–1992* (Antwerp, 1992), 79–81.
43. Poidevin, *Les Relations économiques*, 70, 330.
44. *Le Rentier* (17 May 1899), 13161.
45. See Léon Barety, *L'Évolution des banques locales en France et en Allemagne* (Paris, 1908), 124–5, 127–8, 130–1.
46. AHCL, 158AH 1.
47. In 1908, Barings also underwrote 33% of the 32m. franc City of Moscow 5% loan, exactly the same percentage as the CL, the manager of the issue. Ibid.
48. Ibid.; Girault, *Emprunts russes*, 439–43, 445.
49. AHCL, 158AH 1.
50. The new banks were associated respectively with the SM, the BFCI, the CMF, and the SG. Girault, *Emprunts russes*, 510.
51. AHCL, 158AH 1.
52. *L'Économiste européen* (23 Oct. 1892), 521.
53. Ibid. (11 May 1895), 592–3.
54. More needs to be known about SG relations with Austria-Hungary.
55. In the 1870s, the CL was unwilling to confront the Rothschilds in the Habsburg Empire. Jean Bouvier, *Les Rothschild* (Brussels, 1983; 1st pub. 1967), 265.
56. Bernard Michel, *Banques & banquiers en Autriche au début du XXe siècle* (Paris, 1976), 247.
57. AHCL, 158AH 1. The information in this paragraph and the next two is based on this source.
58. Michel, *Banques*, 253.
59. The General Bank of Hungarian Credit, the Hungarian Commercial Bank of Pest, the First National Credit Union of Pest, and the Banking & Commercial Company of Pest.
60. AHCL, 158AH 1.
61. S. Saul, 'Conjoncture, adaptation et croissance: le Crédit Foncier Franco-Canadien (1880–1979)', *Histoire, économie et société* (Paris), 5/2 (1986), 297–328 (Part I); 5/3 (1986), 427–71 (Part 2).
62. AHCL, 158AH 1.
63. *L'Économiste européen* (8 Dec. 1894), 723.
64. Ibid. (23 Mar. 1895), 369.
65. Ibid. (15 Febr. 1896), 205.
66. Poidevin, *Les Relations économiques*, 74.
67. *Le Rentier* (17 Apr. 1905), 139; (7 Nov. 1907), 436–7; AHCL, 158AH 1. The 1907 loan was for 47m. francs. In 1913, the French portion of the loan was worth 63m. francs; another part, set at 126m. francs, went to the British, Dutch, German, and US markets.
68. *Le Rentier* (7 Dec. 1910), 552.
69. AHCL, 158AH 1.
70. Bussière, *Paribas*, 55.
71. Lewandowski, 'Le Marché de Paris', 238. Ninety-three per cent of the National Bank's capital was in the hands of French investors. Poidevin, *Les Relations économiques*, 716.
72. *Le Rentier* (27 July 1908), 290.
73. AHCL, 158AH 1.
74. *Ibid.*; Poidevin, *Les Relations économiques*, 559.
75. Established in 1905 by the BUP. *Le Rentier* (27 May 1905), 200.
76. AHCL, 158AH 1.

77. Collas, *La Banque de Paris*, 173–4.
78. *Le Rentier* (17 Apr. 1899), 13108; (17 Mar. 1902), 91–2; (7 Dec. 1903), 435.
79. More below.
80. AHCL, 158AH 1; Allain, *Agadir*, 61–5.
81. *Le Rentier* (17 Nov. 1906), 451.
82. AHCL, 158AH 1.
83. The SG's woes in 1905 induced it to accept the assistance of the BPPB in the increase of its capital as well as Paribas directors on its board. See *Le Rentier* (17 Nov. 1905), 426.
84. A substitute for Barings.
85. Saul, *La France*, 315–30, 334–46, 362, 397–407, 464.
86. *Le Rentier* (27 Feb. 1908), 72; Barety, *L'Évolution*, 122–4.
87. Saul, *La France*, 92–3, 105–6.
88. Ibid.; 'La Banque d'État du Maroc et la monnaie sous le Protectorat', *La France et l'Outre-Mer. Un siècle de relations monétaires et financières* (Paris, 1998), 389–427.
89. AHCL, 158AH 1.
90. Thobie, *Intérêts*, 197; *L'Économiste européen* (23 Mar. 1895), 368–9.
91. Autheman, *La Banque Impériale*, 183; *Le Rentier* (7 June 1901), 211.
92. For the BPPB, its 'Table', the BIP, Barings, Cassel, the Banca Commerciale Italiana, the Banque Espagnole de Crédit, the Banque d'Outre-Mer, Bénard & Jarislowsky, etc.; for the SG, its directors, the Société Française de Banque et de Dépôts, Propper, Sauerbach, Périer, Kirschheim, Neymarck, etc. Thobie, *Intérêts*, 233–4.
93. AHCL, 158AH 1.
94. Ibid.; Autheman, *La Banque Impériale*, 163; *Le Rentier* (17 June 1905), 231.
95. Thobie, *Intérêts*, 261; AHCL, 158AH 1.
96. Thobie, *Intérêts*, 264–5, 273–5; Autheman, *La Banque Impériale*, 209; AHCL, 158AH 1.
97. Stockbrokers sold the balance. The IOB local partners were Bardacs and its affiliate, the Société Financière d'Orient. Thobie, *Intérêts*, 337–8.
98. Thobie, *Intérêts*, 294–8; Autheman, *La Banque Impériale*, 228–9; AHCL, 158AH 1.
99. *L'Économiste européen* (18 June 1893), 800.
100. AHCL, 158AH 1; *Le Rentier* (17 Feb. 1903), 64. The Banque Impériale Royale Privilégiée des Pays Autrichiens, another name for the Länderbank, was created in 1880 by Eugène Bontoux's Union Générale.
101. *Le Rentier* (7 Feb. 1907), 56.
102. AHCL, 158AH 1.
103. Poidevin, *Les Relations économiques*, 55–7.
104. *Le Rentier* (17 Sept. 1902), 339–40; (17 Apr. 1907), 155.
105. Collas, *La Banque de Paris*, 155; Poidevin, *Les Relations économiques*, 311, 575; AHCL, 158AH 1; *Le Rentier* (17 May 1905), 188.
106. AHCL, 158AH 1.
107. *Le Rentier* (7 Nov. 1899), 13350.
108. AHCL, 158AH 1.

PART III

From Global Reach to Regional Withdrawal, 1914–1958

8

Established Connections and New Opportunities. London as an International Financial Centre, 1914–1958

PHILIP L. COTTRELL

Standing at the heart of the financial district, the City's War Memorial honours those who died in the Great War. It has come, as elsewhere within the United Kingdom, to commemorate also those who fell in the Second World War and subsequent campaigns. Over the First World War City offices were emptied of young men, and in the Second World War substantial areas within the 'Square Mile' were destroyed by air raids.[1] The two World Wars' grievous, diverse impacts cannot ever be underestimated, and, understandably, they have become many historians' temporal divides. The arising periodization has also been fruitfully applied for understanding London's further development as an international financial centre.[2] However, this perspective clouds an equally important disjunction in the history of the City, and in the world economy that it served, caused by the 'Great Depression'. It was particularly marked by the profundity of the 1931 liquidity crisis. Consequently, while the World Wars' impacts will be fully acknowledged, the following review pivots about the major chronological divide of the 1931 crisis. London's international role was substantially diminished by, first, the immediate shock of that crisis and, then, the world economy's collapse as states' economic policies turned inward. Emphasis upon national self-sufficiency was maintained — and at heightened levels — by the demands of the Second World War and of the subsequent, decade-long period of recovery and reconstruction. A more liberal, internationalist approach was only gradually readopted from the late 1950s, leading to the inception of an entirely new chapter in London's history as a premier global centre.

Section 1 of the ensuing discussion comprises a consideration of the First World War's effects. It reviews opportunities for much greater dealings in foreign exchange, and the 'bill on London's' rapid revival. It also considers the 'echo effects' of the crisis of summer 1914, the authorities' attempts to improve upon City mechanisms, competition and collaboration with New York, and the clearers' turn to overseas banking. The war not only resulted in sterling becoming a floating currency but also caused regulation of the London capital market, which is analysed in section 2. The discussion in section 3 focuses upon how the 1931 liquidity crisis severely affected the City through leading houses' substantial commitments to Central and Eastern Europe. Consequently, it considers the outcomes of the Austrian and German banking crises, and of sterling's own grave problems from mid-July 1931. Section 4 reviews in outline the City's 'long winter' caused by, first, the world economy's prostrate state and, then, the Second World War. In section 5 the discussion pays attention to the recovery of the City's international role over the 1950s and the beginnings of an entirely new foundation for its global importance with the emergence of the Euromarkets. Some reflections upon the City's experience during the first half of the twentieth century are offered in section 6.

1. The Impact of the First World War

The 1920s were characterized by, ultimately, inadequate attempts to re-establish the liberal world economy shattered by the outbreak of the First World War.[3] Rebuilding international finance came to be a very conscious act in which the Bank of England and City merchant banks took leading roles. Their efforts were galvanized by Montagu Norman, after those of Europe's political masters had dismally and cynically failed during 1919. Although central-bank cooperation proved to be a limited force from 1928, and of no avail during the 1931 crisis, over the mid-1920s the considerable efforts involved appeared successful. First, the spectre of hyperinflation was banished and, then, the Entente's currencies were stabilized. Indeed, during the mid-1920s it appeared that the clock could be put back to allow international finance to flourish in its pre-1914 manner and, with it, the City of London. Consequently, continuity was briefly attained between the pre-1914 world and that of the mid-1920s, maintaining the positive momentum of credit and capital within the global economy — at least, for a time.[4]

The immediate post-war years also offered new opportunities, as in foreign exchange dealing, while witnessing a rapid resurgence of the City financing international trade. Nonetheless, there were official, ill-fated initiatives to improve upon its workings. These were undertaken to give a national trade policy, conceived during the desperate depths of war, the support required to counter Germany in a continuing economic confrontation. However, the challenge came from the United States and New York, a consequence of the First World War, arising from the sudden transformation of America's position in world trade and finance. It is this that makes the years 1914 to 1918 a major turning point in world economic history.

The derangement of Europe's foreign exchanges significantly widened opportunities in currency dealing. Within the City, Japhets, Samuel Montagu & Co., and Seligmans were established specialists, and capitalized upon their accumulated expertise. However, by the mid-1920s the market leader was Kleinworts, assisted by the not always audible telephone to ensure the speediest of communications, necessitated by the business's character. The telephone was particularly important for maintaining contact with Goldman Sachs, Kleinworts' New York associates. Kleinworts not only acted as arbitrageurs but also became major operators on the burgeoning forward market — on joint account with Goldman Sachs and also with houses in Amsterdam, Berlin, Budapest, and Paris. Schröders reacted similarly, opening a Foreign Exchange Department in February 1920, an initiative that proved its worth until the restoration of monetary stability.[5] Although Kleinworts developed a very important niche as foreign exchange operators, generally, the merchant banks failed to become dominant principals. As in other areas, the major clearing banks — the newly coalesced 'Big Five' — with their very substantial resources were the main players.[6]

Despite exchange instability, the post-war restocking boom brought about a revival in international acceptances. During 1919–20, foreign-drawn bills stood at £350m., equivalent, nominally, to pre-war levels. However, marked inflation was a complication, another the world economy's increased volatility. Those economies spared the perils of accelerating inflation experienced from mid-1920 the costs of a deep and sharp slump. This inevitably caused a decline in London's international acceptances, down as low as £175–200m. in 1922. The business of the City's leading acceptor — Kleinworts — could only follow this pattern.[7] However, Anglo-German houses — particularly Japhets, Kleinworts, and Schroders — through their historic ties benefited from German undertakings' insistent demand for sterling-denominated credits, indicated by a willingness to pay significant premiums.

After rapidly resolving outstanding debts, Schroders' facilities to German clients reached £5.4m. in 1924. This business was also the mainstay of Kleinworts' acceptances, its German Department's commissions totalling £0.16m. in 1925. The almost insatiable demand from German banks and firms compensated for the decline in the City's American credits. However, post-war German acceptances were no close substitute. Before 1924 they involved considerable uncertainties, but all were granted in sterling and most comprised reimbursement credits, with borrowers specifically shouldering the exchange risk.[8] Kleinworts' partners only declined to grant further credits during autumn 1923 — at the height of the German hyperinflation. Established links played a considerable role in this resurgence but it had a new basis, constituted by the mark's collapse and the void caused by the authorities' closure of Austrian and German banks' London offices in 1914. Summer 1914's financial crisis had diverse echo effects within the City during the early 1920s and, consequently, both its causes and its immediate resolution need to be appreciated to comprehend some post-war developments.

The diplomatic crisis that proved to be the prologue to the First World War led to Deutsche Bank's London agency encountering severe difficulties from 27 July 1914.[9] All City acceptors shared this experience and, consequently, their managements refused new business. Increasing exchange problems, then European governments declaring financial moratoria, aggravated the dire situation through making acceptors liable for their bills. Any failure to meet them would, equally, seriously affect their ultimate holders: London bill brokers, discount houses, and British domestic banks. The Bank of England provided liquidity but demand's extent led to qualitative controls, then an 1847-style Treasury Letter, and, on 2 August, a royal proclamation postponing payment on bills accepted before 4 August.[10] The crisis also provoked the formation of the Accepting Houses Committee. Temporary relief was replaced by the authorities' further responses. On 12 August, the Chancellor announced that the Bank, backed by a government guarantee, would discount all pre-moratorium bills without recourse against holders. This enabled acceptors to postpone payment, but at the cost of 2 per cent over Bank rate. The precise 'period of grace', finally determined on 5 September 1914, was for the hostilities plus a year of peace.

With Britain's declaration of war, the authorities closed the agencies and branches of Austrian and German banks to new business. Their staff could only liquidate debts to nationals of either Entente or neutral countries. In January 1916, the Treasury required the liquidation of their affairs, which consequently came within the jurisdiction of the Controller, appointed under the Trading with the Enemy Act, 1916.[11] From 1921 Deutsche Bank found a substitute for the credits provided by its pre-war London agency in the development of a particularly close connection with Schroders, which also undertook comparable business with both Disconto-Gesellschaft and Dresdner Bank. However, xenophobia persisted even within the cosmopolitan City. Consequently, specifically recruited German-speaking Swiss staff, comprising a sixth of its employees in 1924, handled Schroders' German business.[12] There was also anti-German feeling at the Stock Exchange, even in the early 1930s, when readmittance of traders of German birth was considered case by case, rather than re-election 'en bloc'.[13]

'Germanophobia' within British business had long roots.[14] Nonetheless, the authorities' actions in 1914 against the banks of the Central Powers were not that far removed from applying administrative procedures. Indeed, government remained reluctant to wage economic warfare until 1916, when it was given expression in finance by the Faringdon Committee. This expert group explored deficiencies in the financial system, revealed by comparison with the facilities of the German Kreditbanken—a supposedly unfavourable contrast increasingly highlighted during pre-war years.[15] In many respects, committee members had reached their conclusions before they took a restricted range of evidence that largely supported their particular views. They recommended a new institution to finance trade. Despite the City's lukewarm reception and government increasingly distancing itself from the project, British Trade Corporation was established in spring 1917. Conceived amidst the pressures of war by a myopic group, it proved to be a disaster. Not to compete with City institutions, British Trade Corporation unsuccessfully attempted to give British traders support in markets apparently opened up by the Central Powers' collapse and post-war turmoil within Russia. By the mid-1920s, it was a minor acceptor. From 1926, when reconstituted as Anglo-International Bank, it became a holding for other comparable initiatives that had proved equally fruitless.[16]

Given City hostility to British Trade Corporation, somewhat surprisingly Montagu Norman used from May 1920 the opportunity provided by the 1914 moratorium debts of Anglo-Österreichische Bank's London branch to 're-Anglicize' this Viennese 'great' bank. The conception and unfolding of his initiative may have been due to other impinging developments. The French authorities had embarked from spring 1919 upon a scheme to make Österreichische Länderbank a Gallic institution, which also required settlement of its London 1914 debts. Second, there was Norman's commitment from spring 1921 to Austrian monetary reconstruction. The 'Anglicization' scheme was not realized until March 1922 at the height of Austrian hyperinflation. Furthermore, Norman's expectations for Anglo-Austrian were not fulfilled and, from 1925, its assets were liquidated. Its rump was merged with British Trade Corporation to establish Anglo-International Bank, a frail institution that had a lingering business life until 1944.[17]

Norman's concerns with financing Central and Eastern Europe had some wider impact within the City. For instance, they influenced Satzger, manager of Kleinworts' German Department, who was responsible for this acceptor's involvement in establishing in 1922 Kux, Bloch & Co., a Viennese bank and commission house. It proved successful, unlike Kleinworts' investment in Ceská eskomptní banka a úverní ústav, made in September 1923.[18] Other City initiatives for developing central European business had a longer lineage. British Overseas Bank's origins lay in pre-1914 discussions between Glyn, Mills and Union Bank of Scotland. The venture was further encouraged by the Faringdon Report's somewhat biased views, leading to the bank's establishment in 1919. Initially, it principally operated within the Baltic republics and Poland but, in 1924, it absorbed London & Liverpool Bank of Commerce with a substantial Iberian acceptance business. The consequent realignment of its affairs went along with a rearrangement of ownership, Union Bank and William Deacons becoming principal shareholders together with Prudential Assurance. The bank had an apparently unchequered business life until 1937, when the effects of the 1931 crisis finally brought it down.[19]

It proved almost impossible during the early 1920s to transplant British corporate banking within Europe to benefit the City and British overseas trade. Indeed, the situation after the Armistice proved ironic. On the one hand, various, ultimately unsuccessful, initiatives for further developing a British financial presence in Europe unfolded. On the other, German banks and firms, feared during the war, became increasingly reliant upon City resources. As opposed to a confrontation with Germany, the City's post-war challenge emanated from New York. The dynamic rise of American finance was a product of how the First World War was resourced by the Entente, together with the organizational and structural changes facilitated by the Federal Reserve Act, 1913, the Clayton Antitrust Act, 1916, the Webb-Pomerene Act, 1918, and the Edge Act of 1919.[20]

American bankers were in two minds over how to employ their growing ascendancy, especially vis-à-vis the City of London. Some, like Morgans, were western poles of long-established transatlantic partnerships, and benefited from the shift of power brought about by the Entente's increasing dependency upon the United States for war finance and, then, post-war reconstruction. Its New York partners sought to maintain their established cooperation with European banking associates over the 1920s, although appreciating that they now had the upper hand. While time and resources were on their side, Morgans were nevertheless prepared to challenge immediately the City's sway over China and Latin America through developing both Asia Banking Corporation and Bank of Central & South America. Others, such as Vanderlip at National City Bank, conceived an entirely different strategy — outright competition with London. To this end, National City established International Corporation in 1915 (with Morgan involvement), and trained managers for overseas branches. In 1916, National City acquired International Banking Corporation and made loans to Russia, which Morgans continued to acknowledge to be a client of British finance. National City's entry into Tsarist lending went with establishing Russian branches to join those in Denmark, Italy, Spain, and Switzerland. A network in Argentina, Brazil, and Chile balanced that in the 'Old World'. At the close of 1916, National City had twenty-six overseas branches and sub-branches. Within two further years, International Banking Corp. possessed an Asian complex while National City, in its own right, had forty-five foreign branches.[21]

The American challenge further developed following the Edge Act. Two acceptance banks were quickly established — American & Foreign Banking Corporation and Mercantile Bank of Americas — both linked to the developing 'Morgan group'. American & Foreign opened thirteen Latin American branches during 1920.[22] The promotion of 'Edge Corporations' continued with Paul Warburg's International Acceptance Bank. It was conceived within the strategy largely pursued by Morgans — of modulated cooperation with European finance — as opposed to competition. When International Acceptance opened in April 1921, it was backed in London by National Provincial and Union Bank of London, and Rothschilds.[23]

By the close of 1920 there were 181 overseas American bank branches, of which 81 were linked directly, or indirectly via International Banking Corp., to National City, while 88 were within the 'Morgan group'.[24] This was to prove to be a post-war high point. With the sharp, deep depression that began in mid-1920, $4bn. was locked up in frozen credits, which quickly rebounded upon the newly developed overseas branch systems. During 1921 National City closed five offices and at the end of 1922 its overseas network comprised seventy-two branches. Its reaction chimed with a shift in the general stance of American bankers, whose interest in the ideas and principles of the 'Edge system' waned over 1921. Consequently, their withdrawal continued, particularly on the part of Morgans, which in 1924 sold Asia Banking Corp. to International Banking Corp. and, in 1925, Bank of Central & South America to Royal Bank of Canada.[25]

The post-war American 'invasion' of the City's global realm achieved some permanent results within central and Latin America, and in the emerging Pacific regional economy. These gains would become clearer with the passage of time, forming a foundation for the 'Western hemisphere's' transformation into a dollar area. More immediately, retreat during the early 1920s resulted in a renewed emphasis upon transatlantic cooperation in providing credits and in foreign exchange dealing. For example, from 1924 Kleinworts and Goldman Sachs supplied facilities to Central Europe on joint account. However, from 1928, the lead increasingly came from New York, despite Kleinworts' historic ties, particularly with Germany.[26] More closely integrated were the Morgan transatlantic interlocking partnerships — Morgan Grenfell in London and Morgan Harjes in Paris. Continuity went hand in hand with change, arising from the increasing pull of the New York market after 1918. Directors of Lloyds sat on the board of Park Union Foreign Banking Corporation, formed by National Park Bank of New York and Union Bank of Canada.[27] Schröders went further by establishing J. Henry Schröder Banking Corporation on Wall Street, a strategic move that was to give the London acceptor further, crucial vitality over the twentieth century.[28]

Historians are frequently concerned with illuminating the origins of secular developments but this can often distort understandings and perspectives. The rise of New York-based overseas corporate banking from 1916 was an important new direction that was to foreshadow major changes in international finance. However, it did not immediately replace British overseas banking. Indeed, the number of British overseas branches continued to increase, reaching more than 2,000 by 1928, while the collective assets of British overseas banks doubled between 1913 and 1928. Yet, sustained physical and financial growth was not accompanied by an effective use of resources as, generally, profitability fell from 1918, the most notable exception being 'Eastern Exchange banking'.[29] The decline in returns can be attributed to internal factors, including the poorer quality of human capital employed.[30] Equally important was an almost total change in the operating environment. Following the early 1920s' deep slump, world commerce failed to display its nineteenth-century dynamism, particularly with regard to primary products. This especially affected British overseas banks since they were primarily located in 'New World' temperate lands. Falling or stagnant primary prices, coupled with world trade increasingly comprising the exchange of manufacturers between industrial economies, undercut many British overseas banks' basic rationale.

The world economy's course was far from clear after 1918. Indeed, there were misleading signals, as with the continuing rise of primary product prices for eighteen months, while many considered the early 1920s' deep slump a temporary derangement attributable to the war. These false signs and appraisals were the context for a major organizational change in the City's structure previously based upon functional specialization — the entry of some major clearers into overseas banking. It had a pre-war foundation in the clearers' development of foreign exchange operations together with initiatives for establishing a European presence.

Holden, Midland's chairman, in 1909 developed a plan to acquire a Russian bank. Following Lloyds' acquisition in 1911 of Armstrong & Co. of Le Havre and Paris (reconstituted as Lloyds Bank (France)), and Westminster establishing a French subsidiary in 1913, Midland opened in Petrograd in February 1917. However, this dramatic experience convinced Holden, and his successors, that the best course for Midland's international business was to conduct it through continuing correspondent relationships with foreign banks. These were centralized in 1918 in a specifically formed Midland overseas branch, located in the City.[31] During the 1920s Midland's strategy for international banking was profitable but, nonetheless, proved to be the exception amongst the major clearers.

Barclays and Lloyds became much further engaged in overseas branch banking, not only within Europe but also around the globe.[32] These developments were in part encouraged by the pre-war policies of the German Kreditbanken, with the supposed wider benefits subsequently emphasized in the Faringdon Report. The opportunity for combining home and foreign branch banking was given by the low stock exchange prices pertaining for some British overseas banks from the closing years of the war.[33] Lloyds management took the lead by acquiring London & River Plate Bank in 1918, a takeover possibly welcomed by its board due to declining profitability and the wartime encroachment of American banks upon their business area. The same factors led to London & Brazilian merging with London & River Plate in 1923 to form Bank of London & South America (BoLSA), in which Lloyds had a 57 per cent stake.[34] This major investment accompanied Lloyds continuing to acquire minor, but 'strategic', interests in overseas banks. The policy, initiated in 1906, involved post-war investments in eight institutions, both British overseas concerns and foreign banks. However, some were relinquished during the 1920s, as with Australian Bank of Commerce (acquired in 1910 and augmented in 1925), and P & O Banking Corporation (first taken up in 1920).[35] It has subsequently been acknowledged that Lloyds' post-war Latin American initiative lacked rationale. Its parallel involvement in Indian banking has a more definite explanation. Lloyds' acquisition of Cox & Kings, army agents, was a rescue, undertaken at the Bank of England's behest. Although Lloyds relinquished the two Egyptian branches so acquired in 1926, the Indian and Burmese network was developed and expanded.[36]

The roots of Barclays' creation of Barclays (Dominion, Colonial & Overseas) in 1925 can be traced back to the Faringdon Report and the official, although informal, barriers from summer 1918 to further major domestic bank mergers. Barclays' trenchant chairman, F. C. Goodenough, had a comparable outlook to Lord Faringdon over increasing international economic rivalry and sought to ensure Britain's position by establishing a 'British Empire Bank'. This was given a vehicle through Barclays acquiring an interest in Colonial Bank in April 1918. The platform became wider when Anglo-Egyptian Bank contacted Barclays during 1920, leading to the clearer taking a 90 per cent interest. The project's scope was fully filled out after the increasingly ailing National Bank of South Africa also approached Barclays in 1922. Colonial was transformed into Barclays (DCO), into which Anglo-Egyptian and National Bank were subsumed.[37] The other major investment of this type was National Provincial's full acquisition of Grindlay & Co. in 1924. Like Cox's, Grindlays were army agents but its management had widened its business from 1918 through developing commercial banking in India.[38]

The various, and varying, commitments of Barclays, Lloyds, and National Provincial to overseas banking primarily had the effect of sustaining British global financial presence.[39] However, their support was not appreciated within sections of the City, where from 1923 there was significant opposition to the clearers' further involvement. The cudgels were taken up by Montagu Norman and, when he could not obtain government support for his objections, he turned in 1925 to discriminating against the acceptances of overseas banks linked to the clearers.[40] Fears of the contagion that such investments might generate were given some substance in 1929, when Banca Italo-Britannica's difficulties became known. Lloyds, National Provincial, and the Westminster were significant shareholders and eventually lost possibly as much as £5.4m. due to this particular ill-starred overseas venture.[41]

The establishment of significant equity links between the clearers and some British overseas banks generally had no major effect upon the City's market for international acceptances. Nonetheless, over the first half of the 1920s the clearers on the basis of their domestic structures became major competitors of the traditional acceptance houses. In 1924 Midland's acceptances totalled £40m., and those of all the 'Big Five' £105.3m.,[42] by when they had collectively over half the market.[43]

2. Formal and informal regulation of the capital market

Foreign issues were controlled from 24 December 1914 both to marshal exchange resources and facilitate war financing through domestic long-term borrowing. As war pressures increased, the regulations were developed. Decontrol took place in stages, with the Capital Issues Committee from March 1919 allowed to favour long-term overseas borrowing that would promote British exports, particularly if an application came from within the Empire. As Atkin has demonstrated, the authorities' main concern was not so much the exchanges (with sterling floating), as ensuring that the market would absorb both new and funding issues made on behalf of the British government.[44]

Despite the withdrawal in November 1919 of regulations under the Defence of the Realm Act (in part due to City pressure), foreign borrowing continued to be restricted by the Bank of England. Its regulation had no legal basis, the Bank solely fulfilling this role on behalf of the state through the standing in the City that it had attained during the decade immediately before the war. The 'Old Lady's' control was undertaken through moral suasion, its effectiveness aided by Norman's growing personal ascendancy. Regular meetings with the issuing houses had commenced just prior to the outbreak of war. They resumed after the Armistice and, although primarily concerned with issues of more than £1m., nearly every projected foreign flotation came to be discussed with the Governor. Norman thereby gained an almost complete view of market activity, could express his views, and could influence the timing of issues that he approved.[45] The Bank's prime interest arose from funding the state's vastly expanded floating debt in order to control liquidity. Its control was a factor that allowed both £609m. of the floating debt to be funded and £1,122m. of conversion issues to be made between 1920 and 1924.[46]

Although the resolution of war finance's immediate problems was the prime reason for continued control, regulation also arose because of other difficulties. These were posed during 1920 by the market's congested state that might have constrained the access of local authorities, which, under reconstruction legislation, needed to borrow, in particular for housebuilding. In these circumstances, the Bank established a queuing procedure, with priority for domestic borrowers.

As Table 8.1 shows,[47] new issues declined from 1921 with the onset of a deep slump. In markedly changed conditions, it would appear that all informal restrictions on imperial borrowing were lifted. However, the Bank continued to oppose foreign fixed-interest securities directly competitive with funding and conversion issues. Changes in the Bank's discrimination also included from 1 February 1922 sanctioning loans with maturities of less than twenty years. This was forced by particular issuing houses prepared, despite Norman's opposition, to make ten-year foreign loans. The modified embargo was maintained until 14 January 1924, when foreign issues no longer constituted a significant threat to funding.[48] Nonetheless, Norman maintained his conversations with issuing houses and merchant banks.[49]

Table 8.1 portrays the effects of Norman's control. Between 1920 and 1924, overseas issues amounted to *c.* £581m., of which imperial borrowing, at £368m., accounted for nearly two-thirds. Regulating empire issues caused Norman difficulties. At the close of 1921, he maintained that imperial borrowing was in 'a muddled state', requiring 'unbiased advice from an international standpoint'.[50] Australia was the prime imperial borrower,[51] and its immediate post-war conduct has been characterized as an 'apparently chaotic scramble', confirming Norman's diagnosis. This was the product of conflict between the initiatives of seven state governments and numerous public bodies, pointed up by the smoothness of wartime arrangements when the Commonwealth of Australia had acted as a central, fund-raising body. Subsequent bitter experiences led to the establishment of a Loan Council in 1923/4, which produced some coordination over coupon rates and the timing of Australian state issues. Agreement went so far in July 1924 that further overseas borrowing — primarily on the London market — was limited to £28m. during 1924/5.[52]

Other problems were caused by the Governor's commitment from spring 1921 to bring about European monetary stabilization, which led to a series of related long-term loans from 1922. Norman played little role in the first — for Czechoslovakia, undertaken by Barings at the prompting of the Foreign Office.[53] It was issued by a syndicate, involving Hopes in Amsterdam, Barings' long-standing partners, but also Rothschilds and Schroders, a new City development. This post-war 'trinity' of London merchant banks was to make sixteen issues, their alliance instigated by Schroders as a defensive reaction to New York's increasing power.[54] A further

Table 8.1. *Overseas capital issues made on the UK capital market, 1920–1936* (£m.)

	1920	1921	1922	1923	1924	1925	1926	1927	1928	1929	1930	1931	1932	1933	1934	1935	1936
Grand total for *all* capital issues	384.2	215.8	203.8	223.5	219.9	253.3	314.7	362.5	253.7	236.2	236.2	88.7	113.0	132.9	150.2	182.8	217.2
Of which:																	
Imperial/Commonwealth																	
Public bodies	12.0	78.7	65.8	67.5	57.2	31.5	33.6	56.9	52.1	30.6	56.0	30.6	25.7	25.0	11.0	2.9	0.9
Companies	28.6	12.1	9.7	20.1	16.3	25.9	18.4	30.8	34.0	23.8	14.0	6.2	3.2	4.8	29.4	15.1	22.5
Subtotal	40.6	90.8	75.5	87.6	73.5	57.4	52.0	87.7	86.1	54.4	70.0	36.8	28.9	29.8	40.4	18.0	23.4
% of total	10.5	42.1	32.1	43.0	32.9	26.1	20.5	27.9	23.7	21.5	29.7	41.6	25.6	22.5	26.9	9.8	10.8
Foreign																	
Public bodies	—	5.9	21.3	26.9	43.0	2.3	22.4	19.9	19.8	4.1	12.6	0.2	—	5.3	—	0.5	—
Companies	19.1	19.0	38.4	21.7	7.7	28.1	38.0	31.0	37.5	35.8	26.2	9.0	0.3	2.7	3.1	2.3	3.1
Sub-total	19.1	24.9	59.7	48.6	60.7	30.4	60.4	50.9	57.3	39.9	38.8	9.2	0.3	8.0	3.1	2.9	3.1
% of total	5.0	11.5	25.3	23.8	27.2	13.8	23.9	16.2	15.8	15.7	16.4	10.4	0.3	6.0	2.0	1.6	1.4
Overseas																	
Subtotal	59.7	115.7	135.2	136.2	134.2	87.8	112.4	138.6	143.4	94.3	108.8	46.0	29.2	37.8	43.5	20.9	26.5
% of grand total	15.5	53.6	57.4	66.8	60.1	39.9	44.4	44.1	39.5	37.2	46.1	52.0	25.9	28.5	28.9	11.4	12.2

Source: A. T. K. Grant, *A Study of the Capital Market in Britain from 1919–1936* (London, 1937; 2nd edn. 1967), 134 (drawn from Midland Bank data).

marker of change was Kidder Peabody's sizeable role in the Czech loan, although Barings had been looking to involve transatlantic partners in Russian issues from the 1890s.[55]

Norman had far greater informal control over so-called League loans — issued to support the stabilization plans of the Financial Committee of the League of Nations. He acted in conjunction with this international organ and, through his connections with Benjamin Strong of the Federal Reserve Bank of New York, 'Jack' Morgan, and City merchant banks, attempted to ensure the loans' success.[56] League loans, eleven in all, together with the 1924 Dawes loan, were not subject to the Bank's regulation. Like the Czech 1922 loan, they were made across a number of financial centres, which restricted their impact upon the City. However, Norman's aim of involving the widest range of financial centres primarily arose from ensuring their 'apolitical' character — hence his particular encouragement of participations from the 'neutral' Dutch and Scandinavian markets. The Governor also realized that their achievement required the involvement of American finance, for which he capitalized upon his relationships with Strong and 'Jack' Morgan — as for the 1923 Austrian Stabilization loan and the Dawes loan. So much so, that their particular successes constituted a factor in the subsequent significant involvement of New York houses of varying standings in the finances of Central and Eastern Europe.[57]

In preparing for sterling's return to its pre-war parity, the Bank of England increasingly opposed from mid-1924 foreign lending, other than stabilization and reparations issues, to the extent of effectively shutting the London market from November 1924.[58] To ensure the success of $4.86, this embargo embraced imperial issues from mid-1925, primarily to affect Australian borrowing. Control to support sterling was lifted on 3 November 1925,[59] the only continuing impediment being the 2 per cent Stamp Duty on bearer bonds normally used for sovereign lending. This tax proved an irritant, increasing London issuing costs relative to other centres. However, the resumption of the market's full freedom was not complete. The post-November 1919 informal embargo had given the Bank a further monetary weapon, and it became appreciated during 1925 that its employment was a useful alternative to raising Bank rate. When sterling came under pressure in summer 1929, the Bank reimposed its ban on foreign sovereign loans, maintained until April 1930. Sterling's continuing problems at $4.86 at the close of 1930 led to the Bank intervening again, and Norman extended the embargo's scope as summer 1931's liquidity crisis gathered apace.[60]

3. The 1931 Crisis

During the late 1920s, it appeared that the clock had been turned back, with London's international acceptances standing at £415m. in 1926.[61] Kleinworts remained the leading private acceptor.[62] Both Kleinworts and Schroders continued to benefit from their long-standing ties with Central Europe, although personal sentiment may have unduly affected the directions in which their respective acceptances developed. The further growth in Schroders' German business in 1928 partly filled the 'hole' caused by the withdrawal of American short-term capital. By 1929–30, its German acceptances and related banking business totalled £6.2.m., with a significant amount for industrial companies. German commitments comprised nearly half of the house's activity in this business area. Any arising concerns were calmed by the apparent reassurance that the Young Plan would finally resolve the economic and political tangle of the reparation issue.[63] Although Kleinworts' German acceptances in 1931 at £5.8m. only comprised a third of its credits, it had further German commitments. Like others, it borrowed short term in Paris at 2 per cent and lent these 'cheap' funds at 8 per cent on the long term to German municipalities and commercial firms. By 1931, its municipal loans amounted to £2.7m., while its other German commitments totalled £3.5m.[64]

The continued expansion of merchant bank acceptances during the latter 1920s failed to produce commensurate profits. Significant competition with the clearers became more acute from 1926 with a commission-cutting war, initiated by Midland.[65] Ultimately, the clearers' competitive edge resulted in Kleinworts and Schroders taking on riskier paper — acceptances for industrial firms.[66] Indeed, although bills on the discount market increased markedly in volume at the close of the 1920s, the clearers' greatly enlarged acceptances had caused a marked decline in the availability of 'good' commercial bills from 1922/3.[67] The general problem was the clearers' retention of 'good' bills, given their dominance over acceptances from 1924. The difficulty for private acceptance houses, such as Kleinworts, was the extent to which they were exposed in one area — Germany in particular and Eastern and Central Europe in general. As this became greater, the one safeguard was dealing with only 'A1 concerns', supported by the belief that counterparts — German banks — had learnt a salutary lesson during the 'Great inflation'.[68]

London, through supplying acceptances, developed a considerable risk exposure to Central and Eastern Europe. With the gold exchange standard's inauguration in the mid-1920s, this became larger due to the growing practice of placing deposits with local banks denominated in foreign currencies, primarily dollars. British banks and houses were not alone. This business was equally pursued by American banks, while Belgian, Dutch, French, Italian, and Swiss institutions also participated, so that major Central and Eastern European banks held deposits in dollars, French francs, guilders, sterling, and Swiss francs.[69] The dangers of London's particular commitments first became publicly evident with the collapse of the Credit-Anstalt, Austria's premier bank, on 8 May 1931. The French government's trenchant opposition to the Austro-German Zollunion further complicated the grave situation by affecting the Austrian government's ability to obtain resources abroad to reconstruct Credit-Anstalt.

Arising from the sale of Anglo-Austrian's branches to Credit-Anstalt in 1926, the Bank of England was a significant shareholder in the foundered Viennese bank. Furthermore, Norman would have been aware of Rothschilds' commitment to

Credit-Anstalt, increased by its acquisition of Boden-Credit-Anstalt in autumn 1929. Besides these equity links, there were also the very considerable problems of the City's acceptance credits to, and deposits with, Austrian banks. Following a central-bank governors' meeting at Basle, 17/18 May, Norman tried to discover Credit-Anstalt's exact position, and ways of preventing it from further deteriorating. The latter focused upon constituting a committee of Credit-Anstalt's foreign shareholders and creditors. The Governor aimed 'to control the immediate policy of the Credit Anstalt; to maintain the position vis-à-vis the Credit Anstalt and in some way to exercise the control explicit in the new [equity] holdings [in the proposed reconstruction plan] and implicit in the position of the foreign creditors'.[70] Whether this was Norman's design, recognizing the Achilles' heel of Credit-Anstalt to be its foreign deposits, which were eventually declared at 1,500m. schillings, or a response to an Austrian request for a syndicate of foreign creditors with which to conclude a 'standstill' arrangement, cannot be established. There had been talk of a committee at Basle, while Norman's own actions show that he saw it as a means for exerting pressure in the formulation of policy.

Lists of foreign creditors were to hand by 21 May, but the plans for which they were required needed the consent and goodwill of all involved. A London committee was established firmly enough by 26 May for its existence to be made public and, within two days, its members indicated their preparedness to maintain credits on a daily basis. However, this was on two conditions. First, Credit-Anstalt's management was not to pay any foreign creditor preferentially and, second, effective measures were to be taken to prevent domestic withdrawals, an implicit allusion to the necessity for a government guarantee of Credit-Anstalt's liabilities. Although the foreign creditors had begun what was to become a long dialogue with Vienna, their organization was informal, while there was concern that no parallel moves had been made in New York.[71] American representatives only joined the London committee in late May, a French committee was not formed until 30 May, and a German delegate did not join the London committee until 1 June. Even then, the creditors were not totally concerted as two American banks and one Dutch institution remained uncooperative.

On 29 May the Second Credit-Anstalt Law was passed, empowering the Finance Minister to pledge the security of the Austrian state until 30 June 1933 for loans supporting Credit-Anstalt's reconstruction and current business.[72] Its enactment had caused turmoil within domestic politics, which became apparent to the London creditors as soon as it was applied by Credit-Anstalt's management solely as a reserve power. Furthermore, the bank's officials appeared to allow local withdrawals to take place over the backs of other creditors. Indeed, foreign creditors were threatened with a cessation of payments, coupled with the arising legal complications, while it was well known in Vienna that the West wanted to avoid at all costs a moratorium. At most, the new law was used initially in particular instances to retain individual deposits. More generally, it was unclear whether the statute applied to facilities agreed before the bank had foundered, an uncertainty that made a formal standstill agreement unlikely.

The problem posed by Credit-Anstalt's foreign deposits was solved pragmatically, albeit slowly and grindingly, through applying the government guarantee together with the development of an understanding with the foreign creditors. Nonetheless, withdrawals of deposits continued, met through rediscounting with the Austrian National Bank, the volume of which grew to 628m. schillings by 5 June. Furthermore, National Bank lost 350m. schillings of devisen. A domestic banking crisis was turning into a grave foreign exchange problem.

On 12 June Sir Robert Kindersley travelled to Vienna to conclude an agreement on behalf of the International Creditors Committee with the Austrian government. A partner in Lazards and a Bank of England director, he was 'fully acquainted with the general position and with the exact state of affairs in London'. Gannon, vice-president of Chase National Bank and representative of Credit-Anstalt's American creditors, accompanied him. They found 'a situation which could not continue'. This was because of continuing delays in arranging the external bond issue for financing Credit-Anstalt's reconstruction, upon which further BIS assistance to Austrian National Bank was premissed, coupled with the central bank's growing foreign exchange losses. Consequently, National Bank staff pressed for a moratorium, which would endanger concluding any formal agreements for Credit-Anstalt's foreign deposits. News that Norman would try to place the Austrian Treasury bonds allowed Bruins, the newly installed foreign adviser to National Bank, to take a more optimistic attitude. He agreed to postpone a moratorium declaration for 24 hours. This gave Kindersley and Gannon just sufficient time and the appropriate conditions for finalizing an agreement. Yet, its import was complicated by the Austrian cabinet's resignation some hours after it had been concluded. However, lawyers maintained that the Finance Minister could sign such agreements under the Second Credit-Anstalt Law — the guarantee law — and that related cabinet decisions had force.

Exactly as a standstill for Credit-Anstalt's foreign deposits was arranged in Vienna, the French government formulated the political conditions for issuing in Paris a portion of Austrian Treasury bonds. They were nothing more than an ultimatum designed to disrupt the Austro-German Zollunion plan, and had to be accepted by the Austrian government by, at latest, 8 p.m. that evening. When delivering it, the French Finance Minister merely stated that he understood that, if its stringent political conditions regarding the Zollunion question were accepted by the Austrian government, a substantial portion of the 150m. schilling bond issue would be undertaken in Paris. Yet, this assurance was not given in writing. The French timetable for overturning the Austro-German Zollunion was predicated upon the Austrian National Bank's foreign exchange position. It would give the French merely four hours in which to advance 150m. schillings to the Austrian government so that its proceeds could be included in the National Bank's next return. This was brinkmanship of the most calculated kind, involving the minimum time required for preventing the publication of a central bank statement that, probably, would lead to the automatic imposition of a moratorium and so spark off a panic. Unknown to the Austrian cabinet while formulating its blunt reaction to the French ultimatum — resignation — the Bank of England made a seven-day advance of 150m. schillings secured against the eventual placing of the Treasury bonds.[73]

The Bank of England advance was a holding operation, and proved unsuccessful to the extent that it became a medium-term loan. The Viennese banking crisis widened, leading to further standstill agreements, with one concluded with Wiener Bank-Verein's foreign creditors in August. The crisis also spread through the webs of business that still linked banks situated in the territories of the former Habsburg Empire with the imperial economy's financial centre — Vienna.

There were no major financial links between Vienna and Berlin, but the Credit-Anstalt crisis precipitated a further, very substantial withdrawal of American short-term capital from Central Europe. Its extent resulted in German banks experiencing extreme pressure, only briefly assuaged by the Hoover Moratorium of 20 June. The City reacted by establishing a Joint Committee, drawn from the Accepting Houses Committee and the British Bankers' Association.[74]

On 13 July, Darmstäder u. Nationalbank failed to open, resulting in the declaration of bank holidays on 14 and 15 July in Germany, with Austria and Hungary following suit. The reopening of German banks was accompanied by a very restrictive payments regime that, *inter alia*, froze payments on £64m. of acceptances granted by City institutions. Schroders were particularly affected due to credits to firms and institutions featuring most prominently in the banking crisis: Darmstäder, £0.3m., Nordwolle, £0.1m. and Schulbach Thiemer & Co., £0.1m. However, Norman was not prepared to follow the precedent of August 1914 and develop a moratorium arrangement for London acceptances. In the aftermath of Darmstäder's closure, he was only willing to ensure that City acceptors received sympathetic hearings from their clearing bankers.

The July London Conference, hastily convened by the Foreign Office, failed to formulate initiatives for resolving the German situation. Consequently, Frank Tiarks of Schroders followed in Kindersley's wake by undertaking the onerous task of negotiating a German standstill. After a briefing from Norman, he was, as Kindersley had been, accompanied by Gannon as representative of American creditor banks. At the negotiations which began on 27 July it was proposed that the Hungarian frozen credits scheme might be a model. Subsequent detailed discussions took place from 13 August, with the Wiggin Committee, established by the London Conference, acting as arbitrator. Its intervention led to a standstill being concluded on 19 August, ratified on 9 September. It only covered Rm 6,300m. (£307m.) of short-term commercial debt in terms of freezing principals for six months while ensuring service in convertible currencies. The foreign obligations of the German government, municipalities, and the Reichsbank were excluded.

The Austrian, German, and other standstill agreements, as with the Bank of England's advance to Austrian National Bank, only provided breathing spaces. The severity and length of the economic and financial trauma in Central and Eastern Europe, together with the failure of the January 1932 Lausanne Conference, made necessary repeated negotiations for extending and reformulating the various standstills. These began with talks for the eventual 1932 German Credit Agreement, which ran for a year from February 1932.[75] Similarly, Kindersley regularly visited Vienna from 1933 to participate in successive discussions over the fate of Credit-Anstalt's foreign credits.

The continental European financial crisis of spring and summer 1931 had a very severe and immediate impact upon the City. The problems began with Lazards, the result not of the crisis itself but of misdoings at the house's Brussels office, which caused a £6m. loss. In the circumstances of summer 1931, the Bank of England could not but provide £3.5m. at a penal rate over seven years to prevent Lazards suspending payments. The Bank had to supply a further £1m. in May 1932, when Lazards' Paris house ran into grave difficulties.[76] Directly attributable to the 1931 crisis was six acceptors' technical insolvencies, caused by their respective standstill debts. A further twelve houses were also affected. For Huths, the crisis only increased problems that had first surfaced in 1921/2 following the settlement of its 1914 moratorium debts and the conduct of its post-war business. For very particular reasons, the Bank of England had then provided £1.5m. for restructuring the firm but its new start failed to be profitable, and the standstills constituted another blow. The Bank lost £1m. through its support, and in 1936 Huths' rump business was transferred to British Overseas Bank.[77]

The crisis not only brought down the weakened but also struck mortally at leading houses — Arbuthnot Latham, Goschen & Cunliffe, Japhets, Kleinworts, and Schroders. Schroders' partners lost £1.5m. on business conducted during 1931 despite having restricted acceptances from the opening of the year.[78] There were legal complications over Kleinworts' German frozen debts that gave rise to conflicting valuations—£9.3m. or £7.3m. or £3.298m. Schroders' stood at £4.9m., greater than its capital of £3.7m., but the house was assisted by its bankers, the Westminster, as were Brandts, Goschens, and Hambros. Kleinworts were also affected by a partner's death and needed £3.5m. but, initially, the Westminster's security requirements were found to be too severe. As Norman refused to provide Kleinworts with a guarantee for the sizeable overdraft being sought, Kleinworts had to capitulate to the Westminster's terms. The overdraft was paid off by September 1932.[79]

The crisis and the standstills also affected the discount market. One small house was bailed out by the Bank on very stiff penal terms coupled with subsequent close supervision until its capital had been substantially restored.[80] The more general problem was constituted by standstill bills, which the Bank, despite its objection to renewed bills, continued to accept as eligible paper in order to sustain their circulation.[81] This 'fiction' applied to £61m. of Austrian, German, and Hungarian paper in 1931, and was pointed up by German standstill bills constituting the majority of Bank rediscounts over the first half of 1932. The continued eligibility of standstill bills was threatened in late 1934, when it appeared that an Anglo-German clearing would overturn standstill arrangements. If it had come about, six

City firms would have been endangered, and the Bank with National Provincial began to establish the necessary support operation. The standstill survived but the challenge to it brought about the realization that remaining bills — £40m. German and £3m. Hungarian — were not 'good' for their face value. The Bank consequently looked to a reduction in their volumes on the market. The 'Old Lady's' nudges were formalized on 28 September 1936 with the announcement that only £0.5m. of Hungarian standstill bills per acceptor would be eligible for rediscounting from 15 October 1937. This was followed by the requirement that banks and acceptors should reduce their respective liabilities on German bills by 30 per cent from 30 September 1937. A further 40 per cent of their 1936 volume was required to be removed from the market during mid-1939, when £36m. remained in circulation. This led to two acceptors having to turn to their bankers for support, while another was aided by the Bank but consequently had to withdraw from accepting.[82]

Until mid-July 1931 the retreat of short-term capital from Berlin, Budapest, and Vienna to London benefited sterling. However, sterling came under severe pressure with the failure of the London Conference and the publication of the Macmillan Report on 14 July, which made plain the imbalance between the City's short-term liabilities and long-term assets. A further blow was struck by the May Report that pointed up Britain's fiscal problems — a budget deficit of £120m. Nonetheless, sterling had regained some stability by early August but this was undone by the Bank's mishandling of American and French credits for its support. The arising economic and financial crisis resulted in the formation of a National Government, and the negotiation of further American and French credits for sterling. An emergency budget failed to restore market confidence. Instead, a banking crisis in Amsterdam and the so-called 'Invergordon mutiny' crystallized the underlying situation, and sterling consequently became once more a floating currency from 21 September 1931. It formally became a 'managed' float with the operation of the Exchange Equalization Account, undertaken by the Bank on behalf of the Treasury from 1 July 1932.[83]

The Sterling Area further emerged through governments of a wide range of countries tied politically, or economically, or both to Britain deciding to retain a fixed exchange rate with sterling. Initially, they comprised the British Commonwealth (apart from Canada), Egypt, Eire, Iceland, Iraq, Portugal, and the Sudan. They were joined in 1933 by Estonia, Scandinavia, and Siam. 'Associates' of the Sterling Area included Argentina, Bolivia, Greece, Japan, and Yugoslavia, all of which pegged their currencies to sterling for considerable periods but with various forms of exchange control.[84] Although a currency bloc, the Sterling Area 'proper' was not demarcated by exchange controls until the outbreak of war in 1939. It became a trading bloc with the British government's decision to adopt protection. The way was paved during autumn 1931 by emergency legislation, followed by the Import Duties Act in February 1932, which allowed the development of imperial preference through the Ottawa Agreement. Under this, the United Kingdom gave continued free entry to all Dominion products, except meat, in return for minor concessions and increased preferences for British goods. The various agreements over trade from November 1931 between Britain and countries where there was a political or economic tie were not matched by formal monetary and financial arrangements.

Sterling's float from September 1931 was accompanied by a further embargo upon foreign, although not imperial, lending (see Table 8.1).[85] Furthermore, government decided to pursue a 'cheap money' policy on the grounds that it might do some general good while certainly not inflicting any harm. Bank rate consequently went to 2 per cent on 30 June 1932, where it remained until 24 August 1939. The main, direct advantage lay in the conversion of the National Debt. 'Cheap money' also went towards creating financial insularity to the extent of Norman complaining in 1933 that 'we are now an island financially as well as geographically'.[86] Nonetheless that island was the centre of the world's largest trading bloc during the 1930s. The Bank and the British government had let it be known during the Ottawa Conference that efforts would be made to keep sterling steady on the exchanges, which could be assisted by the Empire maintaining stable exchange rates based upon sterling. Norman was prepared to provide credits, albeit restricted, to aid Sterling Area members undergoing temporary exchange rate difficulties. Thereafter, he toyed with establishing a forum for the central banks of the Empire, finally achieved in 1937.[87]

4. The 'long winter'

The consequences of the 1931 liquidity crisis for the City went with those resulting from the continuing fall in world trade, by February 1933 only a third of its April 1929 level. This had severe repercussions upon British overseas banks, whose prime functions were to finance international commerce and provide exchange. The first casualty was Anglo-South American, the largest British bank in Latin America. It was brought down on 10 September 1931 by a run but was, in any case, structurally weakened through an overcommitment to the Chilean nitrate business.[88] The Bank provided £3m. and four of the 'Big Five' £2m. — to protect the discount market and because of a fear that its failure could lead to a contagious distrust of other British banks. The extent of the subsequent salvage operation resulted in Norman obtaining a Treasury guarantee for the potential losses in November 1931. The need was pointed up by Anglo-South American drawing £8.5m. from its City supporters at the end of January 1932. The bank never recovered, and was sold by Norman to BoLSA in July 1936. Its 'rescue' cost £4.57m., of which £2.35m. was shouldered by the Bank.[89]

Other British overseas banks revealed their difficulties through diminished profits from 1930, when exchange pressures also affected British banks in Australia. Thereafter, some, such as Barclays (DCO), Chartered, and Standard, were adversely affected by sterling's departure from gold and the Union of South Africa following suit in December 1932. With these experiences and the diminution of their traditional business, all British overseas banks turned to increasing their investments — primarily British government stocks that appreciated with 'cheap money'.[90] It proved to give security to ensure their survival. Nonetheless, their geographical scope was reduced; by 1938, British overseas banking was physically and financially concentrated in Asia, Australasia, and southern Africa.[91]

World trade's collapse was reflected in the volume of London international acceptances declining to £134m. by 1933. Thereafter, they failed to recover fully in parallel with trade's hesitant revival over the mid-1930s since a significant proportion of dealings was subject to exchange and payments controls, whereas telegraphic transfers increasingly financed 'unregulated' trade.[92] It was this situation that made standstill bills so prominent on the London money market, especially during the early 1930s. Nonetheless, acceptances remained the core of the private houses' affairs, but the shares of Japhets, Kleinworts, and Schroders fell due to the consequences of the 1931 German banking crisis. Hambros became the lead firm, primarily through its further development of domestic acceptances — a revival of the 'inland bill' — a business in which it was followed by Barings, Erlangers, and Morgan Grenfell.[93]

Accumulated expertise still played a role. Schroders, with Hambros, applied it in establishing Anglo-Foreign Securities, which liquidated standstill credits and dealt in Sperrmarks. This led to the formation of a related subsidiary — Axe Trading — for currency and securities arbitrage and the provision of European credits. Norman blocked the fruition of a comparable development — Compensation Brokers. Schroders' Investment Department also took on a new importance, especially through developing a private European clientele.[94]

The collapse of the City's international dimension from 1931 was also marked out by falls in staffing. Schroders' payroll contracted from 276 at the close of 1930 to 154 by 1939. Kleinworts were in more straightened circumstances and, consequently, undertook a weekly reduction of staff, a dozen at a time, until their numbers had fallen from 400 to 175. Comparably, bonuses ceased to be paid, while salaries were reduced.[95] The lack of buoyant business, coupled with deranged balance sheets produced by the 1931 crisis, meant that economies on operating costs might only minimize losses. Schroders experienced losses not only in 1931 but also in 1932 and 1934.[96] Even Morgan Grenfell, considerably less exposed to German business, only enjoyed net profits at 1920s levels in 1934 and 1936, primarily due to experiencing losses on stocks.[97]

The outbreak of the Second World War was not marked in the City by a financial crisis. Apart from some limited recovery during 1935 and 1936, the international economy was the barest shadow of what it had been during the *belle époque*. Furthermore, as war clouds had gathered during the late 1930s, the authorities prepared, at least financially, for the likelihood of major hostilities through progressively introducing a full battery of regulations, including controls on foreign exchange and capital movements. With the declaration of war, the state took over import purchases, thus dispensing with acceptors' services. Consequently, the City's financial 'motor' barely ticked over between 1939 and 1945. A marker of this is that, amongst Schroders' normal revenue sources, issuing and underwriting made the greatest contribution but only at 11 per cent, whereas the miscellaneous category of 'Other' was by far the largest at 44 per cent.[98] As a consequence, many firms did not merely stand still but markedly retrogressed, and for the personnel who remained in the City, there was little to be done on a daily basis. However, some thought was given to the future, particularly from 1944, when it was becoming clear that the terrible war was drawing to a close. Schroders considered merging with Guiness Mahon and also were approached by Barings over establishing close ties. Nothing came of either initiative but they were indicative of a more positive approach, as opposed to the boredom and melancholy that had characterized the early 1940s.[99]

5. Resurgence

The failure of 1920s monetary stabilization programmes and governments' subsequent reactions to the 'Great Slump' set the context for the Bretton Woods Conference and the less successful International Trade Organization initiative. Nonetheless, measures to re-establish rapidly a liberal world economy proved to be too precocious. This was displayed by the attempt to give sterling current account convertibility from autumn 1946, required by the post-war American loan to the United Kingdom, which resulted in the disaster of the convertibility crisis of summer 1947. However, world trade not only rapidly recovered but enjoyed sustained growth, rising from $53bn. in 1948 to $75bn. in 1951. Despite checks caused by the Korean War, the persistence of inconvertible currencies and high tariffs, and controls over capital movements, together with the Cold War, the global economy gained a renewed momentum over the 1950s. This provided the general context for the re-establishment of the City as a leading financial centre. Its domestic basis came from the devaluation of sterling to $2.80 on 19 September 1949, and the reactivation of monetary policy from 8 November 1951.

From 1953, the increasing, renewed role of the City within the briskly re-expanding world economy was one major factor that affected the Bank's advice to government over further decontrol measures. This counsel first bore fruit in the reopening of the London gold market on 22 March 1954.[100] The Bank gained further ground with what its senior staff regarded as 'technical progress' in February 1955. The government permitted official intervention in the exchange market for transferable sterling, which made transferable sterling, from April 1955, to all intents convertible, although at a discount of 1 per cent to the official rate. Thus, transferable sterling was almost on a par with 'American' sterling, and a unified rate attained for current account transactions.[101]

With progressive decontrol, the City's annual earnings from international financial services increased from £8m. to £30m. over the 1950s.[102] An important waymarker for a number of houses was the settlement of German standstill debts at the London Conference in February 1952.[103] The past's liquidation went along with a buoyant growth of acceptances in which Schroders took a lead, its business expanding from £0.26m. in 1945 to £7.9m. in 1959. From 1951, these primarily financed international trade, although their expansion was halted during 1952 and 1953 with Bank controls to suppress speculation against sterling.[104] Schroders benefited from the assistance of its related New York bank immediately following the war in developing sterling reimbursement credits to local banks in South America.[105] Alongside were sterling credits to Japanese banks from 1950 and banks in West Germany from 1954. The house also consciously attempted to build up a Commonwealth clientele, for which it had little initial basis.[106] This widening of Schroders' acceptances proved prescient as exchange turmoil in summer 1957 forced the authorities to restrict the international use of sterling for trade finance to credits within the Sterling Area.[107] Kleinworts were able similarly to redevelop acceptances, which rose from £4.8m. to £12.15m. over the 1950s. Their growth was driven primarily by Scandinavian credits, an entry into Hambros' traditional market accomplished by Kleinworts dealing directly with borrowers as opposed to local banks.[108]

Sterling remained a key currency during the 1950s but was completely overshadowed by the dollar. The changes in the international economy wrought by the Second World War were far greater than those of the Great War. Britain's international advantages came increasingly to lie in the City's provision of financial services. The domestic economy's problems adversely affected the position of British overseas banks, reflected in a gradual reorganization of their ownership. Some ties between clearers and overseas banking loosened. Lloyds gradually reduced its equity stake in BoLSA from 1943. From 1948 National Provincial withdrew, a process completed by 1955. Barclays retreated from Canada and Italy and, in 1957, sold Eastern Bank to Chartered. There were also mergers amongst independent British overseas banks, which reduced their number in Australia to two. Lastly, three groups developed within 'Eastern Exchange banking', while their respective networks spread beyond their immediate geographical fields of business.[109]

Controls over capital movements limited the City's new issues to largely those for borrowers within the Sterling Area. There was a restricted stream of bond flotations from 1946 but most were conversion issues, undertaken for municipal authorities in Australia and South Africa. Otherwise, the business concerned the finance of the government of Eire and Irish local authorities, together with that of Nyasaland Railways. The geographical pattern of this limited new lending largely coincided with British overseas banks' networks, with, for instance, Barclays DCO undertaking a conversion issue for Pretoria in 1958.[110] The overall data are displayed in Table 8.2.

The head offices, or principal British offices, of British overseas banks comprised about half of the 'foreign' physical aspect of the City's international dimension during the late 1950s. Their place within the 'Square Mile' had developed since the

Table 8.2. Overseas capital issues, 1939–1958 (£m.)

	'Old series': gross issues less refunding and conversions.			'New series': gross issues less redemptions			
Year	Total	Governments and local authorities	Industrial and commercial	Total	Commonwealth	Public and local authorities	companies
1939	23.3	12.6	10.7				
1940	0.4	—	0.4				
1941	0.2	—	0.2				
1942	—	—	—				
1943	1.2	—	1.2				
1944	2.5	—	2.5				
1945	5.2	—	5.2				
1946	16.8	—	16.8				
1947	32.5	8.9	23.6				
1948	38.1	8.2	30.0				
1949	41.9	22.4	19.5				
1950	52.2	28.2	23.9				
1951	50.2	33.1	17.1				
1952	52.4	33.1	19.3				
1953	57.4	30.8	26.6				
1954	79.2	39.0	40.2	47.3	53.4	36.1	11.2
1955	63.6	17.5	46.0	3.4	16.0	−3.8	7.2
1956	52.6	13.8	38.8	10.3	19.5	1.8	8.5
1957	65.1	12.0	53.1	7.3	18.3	1.7	5.6
1958	74.0	48.7	25.3	15.8	23.3	12.8	3.0

Source: 'Capital Issues in the UK', *Bank of England Quarterly Bulletin*, 6 (1966), 154–6.

1830s, so progressively widening the City's global network. Its web of institutionalized connections had further extended from the early 1870s with the establishment of foreign banks' branches and agencies. Yet, their numbers fell from the outbreak of the First World War, in part because of the authorities' actions. During the 1950s, foreign banks once more opened full branches in the City, to number some forty by the end of the decade, so regaining their overall pre-1914 level. The most important, in terms of national groups, were American (eight branches) and French (six branches). Furthermore, twenty representative offices were opened over the decade, primarily by American, Italian, and Japanese institutions. These developments were markers of the world economy's resurgence and, equally, of the City's continuing important place within it, despite sterling's problems.

Foreign banks' long-established role in the City was as foreign exchange operators, and, with the progressive relaxation of controls during the 1950s, they comprised two-thirds of the institutions authorized to deal in specified currencies.[111] British domestic developments also allowed them, along with merchant banks, to act as principals in the emergence and growth of wholesale money markets: the local authority debt market and the nascent interbank market. Most important of all for the revolution that was to take place within the City and world finance from the early 1960s, they participated in the initial development of the Eurocurrency market.

The first stages of the rise of the Euromarkets within the City have only recently begun to be delineated by historians. They were born during the last years of the global dollar shortage, whereas their development within the City was encouraged by the authorities' benign attitude, with no controls placed upon foreign currency deposits held in London.[112] Schroders were an early entrant into the Eurodollar market, exploiting the opportunity to capitalize further on their expertise in forward foreign exchange, while also reacting to the 1957 prohibition on the use of sterling beyond the Sterling Area.[113] Other major City-based principals in the Euromarket's early stages were BoLSA and Kleinworts.[114] The market received a further boost from the general adoption of current account convertibility within Europe at the close of 1958. With business increasingly coming to concentrate upon expatriate currencies, the City lost its historic link with sterling, and was to be entirely reconfigured from the early 1960s.

6. Transformation

The City experienced a 'long winter' after the 1931 crisis. Many institutions' survival was due in part to the decisions taken from 1919 by managements of the clearing banks. The involvement of four of the biggest British domestic commercial banks with some British overseas banks largely ensured the latter's survival over the inter-war period although, ultimately, often at significant costs to the clearers that had established equity links with them. Furthermore, the clearers supported their accepting house clients when they were hit by the 1931 crisis, and engaged in subsequent support operations in association with the Bank of England.

The City's private houses also ensured their survival from the mid-1920s by diversifying their activities, in particular by becoming more involved with domestic finance. This widening of their business scope did not lead to another competitive struggle with the clearers. Managements of the 'Big Five' largely continued to take a very traditional view of their business until the incursion of foreign, particularly American, banks into their domestic market from the mid-1960s totally changed the nature of commercial bank lending. Nonetheless, the City's 'old' houses had earlier suffered from the clearers' competitive edge, arising from their much larger resources. During the 1920s, the 'Big Five' had come to dominate the markets in, first, foreign exchange and, then, international acceptances. This is clear from the experiences of the major private accepting houses, although the respective roles of the 'Big Five' in these particular markets have yet to be fully portrayed and analysed by historians.

As the world economy progressively revived over the 1950s, the City was able gradually to resume its former premier place. The focus in the previous discussion has been solely upon London's banks. However, they were only one part of the major complex that comprised the City's international dimension. Each segment pursued specialist functions, and each seized upon the revival of world commerce and finance. The re-establishment of the play of specialist roles was assisted by the authorities, most particularly in the case of the reopening of London's commodity markets — those for coffee, copper, grain, lead, and wool — from the early 1950s. Similarly, shipbroking and marine insurance recovered and expanded, as indicated, for instance, by Lloyd's net premium income increasing from £149m. to £255m. over the 1950s. Lying behind all these developments was the City's vast pool of human capital, not just the directors and partners of institutions and houses but also the legions of white-collar workers that staffed the rebuilt offices within the 'Square Mile'. This skilled workforce, with its accumulated expertise, was the 'bedrock' of the City that remained intact throughout the first half of the twentieth century. It provided the City with a considerable advantage over other contending financial centres.

What is now clear is that the City's full resumption of its world role was only accomplished through decoupling from its long-standing relationship with sterling — with the problems of the British economy. From the mid-1950s, the 'bill on London' was increasingly replaced by the Eurodollar. The early rise of dealings in Eurocurrencies took the City's cosmopolitanization back to the level that had pertained during the *belle époque* through the opening and reopening of London offices by foreign banks. Thereafter, the City became very rapidly a 'world city' in a totally new, late twentieth-century sense.

Notes

I am grateful to my colleague, Dr B. Attard, for his comments and suggestions during the drafting of this chapter. For a somewhat comparable survey, see R. Roberts, 'The City of London as a Financial Centre in the Years of Depression, the Second World War and Post-war Official Controls, 1931–61', in A. Gorst, L. Johnman, and W. S. Lucas (eds.), *Contemporary British History 1931–1961: Politics and the Limits of Policy* (London, 1991).

1. See S. Bradley and N. Pevsner, *The Buildings of England, London*, i: *The City of London* (London, 1997), 125.
2. Most recently by David Kynaston; see *The City of London*, i: *A World of its Own* (London, 1994); ii: *Golden Years 1890–1914* (London, 1995); iii: *Illusions of Gold 1914–1945* (London, 1999).
3. For one assessment of some aspects of its immediate impact, see T. Seabourne, 'The Summer of 1914', in F. Capie and G. E. Wood (eds.), *Financial Crises and the World Banking System* (London, 1986).
4. See S. Battilossi, 'Financial Innovation and the Golden Ages of International Banking: 1890–1931 and 1958–81', *Financial History Review*, 7 (2000).
5. J. Wake, *Kleinwort Benson: The History of Two Families in Banking* (Oxford, 1997), 213–16.
6. R. Roberts, *Schroders: Merchants & Bankers* (Basingstoke, 1992), 171, 187. See also R. Z. Aliber, 'Speculation in the Foreign Exchanges: The European Experience, 1919–1926', *Yale Economic Essays*, 2 (1962); Battilossi, 'Financial Innovation'. On the origins and pre-war development of Midland's Foreign Department, see A. R. Holmes and E. Green, *Midland: 150 Years of Banking Business* (London, 1986), 133–5.
7. Wake, *Kleinwort Benson*, 211.

8. Ibid. 224–5.
9. M. Pohl and K. Burk, *Deutsche Bank in London 1873–1998* (Munich, 1998), 53–9.
10. E. V. Morgan, *Studies in British Financial Policy, 1914–25* (London, 1952), 6–13; R. S. Sayers, *The Bank of England 1891–1944*, i (Cambridge, 1976), 70, 77.
11. Pohl and Burk, *Deutsche Bank*, 53–9.
12. Roberts, *Schroders*, 170–1, 188–92.
13. R. C. Michie, *The London Stock Exchange: A History* (Oxford, 1999), 193.
14. See C. Buckheim, 'Aspects of XIXth Century Anglo-German Trade Rivalry Reconsidered', *Journal of European Economic History*, 10 (1981); P. L. Cottrell, '"Lo, . . . Nineveh and Tyre.": British Trading Anxieties and Official Reactions, 1870–1929', in D. H. Aldcroft and A. Slaven (eds.), *Enterprise and Management: Essays in Honour of Peter L. Payne* (Aldershot, 1995); R. S. J. Hoffman, *Great Britain and German Trade Rivalry 1875–1914* (Philadelphia, 1933; repr. 1983); P. M. Kennedy, *The Rise of Anglo-German Antagonism 1860–1914* (London, 1988); H. Kieswetter, 'Competing for Wealth and Power: The Growing Rivalry between Industrial Britain and Industrial Germany', *Journal of European Economic History*, 20 (1991); W. E. Minchinton, 'E. E. Williams: "Made in Germany" and after', *Vierteljahrschrift für Sozial- und Wirtschaftsgeschichte*, 62 (1975); D. C. M. Platt, 'Britain and Germany', in id., *Decline and Recovery in Britain's Overseas Trade, 1873–1914* (Basingstoke, 1993).
15. See for example, L. Joseph, *Industrial Finance: A Comparison between Home and Foreign Developments* (London, 1911); H. S. Foxwell, 'The Financing of Industry and Trade', *Economic Journal*, 27 (1917).
16. A. S. J. Baster, *The International Banks* (London, 1935), 193–7; G. Jones, *British Multinational Banking 1830–1990* (Oxford, 1993), 223–8.
17. Baster, *International Banks*, 199–201; A. Teichova, 'Versailles and the Expansion of the Bank of England into Central Europe', in N. Horn and J. Kocka (eds.), *Law and the Formation of Big Enterprises in the Nineteenth and Early Twentieth Centuries* (Göttingen, 1979); P. L. Cottrell, 'Aspects of Western Equity Investment in the Banking Systems of East Central Europe', in A. Teichova and P. L. Cottrell (eds.), *International Business and Central Europe, 1918–1939*, (Leicester, 1983), 316–21; E. März, *Austrian Banking and Financial Policy* (London, 1984), 457–62; Jones, *Multinational Banking*, 228–31; C. Natmessnig, *Britische Finanzinteressen in Österreich. Die Anglo-Österreichische Bank* (Vienna, 1998).
18. P. L. Cottrell with C. J. Stone, 'Credits, and Deposits to Finance Credits', in P. L. Cottrell, H. Lindgren, and A. Teichova (eds.), *European Industry between the Wars* (Leicester, 1992); Wake, *Kleinwort Benson*, 224.
19. Baster, *International Banks*, 202–4; Jones, *Multinational Banking*, 242–4.
20. C. P. Parrini, *Heir to Empire: United States Economic Diplomacy 1916–1923* (Pittsburgh, 1969), 1–9, 22–8, 69, 103, 104, 122; M. J. Hogan, *Informal Entente: The Private Structure of Cooperation in Anglo-American Diplomacy 1918–1928* (London, 1977), 79–80.
21. Parrini, *Heir to Empire*, 56–8, 61–4, 109, 112–14; Hogan, *Informal Entente*, 60. See also T. F. Huertas, 'US multinational banking: history and prospects', in G. Jones (ed.), *Banks as Multinationals* (London, 1990); H. van B. Cleveland and T. F. Huertas, *Citibank, 1812–1970* (Cambridge, Mass., 1985), 76–9, 121–7, 205–8.
22. Parrini, *Heir to Empire*, 80, 91–2, 95.
23. Roberts, *Schroders*, 214–15. See also J. D. Wilson, *The Chase* (Boston, 1986), 12–14, 23–4.
24. Parrini, *Heir to Empire*, 115.

25. Ibid., 75, 94, 117, 118.
26. Cottrell with Stone, 'Credits', 55–6, 59.
27. Parrini, *Heir to Empire*, 115.
28. Roberts, *Schroders*, 213–21.
29. Jones, *Multinational Banking*, 136–7.
30. Ibid. ch. VI.
31. Holmes and Green, *Midland*, 137–41.
32. For the European dimension see G. Jones, 'Lombard Street on the Riveria: The British Clearing Banks and Europe, 1900–1960', *Business History*, 24 (1982).
33. Jones, *Multinational Banking*, 138–9.
34. Baster, *International Banks*, 222–3; D. Joslin, *A Century of Banking in Latin America* (London, 1963), 236; J. R. Winton, *Lloyds Bank, 1918–1969* (Oxford, 1982), 28; Jones, *Multinational Banking*, 139–42.
35. Jones, *Multinational Banking*, 145–7.
36. Winton, *Lloyds*, 22–5, 28, 34, 122–7; Sayers, *Bank of England*, i. 242; Jones, *Multinational Banking*, 142, 145, 239–40.
37. A. S. J. Baster, *The Imperial Banks* (London, 1929), 235; A. W. Tuke and R. J. H. Gillman, *Barclays Bank Limited 1926–1969* (London, 1972), 74; Sir Julian Crossley and J. Blandford, *The DCO Story* (London, 1975), 3–19; Jones, *Multinational Banking*, 147–54.
38. G. Tyson, *100 Years of Banking in Asia and Africa* (London, 1963), 189; Jones, *Multinational Banking*, 156.
39. Jones, *Multinational Banking*, 157.
40. Sayers, *Bank of England*, i. 237–8, 242–4; Jones, *Multinational Banking*, 236–9, 245.
41. Baster, *International Banks*, 197–8; Sayers, *Bank of England*, i. 260–3; Winton, *Lloyds*, 57–9; Jones, *Multinational Banking*, 231–4.
42. Holmes and Green, *Midland*, 166.
43. Roberts, *Schroders*, 184.
44. J. Atkin, 'Official Regulation of British Overseas Investment, 1914–1931', *Economic History Review*, 2nd ser. 23 (1970), 324–5.
45. D. E. Moggridge, *British Monetary Policy 1924–1931: The Norman Conquest of $4.86* (Cambridge, 1972), 201–2.
46. B. R. Mitchell with P. Deane, *Abstract of British Historical Statistics* (Cambridge, 1971), table 5, p. 403.
47. Both Atkin, 'Official Regulation', 325, and Moggridge, *British Monetary Policy*, 203–5, present revised estimates of this series.
48. Atkin, 'Official Regulation', 326–30.
49. Moggridge, *British Monetary Policy*, 205.
50. Bank of England Archive, London [hereafter BoE]; OV 37/20, Norman to Clegg (SARB), 17 Dec. 1921.
51. C. B. Schedvin, *Australia and the Great Depression: A Study of Economic Development and Policy in the 1920s and 1930s* (South Melbourne, repr. 1988), 100.
52. Ibid. 91–2. See also B. Attard, 'Moral Suasion, Empire Borrowers and the New Issue Markets during the 1920s', in R. Michie and P. Williamson (eds.), *The Government and the City* (forthcoming).
53. See A. Orde, 'Baring Brothers, the Bank of England, the British Government and the Czechoslovak State Loan of 1922', *English Historical Review*, 106 (1991).

54. Roberts, *Schroders*, 186.
55. P. Ziegler, *The Sixth Great Power: Barings 1762–1929* (London, 1988), 351–4; Roberts, *Schroders*, 197–8, 376.
56. See P. L. Cottrell, 'Norman, Strakosch and the Development of Central Banking: From Conception to Practice, 1919–1924', in P. L. Cottrell (ed.), *Rebuilding the Financial System in Central and Eastern Europe, 1918–1994* (Aldershot, 1997); K. Burk, *Morgan Grenfell 1838–1988: The biography of a Merchant Bank* (Oxford, 1989), ch. 5.
57. See W. C. McNeil, *American Money and the Weimar Republic: Economics and Politics on the Eve of the Great Depression* (New York, 1986).
58. Moggridge, *British Monetary Policy*, 205–6.
59. Ibid. 209–11.
60. Atkin, 'Official Regulation', 331–4; Moggridge, *British Monetary Policy*, 212–14.
61. T. Balogh, *Studies in Financial Organisation* (Cambridge, 1947), 167.
62. Wake, *Kleinwort Benson*, 237.
63. Roberts, *Schroders*, 192–3.
64. Wake, *Kleinwort Benson*, 243.
65. Roberts, *Schroders*, 185–6.
66. Cottrell with Stone, 'Credits', 56–9.
67. R. S. Sayers, *Gilletts in the London Money Market 1867–1967* (Oxford, 1968), 83, 86, 87, 96, 97.
68. Wake, *Kleinwort Benson*, 247.
69. T. Balderston, 'The Banks and the Gold Standard in the German Financial Crisis of 1931', *Financial History Review*, 1 (1994); Battilossi, 'Financial innovation', 153–4.
70. BoE; 'Message received from Mr Osbourne', 21 May 1931.
71. BoE; 'The Governor', HAS, 28 May 1931.
72. National Archives, Public Record Office, Kew [hereafter PRO]; FO 371 15150 C3745, Phipps to Henderson, 29 May 1931.
73. The above reconstruction of events is based upon PRO; FO 371 15151 C4965, Memorandum by F. Rodd [a Bank of England official seconded to BIS]. See also P. L. Cottrell 'The Bank of England and Credit-Anstalt's Collapse, Spring 1931', in K. Bachinger and D. Stiefel (eds.), with C. Natmessnig, *Auf Heller und Cent. Beiträge zur Finanz- und Währungsgeschichte*, (Frankfurt, 2001), 407–33.
74. Burk, *Morgan Grenfell*, 146–7.
75. Roberts, *Schroders*, 250–62; Sayers, *Bank of England*, ii. 503–11. See also N. Forbes, 'London Banks, the German Standstill Agreements, and "Economic Appeasement" in the 1930s', *Economic History Review*, 2nd ser. 40 (1987).
76. Sayers, *Bank of England*, ii. 530–1.
77. Ibid. 268–71.
78. Roberts, *Schroders*, 262, 264.
79. Wake, *Kleinwort Benson*, 244, 245, 248–9.
80. Sayers, *Bank of England*, ii. 541.
81. Ibid. 537–8.
82. Ibid. 509–12; Roberts, *Schroders*, 265.
83. See P. Williamson, *National Crisis and National Government: British Politics, the Economy and Empire, 1926–1932* (Cambridge, 1992), which supersedes his 'A "Bankers Ramp"? Financiers and the British Political Crisis of August 1931', *English Historical Review*, 99 (1984). See also Sayers, *Bank of England*, ii. 387–430; A. Cairncross and B. Eichengreen,

Sterling in Decline (Oxford, 1983), 27–110; Burk, *Morgan Grenfell*, 147–56; D. B. Kunz, *The Battle for Britain's Gold Standard in 1931* (London, 1987).

84. See D. Williams, 'The Evolution of the Sterling System', in C. R. Whittlesey and J. S. G. Wilson (eds.), *Essays in Money and Banking in Honour of R. S. Sayers* (Oxford, 1969); I. M. Drummond, *The Floating Pound and the Sterling Area, 1931–1939* (Cambridge, 1981); S. Howson, *Sterling's Managed Float: The Operations of the Exchange Equalisation Account, 1932–39* (Princeton, 1980).
85. See J. H. Richardson, *British Economic Foreign Policy* (London, 1936), 69–75; Royal Institute of International Affairs, *The Problem of International Investment* (London, repr. 1965), 76–101.
86. Quoted in Sayers, *Bank of England*, ii. 537.
87. Drummond, *Floating Pound*, 1–27; Sayers, *Bank of England*, ii. 516–18.
88. Joslin, *Banking in Latin America*, 266–8; Jones, *Multinational Banking*, 159–62.
89. Sayers, *Bank of England*, i. 263–7; Jones, *Multinational Banking*, 240–2.
90. Jones, *Multinational Banking*, 177–83.
91. Ibid. 136.
92. Roberts, *Schroders*, 249.
93. Ibid. 266–7; Wake, *Kleinwort Benson*, 248.
94. Roberts, *Schroders*, 267–8, 272.
95. Ibid. 251; Wake, *Kleinwort Benson*, 245–6.
96. Roberts, *Schroders*, 274.
97. Burke, *Morgan Grenfell*, appendix III, 268–9.
98. Roberts, *Schroders*, 275.
99. Ibid. 274–9.
100. J. Fforde, *The Bank of England and Public Policy, 1941–1958* (Cambridge, 1992), 492–505.
101. Ibid. 512–27. On some of sterling's problems, see C. R. Schenk, 'Closing the Hong Kong Gap; Hong Kong and the Free Dollar Market in the 1950s', *Economic History Review*, 47 (1994).
102. W. Clarke, *The City's Invisible Earnings* (London, 1958), 47, 96.
103. Roberts, *Schroders*, 320–3; and Wake, *Kleinwort Benson*, 331–4.
104. Roberts, *Schroders*, 327–8.
105. Ibid. 328–32.
106. Ibid. 333–6.
107. P. L. Cottrell, 'The Bank of England in its International Setting, 1918–1972', in R. Roberts and D. Kynaston (eds.), *The Bank of England: Money, Power and Influence 1694–1994* (Oxford, 1995), 128–9.
108. Wake, *Kleinwort Benson*, 342.
109. Jones, *Multinational Banking*, 255–62.
110. See *The Stock Exchange Official Yearbook 1959*.
111. See 'The UK Exchange Control: A Short History', *Bank of England Quarterly Bulletin*, 7 (1967).
112. See F. Machlup, 'Euro-dollar Creation: A Mystery Story', *Banca Nazionale del Lavoro Quarterly Review*, 94 (1974); B. Scott-Quin, *The New Euromarkets* (Basingstoke, 1975); J. Grady and M. Weale, *British Banking 1960–85* (Basingstoke, 1986), 130–5; J. H. Forsyth, 'Financial Innovation in Britain', in M. De Cecco (ed.), *Changing Money: Financial Innovation in Developed Countries* (London, 1987), 144–9; C. R. Schenk, 'The Origins of the Eurodollar Market in London: 1955–1963', *Explorations in Economic*

History, 35 (1998); and G. Burn, 'The State, the City and the Euromarkets', *Review of International Political Economy*, 6 (1999).

113. Roberts, *Schroders*, table 2: 'Overseas capital issues, 1939–58, £ms.' 324, 341–2.

114. Wake, *Kleinwort Benson*, 344–5.

9

The Challenged Competitiveness of the Paris Banking and Finance Markets, 1914–1958

HUBERT BONIN

Instead of a chronological account describing the evolution of the Paris banking market during the period under review, our study will be dedicated to two main themes: the resilience of Paris and its ability to pursue new ways of development in the face of the reshaping of banking and financial markets. French banks were shaken considerably by the First World War and lost most of their international importance. Given the competition from Belgian, British, German, and even (increasingly in the 1920s) American banks, the very fate of the Paris banking market seemed uncertain. Particularly in 1918, 1930–5, 1940–4, or in the late 1940s, there were many occasions when it seemed close to collapse or to sinking into third-rate status. The question is therefore: how did the Paris banking and financial markets manage to get through such dramatic events whilst not only surviving but also gaining some benefits? The main challenges lie with the assessment of the competitiveness of Paris compared with its counterparts, especially London, with the organization of the Paris market, which fostered the spirit of overseas enterprise and the mastery of risk, and with the subtle balance between the state's concern with national standing and the business world's desires to secure market shares, profits, and power outside France.

1. The Paris market's competitiveness during both post-war periods

Twice France had to face the huge task of rebuilding its economic and financial resources after the world wars. The Paris banking market became involved in this process but not at the expense of its international influence and involvement.

The Paris market and reconstruction after the First World War

The authorities gave priority to the rebuilding of areas destroyed during the fighting; thus exports of capital were forbidden from 1918 to 1928, apart from exemptions to help firms handle limited investments in foreign countries.

However, priority was also given to the rebuilding of the French franc and French state finances. Thus the Paris banking market was somewhat inward-looking. It was concerned with public finances in a certain way. Banks had to subscribe — to invest their liquidities — and promote the subscription of Treasury bills (*bons de la défense nationale*), which were issued on a larger and larger scale even after the peace in order to finance budget deficits — pending German reparations. Banks supported the state by lending huge amounts of cash to the Treasury, with rediscounting at the Banque de France a total of 1,425m. francs in October 1923 and March 1924. They promoted, together with the Banque de France, the purchase of state bonds (worth 16 bn. francs in 1920 alone). The mobilization of savings of the middle classes was thus still gaining momentum — and in the meantime, the Caisse des Dépôts reinforced its key role through the investment of larger inventories of savings banks' assets into state bills and bonds. This continued until the stabilization of public finances in 1926–8, but the process provided the Paris banking market with important operations as Treasury bills had to be consolidated into state bonds following important issues in 1927, 1928, and 1929, crowning Prime Minister Poincaré's efforts to reorganize the state's financial condition.

In any case, the Paris international banking market had to play some role in the battle for the French franc! On the one hand, the banks played an adversarial role, as their foreign exchange departments helped better-off customers and companies to exchange francs into foreign currency, particularly in 1922–3 and in 1925–6 — and some branches of the deposit banks gathered huge profits and commissions from this. The authorities were underinformed about these practices, particularly in 1922-3, and they needed time to understand the realities of the situation. The proof of the weakness of the Paris banking market owing to its lack of foreign currency was the necessity of securing the support of a foreign banking syndicate in 1922 to obtain foreign currency for France (worth about 3,338m. gold francs) and then to have to call for Morgans' help. The well-known 'Morgan loan' in March 1924 provided the authorities with foreign currency (with a credit line of $100m.) needed to survive the crisis — whilst Lazards of London supported the Banque de France with a loan worth £4m. sterling. The latter was repaid at its maturity of three months, the former renewed twice up to December 1924, and then transformed into a long-term loan (twenty-five years) floated in New York by Morgans. The banks also proved their usefulness when they assisted the state's struggle to rebuild the franc; on the one hand Lazards managed to handle foreign exchange for the state account as it was in charge of the management of a first block of $10m. from the Morgan loan, to be converted into francs gradually in 1925. After June 1925, Lazards[1] also kept a reserve of £950,000 sterling at the Banque de France. Finally, Lazards enlarged its mission under an agreement with the leftist government in May–June 1926; it sold the currencies provided by the Morgan loan and transferred the francs thus raised to the Treasury, which was thus able to pay back an important part of its short-term debt; in the meantime, banks provided credits to industrialists called upon to buy currencies on foreign markets for patriotic reasons, and Banque de France rediscounted banks for a part of the amount (May 1926).

On the other hand, Banque de France was equipped with a brand new Foreign Exchange Department, built up by a specialist who had been a manager at Crédit Lyonnais and was thus 'lent' to the central bank. In 1926, a law of 7 August and an agreement of 16 September entitled the Banque de France to buy currencies abroad and manage foreign exchange on behalf of the Treasury. The Treasury had already piled up 2,224m. francs in foreign currencies (pounds, florins, Swiss francs, dollars) since August 1926, often with the help of public-owned companies or friendly industrialists, and Banque de France was scheduled to buy further currency worth 2,900m. francs (around £99m.) up to March 1927. During this time, in 1926–8, the Paris banking market gathered forces to counter-attack: banks played with the franc; they lent money to the Treasury in June 1924 (975m. francs) by buying Treasury bills then discounted at Banque de France; banks and the Banque de France moved almost together to help the government weather the storms and to favour the stabilization of the international flotation of the franc. Thus the Paris market displayed certain signs of solidarity, of transmitting information, and of identifying tracks of speculation. New skills were also developed on foreign exchange markets and Banque de France and other banks sharpened their influence there. This sense of community was somehow confirmed when bankers, financiers, and industrialists often handled common undertakings in order to resist speculative moves by Dutch, Belgian, and German financiers and bankers on the equity capital of certain French firms, as this capital had became cheap owing to the franc's depreciation. Some industrial firms and even Crédit Lyonnais had to protect themselves through intervention on the financial markets (through syndicates buying stocks) and through rules on stocks bearing double voting rights, which small circles subscribed to help management teams and prevent hostile bids. Even so, French bankers failed to prevent British and Italian investors from taking control of the Compagnie Internationale des Wagons-Lits in 1921–3.

The Paris market and reconstruction after the Second World War

As soon as France was liberated from German occupation it had to struggle to rebuild its economy and its financial flows. At first, the banks must have felt trapped within an administrative economy as many rules were imposed on them — whatever their status — in order to force them to subscribe numerous Treasury bills to finance the short-term needs of the state (for example the minimum ratio of Treasury bills to deposits instituted in 1948). Of course, during that period banks also played a key role in selling state bond issues on several opportunities — with famous loans in 1952 (the Pinay loan) or in 1956 (the Ramadier loan). The Paris banking market gradually recovered its investment strengths as inflation was contained, savings grew, and the economy gathered momentum and thus generated assets to be invested. The renewal of the financial market from 1954 to 1962 was a sign of a rekindling of a real and diversified Paris market, but this time for mere domestic goals.

In the meantime, banks had contributed to the rebuilding of the French economy and international links as they gathered their resources in order to finance imports. In a direct line from efforts already shown in 1940–2, with the financing of Vichyist imports from overseas, or in 1941–4 from London and Africa in favour of *France libre*, the banks were deeply involved in syndicates importing commodities and raw materials such as textiles (linen, wool, cotton), and rubber or oleaginous products (the GNAPO syndicate). Owing to its intimacy with its sister bank in the City, Lazards led many such syndicates to set up sums of currency abroad in order to pay for imports; credits were thus extended by these syndicates mainly in the City under the control of the authorities — as exchange controls had been introduced in 1939 (and maintained up to the 1970s). This demonstrated a sense of common responsibility and proved that the Paris banking market had been reborn. Any French bank with a presence in London for trade and exchange activities — Société Générale, Crédit Lyonnais, and BNCI through a branch, CNEP through a subsidiary, British & French Bank — managed to help its customers to get currencies abroad and tried to extend its foreign exchange services. It provided French industrial firms with any facilities to pay in sterling for the raw materials (wool, rubber, tin, and cotton) purchased through Britain.

The struggle was indeed to make ends meet — that is, to pick up foreign currency to finance imports, as the trade deficit was huge — until the time that exports could grow. Of course, currency was obtained thanks to American aid (short-term financing in 1946–7; interim aid in 1947–8; and finally, the Marshall Plan). However, day-to-day operations according to the priorities fixed by the first economic Plan (1946–54) for capital goods imports had to find their own way[2] and bankers were extremely useful in detecting companies with ample currency reserves and in mobilizing them. The rebuilding of the Paris banking market was therefore stimulated by this involvement in financing the import–export trade and exchange operations — which explains the major importance of Forex departments in each big bank, in relationship with the brother department in London or with correspondent bankers. The Paris banking market could thus rebuild somehow its liquidity in foreign currencies, even if that growth had to follow the rhythm of the economic renewal itself.

Last, the economic reconstruction paved the way for the emergence of new methods of financing the re-equipping of France. Up to the beginning of the 1930s mid-term credits were rare and took the shape of renewed overdrafts with only rare refinancing from Banque de France. Some attempts to extend mid-term credit were tried at the beginning of the 1930s, through some refinancing by the Caisse des Dépôts. This soon failed because of the dwindling resources of the Caisse des Dépôts — due to the stabilization and even the shortening of savings banks assets, lodged at Caisse des Dépôts — while the Banque de France refused at that time to assume a new function of a central bank for mid-term credits. However, the post-war period provided the opportunity of building a new mid-term credit system.

The then nationalized Banque de France and the pressures of the authorities, annoyed with the despondent state of the economy and of many enterprises, persuaded the Paris banking market to accept a new scheme. Banks were able to extend mid-term credits to their customers, and then transmit them to Crédit National,[3] a semi-public institution created after the First World War to float bonds in order to finance long-term loans to firms that had suffered during the war. Crédit National thus became the key architect of a mid-term credit system, but the revolution was that the Banque de France itself was entitled to discount the credit bills then emitted as a cornerstone of that system. This helped the French economy and French businesses to accelerate investments and modernization. The Paris banking market became enriched with new forms of credit, which reinforced and diversified it; owing to this progress, French companies were much more able to achieve competitiveness abroad in the face of European and American firms.

2. The Paris market and the world's bankers: Paris versus London, Berlin, Brussels, and New York?

When the First World War broke out, the Paris banking market was the second strongest in the world, even though German and French banks had been fierce competitors in Russia,[4] in south-eastern Asia, or in the Balkans, and also in South America where the French were far less influential apart from some utilities, business, and financing. The First World War destroyed this position and the Paris banking market found itself obliged to struggle to rebuild some of its influence, what had been called 'petty imperialism' ('*l'impérialisme du pauvre*'[5]) or 'imperialism along the French way' ('*l'impérialisme à la française*'[6]). French banks had lost their key interests in Russia, and their influence in the former Ottoman Empire declined little by little during the 1920s — the Ottoman Bank for instance lost its central banking function and most of its industrial banking activities and became a deposit and retail bank in competition with local institutions. Large cash flow activities had to be stopped as correspondent banking was itself deeply curtailed, with Russia or Istanbul first, of course, but also with several institutions overseas or in Germany for a while. Foreign exchange activities, gains in various fees or interest charges (such as transfer, credit lines, or refinancing), were reduced, which weakened the revenues of the Paris banking market. Finally, it is clear from Jean Bouvier's analysis that the French big banks themselves came out of war much leaner and weaker compared with their pre-war positions — even if historians have still to scrutinize precisely the nature of that weakening. Was it because of inflation eating away the value of deposits, the shortening of deposits in Paris from countries benefiting from French cash flows, such as Russia, Germany, or Austria, or was it due to shrinking returns from investments abroad (South America, Ottoman Empire, or Russia)? Conversely, competition increased on the Paris market itself as foreign banks developed their branches there. The key debate lies therefore with the ability of Paris to gain new competitiveness in the face of competition from London and newly emerging New York, in the face of German aspirations[7] to re-establish bridgeheads all over Central Europe, whereas several negative factors prevented the Paris market from asserting its strength on a number of occasions in the 1920s and the 1930s.

The Paris market between crashes and rationalization

The fate of the Paris banking and financial market became critical first in the 1920s because of the crisis of the franc, but secondly when the 1930s crisis shook the stock exchange and stirred up a systemic crash leading to the collapse or near collapse of several big banks. Thus the fourth deposit bank, Banque Nationale de Crédit, failed in 1931 and had to be rescued by the authorities in order to become Banque Nationale pour le Commerce & l'Industrie in 1932. Similarly, Crédit Industriel & Commercial group gathered the pieces of the failed Bauer-Marchal, Banque privée, Banque d'Alsace-Lorraine, and the Banque de Bourgogne, which were then integrated into its network of provincial banks, which thus became reinforced in 1932–4. Finally, the second-largest French investment bank, Banque de l'Union Parisienne (BUP), was on the verge of collapsing in 1932–4, its creditworthiness having crumbled following major credits to Eastern and Central European banks and companies and to other overseas firms, and had to be salvaged through a common action of the Banque de France and the Paris banks.[8] Although these crises severely weakened the French banking market in the 1930s, this very shock led to improvised reforms, which helped reinforce it in the long term. For the time being, the Paris banking market asserted itself as the sole significant banking market in France; and the centralization of rediscounting, of financial flows, and of all other initiatives was achieved in the 1930s.

In fact, no more room was left to local undertakings — local financial markets never reached a high level of turnover in the face of the Paris Bourse. Even the Crédit Agricole entities and *Banques populaires* had to be centralized in the 1930s as many local institutions faced difficulties and were subjected to controls, refinancing, and managers' selection from the Paris mother companies. In the meantime, of course the strength of Crédit Lyonnais, Société Générale, CNEP, CIC, Crédit Commercial de France (CCF), and Paribas increased from the 1930s. The Crédit Lyonnais benefited from Société Générale's difficulties and in 1929 regained the leading rank it had lost between 1921 and 1928 thanks to pushing the policy of extending its network and activities. In fact, like the City clearing banks, neither Société Générale, Crédit Lyonnais, nor CIC were severely shaken by the banking crisis and did not suffer any runs. Merchant banks still existed, but mainly within 'niches' (private banking, the management of some investments abroad, intimate links with some industrialists, transport firms, or wholesale traders), and even Rothschilds seems to have somehow lost ground to Paribas and the BUP in the inter-war period.

Paradoxically, these events did not persuade the financial authorities to set up legislation or rules that could have fostered any systemic organization — in contrast to the measures put in place in the United States, in Switzerland, or in Belgium. In addition, no state management or equity control was instituted over banks as in Germany or Italy. Liberal moods and ideology still prevailed and prevented bankers, civil servants, and Parliament from condemning the liberal banking economy. The emergence of central banking functions at the Banque de France — through intense rediscounting to crippled banks — and the proof that some sense of common interests could gather bankers into salvaging operations might have appeared sufficient reactions in the face of systemic risks. Another paradox was the fact that in 1941, the Vichy regime established new rules paving the way for a plain systemic organization:[9] the same bankers who were liberal in 1930–40 became supporters of interventionism in 1941–4. In fact, the Vichyist centralized economic organization led to state interventionism everywhere; rationalization prevailed among some of the 'modernists' within the corridors of power, as they wished to build the framework of a renewed French economy — pending the German victory and the emergence of some kind of European market managed by Germany, perhaps after some truce or peace with London. Banque de France became officially the central bank with powers of supervision over the banking sector. These rules were in fact confirmed by the post-war democratic regime: the 1946 law became the basis of French banking right up to the 1980s.

The Paris banking market was to be organized along specialized lines: deposit banks and investment banks (and merchant banks) on one side, with separate functions and legal abilities; and most specialized institutions on the other side, linked to the professions (*banques populaires*, Crédit Agricole), social layers (savings banks), or mid- or long-term credits (Crédit National, Crédit Foncier, joined by consumption and mortgage institutions since the 1950s). All had to provide Banque de France (and the Commission de contrôle des banques) with extensive information about credits, customers, and the respect of rules. The Paris banking market was thus rationalized, well organized, and controlled — all the more so because some deposit banks were nationalized in 1945 (Crédit Lyonnais, Société Générale, CNEP, BNCI). At the same time, Banque de France itself became subordinated to the State, as its governor (a high-level civil servant) now exerted extended authority — at the expense of the merchant bankers and industrialists who had been key leaders within its council (Conseil de Régence) from 1800 up to 1936–45. Specialization was considered as the best way to avoid any drift towards 'mixed banking'. This had been practised in the inter-war period by some banks that had pushed 'industrial banking' too far forward while failing to anticipate the deflationary crisis on inventories financed through mid-term discounts. Banks had to specialize along stricter criteria, which explains the growth of BUP, Paribas, Banque de l'Union Européenne (linked with the Schneider then the Empain group), or even the renewed Rothschilds (of Paris). At the same time, the Paris Stock Exchange stuck to its regulation and specialization structures; some reforms in the 1940s enhanced the role of stockbrokers (*agents de change*); their official monopoly on trading was thus reinforced — although controls against insiders' habits were not yet instituted (until 1967).

At end of the period under review everything seemed indeed clear-cut. A well-balanced banking system had taken shape, and had provided money for economic reconstruction — whereas in fact state money sustained a majority of loans required for the renewal of expansion during 1945–55. However, did the Paris banking market appear at that time ready for a competitive foray within the Common Market? The question came up in 1958 as France entered its last year of full protectionism. In fact, several future high-level managers testified that they regarded the Paris banking market as a conservative one. Risk-taking among deposit banks was limited owing to several factors: first, the division of risks between pure discount banks and mid- or long-term credit banks like Crédit National deprived the former of key skills and prevented them from assuming broader functions in the profession of enterprise banking (*banque d'entreprise*). This very profession was somehow false as risk assessment could be hindered by the almost compulsory constitution of syndicates to bear and share the credits pending to each company, as the company was thus the customer of several banks. The final responsibility for the risk assessment was not clearly defined even if one or two lead managers led the syndicate.

Moreover, deposit bankers left room for new emerging forces. These were bankers specializing in credits to consumers, house purchasers, or property developers. They acquired part of their market indirectly as they brought refinancing to these firms (the group led by Jack Francès:[10] Sofinco, Banque de la Hénin, Cogefimo, Sogénin; the group led by Jacques de Fouchier: Cetelem, Union pour le Crédit au Bâtiment-UCB, UFB for leasing),[11] with a smaller group being led by Lazards. Most deposit banks relied for too many functions on what were called 'établissements de place', that is institutions undertaking certain activities on behalf of the whole community of bankers: the *Banques populaires*, Crédit Agricole, Crédit Foncier, Crédit National, and the Francès and Fouchier groups. This division seemed healthy for the Paris market, but did it not encourage some conservatism among bankers? These questions were raised somewhat later, in the mid-1960s, and led to profound reforms between 1967 and 1984.

The market in search of new deployment abroad in the 1920s

When the First World War ended, it gave way to economic warfare,[12] since the victorious Allies had long intended to challenge German economic power following military and diplomatic victory. Besides the repayment of war debts, a new power struggle followed and the Paris banking market became involved — even if the franc suffered severe crises in the 1920s and capital exports were subjected to case-by-case authorizations between 1918 and 1928. On one side, the Paris market benefited firmly from French imperial expansion: cash transfers, credit flows, direct investment (in the 1930s through the consolidation of bad loans), issues of equity and bonds, and international activities depended too heavily, if not decisively, on overseas activities.

Nearer to home, banks resumed their strategy of spreading their skills abroad. Deposit banks (Crédit Lyonnais and Société Générale especially) refrained from launching new foreign offensives and concentrated their efforts on a very few bank markets and on the City. They gradually dismantled operations conducted before the First World War in South America; the French banking market could not even find ways of salvaging the Banque Française du Brésil, which failed in 1921, confirming the retreat of French interests in South America since the war. However, French investment banks (Mirabaud,[13] BUP, and Paribas — joined exceptionally by the deposit bank CIC for some projects in Poland[14]) showed effectiveness in building networks of business relationships in the 'Successor States' — in the territories of the former Austria-Hungary. Paribas, through a half-bank and half-holding company the Banque des Pays de l'Europe Centrale, became influential in several countries there (Romania[15], Bulgaria, Yugoslavia, etc.). BUP intensified its pre-war links with Banque Commerciale de Roumanie[16] and the Banque d'Athènes[17] and, by itself or in alliance with Société Générale de Belgique, conducted business with banks in Hungary and Croatia.[18] Most transactions were conducted in foreign exchange, in financing commodities and raw material imports from this area or equipment exports to it, and in refinancing friendly banks there through correspondent banking — which provided the Paris bank market with fresh flows of cash and fees.

Business and diplomacy were closely linked when the rebuilding of public finances and economies in Central and Eastern Europe became a challenge for Western countries:[19] the international position of France[20] had been ever a challenge for politicians annoyed by competition from Big Powers, as a heritage from old time 'mercantilism'. American bankers and financiers won several contracts and concessions in this area,[21] and British interests struggled to benefit from the temporary exclusion of German competitors there. A subtle struggle thus led in 1923 to the takeover by Western European committees (based in London and Paris) of Banque Impériale Ottomane, which possessed important interests in Turkey[22] and conducted financial business all over Europe. More clues can be found to underline the resilience of the Paris banking market. It thus secured business and profits when bankers followed industrialists into Central and Eastern Europe.[23] Besides aeroplane construction, agribusiness activities, some railway or harbour concessions, and public works contracts, the main industrialist involved there was Schneiders and its financial arm, Union Européenne Industrielle & Financière.[24] This steel, coal, metallurgy, railway, and electrical equipment group took over or reinforced its control over large companies, especially in Czechoslovakia[25] (Skoda, Banska a Huti) and in Poland. This provided broad flows of cash, of foreign exchange (for instance to finance plants exported by Skoda), and of overdrafts as the Schneider group was in a way already 'globalized' and dispatched orders between its subsidiaries either in France or in Central Europe. The leaders in any banking or financial activities linked with Schneiders' trade in Central and Eastern Europe were Union Européenne Industrielle & Financière, Banque des Pays du Nord, a commercial bank specializing in international financing, which Schneiders had bought in 1929 (it merged with Union Européenne Industrielle & Financière in the 1940s in what finally became Banque de l'Union Européenne, a strong commercial bank specializing in the financing of enterprises), or Banque de l'Union Parisienne, intimately linked with Schneiders in Central and Eastern Europe since before the First World War.

The Compagnie Française du Levant was also set up in 1919 by French industrialists to obtain commercial contracts (mainly for railway equipment) in the eastern Mediterranean and Danubian areas, and the banks helped provide credits and currencies. The common point of all these initiatives in Central and Eastern European business was that it generated further fees, revenues, and business for the Paris banking market. Some banks had significant percentages of their balance sheets earmarked to credits to Eastern and Central Europe. For BUP, such credits reached 10 per cent of its total credit position in 1929. It kept refinancing Banque d'Athènes, Banque Commerciale de Roumanie, or Banque Générale de Crédit Hongrois, for instance. The last of these received permanent credits in the 1920s worth 10m. francs and $500,000. To be efficient, economic warfare required the mobilization of the whole banking community. As early as December 1920, French banks had negotiated a contract with Romania in order to finance imports of cereals — through the discounting of Romanian Treasury bills worth 100m. francs. French economic influence was at the same time strengthened by a vigorous policy of mixing banking, insurance, and knowledge management as foreign trade became more and more a linchpin of economic warfare: the Board of Trade diversified and reinforced its tools to help companies conquer outlets abroad. It developed its branches all over Europe and the world (through advisers picked up among businessmen travelling or living abroad), and intelligence was disseminated within France by the Office National pour le Commerce Extérieur.

In March 1920, Banque Nationale Française du Commerce Extérieur was instituted. This was a bank specializing in the financing of foreign trade, using capital from several banks to build an *établissement de place* (a Paris community institution) combining their forces. Credit insurance took shape: to counter the ECGD or Hermes, the SFAC (Société Française pour Favoriser l'Assurance-Crédit)[26] was launched in 1927. After 1928, the state provided the SFAC with guarantees for credits linked to exports — a key weapon in that economic warfare. Finally, a move was made to develop acceptances to finance foreign trade, which were rarely used in France, in contrast to the United States and the City. Banque de France itself favoured the emergence of Paris as a clearance market for acceptances and undertook in 1928 to accept bills remitted by central banks or Bank of International Settlements. The foundation by the Paris banking community of Banque Française d'Acceptations in December 1929, which could accept bills of exchange and thus allow partial refinancing by Banque de France, gave impetus to this policy. In the meantime, bankers and the Banque de France endeavoured to promote the acceptance market among banks and favoured the creation of Compagnie Parisienne de Réescompte in August 1928 as a broker and trader of acceptances. The acceptances market thus grew from 323m. gold francs in 1927 to 1,073m. in 1928 in the balance sheet of Big Banks. However, the financial crisis of 1929–31 occurred much too early to allow the policy to gather real momentum. It is worth adding that the depreciation of the franc between 1922 and 1926 favoured French companies as they could open new markets owing to that indirect source of competitiveness. France became, for instance, an exporter of steel products, something that also generated revenues and fees for bankers and the Paris banking market.

The Paris market through the international crisis of the 1930s: successes and failures

Paradoxically, the Paris banking market prospered on an international level while other markets were shaken by the outbreak of the crisis and although its banks had already endured a systemic crisis. However, this was only a lull before the storm. Since the 1920s, French interests had encountered intense competition from their British counterparts, especially when the League of Nations godfathered the building of a real finance, banking, and commercial law system in several countries. The fight between the French and British central banks[27] is too well known to be studied here. It is sufficient to say that French interests were deeply involved in Romania, Poland, and Yugoslavia; they managed to issue the big loans that accompanied reconstruction, which was the key challenge through all these struggles. Of course, the recovery of the French franc often helped French interests to overcome their British competitors between 1928 and 1932 — something else that provided the Paris banking market with currency flows, fees, and revenues. France took part in the loan to Bank of Poland to sustain the zloty in June 1927 and floated a block of the international loan issued thereafter.[28] Banque de France was allowed by the Bank of England and the American Federal Reserve Board to put up $2m. to the loan to the Bank of Italy in December 1927, as a signal of its rebirth after the recent crisis in Paris.

The crisis of the pound and various uncertainties about the north-western European markets helped the Paris banking market to strengthen its international position: after being so weak in the mid-1920s it became a refuge for call money and harboured volatile funds during 1931–3. It even succeeded in broadening its gold reserves as Banque de France launched a policy of piling up gold bought in the USA — thus incurring discontent from its central banking colleagues. However, patriotic pride prevailed, particularly in the sense of having erased the dire memories of the 1920s: the Paris banking market was then regarded as a geopolitical challenge by the authorities in search of international recognition. While London and Berlin already suffered from financial and/or monetary difficulties, and New York had to surrender in the face of a weakened dollar, the Paris banking market emerged unchallenged for a while. It showed its (admittedly ephemeral) healthiness through its participation in the rescue of its foreign counterparts. It took part in the rescue of the Credit-Anstalt in May 1931 by lending cash (10m. schillings) to Austrian National Bank through a collective credit handled by the Bank for International Settlements (BIS). Then Banque de France took part in several loans set up by BIS to salvage central banks in Eastern and Central Europe: in Hungary (June–August 1931), Germany (June–July 1931, up to April 1933), Yugoslavia (July and August 1931), Czechoslovakia (October 1931 but unused; then again in February 1932 for a project worth 600m.), Poland (August and October 1931), and was involved in credits to Bank of Spain.

Banque de France and a group of French banks were involved in the agreement reached with Bank of England at the end of July 1931. They each provided half of a short-term loan to Bank of England to enable it to buy sterling worth 2,500m. francs; the operation took place on 13 August, with 2,225m. francs being used on 27 August alone. A second agreement was reached on 27 August, with further credit worth 3,100m. francs (£25m.) in August (in parallel with the same amount provided by the Federal Reserve Board). The French banks retained their involvement worth 1,250m. but Caisse des Dépôts added 500m. and together with Banque de France eased the rediscounting of the banks' share, while British Treasury bills worth 2,500m. francs were sold among investors in France. French banks helped Belgium float a loan worth 800m. francs in Paris in August 1932, then a further 500m. loan (in Treasury bills) in January 1933, consolidated into a 600m. FRF long-term loan in 1934, before a foreign loan of 475m. FRF in the same year. Banque de France and other banks also helped Belgium in March 1935 (through a credit of 2bn francs to Banque Nationale de Belgique).[29] Finally, Banque de France had to rescue the Paris branches of several American banks in March and April 1933 — at the time of the dollar crisis — as they needed cash to resist deposit withdrawals and the lack of liquidity. In 1933, French banks also took part in the international loan to Austria, for a share worth 408m. francs. Then in 1937, Czechoslovakia floated a 698m.-franc loan in France (to repay the 1932 loan). Most of the 1928–34 operations were syndicated with the investment bank Paribas as lead manager, sometimes with BUP influence, and deposit banks provided their brokerage edge to implement the purchase of Treasury bills or the floating of bonds. Once again, more fees, interest returns, and cash flows broadened the scale of the Paris banking and finance market.

Nevertheless, the Paris banking market suffered from international storms. First, its foreign trade suffered from the overvaluation of the franc (about 20 per cent) between 1934 and 1936; then uncertainties surrounded the fate of the franc as the state had to finance rearmament, the Paris banking and stock market crises were deepening, and political and diplomatic life seemed unstable. International investors withdrew call money from Paris even if previously acquired gold piles were kept there. In the meantime, the Paris banking market had to face the common problem raised by frozen assets in Central and Eastern Europe and the Balkans because of the German embargo on transfers or drastic clearing agreements (with standstill agreements) that prevented free transfers of currency. The Paris market thus had to cope with frozen credits for several years, which weakened most of its banks (especially Banque de l'Union Parisienne) but also the stockholders, who could not receive interests or dividends. Most banks had to wait several half-years to recover some of the call money they had invested in Germany — and the Société

Générale group especially suffered a confidence crisis over the matter in 1933–4. Indeed, most markets and institutions faced such problems everywhere, but Paris thus lost the market edge it had held at the beginning of the 1930s. Gold fled from Paris after February 1934 (2,426m. francs between 2 and 16 February alone); the FRB and Bank of England bought francs and changed them into gold, and Banque de France restricted credits to banks that intended to export francs to buy gold abroad or to finance customers doing so.

3. Rebuilding international forces, 1945–1958

Although France was one of the victors in the war, it was considerably weakened because of its lack of currency, and its broad trade deficit due to large imports and to its reduced export capabilities, resulting from fifteen years of industrial under-investment. Moreover, the French franc had lost most of its value following several devaluations between 1945 and 1949 — before an ultimate crisis in 1957–8 and a depreciation by more than a third at that time, before the franc retrieved convertibility on 1 January 1959 (although exchange control rules were still active). The challenge for the Paris banking market was thus to regain some room for manoeuvre, to help businesses regain market shares and thus revenues in foreign currencies.

Foreign and imperial outlets

While French banks extended their involvement in overseas imperial markets, commercial outlets in developed or developing countries became a priority. However, in the 1940s and 1950s, the bankers' mentalities remained conservative: internationalization was thus seen as a mere buttress to French traditional trade abroad. After the Second World War, the Société Générale's branch in Buenos Aires remained an active tool either to finance raw material imports from Argentina (wool) or to promote French exports there; Société Générale thus provided important documentary credits. The Société Générale's New York branch undertook multiple activities: as early as the 1950s, it helped finance contracts (for public works and equipment sales) won by French firms in Latin America. CNEP and Crédit Lyonnais reinforced their Egyptian branches — France being Egypt's second largest importer in the 1950s — but lost them because of Nasser's nationalization in 1956. In 1948, CNEP added to its Indian branch in Bombay a second branch in Calcutta, in order to reinforce its market share in raw material exchanges and to propel French firms onto public works markets. As France was the second largest market for Australian wool exports, and CNEP was the sole bank from continental Europe there, its market share was satisfactory in the 1950s. In the meantime, Crédit Lyonnais had opened branches in Anglo-Egyptian Sudan in 1952 in order to finance exports of cotton and various local products.

In Europe,[30] history had left French banks with a somewhat haphazardly distributed network of branches and subsidiaries. Société Générale had been present in Belgium since the beginning of the century owing to a subsidiary, Société Française de Banque & de Dépôts, and Crédit Lyonnais was also present there. Both banks were there to sustain Franco-Belgian trade flows: textiles, and imports through Antwerp, especially cereal imports, which explained the volumes of credit managed by Société Générale's branch there after 1954. Both banks were present in Switzerland to practise currency exchanges, private banking, and the financing of trade in more and more commodities. BNCI's Swiss subsidiary in Basle favoured that bank's branches in eastern France for their textile links with Swiss firms; and it obtained access to international trade financing after the mid-1950s. Société Générale had been established in Spain since the 1920s through a subsidiary, Société Générale de Banque en Espagne, which in fact was concerned only with the financing of Franco-Spanish trade. This bank gathered its forces as soon as trade between France and Spain was re-established in 1948, after some tensions between both countries. Its specialization in credits to agricultural exports to France left room for an enlargement of its activities to the whole of Spain's relations with France.

Crédit-Lyonnais maintained several branches in Spain, evolving from international trade business to local customers, and a subsidiary[31] in Portugal (since 1893). It developed the financing of Portuguese exports, obtained access to textile firms, and expanded its foreign exchange activities, while gaining local customers. It was one of only three foreign banks active in Portugal (with Lloyds and Banco do Brazil). The Société Générale's subsidiary in Alsace-Lorraine since 1871, Sogenal, had closed its branches in Germany in the 1930s. It returned there as early as 1954 with a branch in Cologne, and was then used as the Société Générale's representative in Germany, while also opening a branch in Luxembourg in 1955. In fact, up to the 1980s, French banks did not try to compete directly with their European colleagues: under some unspoken gentleman's agreement or because of legal obstacles, European banks did not launch offensives throughout Europe — apart from some very specialized business carried out by Geneva, Luxembourg, and London affiliates or branches. Paradoxically, bankers' mentalities did not really evolve after the Second World War, even if they did show initiative and therefore entrepreneurship. Colonial prospects were not in fact their sole prospects. However, their projects might seem rather fragmentary when viewed in retrospect. There was no global strategy and only scattered investments were undertaken, for uncertain reasons. The priority was apparently to profit from specific trade relations with some countries or to reinforce traditional French diplomatic presence in these countries, therefore according to a classical geopolitical strategy — without evoking here the branches established in Saar during the unification between that *Land* and France up to 1955.

This classical strategy explained the involvement of French nationalized banks in some Latin American countries, which French diplomacy or firms traditionally favoured as a way of alleviating British or American commercial domination there.

BNCI thus founded a branch in Montevideo in 1951, merely to take part in Uruguayan wool exports to Europe and France. More important was its launch of a subsidiary in Mexico, Banco del Atlantico, by buying a small Mexican bank in 1949. BNCI used this as a handover instrument to help French companies to be informed about industrial projects and to bid for parts of that market. It was followed by a branch in Bogotá in 1954, soon transformed into a subsidiary, Banco Franco-Colombiano. Central America became a target with a subsidiary in Panama in 1955 (Panama Bank & Trust), supplemented in 1958 by a specialized trade and finance subsidiary, Finexia (Sociedad Financiera de Exportaciones e Importaciones). Crédit Lyonnais became the leading French bank in that area, with several subsidiaries acting as bridgeheads for French exporting or purchasing companies; but they also evolved more and more towards 'domestic banking', as they developed their own local customer base besides the transatlantic customers the Crédit Lyonnais entertained. As early as 1948, Crédit Lyonnais established a new bank in Brazil through the takeover of Banco de Metropole in São Paulo. This Banco Frances & Brasileiro appeared in June 1948 and developed a retail banking network. To the west, in 1952 and with Peruvian partners, Crédit Lyonnais founded Banco de Lima, first in order to finance cotton exports to France. Banco Provincial de Venezuela was created in 1953 in Caracas as a partnership between Crédit Lyonnais and local investors. These daughter banks increasingly became ambassadors overseas as they could collect information useful to French exporters and help them when prospecting outlets. As an example, the Banco de Lima was equipped in 1956 with a commercial subsidiary, Panindustria, as a partner to French prospecting firms. In a parallel way, Société Générale maintained its own path in Latin America with the foundation of subsidiaries in various places, though it is not clear why each bank chose one country rather than another. In 1951, Société Générale created Banco Franco-Cubano, as the first European bank in that country, in order to assist Cuban sugar sales in Morocco and Cuban purchases in France. This small bank was closely linked with the Société Générale's New York branch, but it also began to provide services to French firms coming to Cuba to carry out public works.

These scattered entities could not by themselves provide all the services needed for French renewal after the Second World War. In the 1950s, France was obsessed with the rebuilding of its commercial power as it was confronted with a huge currency gap in its efforts to finance imports in times of reconstruction. The banks thus had to ease the operations of their customers, through exchange and through the classical range of credits — documentary credits, sureties for customs, acceptances, etc. They were trusted by the state authorities as weapons in economic and commercial wars. French banks therefore had to assume a specific mission; that of promoting exports and facilitating imports with lower transfer, credit, and exchange prices. The mid-1950s might appear as a turning point, as banks noticed new export trends: public works contracts abroad, capital goods exports, the beginning of wheat surplus exports, and the emergence of commercial relations with Eastern European countries. When BNCI established its service specializing in financing foreign trade relations in 1953, it felt that the time had come to sustain firms in their move from 'Reconstruction' to international competition. BNCI argued that as 'an imperious necessity, French businessmen ought to acquire that export strategy that they too often miss',[32] particularly as France was moving towards the European Common Market. In 1958, BNCI launched Intercomi (Société pour le Développement International du Commerce et de l'Industrie — Society for the International Development of Trade and Industry) as a tool to negotiate export contracts, and in the same year it opened a representative office in Frankfurt, both symbols of its renewed belligerence. The same year, CNEP established its Compagnie Intercontinentale Commerciale & Financière to finance exports. Bankers had once more become internationally minded, after twenty years of near autarky (1930–50), and renewed their commercial fighting spirit. The French banking system became thus open to international currents, as it had been during the 1900–14 period or in the 1920s.

Some proof of the banks' punch can be seen in the case of the investment bank Paribas in the 1950s. Thanks to far-sighted managers (such as Bernard de Margerie), it launched an early policy of re-internationalization. It set up original schemes of financing exports of plants and capital goods, particularly to South America, such as a steel plant in Colombia in 1948–54, and favoured a relationship with an American businessman, Richard Richards, and French industrialists,[33] for whom it rediscounted at the Crédit National. Huge industrial, engineering, and public works contracts were thus secured.

The emergence of Banque Française du Commerce Extérieur

Economic expansion abroad became a target of the French authorities in order to enlarge currency revenues and reduce dependence on American aid. The state entrusted the function of sustaining foreign trade to a specialized institution, Banque Française du Commerce Extérieur (BFCE, the French Bank for Foreign Trade). As stated previously, the French state had laid down a banking strategy of 'specialization', with specialized institutions covering specific market segments as a way to improve the credit supply and promote modernization. BFCE was thus endowed with the task of sustaining foreign trade. Created on 1 June 1946 whilst taking over Banque Nationale Française du Commerce Extérieur, whose success had been limited, and beginning operations on 1 October 1947, BFCE belonged to the nationalized sector as its capital was owned by the nationalized Banque de France, Caisse des Dépôts, Caisse nationale de Crédit Agricole and the four nationalized commercial banks. The BFCE's mission was to 'ease the financing of export or import operations'. In establishing such a tool, France was following a trend common to the United States (EximBank), Spain, and West Germany. It was the sole institution entitled to receive guarantees from COFACE, the body providing official credit insurance for exports, launched by the state in 1946. COFACE was the equivalent of the German Hermes or the British ECGD, and succeeded SFAC for insurance credit activities abroad. A 1949 law reinforced COFACE's role as the state provided COFACE and banks with guarantees for financing capital goods exports.

BFCE instantly became a key tool for the import trade. It provided numerous surety (*caution*) contracts to importers, especially in favour of customs administration. The basic services were of course documentary credits (*crédits documentaires*). Sureties and documentary credits were used intensively to sustain imports under the Marshall Plan during 1948–52. BFCE was involved deeply in import financing, especially for raw materials — particularly wool, oleaginous products, coffee, tea, cocoa, capital goods for transport and agriculture, cotton, and petroleum products. This remained the key role for BFCE throughout the 1947–58 period and beyond. Its basic task — starting in January 1948 — was to offer endorsements to bank credits, and this activity generated 30 per cent of its balance sheet in 1948. Increasingly, credits were extended to the financing of large capital goods projects, as French engineering and mechanics firms took part in international projects.

In fact, BFCE developed a two-tiered activity. On the first level, it was used as a necessary relay for French banks, which had to admit BFCE as an intermediary to obtain guarantees and refinancing; they prepared the borrowing forms themselves for their own customers and presented them to BFCE, the ultimate institution distributing the specialized credits that commercial banks could not extend themselves. BFCE placed itself as 'an auxiliary to banks as it allowed them to lay out their resources, with larger loan facilities and guarantees, in favour of new credits'.[34] By gathering files prepared by banks, BFCE acquired a rare knowledge of French trade activities abroad; it piled up an excellent stock of economic and financial information about foreign activities — particularly by attending the Commission des Garanties & des Crédits au Commerce Extérieur (Foreign Trade Credits and Guarantees Committee), it obtained an acute perception of risks abroad. BFCE organized with Banque de France the collection of statistical data relevant to the French banks' risks abroad. It thus became the cornerstone of the French banking system for any questions linked with exports and imports; and one of its managers, Jacques Chaîne, asserted himself as the key man between 1947 and 1974. He demonstrated acute skills in assessing new types of credit risks abroad because BFCE had to explore new areas of export loans. It thus rediscounted the bulk of credits for exports. It also delivered its signature to banks that asked for Banque de France's discount on credit for exports benefiting from the state guarantee. This eased the growth of such loans for a two-year term (from 1944 to 1948) and then for terms of up to five years (after 1949). International competitiveness increasingly required the extension of credit deadlines, especially when domestic reconstruction was completed and French firms began to prospect foreign markets at the end of the 1950s. The range of financing products failed to comply with international trade requirements, particularly to overcome strong competition in Latin America, Asia, and the Middle East. A national (even patriotic?) challenge was therefore issued, and BFCE became once more a decisive lever to attain foreign trade objectives.

On the second, parallel, level, BFCE acted as a commercial bank by itself, as a competitor to the commercial banks. It was indeed able to deliver loans for foreign trade operations that exceeded the credit ceilings imposed on commercial banks by the credit authorities, thanks to the resources it had gathered on monetary markets — borrowings at call represented 38.5 per cent of its liabilities in 1949 — or on longer terms (18 per cent of liabilities in 1949), notwithstanding its equity capital. Generally speaking, firms found at BFCE credits supplementing their usual bankers' ones: overdrafts, discounts, etc. BFCE was keen on lending currencies to companies as one of its specialities at a time when exchange controls were predominant because of the defence of the French franc and the currency reserves. Little by little, BFCE became a kind of 'second bank' for importing or exporting companies, this 'second bank' role being played in fact over the 'pools' of banks with which any French company was linked, as commercial banks formed 'pools' in order to divide risks borne on each customer. Shortly after its conception, BFCE asserted its pride: 'BFCE is conscious of having answered to public authorities' demand and having efficiently worked in benefit to national interest'.[35] BFCE soon became a useful tool to develop new types of loans and allow French firms to obtain credits as relevant as their foreign competitors; the economic struggle was once more at stake and BFCE had its place in the French range of trade weapons. 'Our studies, developed with the assistance of ministry departments, the central bank, and Crédit National [the medium-term credit institution] are intended presently to set financing techniques for equipment or material supplies outlets which need more and more, because of international competition, extended payment deadlines, and lower credit costs'.[36]

Of course, at that time French exports were lagging behind German and British ones: in 1957–8, monthly French exports reached an average value of $400–450m. while British and German exports were worth $700–800m. For this reason the Paris banking market could not yet hope to challenge London. However, this also explains how BFCE was seen as a fighting instrument in the hands of the French banking and trade systems, servicing 'our industry' at the apex of bilateral trade and bank relations. It helped in experimenting and developing new types of large and medium-term credits owing to its part in the risk-sharing between banking institutions; it therefore spurred these latter to improve their foreign risks assessment and their foreign trade financing skills. At that moment of French banking history, it expanded banks' competitiveness and expertise. It also expressed some ambiguity, as it assumed monopolistic official activities and commercial banking ones, which began to be questioned by other banks in the 1970s.

The non-internationalization of the stock exchange

Lastly, we might consider that the renewed openness and competitiveness of the French banking market was not yet matched by that of the Paris Stock Exchange. In fact, a huge majority of French assets abroad had been sold in the 1944–6 period in order to gather foreign currencies needed by the French authorities to finance imports. Foreign exchange controls, the nationalization of many energy, insurance, and bank companies, and political events could also have limited the lure of the French stock exchange for foreign investors: less than 1 per cent of equity capital there in the 1950s was from foreign investments. The financial market could have suffered too from stabilization, as the state obliged the potential institutional investors — which were insurance companies — to subscribe to several public bonds in order to avoid risks; and their other long-term investments were often earmarked to real-estate projects. In the meantime, habits and legal rules limited the emergence of open mutual or investment funds until the mid-1960s; the French Social Security had favoured since the 1930s some forms of financial redistribution instead of capitalization systems; some rules still favoured the complementary financing of retirement through individual or company contributions; all these reasons might explain why a market of institutional investors could not really emerge in Paris in the 1950s, either orientated towards investments abroad or luring foreign investors. Finally, very few bankers or financiers maintained at that time genuine relations with overseas financial markets, either in London or in New York. Relationship banking with merchant or investment banks had crumbled in the 1930s and 1940s (sometimes in continental Europe because of Nazi Aryanization policies). The weakness of French interests at that time had prevented the Paris finance market from keeping contact with the rapidly evolving structures of the London and New York markets (with new houses, like Warburgs). Very few banks remained involved in transatlantic activities, like CNEP (thanks to the French American Banking Corporation, a subsidiary launched in the 1920s), Lazards of course and Schlumbergers, a merchant bank created in 1919 in order to establish contact in New York.

Some attempts took shape in the 1950s to promote 'closed' investment funds — reserved to a very few large investors — linked to some institutional investors. Compagnie du Canal de Suez, either before or after the nationalization of the canal in 1956, invested some of its reserves either in international funds orientated towards Switzerland or North America (through the investment fund PanHolding) or in a French investment fund, Société Nationale d'Investissement,[37] which had held massive assets since the end of the 1940s. This was a kind of laboratory for financiers and bankers to test collective asset management, which provided some skills that could to be mobilized rapidly in the mid-1960s as soon as mutual funds were set up.

Conclusion

The internationalization of the Paris banking and financial market did not take a regular course between 1914 and 1958: instability prevailed because of wars, several crises of the franc, crises of distrust and runs, the loss of assets abroad in the aftermath of both wars — even before the first anti-imperialist contests in the 1950s (China, Egypt, north Indo-China). In addition, Paris had no way of challenging the dominance of the City over the world's banking and finance —

even if it struggled to be a brilliant second and even a challenger between 1927 and 1934 in Central and Eastern Europe, before the crisis of the franc stopped the momentum and German then Soviet progress led to a drastic shrinking of assets there. We might assert, however, that the internationalization of the Paris banking and finance market had not been a dream. First, in spite of foreign exchange limits and controls for a while, broad foreign exchange activities were carried out by French bankers, either from Paris or from their London subsidiary or branch; they were deeply involved in these international flows of cash, remittances, and clearing, and they shared these high-level skills with their British competitors. Second, owing to industrialists' undertakings in Central and Eastern Europe, overseas, and here and there in Western Europe, or owing to direct foreign investment from banks themselves (in the same areas of Central and Eastern Europe or in Asia through Banque de l'Indochine or else, especially, through networks in imperial France), the Paris market could be the hub for international large-scale refinancing of banks or companies: huge flows of cash and credits were therefore at stake, hundred of millions each year — and most of these credits were at a standstill in the 1931–7 period and sometimes for longer (up to the German international agreement of 1952 for instance). Third, in spite of the collapse of Russian and Ottoman business, French bankers were somehow involved in international finance flows, either to finance some direct investments from companies abroad or to take part in the issuing of important loans in the 1920s and 1930s to new or reborn countries in Central and Eastern Europe: the resilience of the Paris finance market could be seen as a surprise in those very years, besides the floating of oil securities for large sums to the profit of the (Franco-Belgian) Petrofina or the Compagnie française des pétroles groups. Fourth, owing to direct investment in subsidiaries overseas, in imperial France (with a fresh impulse in Black Africa since the 1940s), then in South America, in Central and Eastern Europe in the inter-war period, French bankers could handle decisive transfers of skills abroad, as they had done in favour of Russia before the First World War: three times they proved (in the 1920s in North Africa, Indo-China, and Central and Eastern Europe; in the 1940s in Black Africa; and in the 1940s and 1950s in South America) their resilience, thus also taking part in the permanent capitalist struggle for market shares, the balance of power, and profits.

Notes

1. Cf. Raymond Philippe (a Lazards chief executive manager), *Le Drame financier de 1924–1928* (Paris, 1931).
2. Cf. Gérard Bossuat, 'La Contre-valeur de l'aide américaine à la France et à ses territoires d'outre-mer: la mesure des rapports franco-américains: la mesure des rapports franco-américains', in *Le Plan Marshall et le relèvement économique de l'Europe* (Paris, 1993), 177–200.
3. Cf. Patrice Baubeau, Arnaud Lavit d'Hautefort, and Michel Lescure, *Le Crédit National. Histoire publique d'une société privée, 1919–1994* (Paris, 1994).

4. Cf. H. Bonin, *La Société Générale en Russie* (Paris, 1994) (published in French and Russian).
5. G. H. Soutou, 'L'Impérialisme du pauvre: la politique économique du gouvernement français en Europe centrale & orientale de 1918 à 1929', *Relations internationales*, 7 (1976).
6. Jean Bouvier, René Girault, and Jacques Thobie, *L'Impérialisme à la française, 1914–1960* (Paris, 1986).
7. Cf. Henri Hauser, *Les Méthodes allemandes d'expansion économique* (Paris, 1916).
8. Cf. H. Bonin, *La Banque de l'Union Parisienne. Histoire de la seconde banque d'affaires française (1874/1904–1974)* (Paris, 2001).
9. Cf. Claire Andrieu, *La Banque sous l'Occupation. Paradoxes de l'histoire d'une profession, 1936–1946* (Paris, 1990).
10. About the story of J. Francès's group, cf. H. Bonin, *Suez. Du canal à la finance (1858–1987)* (Paris, 1987).
11. Cf. Jacques de Fouchier, *La Banque et la vie*, (Paris, 1989). *De la 4CV à la video. 1953–1983, ces trente années qui ont changé notre vie* (Paris, 1983).
12. This was the legacy of pre-war habits; cf. René Girault, 'Diplomatie et banque pendant l'entre-deux-guerres', *Relations internationales*, 21 (1980), 7–21.
13. Cf. Alain Plessis, 'Une maison de la haute banque parisienne: les Mirabaud et le financement des entreprises de la fin du XIXe siècle à la Seconde Guerre mondiale', in Philippe Marguerat, Laurent Tissot, and Yves Froidevaux (eds.), *Banques et entreprises industrielles en Europe de l'Ouest, XIXe–XXe siècles* (Geneva, 2000), 239–50.
14. CIC godfathered Banque de Silésie (Slaski) created in Katowice in 1922 with Union des Mines and Sogenal. Cf. G. Soutou, 'La Politique économique de la France en Pologne (1920–1924)', *Revue historique*, 509 (Jan. 1974).
15. Philippe Marguerat, *Banque et investissement industriel. Paribas, le pétrole roumain et la politique française, 1919–1939* (Geneva, 1987).
16. Cf. H. Bonin, 'La Banque de l'Union Parisienne en Roumanie (1919–1935). Influence bancaire ou impérialisme du pauvre?', *Revue historique*, 2 (1985).
17. Cf. H. Bonin, 'La Banque d'Athènes, point de jonction entre deux outre-mers bancaires (1904–1953)', *Outre-Mers. Revue française* (2001).
18. Cf. Eric Bussière, 'The Interests of the B.U.P. in Czechoslovakia, Hungary and the Balkans, 1919–1939', in *International Business & Central Europe, 1919–1939* (Leicester, 1983).
19. Cf. Georges-Henri Soutou, *L'Or et le sang. Les Buts de guerre économiques de la Première Guerre Mondiale* (Paris, 1989).
20. Cf. Maurice Lévy-Leboyer (ed.), *La Position internationale de la France. Aspects économiques et financiers, XIXe–XXe siècles (Paris, 1977).*
21. H. Feis, *The Diplomacy of the Dollar: First Era, 1919–1932* (Baltimore, 1950).
22. Cf. André Autheman, *La Banque Impériale Ottomane, 1863–1924* (Paris, 1996); Jacques Thobie, 'Les Choix financiers de l'Ottomane en Méditerranée orientale de 1856 à 1939', in *Banques et investissements en Méditerranée à l'époque contemporaine* (Marseille, 1985), 57–84.
23. Cf. H. Kernbauer and F Weber, 'Multinational Banking in the Danube Basin', in A Teichova, M. Lévy-Leboyer, and H. Nussbauer (eds.), *Multinational Enterprise in Historical Perspective* (Cambridge, 1986).
24. Cf. Claude Beaud, 'Une multinationale française au lendemain de la Première Guerre mondiale: Schneider & l'Union Européenne Industrielle & Financière', *Histoire, économie, société* (1983), 625–46.

25. Cf. Alice Teichova, 'Les investissements directs français en Tchécoslovaquie entre les deux guerres', in: Lévy-Leboyer (ed.), *La Position*.
26. Cf. Philippe Chalmin, *De la SFAC à Euler, 1927–1997* (Paris, 1997). H. Bonin, 'Aux origines de l'assurance-crédit en France (1927–1939). La création et l'essor de la SFAC et le repli de ses concurrentes', *Histoire, économie et société*, 3rd ser. 3 (2002), 341–56.
27. Cf. Philip Cottrell, 'The Bank of England in its International Setting, 1918–1972', in Richard Roberts and David Kynaston (eds.), *The Bank of England: Money, Power & Influence, 1694–1994* (Oxford, 1994). A. Orde, *British Policy and European Reconstruction after the First World War* (Cambridge, 1990). Cécile Vrain, 'La Reconstruction financière de la Hongrie et l'intervention ou la non-intervention des anciens alliés', in E. Bussière, M. Dumoulin, and A. Teichova (eds.), *L'Europe centrale & orientale en recherche d'intégration économique (1900–1950)* (Louvain-la-Neuve, 1998), pp. 129–42. Nicole Piétri, *La Reconstruction financière de l'Autriche* (Geneva, 1970). A. Teichova, 'Versailles and the Expansion of the Bank of England into Central Europe', in H. Matis (ed.), *The Economic Development of Austria since 1870* (London, 1994), 366–87.
28. Cf. I. Pietrzak-Pawlowska, 'Les Investissements français en Pologne', in Lévy-Leboyer (ed.), *La Position*.
29. Herman Van der Wee and K. Tavernier, *La Banque nationale de Belgique et l'histoire monétaire entre les deux guerres mondiales* (Brussels, 1975), 277–8.
30. Cf. H. Bonin, 'L'Intégration européenne des banques françaises (1796–1996)', *Bankhistorisches Archiv. Zeitschrift zur Bankgeschichte*, 2 (1996), 59–85.
31. Cf. *Le Crédit Lyonnais au Portugal, 1893–1993* (Paris, 1993).
32. BNCI annual report, 1957.
33. Cf. Eric Bussière, *Paribas, l'Europe et le monde, 1872–1992* (Antwerp, 1992). E. Bussière, 'Paribas et les entreprises industrielles des années 1900 aux années 1960', in Marguerat, Tissot, and Froidevaux (eds.), *Banques et entreprises industrielles*, 223–37.
34. BFCE annual report, 1948.
35. Ibid. 1949.
36. Ibid.
37. See Bonin, *Suez*.

PART IV

The Road to Globalization, 1958–1980

10

Crisis and Opportunity: The Policy Environment of International Banking in the City of London, 1958–1980

Catherine Schenk

> The Empire may have disintegrated and the UK may now be a third-rate military power, but the City of London has staged a come-back which would be the envy of any child movie star reaching maturity.
>
> (I. O. Scott quoted by R. J. Clark of Natwest in 1970)[1]

The period 1958–80 falls neatly into two halves: the Bretton Woods era of 1958–71, and the floating exchange rate regime of the 1970s. The years 1958–71 are sometimes characterized as the Long Boom during which OECD countries' GNP grew at an average of 5.4 per cent p.a. While a prosperous time for producers and consumers, this was an even more dynamic growth period for international finance. Nominal net international bank credits by reporting BIS countries increased 33.6 per cent p.a. compound rate compared to 9.6 per cent for GDP and 12 per cent for trade 1964–72.[2] The value of transactions in the Eurodollar market experienced a meteoric rise while the international monetary system crumbled. Fig. 10.1 shows that the growth rate of assets and liabilities in the Eurocurrency market peaked in 1968/9. Even the surge related to the 1973/4 oil surpluses did not cause such a relative increase.

The 1970s, in contrast, witnessed the advent of 'stagflation' with low growth rates and high inflation, but the financial system thrived on the growth of international liquidity and the renewal of capital account liberalization after 1974. Floating exchange rates and the OPEC oil crisis transformed the international financial scene. Even before the oil crisis of 1973/4, domestic recession in the UK and other industrialized countries encouraged bankers to look abroad, especially to oil-importing LDCs. From the second half of 1971 until 1974, the net foreign assets of private banking systems of the industrialized countries exceeded those of their monetary authorities. The bank crises of 1974 and the reduction in OPEC surpluses led to a contraction in the market, and from the beginning of 1976 monetary authorities' assets once again exceeded those of their banking systems.[3] The growth of net international bank lending and bond issues 1971–9 is shown in Fig. 10.2.[4]

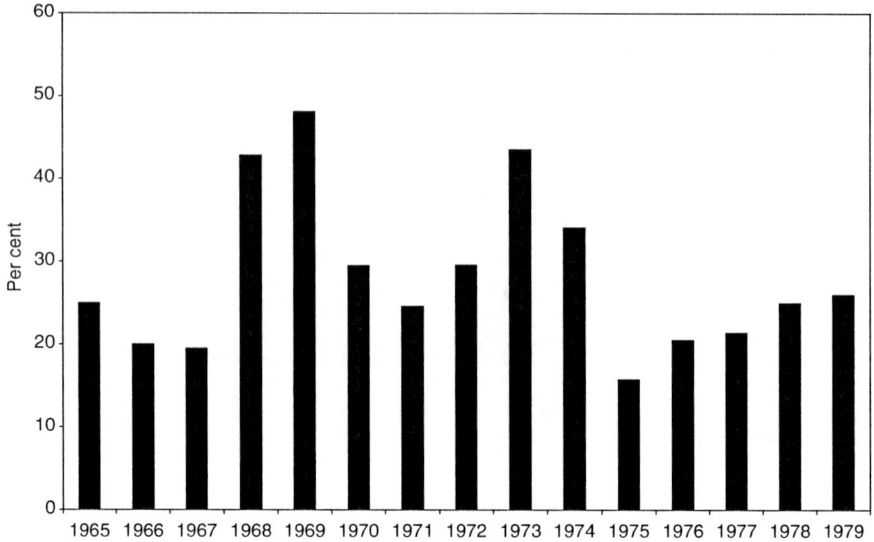

Fig. 10.1. Annual growth rate of Eurocurrency market (net of interbank holdings)
Source: R. C. Williams, *International Capital Markets: Recent Developments and Short Term Prospects* (Washington, 1980).

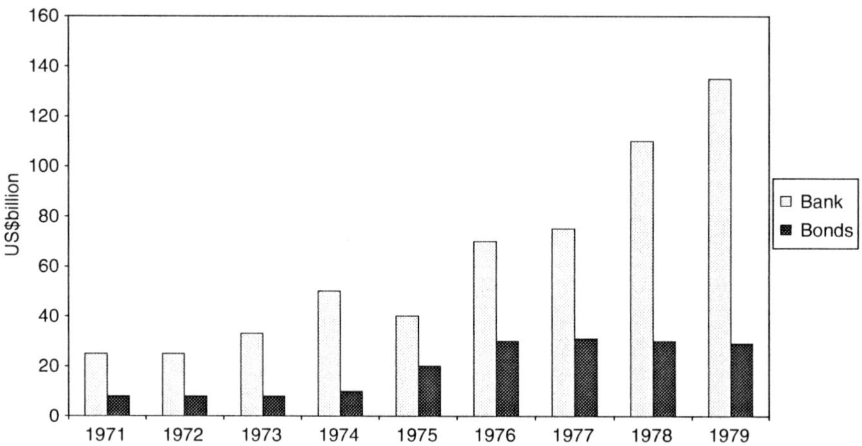

Fig. 10.2. Net new international lending, 1971–1979
Source: Williams, *International Capital Markets*.

The City of London was the main beneficiary of these developments. The increasing complexity of international financial transactions generated greater demand for the services of experts in the City; knowledge of international opportunities and dangers, of loopholes and profitable evasion of controls, and the ability to arrange internationally syndicated loans. The controls imposed on capital markets to prop up the US balance of payments in the second half of the 1960s further enhanced the attractions of London against its main rival, New York, until the mid-1970s when President Nixon began to support the development of New York as an international financial centre. On the other side of the Atlantic, European governments hampered potential rivals to London such as Paris, Zurich, and Frankfurt through their policies to discourage international capital flows in and out of their markets.

Foreign banks rushed into London to take advantage of the regulatory regime and the economies of scale and scope offered in the City.[5] From 1962 to 1970 the number of foreign bank branches or subsidiaries increased from 51 to 129, and then to 214 by 1979.[6] Branches in London also became the leaders of offices operating elsewhere in Europe. At the end of the 1960s, for example, the London branch manager of Chase Manhattan arranged with head office in New York each morning to set amounts to be raised and rates to be offered in the Eurodollar market. These instructions were then passed along to Paris and Frankfurt.[7]

The surge in London banks' foreign assets in the second half of the 1960s reflects this relative increase in activity. Britain's share of world banks' foreign assets peaked in 1969 at 26 per cent of the global total, while the share of the USA fell from 21 per cent to less than 10 per cent from 1966–9 under the pressure of capital restrictions. However, in the 1970s London's relative position declined due to the proliferation of international financial centres in response to the liberalization of capital controls (especially in the USA after 1974) and innovations in products and communications. In 1970 London ranked first in the world in terms of head offices and host to branches, subsidiaries, and representative offices of the world's major banks, but had fallen to third place by 1980 behind New York and Tokyo.[8] Nevertheless, foreign assets as a share of total assets of banks in the UK leapt from 46 to 68 per cent between 1970 and 1981.[9] Among industrialized countries, only Luxembourg banks had a greater share of foreign assets.

The analysis that follows focuses on particular policy responses to the instability of the international monetary system in these decades and how these policies affected the City. First, the collapse of the international monetary system through the 1960s and then the increased risk of the financial market in the 1970s accelerated the pace of financial innovation. Second, as currency speculation grew, policymakers were reluctant to relax controls on the flow of capital, and this had important implications for London's competitiveness. Third, the debate between the state, academics, and bankers over the desirability of floating exchange rates is surveyed. Finally, the era of floating exchange rates and inflation prompted an international and domestic banking crisis in 1974 that drew the Bank of England into more active attempts at prudential supervision.

1. Financial Innovation: Product and Process

The growth of the Eurodollar/Eurocurrency market was the major feature of this period, and London (as the market's main hub) was the primary beneficiary. More than any other, it was this phenomenon that was responsible for the resurgence of the City's importance after the moribund years of the 1940s and 1950s. The market was mainly an interbank market. Initial deposits also came from multinational companies and central monetary authorities—especially of those surplus countries who accumulated reserves as part of their efforts to maintain their fixed exchange rates to the struggling US dollar. The BIS (the market's watchdog) also made large deposits, with the permission of the British Treasury and Bank of England. By the end of 1967 official Eurodollar deposits amounted to $2.2bn.

The growth of the Eurodollar market astounded central bankers everywhere, prompting concerns that it was inflationary and beyond regulatory control. In June 1971 the G10 agreed to stop depositing reserves on the market to avoid swelling it with balances that they believed fed inflation and currency speculation and ultimately ended up back in foreign exchange reserves.[10] This did not, of course, apply to the OPEC countries that were soon to flood the international capital markets with their surpluses. In 1974 the Committee of Twenty of the IMF also proposed limiting state use of the Eurocurrency markets, but the proposal was never formally adopted.[11] The competitive returns in the form of liquidity and high interest rates were too tempting.

On the demand side, the international financial market became the main source of international liquidity for many countries that 'privatized' their balance of payments financing, relying on international capital markets rather than state-negotiated swap agreements. In the early 1960s the USA was particularly keen on using the private capital market to finance international payments imbalances, and it made several proposals to float US government debt in European financial centres.[12] These followed from the US position developed in the early 1960s that there was no need for fundamental reform of the international monetary system. Instead, they hoped to extend the practice of bilateral short-term swaps developed in the 1960/1 crisis, and perhaps include longer-term official bond financing.[13] The British were not enthusiastic because it seemed too ad hoc, especially given the strategic conflict among the G10 at the time, and they sought a more formal and permanent solution to payments imbalances. Furthermore, European capital markets were not considered deep or liquid enough to provide such support. This changed by the 1970s with the expansion of the Eurobond market.

The Eurobond market emerged gradually during 1963. At the end of 1962 the UK Treasury was working with British investment banks to arrange a substantial US dollar loan launched in May for the Belgian state.[14] The July 1963 Autostrade issue for $15m. is generally held to be the first fully fledged Eurobond issue.[15] The market was at first used mainly by state borrowers and European state-owned enterprises. Public sector borrowers raised $44.4bn. on the Eurobond market between 1963 and 1980. In April 1974, for example, the UK government borrowed

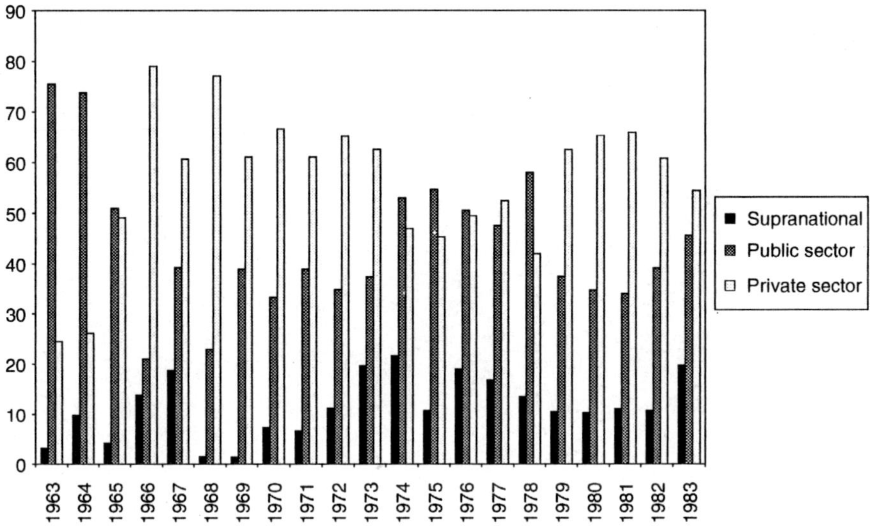

Fig. 10.3. Share of total Eurobond issues by type of borrower (% of total)
Source: I. M. Kerr, *A History of the Eurobond Market: The First 21 Years* (London, 1984).

$2.5bn. from a banking syndicate that included the Chase Manhattan Bank.[16] The move from relying on a pool of foreign exchange reserves to relying on the capacity to borrow in the private capital market marked the beginning of national liability management rather than asset management; an innovation mirroring developments in the domestic banking sector. Fig. 10.3 shows the distribution of public and private issues of Eurobonds.

The Eurodollar market came to maturity with the increased demands arising from the spread of multinational corporations throughout Europe and from the oil crisis of 1973/4. The market was a vital element in the recycling of the OPEC surpluses, and the international banking system at first was widely applauded for accomplishing this in the mid-1970s. In 1974, $23bn. or 40 per cent of OPEC surpluses were deposited in the Eurodollar market, compared with $11bn. invested directly in the USA and $7bn. in the UK. Lending to LDCs, however, began before the oil crisis. In the twelve months after October 1971, lending to developing countries through the Eurodollar market in London increased by £2.5bn., most at long term.[17] These were the seeds of the Latin American debt crisis that was to dominate financial markets through the 1980s.

Although the Eurodollar and Eurobond markets were the most famous innovations of these decades, there were many other new products developed in this period.[18] The dramatic growth of the interbank money market as the major source of bank funds, increased syndicated lending, and new products such as certificates of deposit all helped to transform banking practice. In May 1966 the London branch of the First National City Bank issued the first negotiable $US-denominated certificate of deposit outside the USA. Until 1968, withholding tax was charged on CDs with a maturity over one year, but after this was removed, the CD market flourished as part of the London Eurodollar market. By the end of March 1968, eleven US banks, and fifteen other banks, had issued CDs and a secondary market had developed.[19] By 1981 the value of foreign-currency CDs issued by banks in London exceeded US$75bn.[20] So-called 'roll-over' lending at medium or long term with adjustable interest rates also increased from the late 1960s to amount to perhaps one-third of net international bank claims.[21] Roberts credits the Floating Rate Note, first used in May 1970, as the precursor to the securitization boom of the 1980s and 1990s.[22] Most innovations were in response to an increased demand for products that would spread exchange rate and interest rate risk in these particularly volatile decades as the international monetary system collapsed through the late 1960s, ushering in the inflation and exchange rate volatility of the 1970s.

As well as the new products available, there was considerable innovation in process, mainly to spread risk and capture economies of scale. These included loan syndication, banking groups, and consortia. Between 1964 and 1971, seventeen consortium banks were formed from 110 partner institutions, of fourteen nationalities. A further fifteen consortia were formed by the end of the 1970s. The first consortium bank, Midland and International Bank Ltd., was formed in 1964 by Midland, Toronto Dominion, Standard Bank, and Commercial Bank of Australia. By 1971, three of the seventeen consortium banks were located in Paris, one in Brussels, and the rest in London.[23] By 1979 there were thirty consortium banks based in London.

European banks also tried to promote international cooperation through less formal and binding banking groups or clubs to facilitate syndicated lending. These included EBIC, ABECOR, Europartners, Inter-Alpha, and Unico formed in the 1960s and 1970s.[24] In the early 1960s European banks and finance houses also cooperated in the operation of unit trusts dealing in EEC shares. In June 1962 the most prominent was Eurosyndicat which sponsored two unit trusts, the larger of which, Eurunion, totalled £16m., of which British residents held about 25 per cent.[25] Finally, national distinctions were overcome by the merger activity that characterized the banking structure in Europe in the 1960s. In 1966 US national banks were permitted to invest directly in the stock of foreign banks and by 1971 US banks had bought minority interests in nine British banks.[26]

In the late 1960s European banks began to feel the pressure of competition from large American banks that had access to sophisticated intrabank international communication systems. This prompted efforts to develop formal European information and settlement networks specifically for banking transactions. At this point 80 per cent of international transactions still took place by mail and only 20 per cent by telex.[27] However, the volume of traffic likely to be generated among European banks alone was deemed insufficient, and so North American banks were drawn in to the negotiations. In 1973 SWIFT was launched with 239 member banks from fifteen countries, headquartered in Brussels, with operating hubs in Belgium, the

Netherlands, and later in the USA (1979). It was slow to develop, due partly to heavy line charges by providers who did not want to lose their valuable telex business, and to the need to negotiate terms and common standards, liability, and language.[28] SWIFT finally became operational in 1977, with 518 banks from seventeen countries. By 1979 it was carrying 150,000 messages per day (34.5m. for the year as a whole).[29] West Germany and Italy each had about 20 per cent of the member banks, and Austrian banks were the most intensive users (60 per cent of their international transactions were sent via SWIFT). Only twenty-eight British banks were members of SWIFT by 1980.[30]

Another process innovation was Euro-clear, which was set up by Morgan Guarantee Trust Company at the end of 1968 with initially fifty participants to provide a clearing system for the secondary Eurobond market. It was subsequently turned into a separate company with shares held by 118 banks at the end of 1972, again located in Brussels and not in London.[31] Other banks grouped together to create a rival computerized clearing system, CEDEL, which was established in 1970 by sixty-six banks from eleven countries with its head office in Luxembourg. Examples of initiatives from outside the banking sector were Reuters Stockmaster (1964) and foreign exchange market Monitor (1973) in London, and Telerate in the USA. These systems reduced the cost of information gathering while retaining a near monopoly on this information for banks until the 1980s, increasing the efficiency and profits through capturing economies of scale and reducing transactions costs.

While most of these innovations were responses to the increased risk and scale of international financial activity, they were also affected by continued and sometimes intensified capital controls in the 1960s and early 1970s. This is the subject of the next section.

2. Capital Controls

Through the post-war period a general move towards freer markets prevailed in international trade, but the enthusiasm for freer capital controls was constrained by the balance of payments problems associated with the crumbling of the fixed exchange rate system through the 1960s. The imbalance in the international economy between surplus and deficit countries under the fixed exchange rate regime led to sharp increases in short-term capital flows between developed countries in response to changes in short-term interest rate differentials and expectations of changes in exchange rates. This in turn discouraged further liberalization of capital controls—in the USA and the UK to prevent outflows and in Germany and Switzerland to prevent inflows.[32] The convertibility achieved in Europe at the end of 1958 was external current account convertibility only. Capital account transactions remained closely controlled for a further 15–20 years in most countries.

Towards the end of 1963 prominent defaults on Eurodollar loans in Germany and Switzerland led some in the Bank of England to become very nervous about the potential volatility of the Eurodollar market, prompting a discussion about whether to impose controls to close the market or at least control its growth. The increasing volume of short-term interbank flows seemed to echo the financial crisis of the 1930s,[33] although others believed that the bank losses had been an effective warning for the market and that the banks would rein in the market on their own.[34] The major obstacle, however, was that imposing new controls on inflows would erode the status of London as an international financial centre. As a report by the Bank of England stated in 1963, 'however much we dislike hot money we cannot be international bankers and refuse to accept money. We cannot have an international currency and deny its use internationally.'[35]

Although inflows of short-term capital were left relatively uncontrolled, capital outflows were tightly regulated. Indeed, after current account convertibility at the end of 1958, controls on capital became a greater priority for the British Treasury as a tool to protect sterling from speculative attack and to support the balance of payments. This dichotomy of policy between inflows and outflows reflected a deeper division between controls on sterling and controls on non-resident business in foreign currencies.The latter were left almost completely unregulated and it was this that was the source of London's competitive advantage as an international financial centre in these decades. Controls on sterling, however, remained attractive for the Treasury and successive Chancellors of the Exchequer sought to enhance them, resisting pressure from the Bank of England that sought to free up the commercial and financial uses of sterling.

There were repeated efforts especially among ministers and also some officials within the Treasury to reintroduce capital controls, although the Bank of England usually thwarted these (with some Treasury allies). The main difficulty was that no effective means could be found to stem short-term capital outflows or leaks in existing controls without imposing draconian measures that would threaten sterling area relations, confidence in sterling, or the prospects of the City of London as an international financial centre. Two of the main leaks in the existing system were through the free exchange market in Kuwait and through the emerging international financial centre in Hong Kong, which had a special position as a colony and as part of the sterling area, but also operated freely floating foreign exchange markets.[36]

The main instrument of control on international portfolio investment was through controls on purchase of foreign assets by UK residents and liquidation of sterling assets by foreigners. The only sources of funds for overseas portfolio investment were through the security sterling market, which traded in the proceeds of repatriated foreign investments. In this way it was hoped to create a static pool of funds available for overseas portfolio investment. Due to the demand for such investment, security sterling usually traded at a discount on the official rate.

From 1963 the Bank of England lobbied for the elimination of security sterling since it served little effective purpose due to leaks in the system but was a symbol of capital controls that brought sterling into disrepute.[37] At the beginning of 1965 Callaghan, then Chancellor of the Exchequer, began a general review of ways to tighten exchange controls. In mid-January he told the Prime Minister of his intention to collect a package of measures to tighten up the supply of sterling to the switch market.[38] But the Chancellor did not want to rush new controls while sterling was weak for fear of further disrupting international confidence. Also, from the mid-1960s demand for 'switch' sterling from the Bank of China through the Hong Kong and Shanghai Bank kept the security sterling rate close to the official rate, which made it seem less of a signal of sterling's weakness. By 1966, however, Treasury officials agreed with the Bank that the market should be eliminated, but found it difficult to convince the Chancellor (and his adviser Thomas Balogh), who were reluctant to relax controls when sterling was under pressure. Callaghan was finally convinced by another inquiry in February 1967 and security sterling was finally eliminated in the budget of April 1967. This was the only relaxation of capital controls in the budget.

Despite the limited progress until the mid-1970s, the theoretical case for liberalization seemed clear and required lip service at least to be paid to the process. The gap between theory and practice, however, merely widened. In 1961 the OECD adopted the Capital Movements Code. This was revised and broadened in 1964 but excluded most short-term operations except for commercial purposes (i.e. related to international trade). Also, not all restrictions were included in the Code: for example, taxes on transactions and payments, two-tiered exchange rate systems, and currency deposit requirements were all excluded.[39]

Capital account liberalization was also part of the EEC arrangements to reduce barriers between members. In 1959 Robert Marjolin, through the European Commission, proposed a fast track towards capital liberalization as part of the creation of the Common Market, but only Germany was enthusiastic. The other members of the EEC were more cautious, mainly because of their fears of destabilizing short-term capital flows, but also because of the desire to retain monetary policy sovereignty.[40] This caution was reflected in the limited range of relaxation included in the First Directive on capital controls in 1960. Only capital flows linked to trade within the EEC, direct investment, and investments in listed shares were liberalized. In December 1962, the European Council adopted a weak Second Directive on capital controls. Bakker describes how this document was of little substance, but was promoted in order to sustain some semblance of momentum over liberalization.[41] The enthusiasm of European governments for greater liberalization was extinguished by the currency pressures of 1960/1 that had prompted the reintroduction of capital controls in Germany. A proposed Third Directive foundered on the increasing caution of the European partners and the disintegration of the international monetary system.

The USA also constrained the outflow of capital until 1974 through the Interest Equalization Tax of 1963 and subsequent constraints on foreign investment to protect the balance of payments. US policy particularly targeted the Eurodollar market in September 1969 by introducing a 10 per cent reserve requirement on liabilities to foreign branches of US banks in excess of the average amounts outstanding in May 1969. France, Germany, and Switzerland also prevented the development of Eurodollar markets through a combination of taxes on withdrawals of overseas deposits, prohibition of interest on such deposits, and gentleman's agreements not to accept Eurodollar deposits. This greatly enhanced the attractions of London.

In the 1970s, inflation and slow growth increased the protectionist tendencies of many governments, and restrictions on capital account transactions did not begin to relax on a global basis until 1975. When the crises of 1970–3 hit the currency markets, the pretence of coordinated liberalization in Europe was abandoned as members raised their exchange controls unilaterally. In June 1971 the European Commission advised members to use capital controls to protect against exchange rate speculation, particularly through the Eurocurrency market. Germany, France, Belgium, Luxembourg, and the Netherlands all introduced a combination of reserve requirements on Eurodollar deposits and prohibition of interest on short-term foreign deposits.[42] Germany dismantled these controls in 1974. France also introduced controls, first on inflows (including 100 per cent reserve requirements on new non-resident franc deposits) and then on outflows from 1974, which were retained throughout the rest of the decade. The USA led the way with the liberalization of capital outflows in 1974 as part of Nixon's effort to rehabilitate New York as an international financial centre.

In this turbulent period the UK finally joined the EEC, and it was agreed that capital account liberalization could be postponed until 1975. When the time came, however, Britain was facing a balance of payments crisis and requested a further delay, initially granted for one year but then extended after the sterling crisis of November 1976. It took Margaret Thatcher's Conservative government to break the protective crisis measures of the Labour governments. All exchange controls were finally abolished in October 1979.[43]

In summary, during the 1960s and 1970s European countries maintained tight controls on capital flows, especially short-term financial flows. The UK tried, but was unable to further restrict short-term outflows to any great extent, and considered but abandoned plans to monitor inflows. The reason for the UK position was the commitment to sustaining London as an international financial centre, and to avoid changes in policy that might affect confidence in sterling.

3. Floating Exchange Rates; Academics vs. Bankers vs. Policy-Makers

As early as 1953 Milton Friedman began to advocate floating exchange rates[44] and his position gradually attracted more followers among the academic community.[45] In 1963 the Brookings Institute published an influential report recommending fluctuating exchange rates along with increased liquidity as a solution to the problems of the international monetary system.[46] Within policy-making circles and among international bankers, however, the sea change was much slower.

Bankers are generally a cautious lot, and they feared the destabilizing impact of more flexible exchange rates. In March 1969 members of the Treasury and Bank of

England met with various bankers in New York who argued vigorously against greater flexibility of exchange rates and stressed the dangers of discussing the issue publicly.[47] In July 1969 G. Pelli of the Swiss Bank Corporation noted that 'I am convinced that the uncertainty wider bands would create in the monetary system would be destructive'.[48] Writing in the same year, John E. Nash, then executive director of Samuel Montagu, warned that 'The most dangerous illusion about the adoption of a floating pound is that it would give a British government more time to work out a sensible economic strategy by removing the immediate balance-of-payments constraint.'[49] He viewed the proposals for floating exchange rates as an easy but dangerous escape route for domestic policy integrity. The devaluation of 1967, far from leading to rapid adjustment, had generated considerable speculative capital flows that led to changes in the exchange rates of the DM and the franc.[50] This tendency was exaggerated by the dramatic expansion of what he termed 'mobile money' or short-term capital flows. Nash argued strongly that the expansion of this type of business must be sustained and that it relied on a stable pound.

Efforts to bring economists and practitioners together to forge a consensus were not completely successful. A series of four meetings of economists and bankers from ten countries in 1969 studied the possibility of greater flexibility of exchange rates. The communiqué from the June meeting cautiously noted that a majority of participants advocated slightly wider bands for exchange rate fluctuations 'within the existing framework'.[51] One academic participant later noted that it was 'those who have been directly concerned with the operation of the present system' (i.e. bankers) who were most dubious of the benefits of such flexibility.[52]

Ministers and government officials also tended to be more cautious than the academics. In August 1964 the G10 ministers reasserted their conviction that the fixed exchange rate system should be maintained.[53] Partly this reflected the fact that ministers could not openly discuss changes in exchange rates for fear of precipitating speculative attacks on weaker currencies. But it also reflected an aversion to exchange rate flexibility since it did not promise to resolve underlying difficulties and would not contain speculative pressure. In Britain in November 1965, the virtues of a wider spread of exchange rates as a way of damping speculation were rejected by the Treasury and the Bank of England on the grounds that 'while squeezing existing bears it would create new ones'.[54]

Pressure from the academic community mounted as the fixed system weakened. In 1964, the US Joint Economic Committee of the Senate recommended that the USA should consider more flexible exchange rates. The JEC was more allied to academic economists, and persisted in their pressure through subsequent reports, including a plea in August 1965 that the possibility of wider exchange bands 'receive the serious consideration which it merits'.[55] In Germany at the end of 1964, the academic economists of the official Council of Economic Advisers also advocated more flexible exchange rates. Emminger of the Deutsche Bundesbank later explained that policy-makers chose to ignore such proposals because there were no serious external problems until 1967.[56]

Wide-band proposals gained a new lease of life after the dramatic devaluation of sterling in 1967 brought exchange rate regimes back to prominence in the media and among academics. Dissatisfaction with the existing system was also prompted by the increasing pressure on the US dollar and the collapse of the gold pool. In March 1968, as the gold pool crumbled, floating sterling was seriously considered by the Bank of England, but it was dismissed after the central-bank governors' crisis meeting in Washington developed a more moderate short-term solution based on mutual support.[57]

In September 1968, as European and American central bankers began to advocate wider bands, the Treasury scrambled around for an official view but could find no papers on the topic since the 1950s. Furthermore, nobody was even sure from where the 1 per cent Bretton Woods margin originated beyond an assumption that it was the product of a deal between White and Keynes over which the latter did not consult London.[58] In February 1969, the Treasury concluded that a 5 per cent band would be technically feasible but would be difficult for the EEC to accept, and that the UK should not take a fixed position on the issue.[59] At the same time they dismissed a crawling peg as a non-starter. It would require countries to use domestic interest rates to counter speculative capital flows, it would not solve the imbalance in the international monetary system, and it would require too much international cooperation. Furthermore, the EEC countries could not use flexible rates because it would undermine their efforts at economic integration, and the USA could not use them since the US dollar was officially pegged only to gold. Finally, the transition from the adjustable peg system to a crawling peg would generate unsustainable speculative pressures.[60] In July 1969 the Australians were briefly consulted, and they also expressed their antipathy to greater flexibility.[61]

The new administration in the USA was somewhat more open-minded and opinion gradually strengthened that greater flexibility was a solution to the recurring pressure on the US dollar and the inability to correct the balance of payments deficit. In April Ryrie opined:

> The talk about greater flexibility is in fact an effort to get surplus countries to accept some of the burden of adjustment ... The Americans are, in effect, saying 'either help us reduce the deficit or finance it'. There is rather less of the feeling which one felt with the Johnson Administration that the European thesis that it is up to the US to deal with its deficit had been accepted.[62]

Ryrie, therefore believed that the US discussion of floating was merely a bluff, a possibility that is confirmed by the tenacity with which the USA clung to fixed exchange rates in 1971.

Meanwhile, the DM was floated briefly in September 1969 and then repegged in October with a revaluation of 9.3 per cent. In the same month, the Chancellor of the Exchequer made a speech to the joint IMF/World Bank meeting against wide bands of +/ −5 per cent, arguing that they brought the disadvantages of the abolition of obligations over parities but would not deliver the advantage of eliminating speculation. He suggested, however, that a margin of +/ −2 per cent could offer the needed flexibility for the pursuit of national policies.[63] Jenkins then added to his speech a proposal that was his own invention and surprised his advisers—an extended version of the Basle agreements of 1968 to support the value of currencies other than sterling in order to check speculative capital flows, and a proposal to eliminate the profits of speculators through selective taxation.[64] Neither proposal was supported by the Treasury.

At the same time as the Chancellor was dismissing the wider bands, pressure was building in Europe and the USA for a crawling peg system. At the beginning of September 1969, Schiller, the German Economics Minister, advocated the immediate introduction of a crawling peg system.[65] Carli, Emminger, and d'Estaing had all earlier supported such a scheme. At the IMF meetings later in September 1969 Volcker of the US Federal Reserve Bank called for an international study of the prospects for a crawling peg. Van Lennep was sceptical and worried that such an enterprise would generate exchange uncertainty. Nevertheless, there was general support for an IMF Board study and perhaps also an inquiry within the G10, especially dealing with the impact on the EEC. It was agreed, however, that there should be no public reference to such studies because of the detrimental effect on confidence, and the probability of antagonizing the LDCs with yet another initiative that excluded them. The USA alone wanted the studies to be more public in order to satisfy domestic public opinion that was pressing for a bolder policy departure.[66]

The Smithsonian Agreement of 1971, however, showed the resilience with which US policy-makers clung to pegged or at least stable exchange rates. Nevertheless, the softening attitude of the USA to fluctuating exchange rates, the increasing reluctance of Germany to accept inflationary pressure, and the loss of market confidence in the US dollar eventually drove policy-makers to accept the inevitable. Exchange rates floated from 1972/3 after the ill-fated attempt to rescue the system in 1971. The new era of international finance had begun, creating challenges for the market and for regulators.

4. Prudential Supervision

One of the major implications of the expansion of the financial markets and the introduction of exchange rate instability was the challenge that it posed to regulators. After all, the Eurodollar market had been spawned largely by the desire to evade regulations in the late 1950s (Regulation Q in the USA and ceilings on deposit rates in London).[67] As noted above, a series of runs on European banks and a major default by Ira Haupt in 1963 sparked shivers down the spines of some at the Bank of England with memories of the 1931 financial crisis.[68] City bankers, in particular Sir Charles Hambro, were also concerned about the rapid and uncontrolled expansion of the market.[69] At the time, the Bank of England was wary but opted to turn a blind eye to the banks' violation of the spirit of exchange control, while hoping to manage the market informally through personal contact with participant banks. Imposing formal controls would cause this profitable business to move elsewhere, to the detriment of the City. Mynors stated that 'It is par excellence an example of the kind of business which London ought to be able to do both well and profitably.'[70]

The Americans apparently agreed that there was no need for external supervision or new regulation of the market. At the end of 1963, R. L. Workman of the UK Treasury reported that the American view was that 'Some people had burnt their fingers, even bankers, and would be more cautious in the future. Some corporate treasurers had not quite realised the risks they had been taking in placing short term dollar funds abroad, thinking of them as deposits with a liquidity corresponding to that of deposits with the domestic banking system rather than as short term loans.'[71]

While, in the 1960s, the Bank of England came shy of imposing controls on inward flows of Eurodollars into London, the major banks were asked periodically to report their activity in the market. They were warned by the Bank to maintain adequate liquidity ratios and to ensure suitable geographical spread of deposits and maturity dates. As the market grew, however, these informal arrangements proved inadequate. The City had become considerably more heterogeneous with the surge in foreign and especially American banks who were less amenable to the cosy relationship that had characterized the Bank of England's relationship with the City in the 1950s. After the relaxation of controls on domestic lending in September 1971, the City's activity soared, particularly lending related to equity and property markets.

The introduction of floating exchange rates combined with the OPEC oil surpluses after 1973 increased the size and potential risk in the market. Worries about the liquidity and transparency of the Eurodollar market and other short-term financial flows led to increasing emphasis on prudential regulation. As the surge in foreign lending mounted, efforts at international regulatory coordination were begun. The G10 Eurocurrency Standing Committee met regularly in Basle, mainly to exchange information and discuss the standardization of market statistics. Their efforts from 1971 to restrain central banks from placing foreign exchange reserves in the Euromarket met with mixed success outside the G10 themselves.[72] The EEC set up a Contact Group of national banking supervisors in 1972 to develop cooperation and exchange information on banking supervision, but again progress was slow. It was not until the end of 1977 that they published their First Directive to coordinate laws, regulations, and administrative provisions of credit institutions.

In the UK, a credit squeeze in 1973, following two years of expansionary policy, threatened domestic financial institutions, prompting the so-called secondary banking crisis at the end of the year. The closure of some of the new wholesale banks and the near failure of many others highlighted the dangers of the rapid expansion of small illiquid banks, and prompted the Bank of England to organize a 'Lifeboat' fund among clearing banks to support them over the next two years.[73]

Crisis also struck international banking. At the beginning of 1974 the USA relaxed capital controls, prompting a significant capital outflow and rapid depreciation of the US dollar that caught out some foreign exchange dealers. Doubts about the soundness of many new small and medium-sized banks in the market prompted the emergence of a tiered interest rate structure in the spring and summer of 1974.[74] David Rockefeller, head of Chase Manhattan Bank, warned the IMF's managing director about the dangers of 'increasing lending risks' in this environment.[75] Small banks faced a liquidity squeeze as the market contracted, and on 26 June 1974 the Herstatt Bank was forced to close due to foreign exchange trading losses amounting to over US$100m., while carrying deposits of US$760m.[76] The market panicked and the rate on three-month Eurodollar loans soared to an unprecedented 14 per cent in mid-July. At the end of September the New York Reserve Bank had to take over the foreign exchange obligations of Franklin National Bank. Much larger than the Herstatt, the Franklin was left with 300 contracts outstanding, amounting to forward transactions of US$725m.[77] The willingness of the Bundesbank to allow the failure of the Herstatt contrasted starkly with the Fed's support of the Franklin, throwing up the inconsistency of international practice of lender of last resort.[78]

The Bank of England took the position that it had no responsibility for the solvency of subsidiaries of foreign banks in London and so the Israel-British Bank was allowed to fail in July 1974 with outstanding debts of £43m. Negotiations with the Israeli banking authorities, however, eventually produced a fund to which the Bank of England contributed £3m. to honour creditors.[79] As well as these spectacular cases, many other international banks suffered foreign exchange losses during 1974, including Westdeutsche Landesbank, Union Bank of Switzerland, and Lloyds through its Swiss branch.[80]

Analogous to the response to the domestic crisis of 1973/4, the international crisis prompted efforts to coordinate lender of last resort facilities to international banks. In September, the central-bank governors of the G10 announced that, although detailed rules governing lender of last resort to the Eurodollar market were not practical, the market should be reassured that 'means are available for that purpose and will be used if and when necessary'.[81] They also set up the Committee on Banking Regulations and Supervisory Practices in Basle, chaired first by George Blunden and then by Peter Cooke, both of the Bank of England.[82]

National regulatory changes also ensued. In the City, the Bank of England urged the consortium banks to agree in letters to the Bank of England that their shareholders would agree to act as lenders of last resort. Foreign banks were asked similarly for commitments that they would support their UK subsidiaries, although these undertakings were not enforceable.[83] At the same time the Fed announced that it was ready to act as lender of last resort for member banks to protect them against abrupt withdrawal of petro-dollars or any other deposits. Together, these measures reassured the market and the tiered interest rate structure contracted early in 1975 as confidence returned. Interest rates on three-month deposits fell back below 6 per cent for much of 1976 and 1977. The growth of the market, however, did not recover the heady days of the late 1960s and in 1975 the Eurocurrency market grew by less than 16 per cent.

This crisis prompted a change in the Bank of England's relationship with the City. Ten years earlier, similar crises in Europe related to the Eurodollar market had been contained through informal and ad hoc advice. By 1973/4 the volume of capital flows, greater public sensitivity to the interests of depositors, and membership of the EEC were all deemed to require a more formal and interventionist response. In addition to the traditional personal meetings with individual bank officers, more detailed and continuous statistical reports were required from banks in London to enhance prudential supervision. At the end of 1974, the Bank of England sent a letter to all banks in the City advising them to tighten up their internal control systems, in particular with respect to the control of foreign exchange operations by branches and subsidiaries overseas. This was the first time such a formal and public instruction had been made. British overseas banks were also asked for the first time to report to the Bank of England on their overseas offices. Blunden noted that 'the reaction of most banks to our letter has suggested to us that we were right in judging that the banking community as a whole was ready for us to take this new line'. Blunden, nevertheless, promised, 'Our approach remains flexible, personal, progressive and participative.'[84]

By 1977 the Bank of England was urging private financiers to move out of the market for long-term loans to make way for official financing. The private market was no longer considered an appropriate source of longer-term debt now that the problems of adjustment in LDCs appeared more protracted. In a speech to the Financial Times Euromarkets Conference in February 1977, J. A. Kirbyshire, chief adviser of the Bank of England, urged that

> If the banks are to be able to continue in their proper role beyond the next few years, and if the danger of a sudden freezing over of private international finance is to be avoided at some point in the future, then we must begin now to envisage a gradual shift of emphasis towards official financing, which in turn will underpin a continued major role for the banks.[85]

At this point the Bank advocated closer links between private banks and the IMF and World Bank. Meanwhile in 1976 and 1977 Witteveen, managing director of the IMF, warned that easy credit from private banks could delay the necessary adjustment of the national borrowers and could add to liquidity creation, advising that 'a very careful and balanced policy by the international banks is needed'.[86]

The Basle Committee on Banking Regulations and Supervisory Practices issued its Concordat in 1975 setting out the supervisory responsibility for multinational banks, concluding that solvency of foreign branches was 'essentially a matter for parent supervisory authorities', while foreign subsidiaries and joint ventures lay within the responsibility of the host authorities.[87] The subsequent recommendation of 1978 that solvency should be based on consolidated accounts put greater emphasis on parent authorities than on hosts to ensure the collection and publication of this information.

The Basle Committee also considered how it could help with risk management, perhaps through central agencies that collected information on total liabilities of particular borrowers that could be accessed by potential additional borrowers. In the late 1970s, however, the problem of customer confidentiality and the different standards of disclosure among the various jurisdictions made this impossible.[88] In 1977 a proposal by Arthur Burns, chairman of the Fed, to collect information on the direction and volume of international bank lending met strong resistance from banks, who viewed this as unnecessary meddling in their affairs.[89] Instead, from 1974 the BIS reported quarterly data on countries' external debt and from 1978 included maturity distribution on a half-yearly basis. From the end of December the Bank of England began to publish the consolidated exposure of banks in the UK. In May 1982 the Basle Committee finally agreed on guidelines for banks to consider regarding country-risk analysis—just in time for the LDC debt crisis.

The progress of these efforts at international coordination was limited by the problems that still confront those seeking to develop global financial standards; different political, legal, and institutional structures of financial systems and an antipathy to supranational harmonization. As noted above, the EEC harmonization programme, surely most suited to supranational coordination, made little progress in the 1970s. At the International Banking Summer School of 1977 Blunden expressed the Bank of England's dim view of such efforts.

> The banking system of a country is central to the management and efficiency of its economy; its supervision will inevitably be a jealously guarded national prerogative. Its subordination to an international authority is a highly unlikely development, which would require a degree of political commitment which neither exists nor is conceivable in the foreseeable future.[90]

After relatively smooth and cautious sailing during 1975–7, international bank lending surged again in 1978. A run on the US dollar in the second half of 1978 also increased international transactions. Interest rate hikes in the USA were felt in higher rates in the Eurodollar market. Into this volatile environment came the second oil crisis sparked off by the Iranian revolution at the end of 1979. The decade ended in another spirit of crisis that was ultimately to lead to international banking's greatest challenge; the Latin American debt crisis. The prudential regulation introduced in the 1970s proved inadequate to cope with these pressures, particularly on the assessment of country risk, and the prevalence and dangers of syndicated lending. Bank lending as a proportion of LDC debt rose from 15 per cent in 1970 to 27 per cent in 1980, contributing to the Latin American debt crisis of 1982.

5. Conclusion

The 1960s was a period of globalization of business enterprise generally, and banks followed these customers internationally. In the 1970s, however, international finance took on a lease of life of its own as fluctuations in exchange rates, OPEC surpluses, and innovation offered greatly expanded opportunities. The financial markets thrived on inflationary crisis and disparity in regulatory regimes in a rising market. Banks responded to the collapse of the international monetary system with financial innovations that considerably increased the scale of their activity. This increase in activity in turn generated further innovations to capture economies of scale. This chapter has focused on the changes in the policy environment that responded to these new challenges. Regulators continued to try to contain the acceleration of the market through capital controls throughout the 1960s, especially in Europe and the USA to the advantage of the City of London. Prudential supervision, however, was relatively informal and relaxed. From 1975, as the new floating exchange rate system became established, the tide turned and capital controls were liberalized while prudential supervision was formalized to try to offset possible market failure. In the end, however, this proved too late and too little to contain the mounting debt crisis that broke in 1982.

Notes

1. The comment was written by Scott in 'That Controversial Eurodollar Market', *Natwest Bank Review* (Aug. 1969), 2–22. Quoted in R. J. Clark, 'The Evolution of Monetary and Financial Institutions', in D. R. Croome and H. G. Johnson (eds.), *Money in Britain 1959–1969* (Oxford, 1970), 138.
2. R. C. Bryant, *International Financial Intermediation* (Washington, 1987) 22.
3. *International Financial Statistics*, Supplement 14.
4. R. C. Williams et al., *International Capital Markets: Recent Developments and Short-Term Prospects* (Washington, 1980), 27.
5. Domestic banks in the City also mushroomed as restrictions on their activities were relaxed after 1971.
6. R. M. Pecchioli, *The Internationalisation of Banking; The Policy Issues* (Paris, 1983), 69.
7. J. D. Wilson, *The Chase: The Chase Manhattan Bank, N.A. 1945–85* (Cambridge, Mass., 1986), 182.
8. S. R. Choi, D. K. Park, and A. E. Tschoegl, 'Banks and the World's Major Banking Centers, 1990', *Weltwirtschaftliches Archiv*, 123 (1996), 774–93.
9. Pecchioli, *The Internationalisation of Banking*, 19.
10. B. J. Cohen, *Banks and the Balance of Payments* (Montclair, NJ, 1981), 65.
11. A. Teck and W. B. Johns, 'Portfolio Decisions of Central Banks', in A. M. George and I. H. Giddy (eds.), *International Finance Handbook*, ii (New York, 1983), 10.
12. Report of Anglo-US Working Party meeting by Hubback, 16 July 1963. Bank of England Archives (hereafter BE) OV53/20.
13. In early 1962 the US Treasury issued 3-month lire bonds bought by the Bank of Italy and then rolled over into 15-month bonds. Letter from C. A. Coombs, vice-president of the Federal Reserve Bank of New York, to R. A. O. Bridge, 1 Feb. 1963. BE OV53/15.
14. See correspondence in BE C40/773. Warburgs is mentioned by the Bank as a participant.
15. On the origins of the Eurobond market see I. M. Kerr, *A History of the Eurobond Market: The First 21 Years* (London, 1984). K. Burk (ed.), 'Witness Seminar on the Origins and Early Development of the Eurobond Market', *Contemporary European History*, 1/1 (1992), 65–87. G. Burn, 'The State, the City and the Euromarkets', *Review of International Political Economy*, 6/2 (1999). 225–61.
16. Wilson, *The Chase*, 212.
17. *Bank of England Quarterly Bulletin*, 3 (1972).

18. S. Battilossi, 'Financial Innovation and the Golden Ages of International Banking: 1890–1931 and 1958–81', *Financial History Review*, 7/2 (Oct. 2000), 141–75.
19. 'Overseas and Foreign Banks in London', *Bank of England Quarterly Bulletin*, 8/2 (June 1968), 158.
20. Pecchioli, *The Internationalisation of Banking*, 28.
21. Ibid., 32–4.
22. R. Roberts with Christopher Arnander, *Take your Partners: Orion, the Consortium Banks and the Transformation of the Euromarkets* (Basingstoke, 2001), 11–12, 113–14.
23. R. Pringle, *Banking in Britain* (London, 1973), 163. For a general survey as well as a specific case study see Roberts, *Take your Partners*.
24. See Roberts, *Take your Partners*, appendix III for a description and D. Ross, 'European Banking Clubs in the 1960s: A Flawed Strategy', *Business and Economic History*, 27/2 (1998), 353–66 for analysis of the early initiatives.
25. *The Economist* (30 June 1962), 1339. Other associations were Eurofin, Euroinvest, Negit, and Sogefina. In 1962 these five groups involved 27 financial institutions from 9 European countries.
26. Pringle, *Banking in Britain*, 162.
27. J. R. S. Revell, *Banking and Electronic Fund Transfers* (Paris, 1983), P 149.
28. Veith also cites problems with software. R. H. Veith, *Multinational Computer Nets: The Case of International Banking* (Toronto, 1981), 47.
29. See SWIFT website, www.swift.com.
30. Veith, *Multinational Computer Nets*, 48.
31. Kerr, *A History of the Eurobond Market*, 98–100.
32. OECD, *Liberalisation of Capital Movements and Financial Services in the OECD Area*, (Paris, 1990), 34.
33. Note by Preston to Bridge, circulated to Selwyn, O'Brien, and Parsons, 4 Dec. 1963. BE EID10/22.
34. Bridge to Parsons and O'Brien, 5 Dec. 1963. BE EID10/22.
35. Report by J. M. L. for Hamilton, 19 Oct. 1961. BE EID10/19.
36. On the reasons why the Hong Kong Gap was tolerated see 'Closing the Hong Kong Gap: The Hong Kong Free Dollar Market in the 1950s', *Economic History Review*, 47/2 (1994), 335–53. For a description of the Kuwait Gap see S. Smith, *Kuwait 1950–1965: Britain, the al-Sabah, and Oil* (Oxford, 1999), 75–6.
37. 'The Exchange Control Gap and Security Sterling', 18 Dec. 1963. Public Records Office, Treasury [hereafter PRO T]295/27.
38. Note from the Chancellor to the Prime Minister, 13 Jan. 1965. PRO T295/65.
39. OECD, *Liberalisation of Capital Movements*, 39.
40. A. F. P. Bakker, *The Liberalization of Capital Movements in Europe: The Monetary Committee and Financial Integration 1958–1994* (Dordrecht, 1996), 80–5.
41. Ibid. 92–4.
42. Italy and Switzerland did not introduce new restrictions. D. Kane, *The Eurodollar Market and the Years of Crisis* (London, 1983), 68.
43. Bakker suggests that a major motivation from the Bank of England's point of view was to maintain London's position as an international financial centre. Bakker, *The Liberalization of Capital Movements in Europe*, 139.
44. 'The Case for Flexible Exchange Rates', *Essays in Positive Economics*, (Chicago, 1953).

45. J. E. Meade, in *Three Banks Review* (Sept. 1964, June 1966). H. G. Johnson, 'The Case for Flexible Exchange Rates, 1969', in *UK Floating Exchanges: A Debate on the Theoretical and Practical Implications* (London, 1969), 9–37.
46. W. S. Salant et al., *The United States Balance of Payments in 1968* (Washington, 1963).
47. Rawlinson, Figgures, and Maude met with representatives of Morgan Guarantee Trust, Chase Manhattan Bank, the New York Federal Reserve Bank, Discount Corporation, Brown Bros. Harriman, and Manufacturers Hanover Trust on 7 Mar. 1969. BE OV53/40.
48. Paper by G Pelli, 15 July 1969. BE OV53/40.
49. J. E. Nash, 'UK Policy and International Monetary Reform', in *UK Floating Exchanges* 64.
50. Ibid. 63.
51. For a text of the Communiqué of 30 June 1969, see S. Marris, *The Burgenstock Communique: A Critical Examination of the Case for Limited Flexibility of Exchange Rates* (Princeton, 1970).
52. Ibid. 1.
53. For a contemporary survey, see G. N. Halm, *The 'Band' Proposal: The Limits of Permissible Exchange Rate Variations* (Princeton, 1965), 35–46.
54. Note for record 3 Nov. 1965, Ruess and Ellsworth (2 US Congressmen) meeting with Rickett. BE OV53/33.
55. Joint Economic Committee of US Congress, *Guidelines for Improving the International Monetary System* (Aug. 1965). Quoted in G. N. Halm, *Toward Limited Exchange-Rate Flexibility* (Princeton, 1969), 3.
56. O. Emminger, *The D-Mark in the Conflict between Internal and External Equilibrium, 1948–75* (Princeton, 1977), 20–1.
57. Memo by CWM for Governors, 14 Mar. 1968. Note for the record of meeting of Deputy Governor of Bank of England with Chancellor of Exchequer, 18 Mar. 1968. BE OV53/38.
58. Paper by C. J. Carey on Wider Margins, 18 Sept. 1968. PRO T312/2329.
59. Paper by W. S. Ryrie for the Group on the International Monetary System, 12 Feb. 1969. PRO T312/2329.
60. W. S. Ryrie to F. E. Figgures, 21 Feb. 1969. PRO T312/2329.
61. Talks between W. S. Ryrie and Australians, 23 July 1969. BE OV53/40.
62. W. S. Ryrie to J. A. Kerbyshire, 8 Apr. 1969. BE OV53/40.
63. Widening the margins to +/ − 2% was believed to be supported also by Giscard d'Estaing. Brief for visit of G. d'Estaing, Oct. 1969. PRO T312/2327. The Bank of England had supported this band from July 1969.
64. Report of Chancellor's speech to the Bank/Fund meeting, Sept. 1969. PRO T312/2327. The Treasury determined that his proposals were unworkable. J. H. Williamson (then advising the Treasury) agreed that the plan would merely be introducing a formal US$ standard. Any effective elimination of capital profits from speculation would require intolerable regulations. J. Williamson, 3 Oct. 1969. PRO T312/2327.
65. Extract from *The Guardian*, 4 Sept. 1969, PRO T312/2327.
66. F. E. Figgures to Hudson for PM, 17 Sept. 1969. PRO T312/2327.
67. C. R. Schenk, 'The Origins of the Eurodollar Market in London, 1955–1963', *Explorations in Economic History*, 35 (Apr. 1998), 221–38.

68. Note by Preston to Bridge, circulated to Selwyn, O'Brien, and Parsons, 4 Dec. 1963. BE EID10/22.
69. Hambro had expressed concern at the growth of Eurodollar deposits and had asked for the Bank of England's view. Despite the chairman's concern, Hambros was a significant participant in the Eurodollar market. Schenk, 'The Origins'.
70. Letter from H. B. Mynors to Sir Charles J. Hambro. Drafted and vetted by Governor Cobbold. 29 Jan. 1963. BE EID10/22.
71. Note by R. L. Workman (HMT) of a trip to New York and Washington. BE EID10/22.
72. G. G. Johnson and R. K. Abrams, *Aspects of the International Banking Safety Net* (Washington, 1983), 24.
73. For a detailed account of the crisis, see M. Reid, *The Secondary Banking Crisis, 1973–75*, (Basingstoke, 1982).
74. Johnson and Abrams, *Aspects of the International Banking Safety Net*, 18. They also suggest that this encouraged Japanese banks to maintain stricter standards for matching maturities. For a description of the tiers at various points see I. H. Giddy, 'The Eurocurrency Market', in A. H. George and I. H. Giddy (eds.), *International Finance Handbook*, i (New York, 1983), 18.
75. Quoted in H. James, *International Monetary Cooperation since Bretton Woods* (Washington, 1996), 320.
76. Reid, *The Secondary Banking Crisis*, 115. Wilson, *The Chase*, 213.
77. *Federal Reserve Bulletin*, Mar. 1975. Franklin National had been in difficulties since May. Its assets (valued at US$3.6 bn.) were subsequently sold to a consortium bank, European-American Banking Corporation, in Aug. 1974. S. J. Weiss, 'Competitive Standards Applied to Foreign and Domestic Acquisitions of US Banks', in Comptroller of the Currency, *Foreign Acquisition of US Banks* (Washington, 1981), 324.
78. For the implications of this see Johnson and Abrams, *Aspects of the International Banking Safety Net*, 22–3. They argue that the US action ameliorated the international repercussions of the Franklin crisis. Governor Richardson of the Bank of England subsequently noted that the German authorities took a more prudent and supportive attitude to banks with liquidity problems from Sept. 1974. Quoted in Reid, *The Secondary Banking Crisis*, 117.
79. Johnson and Abrams, *Aspects of the International Banking Safety Net*, 21–2. Reid, *The Secondary Banking Crisis*, 115.
80. Reid, *The Secondary Banking Crisis*, 114.
81. Quoted in Johnson and Abrams, *Aspects of the International Banking Safety Net*, 23.
82. G10 plus Switzerland and Luxembourg.
83. By the end of February 1975 all consortium banks had given such an undertaking. In 1976/7 Western American Bank (owned by Hambros, Bank of Tokyo, National Bank of Detroit, Wells Fargo, and Security Pacific National Bank) drew on its shareholder banks. It was then transformed into Bank of Tokyo International. Reid, *The Secondary Banking Crisis*, 119.
84. Speech of George Blunden to the Institute of European Finance of the University College of North Wales, Mar. 1975, in London, *Bank of England Quarterly Bulletin*, 15/2 (June 1975), 190.
85. Speech by J. A. Kirbyshire, 23 Feb. 1977, *Bank of England Quarterly Bulletin*, 17/1 (Mar. 1977).

86. James, *International Monetary Cooperation*, 320. This advice was resented by some borrowers, ibid. 321.
87. Quoted in Johnson and Abrams, *Aspects of the International Banking Safety Net*, 16.
88. Speech by Blunden to International Banking Summer School in Stockholm in June 1977, *Bank of England Quarterly Bulletin*, 17/2 (1977).
89. James, *International Monetary Cooperation*, 321.
90. *Bank of England Quarterly Bulletin*, 17/2 (1977).

11

The International Opening-up of the Paris Bourse: Overdraft-Economy Curbs and Market Dynamics

Olivier Feiertag

The generally accepted view of the relatively insignificant part played by the Paris Bourse on the international scene after the Second World War was first formulated in the 1950s and has been more or less continually put forward until our own time.[1] In comparison with major international financial centres like London, New York, or even Zurich,[2] the French financial market in the 1950s and 1960s was 'parochial and, first and foremost, concerned with the protection of its members' privileges'.[3] From this point of view, the contrast with the situation prevailing before 1914 and even to a great extent in the 1920s is quite obvious.

The observation refers more widely to the 'long depression' of the Paris Bourse after 1945.[4] The decline, however, was part of a more general downwards trend in every financial market in Europe at the time,[5] which over a long period the London Stock Market was unable to escape.[6] The widespread nature of the phenomenon is not without importance when accounting for the low level of the Bourse's international involvement. Indeed, in the continued absence of any overall and really integrated financial market, the opening-up of any specific national one to the outside world was still very closely linked to the degree to which all the others were becoming more international.

Nevertheless, the main reasons for the relative insularity of the French financial market after 1945 and until the 1980s at least are to some extent specific to France. They have been known and analysed for many years, and are connected with both what has commonly been referred to as the *dirigisme* of the state during the period and the archaic structures and rigid rules governing the way the market worked.[7] As Jean Guyot, a partner in Lazard Frères and a member of the Baumgartner Commission on the financial market, set up in 1971, rather ironically pointed out, all the obstacles to the internationalization of the Paris Bourse ultimately came from 'the attitude nicely described some years ago by the British diplomat who observed that what the French cannot forgive foreigners for is not being

French'. So, Guyot concluded, 'the French were so disappointed at the failure of foreigners to understand them that the French market tended to hide away in a complex network of protective measures, regulations, and checks that created the illusion of a job well done and the cosy attitude of mind that made it possible to resist change'.[8]

In the circumstances it is rather remarkable that the Bourse managed to maintain a level of international activity over the period. The development of that no doubt marginal but nevertheless persistent level from the late 1950s and the return of the franc to external convertibility to the liberalization of the financial market in the second half of the 1980s is what will be examined here. By considering the ebb and flow of the dynamics of the international markets in their effect on capital markets, it might be possible to throw some particular light on, and perhaps even to highlight, the changes within the whole of the French financial system. For the Bourse, however important it may be in that system, is not something isolated from its other components, such as the banks or the Treasury, and can indeed quite validly be seen as a *precipitate* of the financial, and hence the economic and social, history of a country.

On these bases, we shall first try to grasp and measure the rhythms of the dynamics of the limited but recurring internationalization of the Bourse from the late 1950s to the early 1980s, in particular within the totally new context of the process of constructing Europe. This will subsequently lead to an analysis of the reality of the curbing processes proper to the forms of overdraft economy which overall remained permanent in France as the country began to move into the 1980s.[9] These help to show clearly that the remarkable stability of the system was as much a result of the unity of purpose of the great majority of its mixture of public and private agents as of its relative imperviousness to the international world. In the light of this kind of empirical approach to the working of the French financial system, our final concern will be an examination of the relevance of the state–market tensions so often proposed as an explanation of developments in the French economy in the twentieth century. The result will be the working hypothesis that the coupling, however compellingly real it may be perceived to be, could be replaced by the more operational tension that in the real world has always, right down to our own times, pitted national needs against international relations on the international capital market. This led to the specifically contemporary innovation of the emergence, as a result of the growth of Eurocurrency, of a truly comprehensive and integrated financial market.[10]

1. Assessing the international dynamics of the Bourse, 1958–1983

The extent to which the Bourse opened up to the international market can be mainly seen at the two levels of foreign stocks and shares quoted and the proportion of non-resident portfolios handled in Paris. At the wider market-place level, the data can usefully be complemented by taking into account, wherever possible, the portfolio investments of French residents on foreign financial markets. Similarly, even if it initially seems that the direct part played by foreign traders on the market up to the gradual increase in the capital of *agents de change* from 1988 onwards was virtually nil, it must also be borne in mind that foreign banks and brokerage houses had been set up on the Paris financial market.

The number of stocks and shares officially quoted gives, as a first approximation, an often pointed-out reading of the decline of the Bourse in the late 1950s, since overall the figure is divided by two between the eve of the First World War and the end of the 1950s, with 226 foreign securities registered on- and off-floor in 1957.[11] The number fell regularly and consistently, settling at 179 foreign securities registered in 1983. But the real significance of the figure is limited, for despite frequent attempts to rejuvenate them, listings largely remained a museum of sometimes totally inactive securities mostly registered before 1914. Indeed, over the period relatively few foreign securities (South African gold mines, and certain oil securities like Royal Dutch, a quarter of whose capital was in French hands) and American stocks and shares (ATT and Du Pont de Nemours) accounted for most of the investments. Consequently, it is hard to establish a hierarchy of international finance centres on the basis of the number of foreign securities quoted, as is shown by the two contrasting examples of the New York Stock Exchange (which quoted a mere twenty-six foreign securities in 1964) and its Amsterdam equivalent (with close to three hundred in the same year). In addition, counting the securities officially quoted necessarily takes no account of those traded off-floor, the number of which continually changed from around forty to around sixty between 1962 (the year in which on-floor and off-floor trading were combined) and 1983.

What casts rather more light on the matter is the in fact ever-marginal share of foreign securities in the structure of the nominal capitalization of the Bourse at the time. Between 1963 and 1982, it was barely more than 10 per cent, as against 58 per cent in 1913 and still almost 30 per cent in the late 1920s.[12] But the most accurate way of assessing the international opening-up of the Bourse is to take into account the value of transactions effectively brought about by quoted foreign securities and to compare them with the value of those involving French securities (Fig. 11.1).

The persistently low overall level of transactions in foreign securities on the Bourse, which during the period amounted on average to scarcely 10 per cent of the value of transactions in French securities, is certainly the most significant fact. There is no doubt that this situation, which went hand in hand with the collapse of the share of foreign securities in French portfolios,[13] shows a completely opposite trend to the dynamics of increasing internationalization underlying the rapid development of the Paris financial market during the second half of the nineteenth century.[14]

First and foremost among the most frequently quoted causes of the reversal in the trend is exchange control, which was the normal situation in France from the First World War until it was completely abolished in 1990. With regard to the Bourse, the long-lasting legal constraint is perfectly illustrated by the persistence of exchange securities, that is, the creation of an administered, self-contained market disconnected from the national exchange market and supplied exclusively by foreign currency produced by realizing securities abroad. The device, which was

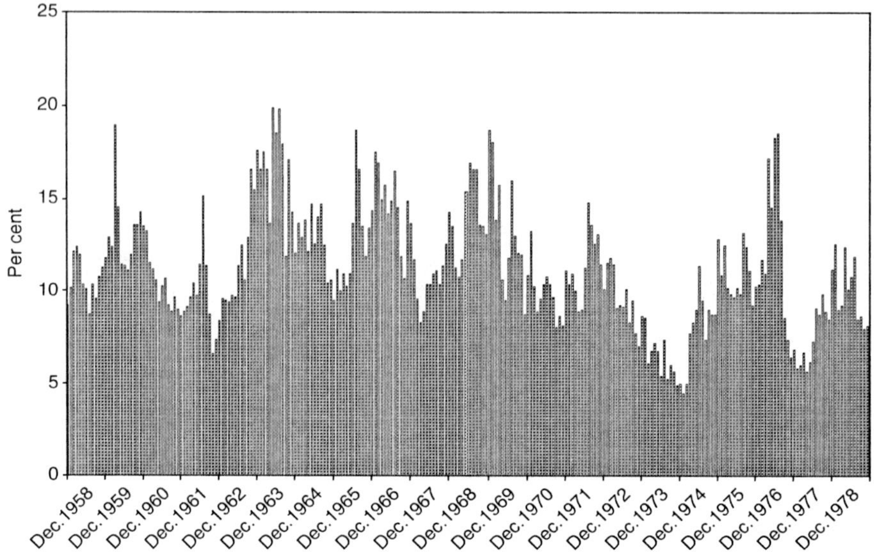

Fig. 11.1. Average monthly transactions on foreign securities compared with those on French securities in the share market 1963–1983

Source: *L'Année Boursière*, 1963–1983.

introduced at the Liberation, was first abolished in 1962 and then re-established from 1968 until 1971. It was reintroduced in 1981 and finally abolished in 1985. Notably, it has always risen higher than official rates for the franc, being worth 40 per cent more in 1957–8 for example, when the increase in the capital of Royal Dutch was announced in February 1958,[15] and in 1983 it was still worth 36 per cent more than the official rate for the franc on the exchange markets. The higher rate is quite a good illustration of the part played by safety-net shares when inflation is high and there is a risk of devaluation. It provides another acceptable way of assessing the international dynamics which were no doubt just as much a feature of the financial market for the whole of the period in question, both despite and because of the existence of exchange control. A more detailed analysis of the share of transactions involving foreign securities confirms the coexistence of the international dynamics and the instruments of control used by a highly nationalized market. Thus the growth that was a feature of 1968 can be seen as both the consequence of the increased search for safety-net investments in the context of the social crisis of May and June of that year, and the fear of a 'hot' devaluation (a stratagem which also brought about the reintroduction of the exchange bond on 25 November), but also as the automatic effect of the sharp rise on the main Western financial markets, which was the opposite of what was happening in France. Generally speaking, foreign share prices in Paris over the period mostly evolved counter-cyclically in relation to French ones. It can be said that the inward-looking nature of the Bourse was marked but far from total between 1958 and 1983. From this situation arose the tension between the domestic and the international aspect of the financial market, with its national centre and its international fringes, which has been a prevalent feature of the French financial system as a whole throughout the time in question.

Non-residents' portfolio investments on the Paris market provide an alternative approach to the reality of the situation. The decision in late 1958 that the franc, along with all European currencies, should once again be convertible meant that the Bourse was opened up to foreign capital. This took place within the context of the effective establishment of the EEC, which put the question of the internationalization of the financial markets of member states on a new footing.[16] Thus article 67 of the Treaty of Rome stipulated, albeit in still rather guarded terms, that in principle there should be a gradual freeing-up of movements of capital 'insofar as is necessary for the proper functioning of the Common Market'. The first directive regarding the implementation of article 67, which was adopted by the Council of the EEC as early as 11 May, more specifically recommended an 'irreversible and unconditional' liberalization for the securities traded on financial markets, whilst however retaining the possibility of transferring capital at flexible exchange rates. This new environment explains the major growth in foreign investments characterizing the Bourse and indeed all the major EEC stock exchanges between the end of 1958 and the first quarter of 1962. The flow of investments, which was largely the result of joint German, Belgian, Dutch, and Swiss investment funds, but also of the return of funds that had been invested abroad, amounted on average to between \$100m. and \$150m. a year.[17] This contribution from abroad thus represented between 3 and 4 per cent of total transactions involving French shares and no doubt helped to raise their value to record levels.

Yet it is difficult to give precise figures for the growth in the share of foreign capital on the securities market, and most practitioners in the field had little faith in them.[18] Indeed, the Bank of France's balance of payments figures, which are the only ones available, are based on varying exchange control regulations, and do not distinguish clearly enough between portfolio and the much greater direct investments. Using that basis, the Commission des Opérations de Bourse (COB) (Stock Exchange Operations Commission) tried, as soon as it embarked on its activities in 1968 and in the context of an often expressed desire for internationalization, to asses the impact of foreign traders on the Bourse. After an initial spurt in 1959–62, there was a clear trend towards disinvestment until 1965. This was followed by a second spurt in the late 1960s and early 1970s, when there was a marked decrease in activity on the London and New York stock exchanges, with a 7 per cent increase on the total transactions in 1972, despite the measures taken against foreign investors in late 1971.[19] Once again, however, the trend was dramatically reversed in 1973, and it was not until the late 1970s that a new high—representing, according to Pierre Balley, 16 per cent of total investment in French shares[20]—was reached, only to decline again from 1981 to 1983. The bond market, however, benefited far less from such external support, since the share of foreign investment, estimated by the

Ministère de l'Économie et des Finances at the end of 1963, amounted to no more than 1 per cent of the total offer on that market between 1959 and 1963, as against 10 per cent on the German and 37 per cent on the Netherlands market.[21]

However accurate or inaccurate such estimates may be, they do confirm that in the period in question the volume of foreign intervention remained marginal. Yet its role was not negligible, since on stock exchanges it is the nature of marginal transactions to be the most determining factor. Using international comparisons, it can be seen that the intervention of foreign investors goes hand in hand with and accentuates movements occurring at the national level. Such an effect was very evident in, for example, the upward movement after the 1978 general election, particularly under the influence of British dealers acting on behalf of North American investors.[22] The other side of the coin, however, is that such capital is soon withdrawn, as when profits were taken in the second half of 1962 after the 1959–61 boom or a fall in prices was expected in 1973 and 1981.

Like the fact that the major part of foreign investments is concentrated in the variable income sector, such short-term fluctuations reflect the hardly surprising fact that the main aim of non-resident portfolio investments on the Bourse is to make a profit. As P. Balley, the former head of the Stock Market Department at the BNP, who became a member of the COB and first president of the MATIF, explained in 1986, however, 'investors of that type are not subject to any social feeling or even to the force of inertia typical of many French shareholders'.[23] The difference between international transactions and strictly national ones on the Paris market is ultimately a matter of the more or less explicit formation of a hierarchy of preferences largely proper to the period in question, but which in the case of France had been established before the First World War and thoroughly consolidated during the 1930s slump and again by the Vichy regime from 1940 to 1944. Seen in this light, both the 'patriotism' so often invoked in the nineteenth century by the shareholders and the recurrent denunciation of ('inevitably') cosmopolitan speculators have helped to make the profits hoped for from stocks and shares perhaps not a secondary motivation but at least a more moderated and controlled one *de facto* as well as *de jure*.

In this context, it was certainly on the margins of the system, at the point of contact between the national level and the international environment, that the possibility of profits was least restricted. The pattern seems valid for the working of both the Bourse and the financial system as a whole, a hypothesis which is confirmed by, for example, the strategy developed from the 1960s by the private banks, the heirs to the *haute banque*, which were still constituted as partnerships (e.g. Neuflize, Schlumberger & Cie or indeed the Compagnie Bancaire) which, marginalized after the war, had sought to ensure their survival by an early internationalization, particularly in securities transactions.[24] In their case, it was a matter of using their higher profit level on the international market to compensate for their very small size in comparison with the major nationalized banks located in the midst of an overdraft economy receiving major support from the national monetary authorities.

2. The Bourse and French *dirigisme*

'Quite apart from its own interventions on the capital markets, the Treasury has found itself, by circumstances rather than by deliberate intention, charged with the responsibility of supervising such markets.' The kind of administrative supervision referred to by Jean-Yves Haberer, the director of the Treasury at the Finance Ministry at the time, did indeed take the form of a strict control of every new introduction of foreign securities quotation in the whole of the period.[25] Under the law of 31 May 1916, which was still in force throughout the period we are considering, any such introduction was prohibited in order to protect national savings. This meant that any admission of foreign securities during the period required a dispensation from the provisions of the 1916 law, which could be granted or refused by the Finance Minister after an examination by the Bourse's Shares Committee until 1968 and thereafter by the COB.

Although we have seen that the total number of officially quoted foreign securities was not really significant, the rate at which new foreign securities were introduced does in fact show the trend towards the internationalization of the Bourse between 1963 and 1983 and means that a valid comparison with other financial markets can be made (Fig. 11.2).

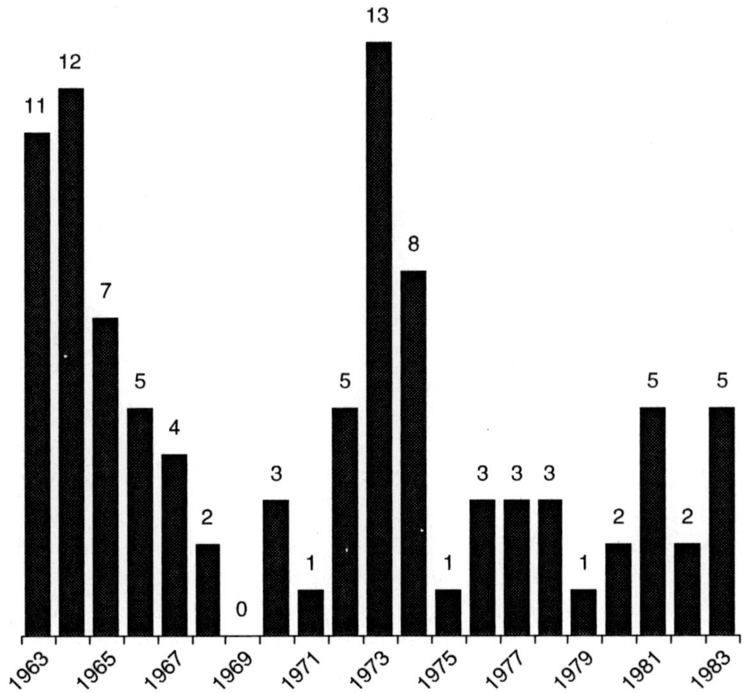

Fig. 11.2. Admission of foreign securities to the official Bourse list, 1963–1983
Source: *L'Année boursière* and annual reports of the COB.

Between 1963 and 1983, ninety-six new foreign securities, on average between four and five a year, were admitted to the Bourse's official list. The renewal was far from negligible, since during the period covered the combined French and foreign average annual increase was a mere ten or so securities. There is thus no doubt about the importance of the new foreign securities at a time when the Bourse's official list had been tending to shrink drastically since 1945 as a result of nationalizations and the tendency towards industrial concentration. In addition, the new foreign securities were very largely industrial stocks and shares, particularly in growth sectors, and helped to fill certain gaps largely inherited from the nineteenth century, when state funds were always predominant.

On the other hand, however, the internationalization of the Paris market's official list certainly progressed more slowly than was the case on all the other major European stock markets, with the exception of Milan, where it was forbidden to quote foreign securities during the period. Thus in 1973, a year when internationalization increased greatly on the financial markets as a result of the enlargement of the EEC to include Great Britain and Denmark, the Bourse exceptionally admitted 13 new foreign securities, including 6 British (among them BP, Marks and Spencer, Phoenix) and 2 Japanese companies (Hitachi and Matsushita) thus bringing the number of Japanese companies on the list to 3 (Sony had been admitted the previous year). The new impetus this gave to Paris in 1973 was remarkable, since the list had not seen such an influx of new foreign securities since 1963–4. During the same year, however, internationalization was an even more marked feature in London, with the admission of 47 new foreign securities of which only 3 were French, Amsterdam (31 foreign securities including 2 French), Frankfurt (28 including 2 French), Zurich (20 including 2 French), and even Brussels (14 including 1 French). The Tokyo Stock Exchange admitted foreign securities for the first time (6 including 1 French, the Compagnie Financière de Paris et des Pays-Bas, 360,000 of whose shares had been previously sold directly on the spot in 1972.[26]

These figures thus generally confirm the Bourse's relative difficulty in opening up to foreign trading. One of the reasons for its isolation has to do with its lack of attraction for foreign dealers in a market chronically subject to currency controls, the reintroduction of which in November 1968 directly accounted for, for example, the absence of any new foreign quotations in 1969. Yet currency control in Britain between 1939 and 1979 was at least as rigorous. In addition, that country's taxation on stocks and shares and the high cost of transactions on the London Stock Exchange as a result of the 2 per cent stamp duty introduced in 1947[27] meant that the frequently proposed explanation of on average higher costs in Paris and the less attractive income tax burden in France needs to be qualified. It is certainly true that in comparison with the situation in London, the taxation on a securities transaction in Paris in 1971 was twice as high on the cash market and three times as high on the term market. On the other hand the cost of the remuneration of the brokers was much lower in Paris at the same date, being 60 francs on a 10,000-franc transaction, as against 70 in Amsterdam, 87 in Frankfurt, and 125 in London.[28] The French tax system governing income from foreign securities was on the whole disadvantageous for non-residents, as the system of taxable assets introduced in 1966, which benefited only residents, meant a 25 per cent discrimination against non-residents. There is no doubt that such factors were influential and played a large part in shaping foreign traders' investment strategies, which were inevitably based on comparisons between countries. In the current state of properly historical research, i.e. that based on primary archives, it cannot be stated however that the motivation of actors on the financial markets exclusively obeyed rules for selecting portfolios that were purely rational and exclusively based on a calculation of the short-term profitability of capital.[29]

Although any analysis of the strategies adopted by foreign traders is still largely terra incognita, the policy of supervising the market carried out by the monetary authorities can be described more fully. Amongst the range of ways of controlling access to the financial market, the Bourse Securities Committee played an important part as the penultimate deciding body, with the final decision on whether or not to admit special cases falling to the Finance Ministry. The Committee, which had been set up under the Vichy regime by the law of 14 February 1942, was chaired ex officio by the Governor of the Banque de France, which also provided its secretariat, which was managed by one of its inspectors. The small number of permanent members of the committee also included the syndic of Compagnie des Agents de Change, a representative of the banking profession, one from the shareholders' association, and the director of the Treasury acting as the government's commissioner. His power to curb developments emerges very clearly from the 1961 discussions on the Commerzbank's application for admission to the Bourse's list, submitted in August with the support of the Crédit Lyonnais. It was considered on the occasion of the one hundred and eighteenth meeting of the Bourse's Securities Committee on 12 December of that year, when Pierre Calvet, a deputy governor of the Banque de France and chair of the committee, made his reluctance clear from the start: 'For my part, I would not like to oppose the application, but I feel that I should like certain reservations to be recorded in the minutes. We have no banking securities at all, but I wonder whether as a general rule it is really appropriate—given that everywhere in the world banking activities are after all closely supervised and regulated by the public authorities—to admit banking securities, whether German or from other countries ... Personally, I would like to say quite honestly that I have no great enthusiasm for it.'[30]

The position of Olivier Moreau-Néret, the president of the Crédit Lyonnais and the banking profession's representative on the committee, was rather lukewarm at the time, even though his establishment had just begun to establish working relations with the Commerzbank through its Securities Department.[31] He explained to the committee that the Commerzbank's application 'was presented at the urgent request of a company which at the same time was asking for its shares to be registered on the London stock market's list', the application having been submitted by a group of banks including Warburgs, Rothschilds, Schroders, and Kleinworts.[32] Sellier, the *agents de changes*' representative, then pointed out that if the firm was listed in London, there was a reason for listing it in Paris, since London would soon be in the Common Market.[33] Calvet accepted the Common Market argument, and that of the prosperity of the German economy, currency, public finances, and the solidity of the mark.[34] These lively debates show very clearly the reality of the curbs on the internationalization of the Bourse right from the start. As a matter of fact, the admission of the Commerzbank was finally turned down by the Finance Minister at the very beginning of 1962,[35] provoking lively reactions in German financial thinking, which could make no sense of the refusal, when even the London Stock Exchange had admitted the German bank to its listing without the slightest difficulty.[36] It was to take until 1971 for the Finance Minister finally to admit the Commerzbank to its official list, on the basis of a favourable report from the COB. It was the first German bank to achieve this, shortly after the 1972 partnership agreement between it and the Crédit Lyonnais in October 1970.

The reasons for such tardiness on the part of the French may initially be seen both as the supervisory function of the Finance Ministry and the filtering-out by the Bourse's Securities Committee, consisting predominantly of representatives or nominees of the state, such as the president of the Crédit Lyonnais, which was of course also a nationalized bank. It is significant that the committee chaired by Pierre Fournier, a former governor of the Banque de France, set up in 1960 by the then Finance Minister Wifrid Baumgartner, himself also a former governor of the Banque de France, with the task of examining chiefly 'whether the Paris market place was sufficiently well organized to take on the role it was being offered following the setting-up of the EEC', came to conclusions that tended to lead to a more marked *dirigisme*.[37] Amongst the arguments leading to the combining of on- and off-floor trading in 1962 was the major one that first-rate foreign securities such as Olivetti or Hoechst were still not quoted, 'being either granted a dispensation from the refusal in principle provided for by the 1916 law and having to be listed, or still subject to it, and in no circumstances can the refusal of admission by the public authorities be overcome by the expedient of resorting to an unofficial market'.[38] In the early 1960s the attempt to 'organize' the financial market within the new institutional framework of the EEC essentially amounted to increasing the public authorities' control over it. In this context, the Fournier Commission aimed at giving the Bourse's Securities Committee greater powers, to enable it to 'impose from every point of view the solutions based on the general interest as well as the monetary and economic policy marked out by the government'.[39]

The desire to subordinate the financial market closely to the major options of national monetary and economic policy by isolating it from major dynamics at the international level was completely in line with the reasoning behind the 1941–2 Bourse reforms,[40] and also echoed the concerns of many public financiers in the inter-war years. It surfaced again in 1961, when the beginning of the construction of Europe brought national frameworks into question, and lay at the heart of Calvet's arguments for refusing to admit the Commerzbank, when he maintained that the major banks, given the mechanisms linking them closely to monetary policy, were too tied up with individual states to be admissible to a foreign stock exchange without the risk of causing some kind of damage to the national sovereignty as seen in the monetary and economic policy of the host country. So French *dirigisme* in the Bourse during the period considered, which was particularly obvious in the reserved area of international financial relations, can be seen as a means rather than a cause. Overall, the major reason for the closed nature of the Paris capital market at the international level has more to do with the very structures and conditions of the working of the overdraft economy, which was still a feature of France at the time, and *dirigisme* was essentially an effect rather than a cause.

3. Financial markets, overdraft economy, and national cohesion

Any financial system is naturally conservative. It functions on the basis of a distribution of risks and profits which inevitably tend to be self-perpetuating. The curbs on the internationalization of the Bourse between the late 1950s and the early 1980s show that the French financial system was no exception to the rule. Within it, the closed nature of the financial market sector can be seen as the sine qua non of the functioning of the overdraft economy set up in France from the First World War. The hypothesis is helpful in many ways, since it makes it possible to go beyond the idea of the Treasury (and hence the state) as the sole beneficiary of the system and to replace the classical opposition of private and public finance with a more universal explanation based on the dynamic confrontation of national ways of thinking and international realities.

That kind of approach is remarkably echoed in a good number of successive studies by expert commissions set up at the time by the public authorities to examine the conditions for a reform of the French financial market. Bringing together both public and private actors in the financial system, and moving easily between one sphere and the other (thanks to the practice of transferring senior civil servants into the private domain, and creating groups that on the whole were very restricted and rather infrequently changed over the period) these small committees provide a marvellous picture of a remarkably homogeneous and cohesive French financial milieu, particularly in the face of the dynamics of the international situation. These features can be clearly seen in an examination of the work of the commission set up by Valéry Giscard d'Estaing, the then Finance Minister, at the very beginning of 1971 and chaired by Wifrid Baumgartner, who moved on to head Rhône-Poulenc shortly after leaving the Finance Ministry in 1962. There was a striking continuity of men throughout the period, as there was also in the make-up of the commission, which brought together a number of public and private financiers in powerful positions in the financial system since the end of the war and even the pre-war period. The continuity alone does not explain the conservative nature of the management of the French financial system, but it is a fact that the reform movement that followed in the mid-1980s was accompanied by change in membership accentuated by the shift in political power in 1981 but was also ushered in by changes in monetary theory during the 1970s.

Equally remarkable is the heavy representation of banks on both the Baumgartner and indeed all the successive Bourse reforming commissions since the early 1960s: deposit banks (the Société Générale), merchant banks (Paribas, Lazards, and Suez) and also the heirs of the *haute banque* (Neuflizes, Schlumberger & Mallet). If public and semi-public establishments like the Caisse des Dépôts and the Crédit National are included, the preponderance of banks in the widest sense becomes apparent. It exactly reflects their position in the financial system at a time when the overdraft economy in France was reaching something of a peak between the late 1960s and the early 1970s. The structural importance that banks, and especially big deposit banks, assumed within the French financial system was the final result of a long-drawn-out process set in motion as early as the last third of the nineteenth century. It was not until the end of the Second World War, however, with the wave of credit nationalization and the radical transformation of the place of the issuing bank into what was in a certain sense the lender of *first* resort in the banking system,[41] that the bases for a largely characteristically French overdraft economy were laid. That specifically French feature was no doubt one of the main reasons for the long depression endured by the Bourse and its limited international opening-up between the 1950s and the 1980s.

The work of the Baumgartner Commission had clearly shown the reality of the situation: 'the banks play a fundamental and specific part in the securities market. Financial organization in France is different from that in the United States and Great Britain, where banking networks are dense and collect three-quarters of the orders'.[42] The strategy of the major deposit banks, however, was in fact not to any great degree orientated towards the financial market, which they rightly saw as not being very profitable, since the average return on shares (including the taxable element) since the early 1960s could be estimated at 3.1 per cent per annum at most. 'Given their many and varied activities', concluded Jean-Jacques Burgard, the secretary-general of the COB, 'banks do not pay any special attention to the securities sector of their activities, which is complex and not very profitable'.[43] Even more explicitly, Pierre Balley confided to Gilles Brac de la Perrière, the financial director of Rhône-Poulenc and the nominated secretary of the Baumgartner Commission, 'that one of the reasons for his scepticism with regard to our work for reanimating the Bourse was connected with the big nationalized banks' lack of interest in it (including his own firm)'.[44]

There can therefore be very little doubt that the importance of banks, particularly of the major deposit banks (but also, since 1966, of the merchant banks), within the financial system goes some way towards explaining the long depression of the financial market. The true cause of the blockage was not really a theoretical distinction between direct and mediated types of financing, since, as we have seen, by the 1960s and 1970s the major share of transactions on the secondary market was already based on banks rather than *agents de change*, whose resources, unlike those of the London brokers, had always been limited. The persistence of an overdraft economy in France was much more attributable to the undeniable mutual interest of the majority of actors in the financial field, including no doubt the Treasury, but also banks as a whole and the combination of borrowers, enterprises, and households in general. That community of interest is the only factor which in the last analysis explains the system's remarkable cohesion and astonishing medium-term stability, and it suggests the need to take a more relative approach to the reality, in the practices of the financial system both pre- and post-1945, of the split between 'state and the market' and 'public' and 'private' finances that so heavily marks the theory and even the perceptions of the financial actors themselves. More relevant, although in a different way, however, as an explanation of the functioning of the overdraft economy prevailing in France until at least the 1980s is the clash between its closed nature at the national level, a sine qua non of the viability of the system, and the openness at the international level which threatened its very foundation, the closed monetary circuit.

The clash was at the heart of the work of the Baumgartner Commission, which had been explicitly set up, in the words of the letter setting out its terms of reference, 'with the aim of widening the Common Market and freeing the movement of capital and obliging the Paris market to adapt to the demands of the much larger market and prepare itself to face up to competition from European financial centres'.[45] In other words, and more openly, the main concern of financial circles at the time was the need to meet competition from the London market, which the perceived inevitability of Great Britain's entry into the EEC would certainly bring. Such was clearly the sense of Brac de la Perrière's note of guidance at the time: 'The urgent need for improving the mechanisms of the Paris market is made obvious by Britain's imminent entry into the Common Market, the power of Anglo-Saxon financial institutions and the technical expertise of the City.'[46] And Jean Guyot, who had been given the task of coordinating work within the commission on the internationalization of the Bourse, had clearly seen that the opening-up was leading up to 'a fresh look at our whole financial system in the light of economic and monetary union at the technical level (bank and stock exchange activities), the regulatory level (exchange control) and the taxation level (status of non-residents)'.[47] It was a reminder that the development of the Bourse could not be separated from that of the financial system as a whole. The question of its internationalization at the time was far less a matter of a natural market trend than of international relations.

In his analysis of the superiority of the London to the Paris market, Jean Guyot mentioned primarily the history of the City, which is 'its participation since the eighteenth century in foreign financing, a role scarcely reduced by the First World War.[48] Thinking along the same lines, he explained that London's financial pre-eminence was primarily explicable by the fact that 'the American banks had moved into the City, carrying out two thirds of their Eurodollar transactions there.[49] In the same way, the relatively closed nature of the Paris market place was ultimately due more to a certain international balance of forces than to pure market logic. André de Lattre, the deputy governor of the Banque de France at the time, had made the same forthright observation in his 1965–6 lectures at the École des Sciences Politiques: 'The risk of French firms being taken over by means of a stock-market purchase cannot be ruled out theoretically.'[50] In his opinion, there was almost as great a 'risk of colonization' from foreign portfolio investments as from the direct investments currently attracting all the attention of the public authorities in France in the Gaullist era. As is known, in that very same year, 1966, the General decided to take France out of the integrated NATO command. In a similar vein Claude Pierre-Brossolette, the director of the Treasury, speaking before the Economic and Social Council in 1971, justified the higher tax rate on income from securities held by non-residents by the fact that fiscal dumping might be fine for Luxembourg, as it once was for Tangier, and perhaps now was for the Bahamas, but could not be suitable for a country like France.[51]

The director of the Treasury's words very early in the 1970s, with their nationalism scarcely toned down by references to the 'international brotherhood of financial markets', were no doubt a fairly considerable factor in the Bourse's persisting isolation in the period, for the culture of a closed financial system on national territory was not the monopoly of senior civil servants in the economic and financial fields. It was shared by most heads of firms, including some of the largest ones, who, as Serge Varangot, the Bourse manager at Paribas, pointed out, 'were not "stock-market minded" and in general cared rather little about increasing the distribution of their company's shares, particularly abroad'.[52]

But for all that, we need to put the analyses of the French financial system's resistance to an opening-up to the outside world firmly back into the situation of the shortages of capital that characterized the whole period of exceptional economic growth in every country except the United States and into the context of international financial relations at a time when the overall, truly integrated financial market, which was to develop only in the last quarter of the twentieth century, had not yet emerged. Even in the 1960s and 1970s, the international financial market was still essentially no more than the sum of capital flows from one national market to another, in the narrow accounting and theoretical balance of payments of each one. The implementation of the interest equalization tax from 1963 in the United States was entirely a part of the same way of thinking. In the end, as G. Rendu of the COB emphasized in 1971, the regulations made selling foreign securities on Wall Street 'practically impossible'. 'Putting securities on the American market', he concluded, 'is something of a major feat if the company in question does not act through a subsidiary enabling it to avoid equalization tax.'[53] The problem of the internationalization of the Bourse is clearly not endogenous to the French financial system, but is connected, perhaps chiefly, with a specific world situation, that is, to a certain configuration of relative international economic and political strengths.[54] From this point of view, in a world profoundly marked by the structural asymmetry in the Western bloc resulting from American superpower status, there is virtually no doubt that the greater or lesser opening-up of the various financial markets in Europe was largely dependent over the period on the nature of its transatlantic relations, of which the City is an excellent example. The effects of the suspension of dollar/gold convertibility, which were long felt on the range of European stock exchanges, also offer support for the hypothesis.

4. Conclusion

The historical problem of the international role of the Paris Bourse from the late 1950s to at least the 1980s cannot easily be reduced to a list of the multiple controls imposed by a *dirigiste* state on the free play of market forces. The case of the Paris financial market offers an encouragement to go beyond the narrow confines of the most frequently used explanatory framework for the development of international financial centres in the twentieth century. That framework is based on the notion of international competition, where the competitiveness of the dominant centres is assumed to be the result of a range of technical criteria such as language or, more generally, the quality–price relationship of the benefits offered to 'international traders', an abstract entity supposed to be exclusively motivated by a rational calculation of maximum utility.[55] Such an approach may in some as yet undefined way correspond to the reality of the overall financial market that has emerged over the last twenty years or so, but it does not adequately explain, except perhaps anachronistically, the issues involved in the process of financial internationalization in the preceding period.

The various assessments of the opening-up to the outside world of the Bourse from 1958 to 1983 have shown that the flows of international capital, which all remained marginal in the period, nevertheless exerted a not insignificant continuous pressure, varying in strength from time to time, which considerably increased the dynamics of the securities markets in boom periods and contributed to a fall in prices when things were going less well, with foreign securities quoted in Paris at such times serving as a safety net. Given the constraints of a whole range of rules and practices on the periphery of the financial market, studying such international dynamics has helped to make it possible to look beyond the Bourse itself to the major features of the French financial system as a whole. Its remarkable cohesion and equally remarkable medium-term stability were ultimately a result of its closed nature. Essentially, a overdraft economy is a national, and perhaps even a nationalistic, phenomenon.

It is thus in the narrow borderland between the closed nature of national systems and the dynamics of the opening-up of the international financial system that the mechanisms of financial change and innovation were concentrated. This development was primarily an effect of the transformation of the international balance of power and changes in the institutional framework, particularly as regards the two key features of the period, European construction and the vagaries of the super power status of the United States. The surge in Eurocurrencies in the 1970s took place in precisely such conditions, where national markets and the dynamics of the international situation met, and in a certain way created the bases of the global financial market of the late twentieth and early twenty-first centuries.

Notes

1. Georges Lutfalla, 'Le Marché financier, son rôle économique, sa situation actuelle, les réformes que celle-ci appelle', *Journal officiel, avis et rapports du Conseil Économique* (14 Nov. 1952), 409.
2. *Les Principales Places financières du monde* Chambre de Commerce Suisse en France (n.p., 1959).
3. Richard Roberts, (ed.), *International Financial Centres of Europe, North America and Asia*, (Aldershot, 1994), p. xiv.
4. Françoise Marnata, *La Bourse et le financement des investissements* (Paris, 1973), 38.
5. Alexandre Lamfalussy, *Les Marchés financiers en Europe* (Paris, 1968).
6. Ranald C. Michie, *The London Stock Exchange: A History* (Oxford, 1999), 326 ff.
7. Philip G. Cerny, 'The Little Big Bang in Paris: Financial Market Deregulation in a Dirigiste System', *European Journal of Political Research*, 17 (1989, 169–192: Pierre-Cyrille Hautcoeur, 'Le Système financier français depuis 1945', *Risques*, 25 (Jan.–Mar. 1996), 135–51.
8. Jean Guyot, 'Le Marché de Paris, la City de Londres et le Marché Commun', typed note, Apr. 1971, Archives Wilfrid Baumgartner (AWB) 4BA33, Dr6.
9. Michael Loriaux, *France after Hegemony, International Change and Financial Reform* (Ithaca, NY, 1991); André Straus, 'Structures financières et performances des entreprises industrielles en France dans la seconde moitié du XXe siècle', *Entreprises et histoire*, 2 (1992), 19–33; Olivier Feiertag, 'Finances publiques, mur d'argent et genèse de la libéralisation financière en France de 1981 à 1984', in S. Berstein and P. Milza (eds.), *François Mitterrand, les années du changement, 1981–1984* (Paris, 2001), 431–55.
10. Henri Bourguignat, *Finance internationale*, 3rd edn. (Paris, 1997), 39 ff.
11. Henri Ardant, *Le Marché financier international*, lecture notes, Conservatoire National des Arts et Métiers, fascicule 2 (1958).
12. Oliver Moreau-Néret, *Les Valeurs mobilières* (Paris, 1939), vol. 2 296–7.
13. Charles-Albert Michalet, *Les Placements des épargnants français de 1815 à nos jours* (Paris, 1968), 249.
14. Lutfalla, 'Le Marché financier, 411.
15. André de Lattre, *Les Finances extérieures de la France (1945–1958)* (Paris, 1959), 88.
16. Jean Carrière, 'Les Places financières du Marché Commun devant la libération des mouvements de capitaux', *Revue du Marché Commun*, 6 (May 1961), 202–14.
17. Lutfalla, 'Le Marché financier', 48; A. de Lattre, *Politique économique de la France depuis 1945* (Paris, 1966), 302.
18. Commission des Opérations de Bourse, *Deuxième rapport annuel au président de la République* (1969), 302; Pierre Balley, *La Bourse: mythes et réalités* (Paris, 1986), 74.
19. COB, *Cinquième rapport annuel au président de la République*, (1972), 61–2.
20. Balley, *La Bourse* 74.
21. Service des Archives Économiques et Financières (SAEF) du Ministère des Finances, Z 13533, structure de l'offre de capitaux sur le marché des valeurs à revenu fixe, 1959–63.
22. Balley, *La Bourse* 75.
23. Ibid.
24. See for example Henri Freppel, 'Département financier' note no. 1 pour Rémy Schlumberger, 8 Janv. 1963, Archives de Neuflize, Mallet, Schlumberger (ANSM) & 1412.
25. Jean-Yves Haberer, *Les Fonctions du Trésor et la politique financière*, Institut d'Études Politiques, 1975–6 (Paris, 1976), fascicule 1, 451.

26. COB, *Cinquième rapport* 78.
27. Lord Ritchie of Dundee, 'The London Stock Exchange and International Investment', in *The City of London as a Centre of International Trade and Finance* (London, 1961), 159.
28. AWB, 4BA32, working pages of the Baumgartner Commission, Tableau comparatif des frais fiscaux perçus sur diverses places boursières, Tableau comparatif des rémunérations perçues par les intermédiaires de diverses places boursières, 1971.
29. Michel Aglietta, and André Orléan, *La Monnaie entre violence et confiance* (Paris, 2002), 35 ff.
30. SAEF, 22D-178/1, Minutes de la 118e séance du comité des Bourses de valeurs, 12 Dec. 1961, 56.
31. Eric Bussière, 'La Stratégie européenne du Crédit Lyonnais de l'après-guerre à Europartenaires (des années 1950 aux années 1970)', in *Le Crédit Lyonnais, 1863–1986* (Geneva, 2003), 679–701.
32. SAEF, 22D-178/1, letter of Moreau-Néret to Calvet, 23 Nov. 1961 and procès-verbal de la 118e séance du Comité des Bourses de Valeurs.
33. Ibid. 57.
34. Ibid.
35. SAEF, 22D-178/1, Letter of Baumgartner, Finance Minister, to Calvet, 4 Jan. 1962.
36. SAEF, 22D-178/1, *Hamburger Abendblatt*, 20 Jan. 1962.
37. SAEF, Z13661, *Rapport sur l'organisation des bourses* (Feb. 1961), 4.
38. ANSM,&145, working of the documents Fournier Commission, 'Etude sur la fusion éventuelle du Parquet et du Marché, des Courtiers', note by Lansieux, inspector of the Banque de France and secretary of the Bourse Committee, 25 Nov. 1960, 5.
39. Ibid. 6.
40. Bertrand Hommey, 'La Bourse des Valeurs et l'économie dirigée', thesis (Paris, 1942).
41. O. Feiertag, 'Les Banques d'émission et la croissance, 1945–1973', in *Politiques et pratiques des banques d'émission (XVIIe–XXe siècles)* (Paris, 2003).
42. AWB, 4BA35, Dr1, 'Les Banques et le marché des actions', note of Renaud de la Génière, 25 May 1971, 1.
43. AWB, 4BA34, Dr2, J. J. Burgard, 'Note sur le fonctionnement du marché boursier au cours de la prochaine décennie', 28 Apr. 1971.
44. AWB, 4BA33, Dr6, G. Brac de la Perrière, to W. Baumgartner, 'Notes prises aprèsune conversation avec M. Pierre Balley', 16 Apr. 1971: see also COB, *Quatrième rapport annuel au président de la République* (1971), 83.
45. AWB, 4BA33, Dr1, Letter of France Minister to W. Baumgartner, 4 Mar. 1971.
46. AWB, 4BA32, 'Orientation et méthodes pour le groupe Marché financier', note from G. Brac de la Perrière to W. Baumgartner, 19 Jan. 1971.
47. AWB, 4BA/33, Dr6, note quoted, 9.
48. Ibid. 5.
49. AWB, 4BA34, J. Guyot, groupe de travail sur les aspects internationaux, compte-rendu de la réunion du 19 avril 1971, 3.
50. de Lattre, *Politique économique*, 302.
51. AWB, 4BA37, Dr3, typescript of the hearing of C. Pierre-Brossolette before the finances section of the Conseil Économique et Social, 8 July 1971, 26.
52. AWB, 4BA34, Varangot, 'La Faible Distribution des actions françaises à l'étranger: aspects commerciaux' (in English in the text).
53. Ibid.

54. This possible method of analysis, now rather neglected when the history of economic and financial international relations increasingly tends to fit into the framework of a strictly 'Paretian' world, was interestingly explored immediately after the Second World War by François Perroux for example: 'Esquisse d'une théorie de l'Économie Dominante', *Economie appliquée* (1948), 2–3. See also Alain Cotta, 'Le Déclin de la domination économique d'une nation', *Revue d'économie politique*, 70, (1960), 35–8. The end of the Cold War does not mean that such an approach is now irrelevant for an understanding of the past and present development of international financial markets.
55. See for example Geoffrey Jones, 'International Financial Centres in Asia, the Middle East and Australia: A Historical Perspective', in Y. Cassis (ed.), *Finance and Financiers in European History, 1880–1960* (Cambridge, 1992), 405–28.

12

London as an International Banking Centre, 1950–1980

MAE BAKER AND MICHAEL COLLINS

1. Introduction

It is clear that the late 1950s and early 1960s marked the beginning of a period of important structural change and innovation within British banking. After the war, of course, the City's fortune was far from assured—with the UK's relative economic weakness, with the weak international financial legacy from sterling's experience in the 1930s and during the war, and with the continued unfavourably restrictive international financial environment facing City institutions. This chapter examines the re-emergence of London as an international banking centre by focusing on the rapid growth of foreign banks locating in the City in the 1950s, 1960s, and 1970s, and the consequent competition they posed for indigenous British banks. The size of an international banking centre, and its relative importance, can be assessed on a variety of bases. In this chapter, we employ traditional measures: the number of overseas banking establishments which have located in the centre; the scale and share of deposit taking; and the scale and share of international bank lending advanced. Because it is difficult to isolate any particular thirty-year period from events shaping the preceding and following years, we begin with a brief precursor to the period in order to set it in context.

2. Historical background

Foreign bankers have long been attracted to London. Thus, during the nineteenth century there were an increasing number of examples (such as Allied Irish in 1825, and Algemene Bank Nederland in 1858). However, a fair number of 'foreign banks' in fact had strong British connections (for example Bank of New South Wales in 1853, Bank of New Zealand in 1862, Hong Kong and Shanghai Banking Corporation in 1865), and also many British merchant banks were formed by foreigners who came to Britain. It was not until around 1870 that a noticeable inflow of foreign banks proper started—that is, foreign banks which resisted absorption by British banks, and retained their identity as outposts of their overseas parents.

By the start of the First World War, there were twenty-nine such banks in London—one measure of London's importance as an international financial centre. The core attraction of the City stemmed from the size and international importance of the British economy and the widespread multilateral trading and financial arrangements that had been firmly established under Pax Britannica.[1] Critically, a large share of world trade was conducted in sterling, and the bill of exchange drawn on London was the premier method of financing it.[2] Such business, and the associated foreign exchange business, was a lucrative magnet, pulling in foreign banks eager to gain a share of the market.[3] Furthermore London was the main supplier of capital—both short and long term—to the rest of the world. Between 1870 and 1912 annual capital exports rose to a remarkable degree from £32m. to £226m.[4] Helping to float these loans, and—more frequently—acting as paying agents for them, was lucrative business for foreign banks in London. Amongst the first to arrive were the French. Comptoir National d'Escompte opened a London branch in 1865, followed by Société Générale and Crédit Lyonnais in 1871, and Banque de Paris in 1873. The first German bank also entered in 1873—Deutsche Bank, followed by Dresdner Bank in 1895, and Disconto-Gesellschaft by 1900. By 1914 these banks had been joined by Russian, Japanese, Belgian, Chinese, Swiss, Italian, and American banks—although the German banks at this time took their leave (indeed, Dresdner Bank was not to reappear in London until 1967).

In the 1920s the growing hegemony of the United States had a strong impact with a wave of new entrants to the London banking scene from across the Atlantic—Bankers Trust Company, First National City, and the forerunner of Manufacturers' Hanover Trust. As elsewhere in the financial world the economic crises of 1929–33 severely affected developments. Banking business suffered a sharp decline,[5] exacerbated by German and other Central European payments defaults and the collapse of the gold standard, with Britain suspending gold payments in September 1931. The UK's traditional role of international financing was severely curtailed and the outflow of capital overseas almost ceased.[6] The collapse of international trade during this time also severely damaged the international acceptance business, a mainstay for a core of London-based financial institutions. Not surprisingly, few new foreign banks opened in London during this time; the Bank of America being a notable exception in 1931. Just as the German banks had left London during the First World War, the Italian and Japanese banks left during the Second. Thus, it was not until the post-war period, with the eventual return to convertibility and the increased prosperity of the 1950s, that the inflow of foreign banks into London became once more pronounced.

3. 1955–1980: The growth of foreign banks in London

The return to full convertibility in 1958 saw the magnetism of London attracting foreign banks once more. Convertibility, followed by the development of London's new money markets—especially the Eurodollar market—proved irresistible.

In 1950 there were 53 foreign banks in London. By 1960 this had risen to 77, and by 1966 to 103. The succeeding years saw acceleration in the rate at which foreign banks established themselves in London, and by 1970 the total of foreign banks amounted to 159, an average of eight per year over the decade. But it was in the final decade of the period of this survey—that is, 1970 to 1980—that the arrival of foreign entrants reached its pinnacle, at just over nineteen per annum, bringing the total of foreign banks in London to 351 by 1980 (see Fig. 12.1).

In the one hundred years from 1870 to 1970 the number of foreign banks directly represented[7] in London had risen from 10 to 159. It took less than eight years to add this number again. By 1978 the number of foreign banks had risen to 311, and by the end of the decade it stood at 351. As can be seen from Fig. 12.1, 'take-off' can be dated to the 1960s. Thus, in the post-war years, the number of foreign banks increased by just 24 from 1950 to 1960; and then by 82 in the 1960s.

The origin of these banks is illustrated in Fig. 12.2 and Table 12.1. Historically, in the nineteenth and early twentieth centuries, the Commonwealth banks had had the largest presence in London in terms of numbers of banks. By 1950, however, the European banks had taken the lead, and have held it ever since. Thus, during the 1960s there was a notable increase in European banks, from 28 in 1960 to 50 by 1970—by then they were the largest group, having pushed the Commonwealth banks to third place behind the USA (which had 37 banks in London). Japanese banks had still to make their mark. In 1960 the number of Japanese banks present in London was slightly below that of the USA, with 8 compared to 10 banks, but whilst US banks had increased to 37 by 1970, Japanese banks had grown to just 13 (Table 12.1).

Overall, the decade of the 1960s saw the number of foreign banks in London more than double from 77 to 159. In terms of scale, London was exceptional.

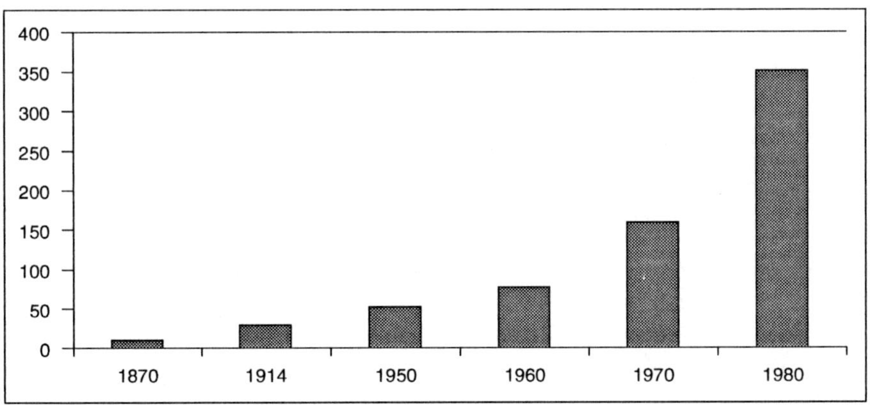

Figure 12.1. Foreign banks in London, 1870–1980 (direct representation)
Source: complied from various issues of the *Banker*.

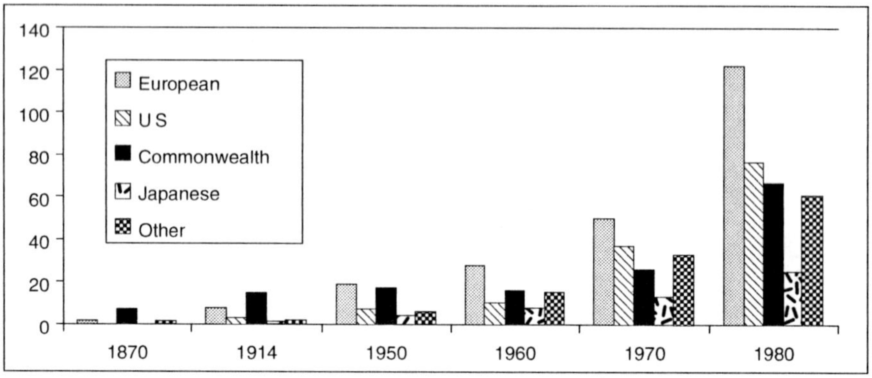

Figure 12.2. Origins of foreign banks in London
Source: Compiled from various issues of *The Banker*.

Table 12.1 *Foreign banks in London, by country*

	Total	European	US	Commonwealth	Japanese	Other
1870	10	2	—	7	—	1
1914	29	8	3	15	1	2
1950	53	19	7	17	4	6
1960	77	28	10	16	8	15
1966	103	34	14	21	12	22
1970	159	50	37	26	13	33
1980	351	122	76	67	25	61

Source: Compiled from *The Banker*, various issues.

Indeed, the importance of London as an international banking centre can be judged by the fact that by 1970, London (with 159) had double the number of foreign banks of any other financial centre in the world, including its closest rival New York, with 73 (see Table 12.2), and Tokyo, with 19. Although the 1970s saw an expansion in foreign operations of banks throughout Europe, London still held the lead. By the end of 1975 there were 244 foreign banks directly represented in London (and a further 87 foreign institutions which were indirectly represented through bank consortia). In comparison Frankfurt at that time had 133 directly represented foreign banks, and Switzerland (with financial centres in Basle, Zurich, and Geneva) in 1974 had 101.[8]

The 1960s saw an expansion, not only in the numbers of foreign banks in London, but also in the range of activities in which they were engaged. Many continued to be primarily engaged in the financing of trade, via acceptance and discounting business, or cash advances, generally in trade between Britain and their

Table 12.2. *Foreign banks in New York and London*

	New York	London
Before 1971	73	161
1971	79	174
1972	83	213
1973	96	230
1974	112	262
1975	124	261
1976	139	263
1977	172	298
1978	202	311
1979	234	328

Source: *The Banker*, Feb. 1980.

home countries. However, the more rapid growth of business lay elsewhere, in foreign currency dealing and banking business that had previously been the preserve of the domestic banks.

One reason for this influx was that the City of London was characterized by a more liberal regulatory environment than was usual in other international financial centres at the time.[9] There was nothing in London akin to the American Glass–Steagall Act which in America imposed a separation of commercial and investment banking functions, or to the similar arrangement in post-war Japan or the French separation (up to 1966) of the banking sector into *banques de depôts* and *banques d'affaires*. Indeed, in America the existing restrictions on banking function wrought by the Glass–Steagall Act and on location by the McFadden Act were intensified with regulations limiting interest rates on deposits under Regulation Q and imposing taxation upon the interest on loans made overseas under the Interest Equalization Tax introduced in 1963. The latter is credited with having a dramatic impact—diverting business from New York to London.

> Almost overnight, the New York market was closed to foreign long-term borrowers. From then on, any American who bought foreign bonds in New York had to receive his interest with tax lopped off. This became an intolerable situation when there were richer pickings in international lending to be found elsewhere ... in London.[10]

In Britain, the government did impose restrictions on bank and consumer credit in pursuit of its macroeconomic objectives, but they impinged largely on the business of the domestic banks. Moreover, whilst the Bank of England might, from time to time, make requests to the banks to limit advances or even call for special deposits, the controls on the banks operated largely through 'persuasion' rather than legislation. There was nowhere else in the developed world where such flexibility of action existed, and where bankers could adapt their thoughts and practices to new possibilities of earning a reward. Thus the inflow came from all corners of the world, but the largest single source was the world's largest economy, the USA. The attraction of flexibility of action was stressed by the contemporary financier, Paul Bareau.[11]

There is ... the informality and freedom of the system—or rather of the state of affairs, for there is no system. Our financial structure is far freer of statutory restriction than it is, for example, in the United States, the home of the free enterprise. At the head of the community stands the Bank of England ... It can now require other banks to do its bidding [as a result of nationalization] but it has never had to resort to that ... The position today remains in all its essence what it was in the days of the Governorship of Mr Montagu Norman, of whose reign it used to be said that the most powerful instrument of credit control in Britain were the eyebrows of the Governor.[12]

The American banks went to London partly to bypass domestic restrictions. Over the thirty years from 1938 to 1968, major USA banks had grown rapidly, but expansion within the USA (both geographically and by function) was limited by federal and state authorities. For example, by the Glass–Steagall Act of 1933 which rigidly separated out investment banking activities from commercial banking, and by the McFadden Act of 1927 which effectively prevented inter-state branching. Consequently, American banks were unable to match the expansion of their client companies, and those banks which concentrated on domestic banking business were unable to provide the range of services that their large, internationally orientated clients required, with the risk of loss of business and clients to other banks. By 1961, 800 subsidiaries of American multinational companies had already located in the UK.[13] It was hardly surprising, therefore, that establishment of a branch in London—a financial centre pre-eminent in world financial affairs—proved attractive to American banks. They could offer international banking facilities to their US client companies, service the banking requirements of UK-based subsidiaries of US companies, and gain access to the rapidly developing parallel money markets and the Eurocurrency markets. Contemporary financier Bareau offered one further explanation for the attraction of London—the networks and philosophy of the City which facilitated speedy decision-making, accompanied by the assistance given to flexibility and adaptability by the relative lack of obsession with lawyers:

One reason [for the attraction] ... is to be found in the compactness as well as in the composite whole represented by the City of London. The people who matter within this square mile know one another intimately ... They have often been to the same schools, they belong to the same clubs; on the whole they tend to trust one another. As a result of this proximity and compatibility, they find it possible to reach decisions quickly, probably more quickly in the case of transactions which need the consent of many parties, than is possible in any other financial capital ... In such markets as the discount and money markets, business running into millions of pounds is transacted wholly by word of mouth and never confirmed on paper. Speed of decision is also helped by the fact that we are less obsessed by lawyers and legal formalities in London than they are in other capitals. I well remember the late Lord Keynes appearing at the United States Treasury building in Washington at the start of one of the wartime negotiations between the two countries and being asked by his American counterpart, Dr Harry White, 'Where is your lawyer?' 'We haven't one,' said Keynes. To which Harry White replied, 'Who then does your thinking for you?'.[14]

One might be led to conclude that the foreign bankers operating in London were themselves at something of a disadvantage, being 'outsiders', lacking familiarity with the 'trust ethic', and not, initially at least, part of 'the club'—indeed London's openness to outsiders eventually destroyed 'the club'.[15] However, the same commentator goes on to note how the newcomers to the City were quick to adapt to the City philosophy and way of conducting business: 'they quickly became imbued with the atmosphere and philosophy of the City. They tend to become *plus royaliste que le roi*.'[16]

As more and more foreign banks located within the City, the concentration of banks—which was already the greatest in the world—naturally increased. This concentration, along with an unrivalled network of international contacts, and the growth of the interbank markets, served as a magnet for further foreign banks. 'London had the critical mass necessary to attract banks, and by doing so it became even more attractive to other banks.'[17]

4. The parallel money markets

Another major reason for the inflow of American banks in the 1950s and 1960s was to gain access to London's burgeoning money markets. In London, a second money market, or group of parallel money markets, developed from the late 1950s. These new markets initially developed from the activities of existing institutions taking on extra business as the opportunities occasioned by changing regulations and official policy presented themselves. In the early 1950s an initial impetus had been provided by the change in monetary policy from cheap money to the use of interest rates as a control device.[18] Initially the main participants in these markets were UK merchant banks and overseas banks with offices in London, and much of the subsequent growth of these institutions is bound up with the continued development of the parallel money markets.

The rationing by the authorities of conventionally supplied bank funds, and the retention of cartelized prices by the clearing banks, encouraged potential borrowers to find other sources of funds—and also facilitated a more efficient interest rate mechanism in these markets—which, in turn, attracted other supplies of money into these new markets. The result was the emergence of new and highly competitive markets which were free from the restrictive practices that continued to govern the clearing banks and discount houses until 1971. The periodic application of monetary squeezes, which concentrated on restricting clearing bank advances, gave further impetus to the development of the parallel markets. A major consequence of the development of these new markets was a large expansion in the total and types of short-term instruments available to banks. At the time of the Radcliffe Report in 1959, the assets of the UK merchant banks for the most part had consisted of loans to the discount market, loans to local authorities, and holdings of short-term government debt. Since then, in addition to their acceptance business, they had become extensively engaged in wholesale banking, with market loans (certificates of deposit, interbank loans, and marketable loans to local authorities) being the predominant asset category—accounting for over 53 per cent of total assets by 1981. Over the period from 1951 to 1981, the liabilities of UK merchant banks (mainly in the form of time deposits and certificates of deposit) rose seventy-five-fold, climbing from 1 per cent of total deposit liabilities in the UK banking sector in 1951, to 5 per cent by 1979 (see Tables 12.3 and 12.4).

The expansion of the UK merchant banks' deposit liabilities was, however, overshadowed by those of the overseas banks in London (see Table 12.5). For these latter banks, deposit liabilities rose from 9 per cent of total deposits in 1951 to a staggering 61 per cent by 1980. The business conducted by these banks shifted from being predominantly trade related to operations in the wholesale markets—to the extent that the vast bulk of the business conducted by these banks took place in the parallel markets.

The clearing banks, on the other hand, were relatively slow starters in the parallel markets. Their resources consisted overwhelmingly of retail deposits, accumulated at their nationwide branching networks. Besides, during the 1960s, the clearing banks were under-lent as a result of government imposed restrictions. Consequently they had no immediate need to seek or attract additional funds. They did partake, however, to a limited extent through merchant bank subsidiaries, where these existed—for example Lloyds Associated Banking Company. The active involvement of the clearing banks did not really begin until the liberalization of the credit control regime in 1971. From thereon the importance of the new money markets rapidly increased such that by the mid-1970s wholesale deposits amounted to 40 per cent of the London clearing banks' total deposits.[19]

A key feature of the parallel money markets was interbank business; indeed by the 1970s the interbank market had become by far the largest of the sterling parallel markets, with interbank deposits dwarfing all other sterling short-term instruments

Table 12.3. *Ratios of deposits of domestic banks and deposits of foreign banks to total deposits*

	Total domestic (£m.)	Total foreign (£m.)	Domestic as % of total	Foreign as % of total
1951	7,347	713	91	9
1955	7,673	808	90	10
1960	9,216	1,467	86	14
1965	11,653	4,553	72	28
1970	15,064	24,520	38	62
1975	53,206	75,888	41	59
1980	111,554	172,171	39	61

Source: Compiled from the *BEQB*.

Table 12.4. *Deposits: domestic banks*

	British clearing banks (£m.)	Other UK banks (£m.)	Accepting houses/ merchant banks (£m.)	Total (£m.)
1951	6,333	878	136	7,347
1955	6,612	909	152	7,673
1960	7,831	961	424	9,216
1965	9,454	1,168	1,031	11,653
1970	10,606	1,452	3,006	15,064
1975	26,551	21,590	5,065	53,206
1980	53,596	46,482	11,476	111,554

Source: Compiled from the *BEQB*.

Table 12.5. *Deposits: foreign banks*

	US (£m.)	Japanese (£m.)	Other (£m.)	Commonwealth (£m.)	Consortium (£m.)	Total (£m.)
1951	96	—	75	542	—	713
1955	123	—	140	545	—	808
1960	389	—	311	767	—	1,467
1965	1,432	—	523	922	—	4,129
1970	11,567	—	7,156	5,797	—	24,520
1975	36,767	11,816	22,043		5,262	75,888
1980	59,591	40,734	60,601		11,245	172,171

Source: Compiled from the *BEQB*.

(money at call, Treasury bills, commercial bills, local authority temporary debt, deposits with finance houses, and sterling CDs). In the early 1960s interbank deposits stood at 8 per cent of amounts outstanding in the London sterling money markets. This contrasted with the traditionally important Treasury bills, which were still the largest category at 67 per cent of the total. By 1979, though, the situation had been completely reversed. At that time, Treasury bills accounted for 6 per cent of amounts outstanding whilst interbank deposits were the largest category at 42 per cent. These interbank transactions were typically on an unsecured basis, in amounts of £0.5m, £1m., or more, for less than three months' duration, with deposits not transferable or negotiable.[20] The advantage which interbank dealing conferred upon the participating banks was the ability to adjust liquidity positions very easily and quickly through borrowing or lending amongst themselves, rather than relying on adjustments to call money and bill discounts as they had done previously.

5. The Eurodollar market

Alongside the development of the parallel markets ran that of the Euromarkets.[21] Some British banks had accepted foreign currency deposits on a small scale even before the Second World War, but it was not until after the 1950s that the transactions became large scale.[22] According to Burn,[23] London-based banks in 1957 were the starting point of the Eurodollar market as a result of the domestic credit squeeze, when Bank rate rose sharply to 7 per cent and the authorities imposed curbs on UK banks' overseas lending of sterling to finance trade between non-sterling area countries. The rise in Bank rate allowed British banks to offer internationally favourable terms for dollar deposits whilst the curbs on sterling credit of overseas trade induced the banks and accepting houses to find alternative means of providing such trade credit. This gap in trade finance was initially bridged by the dollars deposited with British merchant banks arising from Regulation Q in the USA, which limited interest payments on deposits. Thus, there was a conjunction of factors in 1957—whilst US interest rates on deposits were artificially depressed, UK rates were at a historic high. Additionally, borrowers from American banks in the USA were customarily required by the banks to re-deposit a proportion of each loan into a non-interest-bearing account at the bank, thus, effectively, increasing the cost of borrowing.[24] The predictable result was that dollar holders placed their dollar deposits with British banks.

This early Eurodollar business was conducted for the most part by the London merchant banks and the Midland Bank.[25] The years between 1958 and 1963 saw a quadrupling of such deposits by the accepting houses such as Barings, Rothschilds, etc. As these dollar deposits did not need to be switched into sterling and, therefore, did not fall under the umbrella of exchange control regulation, this gave a significant fillip to London as an entrepôt centre and marked the beginning of the offshore Eurodollar market proper.[26] The subsequent growth in the Eurodollar markets is traditionally held to have been fuelled by three further factors. First, the US balance of payments deficits at the end of the 1950s meant there was a general growth in dollar holdings outside the USA. Second, East European countries who were accumulating dollars had no wish to reveal the scale to the Cold War enemy, the USA, by depositing them in US banks, and they feared the possibility of them being blocked or seized for political reasons. Therefore, they sought other, non-American repositories. Thirdly, and significantly, the return to convertibility of the major European currencies in 1958 led to an associated revival of foreign exchange markets.[27] By mid-1958 the Eurodollar market operating through London was well established and (as noted above) there began the influx of American banks, eager to avoid Federal Reserve regulations.

The arrival of the American banks *en masse* ended the dominion of the British merchant banks.[28] The American banks not only fostered further dealing in Eurocurrencies, but also developed new instruments, most notably the certificate of deposit. In fact, by 1967 American banks operating in London had the lion's share of Eurodollar business. This was not altogether surprising, of course, as these banks were perceived to have an advantage over UK clearing banks in that they were all large institutions dealing in their own currency and with established ties with American corporations. Indeed, repeated bouts of monetary constraint in America left an unsatisfied demand for bank loans—and, so, for some US corporations, borrowing dollars from American banks based overseas became an attractive proposition.[29] Thus, these banks had a ready outlet for their dollar deposits via their head offices in the USA. According to *The Banker*, during the US credit squeeze of 1966, around $4bn. was taken in from their overseas branches by the head offices. During the 1968 credit squeeze, the total of Eurodollars remitted back to US head offices in this way was reported to have been around $6bn., and in just three weeks of June 1969, American branches in London found $3bn. for their fund-hungry head offices![30] These dollar deposits came not only from the USA but also from Europe and throughout the world as the chronic US current account deficit continued to add to the supply of international liquidity. An outlet for funds on such a scale enjoyed by the American banks in London was not one shared by non-American banks. Consequently, the strains caused by this huge flow of dollars to American banks in the USA (for example, forcing up the short-term Eurodollar interest rate to an unprecedented 13 per cent in June 1969) aroused disquiet amongst European bankers and the Federal Reserve alike, leading to renewed calls for some control of the market. Indeed, during the 1960s several European countries, including France, Switzerland, Germany, and Italy, had placed restrictions on the transaction of Eurodollar business, whilst the Bank of England and the UK Treasury resisted the pressure to restrict Eurodollar business.[31] On the other hand, experience in the 1960s also demonstrates that a huge volume of funds could be found at short notice through the Euromarkets at that time. Furthermore, the development of the Eurodollar markets enabled European banks, as well as American branches in London, to finance a great variety of needs and borrowers, from corporations to governmental and quasi-governmental agencies.

It is difficult to assess the extent of the London banks' (both domestic and foreign) involvement in the Eurodollar market as this involves separating out Euromarket business from the rest of the banks' business. However, during this period, the Bank for International Settlements (BIS) Annual Reports did try to estimate the size of the market by both user and source of funds. At the end of 1968, on the 'users' side, the USA and Canada accounted for 40 per cent of the total—or $10bn. of a total of $25bn.; with $7bn. of that $10bn. attributed to US banks. By June of 1969 this figure had risen to $13.4bn., out of a total of $30bn. The overwhelming mass of that US bank borrowing was channelled through their London branches, and as that figure relates solely to repatriations, it understates total borrowing by American banks. Of course, in addition to sending Eurodollars back to head office, the American banks in London also lent Eurodollars to corporate borrowers. It is estimated that the American banks in London accounted for around 60 per cent of the Eurodollar business by the end of the 1960s, and that together with the Eurodollar business transacted by other foreign banks in London, and by the London merchant banks, the extent of the London share of the Eurodollar market amounted to 80 per cent—that is, 80 per cent of the Eurodollar pool of funds was borrowed through London-based banks.

The 1970s saw a combination of factors bring about a shift in the Eurocurrency market away from the dominance of the foreign branches of US banks towards European banks, principally Swiss, UK, Italian, and French. Amongst the reasons were the monetary easing in the USA, the repayment of Eurodollar borrowings by US banks, the inflow of Deutsche Marks to the Euromarkets, the inflow of funds from official monetary authorities, tight credit conditions in Europe, and increased borrowing by European corporations. This shift is reflected in the share of currencies other than dollars in the market. That share rose from 15 per cent to almost 35 per cent between 1969 and 1970.[32]

The Euromarket continued to grow throughout the 1970s. Estimates by the BIS of the size of the Euromarkets shows a greater than ninefold growth, from $44bn. in 1969 to around $475bn. by 1979.[33] The growth of business was, according to the BIS, particularly marked in Luxembourg and the UK. Although London banks had experienced some relative decline in Euromarket business as the other European banks expanded, by the end of the decade Eurocurrency business was once more expanding strongly in London, up by 33 per cent in 1979 alone, in total amounting to 42 per cent of the world market. A large part of this new business was attributed to Japanese affiliates located in London. In terms of total international lending attributed to principal international banking centres, London's share (which had varied between one-third and one-quarter from the 1960s to the early 1970s) stood at just over one-quarter of the market (27 per cent) in 1975 and 1980. This was still significantly above that of New York—13.5 and 13.4 per cent respectively, and that of Tokyo—4.6 and 5 per cent.[34] However, the continuing pre-eminence of London as an international banking centre was not paralleled by that of British banks.

6. The impact of foreign banks on British banking

During the 1960s, London bankers had four complaints to make about the foreign banks—and in particular American banks—in London. These were the siphoning-off of Eurodollars to banks in the USA; the impact on property prices and rentals in the City (as they all wanted to be within the Square Mile); the poaching of trained staff with inflated salaries; and their lack of timidity in touting for new business. This last practice was looked upon with disdain by the native London bankers. The commercial banks had always claimed that they engaged in some competition for new business, but there was a general tacit agreement between British bankers that direct soliciting of customers of other banks was not acceptable; that it would lead to questionable tactics, and result in the 'law of the jungle'.[35] American bankers, reared in the 'land of the hard sell', had no such inhibitions. American banks in London were not retail banks garnering in deposits through a branch network; instead they bid directly for money in the competitive money markets. Thus, they did not have the considerable costs of maintaining a branch network. Consequently, they could offer highly competitive rates on domestic and foreign business, attracting previously long-term customers of British banks. Any remaining complacency of the Big Five was shattered as they experienced a loss of market share in the area of the business they had once thought sacrosanct—foreign banks in London now began taking a growing share of domestic deposits.

In 1955 British banks had held 90 per cent of the total deposits in the UK banking sector. By 1965 this had already slipped to 76 per cent, with foreign banks accounting for 28 per cent of total deposits. In 1967 *The Banker* reported with alarm the rate of growth of deposits amongst foreign banks in London, reporting that 'there is little sign of any slackening. At this pace it will be only a few years before the branches of foreign banks in London have combined deposits approaching those of the clearing banks themselves.'[36] The prediction was correct. Just three years later (1970), the foreign banks had not only equalled, but overtaken domestic banks, with deposits amounting to 62 per cent of total deposits (Table 12.3). Thereafter, the foreign banks maintained this lion's share of total deposits, of about two-thirds of the total, to the end of the period (Table 12.6). Even a comparison with British merchant banks— who like the foreign banks in London did not have domestic branch networks and engaged in wholesale markets—shows the deposits of the foreign banks increased at a faster rate (Tables 12.4 and 12.5).

Although the European banks had taken the lead from 1950 in terms of numbers of banks in London, it was the American banks that secured most of the deposits. Official figures do not distinguish between Commonwealth banks and other overseas banks (which includes European banks) after 1970, but until that time the Commonwealth banks had accounted for 88 per cent of the combined deposits of Commonwealth and other foreign banks in 1951, falling to 80 per cent by 1955, 71 per cent by 1960, 54 per cent by 1965, and 45 per cent by 1970. Even assuming

Table 12.6. *Ratio of deposits to total deposits, by origin*

Percentage of deposits held by				
	US banks	Japanese banks	Other overseas banks	Domestic banks
1951	1		8	91
1955	1		8	90
1960	4		10	86
1965	9		19	72
1970	29		33	38
1975	28	9	21	41
1980	21	14	25	39

Source: Compiled from the *BEQB*.

that the Commonwealth banks' share continued to fall—as the category 'other overseas banks' after 1970 includes not just Commonwealth and European banks but the rest of the world—it is unlikely that the European banks would have had a larger share of total deposits than the US banks (Table 12.5). A reflection of the growing importance of Japanese banks is the inclusion of separate deposit figures for Japanese banks in official reporting (Table 12.5).

A significant amount of the rise in total deposits took place in the deposits of overseas residents—largely in foreign currencies, and particularly into foreign banks (see Fig. 12.3). In 1970, the deposits of overseas residents' accounts with the UK deposit banks amounted to just 4.4 per cent of the deposit banks' total deposits. In contrast, the foreign currency deposits of foreign banks averaged around 83 per cent of their deposits, with a staggering 92 per cent of US banks' deposits coming from overseas residents. Even the UK merchant banks—with 54 per cent of their total deposits in the form of foreign currency deposits—did not come close to the share of the foreign banks, especially the Americans, much of which can, of course, be attributed to the growing Eurodollar market. Significantly though, the British clearing banks were also losing domestic deposit business to the foreign banks. Between 1955 and 1970, sterling deposits by UK (non-bank) residents at American banks alone rose over seventeenfold from £27m. to £468m.

Similar inroads were achieved by foreign banks into the UK advances business. As Table 12.7 shows, advances made by foreign banks to UK residents between 1964 and 1970 increased by 133 per cent (from £889 to £2,069), compared to an increase of just 22 per cent by the British clearing banks. British merchant banks fared better than the clearing banks, although still behind the foreign banks, with a rise of 117 per cent over the same period. However, the overwhelming growth in the lending business of both British banks and the foreign banks was focused on overseas borrowers. Advances made by British clearing banks to overseas borrowers rose by 338 per cent between 1964 and 1970 whilst those of the British merchant

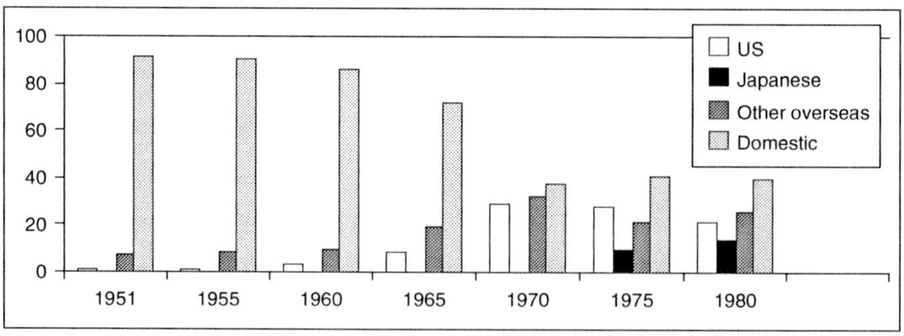

Figure 12.3. Percentage of deposits to total deposits, by origin
Source: Compiled from *BEQB*.

Table 12.7. *Advances by British and foreign banks to UK residents and overseas residents (£m.)*

	British banks				Foreign banks to	
	Clearing banks to		Merchant banks to		UK residents	Overseas residents
	UK residents	Overseas residents	UK residents	Overseas residents		
1964	5,130	112	221	248	889	1,845
1970	6,282	491	480	1,041	2,069	12,831
1980	25,380	5,913	1,831	2,045	9,260	33,357

Source: Compiled from the *BEQB*.

banks rose by 320 per cent and those of the foreign banks in London rose by 595 per cent (Table 12.7).

The remarkable achievement of these foreign banks in securing UK advances business is in part due to the foreign banks' low overhead costs and their smaller operating margins. They had no large-scale retail branch network to maintain, or myriad of small accounts to service, and thus they could afford to offer higher rates on deposits whilst remaining competitive on advances. They also received higher rates on their liquid resources. Whereas the clearing banks put their liquid (non-cash) reserves into Treasury bills, loans to the discount market, and commercial bills, the foreign banks instead invested their liquid reserves mainly in London's 'new' money markets—especially the local authority market and the interbank market—where yields were higher. Table 12.8 illustrates the movement of liquid reserves in this way from 1955 to 1967. In 1955 the foreign banks' balances with other banks amounted to 15 per cent of liquid reserves, loans to UK local authorities to 2 per cent, 'money at call' to 59 per cent, and 'sterling bills discounted' to 24 per cent. By 1967 the proportions were 62, 23, 11, and 4 per cent respectively, a reversal in importance. It was the existence of such large short-term money markets that was one of the principal attractions of London to the foreign banks.

The inroads made by foreign banks into the UK advances market continued throughout the 1970s. The decade between 1970 and 1980 saw an explosion of foreign banks in London as all the categories of foreign banks saw their numbers just about double, and some—the European, US, and Commonwealth banks—more than double. The growth of the Eurocurrency markets, the end of the 'corset' restrictions on credit, and, finally, the removal of exchange controls in 1979, all provided more favourable conditions. These prompted banks to launch new campaigns in the retail market, simplify operations, and open up new avenues of business. Following the removal of UK exchange controls, the completely free flow of capital now possible in London's markets further enhanced its attraction as an international financial centre. During the last five years of the period, the foreign

Table 12.8. *Investment of foreign banks' liquid reserves*

	1955 (£m.)	1960 (£m.)	1965 (£m.)	1967 (£m.)
Balances with other banks	24	70	523	737
Loans to UK local authorities	3	66	200	272
Money at call and short notice	94	67	109	129
Sterling bills discounted	39	49	47	50

Source: *The Banker*, (Nov. 1967).

banks in London maintained their share of foreign currency advances at around 72 per cent, most of which were loans to overseas residents, whilst continuing to make steady inroads into the advances market to UK residents, with their share growing from 14 per cent in 1975 to 19 per cent by 1980.

7. Conclusion

The decade immediately following the Second World War marked a turning point for British banking, for this was a period of important structural change and innovation within the banking sector. The immediate post-war picture had appeared far from rosy for the City, because of the UK's relative economic weakness, with the weak international financial legacy from sterling's experience in the 1930s and during the war, and with the continued unfavourably restrictive international financial environment facing City institutions. Nevertheless, the City of London proved to be resilient, climbing once more to the position of foremost banking centre in the world. With hindsight we can identify a number of significant, favourable factors when compared to other financial centres.

The City of London's existing financial experience and international banking links helped attract new business to London, where the opportunities for remunerative and secure investment were either available or were developing rapidly (for example in the interbank and local authority markets) and an active foreign exchange market already existed. As we have seen, the interbank transactions quickly established a secondary market in Eurocurrencies where funds—generally foreign currency deposits at London offices of banks from the currency's country of origin—could be lent and re-lent. Once the specialist facilities were established in London the process developed its own momentum, with new facilities attracting an influx of overseas banks. The development of the Euromarkets provided a crucial boost to the City's regeneration. The oil crisis of the 1970s generated great increases in financial imbalances in the world economy. The recycling of the surplus revenues of the oil-exporting nations to the deficit and borrowing nations took place largely through the Euromarkets—underpinning the sharp growth during the 1970s. Another significant factor in the revival of London as an international banking centre was the benign attitude of the British monetary authorities. The Bank of England welcomed the expansion of the City's international business: foreign currency business was exempted from the constraints applied to sterling deposits and advances in the pursuit of monetary and credit policy. The geographical compactness with its attendant proximity of contacts, accompanied by a breadth and depth of services, markets, experience, and expertise, plus a philosophy and manner of doing business—which generated both flexibility and speed of decision-making, all combined to produce a package of benefits unrivalled in any other financial centre.

Notes

1. R. C. Michie, 'The Rise and Rise of a Global Financial Centre: The City of London since 1700', University of Durham, inaugural lecture, 25 Nov. 1999.
2. R. C. Michie, *The City of London: Continuity and Change, 1850–1990* (London, 1992); W. M. Clark, 'The World's Banker', in R. C. Michie, *The Development of London as a Financial Centre* (London, 2000).
3. W. F. Spalding, 'The Establishment and Growth of Foreign Branch Banks in London, and the Effect, Immediate and Ultimate, upon the Banking and Commercial Developments of this Country', *Journal of the Institute of Bankers* (Nov. 1911), 436–7.
4. *The Banker* (Nov. 1967), 117, 501, 937–59.
5. For example, the deposits of British and Continental Banking dropped from £7m. in 1930 to around £600,000 by 1931.
6. New capital issues for overseas countries, which had amounted to over £60m. in 1924, had fallen to £348,000 by 1931.
7. By a branch, representative office, or subsidiary.
8. E. P. Palzer, 'Internationalization of Banking by Foreign Bases and Addresses', in J. E. Wadswarth, J. S. G. Wilson, and H. Fournier (eds.), *The Development of Financial Institutions in Europe, 1956–1976* (Leiden, 1977).
9. R. Spiegelberg, *The City* (London, 1973); G. Jones, 'Concentration and Internationalisation after the Second World War', in S. Kinsey and L. Newton (eds.), *International Banking in an Age of Transition* (Aldershet, 1998); C. T. Schenk, 'The Origins of the Eurodollar Market in London: 1955–63', *Explorations in Economic History*, 35 (1998).
10. Spiegelberg, *The City*, 93–4.
11. Paul Bareau held positions as a financial journalist, editor of the financial periodical *The Statist*, economic consultant to Barclays Bank, director of a number of investment trusts, and member of the wartime UK Treasury delegation to Washington, working on the Bretton Woods project.
12. P. Bareau, 'The Financial Institutions of the City of London', in *The City of London as Centre of International Trade and Finance* (Institute of Bankers, July 1961), 14–15.
13. J. Coakley, 'London as an International Financial Centre', in L. Budd and S. Whimster (eds.), *Global Finance and Urban Living* (London, 1992).
14. Bareau, 'Financial Institutions', 19.
15. D. Kynaston, *The City of London*, iv (London, 2001).
16. Bareau, 'Financial Institutions', 19.
17. Michie, *The City of London*, 91.

18. M. Collins, *Money and Banking in the UK: A History* (Beckenham, 1988), 365.
19. Collins, *Money*, 368; Committee of London Clearing Bankers, *The London Clearing Banks: Evidence by the Committee of London Clearing Bankers to the Committee to Review the Functioning of Financial Institutions* (London, 1978).
20. Wilson Committee, 'Report of the Committee to Review the Functioning of Financial Institutions', Cmnd. 7937 (London, 1978).
21. For a detailed account of the origins of the Eurodollar market see Schenk, 'Origins'.
22. Collins, *Money*.
23. G. Burn, 'The State, the City and the Euromarkets', *Review of International Political Economy*, 6/2 (1999).
24. P. Bareau, 'The International Money and Capital Markets', in E. V. Morgan, R. A. Brealey, B. S. Yamey, and P. Bareau (eds.), *City Lights: Essays on Financial Institutions and Markets in the City of London* (Institute for Economic Affairs, July 1979).
25. S. Mason, *The Flow of Funds in Britain: An Introduction to Financial Markets* (London, 1976); Schenk, 'Origins'.
26. Collins, *Money*; Burn, 'The State'.
27. Collins, *Money*.
28. S. Strange, *Sterling and British Policy: A Political Study of an International Currency in Decline* (London, 1971).
29. Kynaston, *The City*, 269.
30. *The Banker* (Aug. 1969), 773.
31. Schenk, 'Origins', 234.
32. BIS 41st *Annual Report* (1970/1).
33. BIS 45th *Annual Report* (1974/5), 50th *Annual Report* (1979/80).
34. Coakley, 'London'.
35. *The Banker* (Oct. 1969), 1067.
36. *The Banker* (Nov. 1967), 941.

13

French Banks and the Eurobonds Issue Market during the 1960s

Eric Bussière

This contribution, which is based on unpublished material from the archives of the Paribas and Crédit Lyonnais banks, sets out to analyse the determining factors in the paradox of how the two French banks managed to build up a considerable activity during the initial phase of the increase in Euro-issues between 1963 and the end of the decade, at a time when the French authorities did not really encourage either the international role of the Paris market or the use of the franc at the international level. Both Paribas, a private merchant bank, and the Crédit Lyonnais, a deposit bank nationalized since 1945, were to some degree leaders in the field. Each had, along with the British banks, dominated the international issues market until 1914. In the inter-war years, however, such activity had decreased significantly and practically ceased since 1945.

The first section of this contribution analyses the way in which the two banks fitted into the international market and managed, by putting their advantages and international alliances to good use, to win an enviable position in the Euro-issues sector. The second analyses the options open with regard to the positioning of French banks on that particular market once the initial leadership of the City banks had been challenged. A number of them were tempted to adopt a continental strategy alongside their German counterparts, whilst others remained faithful to their Anglo-Saxon alliances. The continental strategy, however, was of interest only insofar as there was a prospect of an opening-up of the French market to foreign issues by means of the creation of a European capital market, which was in fact blocked by the French government, despite pressure from the banks. The opening-up was embryonic and too short term, as is shown in the third section. In the fourth section, however, it emerges that the activity of French banks on the international market was one of the means by which rivalry and competition were reintroduced, and that fairly widespread analyses of the role of the state in the liberalization of French banking and the development of the French economy that have appeared to date therefore need some amendment.

1. French banks and the beginnings of the international market

Paribas: rapid integration based on Anglo-Saxon alliances

Initially, given its long and ancient tradition and above all its ability to re-establish strong links with American and British firms and markets after the slack period immediately after the war, Paribas was the most active French bank on the international market. Setting up branches in New York and London both strengthened the essential alliance and brought Paribas into contact with the two great international capital markets.

The idea of setting up a branch of Paribas in New York in 1960 had been studied during the preceding year. All the possibilities put forward set out to define the forms a close association with Lehman Brothers, with whom excellent personal relationships had been established, might take. At one point, acquiring shares in the American company was considered, but the project was abandoned for legal reasons. It was finally decided to create a Paribas Corporation, with its development being sponsored by Lehman Brothers. The main objective was to seal an overall alliance between the two banks taking advantage of the growth of transatlantic relations by helping American firms wishing to establish themselves in France, the Common Market, or Africa, and European firms to do the same or to find financial support in the USA.

Lehman Brothers' support in launching Paribas Corporation was to be significant. They introduced the Paribas branch to operations closely linked to the US securities market as a sub-participant in the underwriting syndicates they managed, helping it to invest securities and putting it in touch with its industrial customers. For its part, Paribas became Lehman Brothers' special representative in its European operations and entrusted them with the handling of the group's financial affairs in the USA.

One of the chief results of the association was therefore to introduce Paribas to the American market, thus enabling it to master the techniques and practices of issue transactions on the world's main financial market and to establish, or re-establish, alliances that would be extremely useful once the international financial market was flourishing again. This capital of relations was to be outstandingly valuable when American firms sought finance in Europe.

The establishment of a branch of Paribas in London made the links with Anglo-Saxon firms even stronger. After careful monitoring involving Paribas and teams from S. G. Warburg & Co. during 1963, Paribas Ltd. was set up on 6 February 1964. The shareholders included insurance companies, investment trusts, several City firms including Barings, R. Fleming, Samuel Montagu, M. Samuel, and, above all, S. G. Warburg & Co. The participation of Lehman Brothers was aimed at placing the new organization firmly in the New York–London–Paris triangle. Amongst the activities it expanded as soon as it was in place was underwriting in the field of British and international issues.

The fact that it was in London increased the already active cooperation in the issues sector and consolidated the experience gained in the USA. It also made it easier to maintain fairly close contact between teams, as shown by Pierre Haas's time at Warburgs soon after his arrival at Paribas. He was to play a major part in the development of international activities at Paribas in the following years.

Although the participation of Paribas in the very first operations on the international market was obviously greatly facilitated by such alliances, the bank's own strengths and new departures also played a part. In late 1960 the long-standing relations between Paribas and the American bank Kuhn, Loeb & Co. were renewed during preliminary discussions concerning a Mexican loan on the American (Kuhn Loeb), British (Warburgs), and continental European (Paribas) markets. That issue, carried out in 1963 in rather difficult circumstances, enabled Paribas to establish itself alongside the above-mentioned concerns and the First Boston. Relations with Lehman Brothers on the one hand and the Kuhn Loeb/Warburgs axis on the other, together with its friendly relations with Samuels in London, was the basic means by which the bank moved into the first issues on the international market.[1] There are many instances of the advantages for Paribas in such cooperation as a link between the American banks and the banks or issuers in continental Europe. In 1963, for example, Paribas and Warburgs combined to canvass the Italian IRI and in 1964 Lehman Brothers and Paribas jointly approached the Spanish governement.[2] The results of the 1964 and 1965 Euro-issues show the real value of such alliances: both the co-managerships Paribas obtained in 1964 were alongside Warburgs, which appeared with the French bank in nine underwriting syndicates out of the twenty-five in which the latter took part in 1964, and in 1965 Paribas once again featured with Warburgs, Lehman Brothers, or Kuhn Loeb in fourteen operations out of the thirty-four such syndicates Paribas was involved in.

Alliances of this kind were flexible, adaptable to circumstances and the wishes of the issuers, and, despite their preferential nature, non-exclusive, as is clear from correspondence between the French bank and Warburgs: 'We are well aware of the efforts you have always made to give the Banque de Paris et des Pays-Bas a part to play in the transactions you manage'; while as far as possible Paribas did the same in, for example, the Transalpine pipeline affair, in which it was acting as co-leader with Warburgs and N. M. Rothschild.[3]

The strategy followed was of course an Atlantic one, specifically based on the desire to meet the needs of American firms for financing in Europe. But Paribas had no wish to restrict itself to simply making use of the Warburgs network, which was not enough to enable it to become a leading institution in the field. What it wanted was to create its own clientele by making itself known to American firms with little experience of European banks and finding it difficult to understand why French banks should be involved in issues in which the French market could play no part: 'Federated Stores would prefer to have Morgan and Co as co-manager, since the name is well known to them and the firm has English-speaking executives in Paris who are acquainted with Wall Street practices.'[4] Paribas thus emerged as a leading institution with expert knowledge of the international market in the eyes of inexperienced American banks by means of a canvassing operation initially guided by Lehman Brothers. On their advice, it was decided to make a coordinated approach to American firms with their main banker, provided that he needed support in Europe: 'The best chance for the Banque de Paris would be to offer its services to American firms and their traditional bankers when the latter have no special international function.'[5]

Paribas also based its activities on its international presence in Europe. Paribas-Luxembourg, which was set up in 1964, enabled the bank to offer facilities in terms of quotation on one of the busiest places on the international market in continental Europe, and the activities of the Geneva branch meant that the placing capacity of that particular market became particularly attractive.[6]

The achievements of Paribas on the international market show how quickly the bank had become an important institution on it (Table 13.1). In 1967 Paribas obtained twenty-one leaderships or co-leaderships and participated to a total of \$30.7m. in the placing syndicates and \$39.9m. in the underwriting syndicates it has been possible to list. The major part of the placing was provided by the group's international network (74.35 per cent) with the Geneva branch contributing the largest amount (46.58 per cent, or 62.65 per cent of the group's investment capacity abroad).

The Crédit Lyonnais: Maurice Schlogel's voluntarism

What the Crédit Lyonnais wanted was to return to what had been its tradition at the beginning of the century and to take its place again amongst the great securities issuers on the international market. By 1964 it was attempting to make its presence felt on the international issues market by acting as a full partner and not a mere sub-participant, but that could really be possible only insofar as the bank's placing capacity, which was very real primarily at the national level, could be widely used. The Crédit Lyonnais did everything it could to promote that possibility at the time of two community organizations'—the European Investment Bank (EIB) and the European Coal and Steel Community (ECSC)—issues in 1964. Given the nature of the two borrowers, a relatively open attitude to the market on the part of the French government might have been expected, but the Treasury was not to allow the bank to make use of its placing capacity in France. That meant that the

Table 13.1. *The achievements of Paribas on the international market, 1964–1965*

1964 (out of 39 operations identified)	1965 (out of 39 such operations)
14 placing only	1 placing only
23 underwriting and placing	35 underwriting and placing
2 co-leadership	3 co-leadership
Total placing \$15,585,000	Total placing \$13,510,000
Total underwriting \$13,385,000	Total underwriting \$16,270,000

Crédit Lyonnais was to play a minor part in the two operations, having a merely retrocessionary role in the ECSC loan and not achieving its ambition of acting as a leader in the EIB issue.

Faced with that situation, the bank did what it could, taking an interim decision and adopting a suitable strategy with relatively modest short-term but more ambitious medium-term objectives. On the one hand, it had to retrict its participation in syndicates to the capacities provided by its international network. The particular problem it faced was that of moving fully into the circuit already partly made up of the Anglo-Saxon banks, within which it did not have the same excellent relations as Paribas. Its strategy, which was defined by autumn 1964, was rather like tracing the leaders of a ring, and involved establishing contacts with Anglo-Saxon, and especially American, banks at the point of origin of business, initially at least avoiding questioning the pre-eminence of the French merchant banks, while at the same time making its own claims clear. On the Boulevard des Italiens, they felt that they were just as entitled as Paribas to move into international operations.[7]

The visit the directors of Hambros paid to Maurice Schlogel on 15 March 1967 saw a relative clarification of the strategy and its first results. Between 1964 and 1967, the bank had followed a policy of establishing a presence, standing out amongst the most serious French operators in international transactions, and making good use of its branches abroad, thus playing an important but not decisive part. At that point, the beginnings of a move towards a freer French market would enable the institution to play a more serious one, 'providing even greater vindication of our demands'.[8] These growing demands had gradually become obvious, and little by little the bank had managed to gain a place not only in investment but also in underwriting syndicates, demanding increasingly significant shares. Hence in early March 1966, a $150,000 participation in an underwriting syndicate offered by an American partner was refused: 'the $150,000 offered are rather unworthy of the Crédit Lyonnais.'[9]

The bank strengthened its increasing power in the syndicates primarily by making use of its placing capacity, which was increasing at the same rate as its international network was growing stronger. In addition to the quantitative limits imposed by the closing of the French market, however, the working methods of the syndicates were penalizing French banks. Since the syndicates were mostly organized on the basis of responsibility for a specific geographical area, the Crédit Lyonnais acted as a sub-participant, with all the consequences that that entailed for its standing and size of participation.[10] Despite such restrictions, however, the bank gradually managed to make progress. The Tokyo City loan, for instance, issued in April 1964 was sold by London ($134,000), Brussels ($27,000), and Luxembourg ($14,000). In February 1964 the Crédit Lyonnais succeeded in investing $100,000 of the Council of Europe's loan, but could have invested $500,000.[11] When a Swedish issue was launched in New York in 1965, the Crédit Lyonnais was allocated $235,000 of the investment when it could have handled at least $480,000.[12]

Table 13.2. *Crédit Lyonnais: a comparison of the results obtained in the international issues field, 1964–1965*

1964 (out of 44 transactions)	1965 (out of 62 transactions)
Underwriting $4,600,000 Placing $9,260,000	Underwriting $12,273,000 Placing $14,135,000

In 1964 the bank's concern was often to obtain enough securities, given its desire to extend and consolidate its placing capacity even if costs were sometimes high, and on several occasions it was badly served by the leaders of a syndicate and had to redeem itself on the market to do the best for its clients.[13] That deliberate strategy, aimed at strengthening its position as a skilful investor amongst its syndicates and clients, enabled the bank to play a larger part in underwriting syndicates. In September 1964 the vice-president of First Boston was informed that the Crédit Lyonnais had no intention of merely placing loans.[14] A comparison of the results obtained in the international issues field in 1964 and 1965 show the growth in power, with the underwriting/placing ratio rising from 49.7 per cent in 1964 to 86.8 per cent in the following year (Table 13.2).[15]

The bank's position gradually grew stronger, as shown by a symbolic climb up the pages of prospectuses. In November 1965, at the time of the AB Götaverken loan, it was listed just below the three leaders, the three American banks, Amro, and Hambros.[16] In December of that same year, however, at the time of a Philips Petroleum issue, it was refused guarantor parity with the Deutsche Bank, and was obliged to accept a share of $400,000 instead of the $700,000 granted to its competitor.[17] During 1966 the Crédit Lyonnais increased its efforts to obtain leadership positions.[18] In the end, the attempt paid off: in 1966 it bank managed, in conjunction with Goldman Sachs, a Motorola loan on the international market.[19] At the end of the same year, it negotiated a Sumitomo loan with Daiwa Securities and White Weld.[20]

The *Times* ranking for the ninety-one international issues in 1967 shows the increasing strength of the Crédit Lyonnais (ranked twentieth with five managerships or co-managerships involving a total of $122,000,000) whilst confirming the outstanding performance of Paribas as number one (with twenty-one managerships or co-managerships involving a total of $490,000,000). During the first half of 1968, the Crédit Lyonnais rose to ninth.

2. Cooperation with British and continental banks

French regulatory constraints encouraged the Crédit Lyonnais to move into the international financial community, initially towards Anglo-Saxon partners. This was the purpose of Maurice Schlogel's visit to the USA in summer 1964, where he met the directors of White Weld and Dillon Read.[21] On a further visit to London in December 1964, a representative of the Crédit Lyonnais met his opposite numbers from Warburgs, Hambros, Schroders, and Philip Hill. He reminded them of the Scandinavian issues made jointly with Hambros at the beginning of the century and expressed his bank's wish to work together in future.[22]

French and Anglo-Saxon relations were not always very good, however, and the French banks were not always well served, as had happened with the Cyanamid loan of September 1965.[23]

The gap between placing capacity and the banks' worldwide responsibilities very quickly became a problem, as is shown by the structure of the Enzo Gutzeit issue syndicate set up in January 1965[24] and managed jointly by Warburgs, the Svenska Handelsbank, and the Crédit Lyonnais as below:

• Underwriting:	Warburgs and European syndicate:	13.125% + 31.25% = 44.375%
	Commerzbank and German syndicate:	13.125% + 31.25% = 44.375%
	Crédit Lyonnais:	5.625%
	Svenska Handelsbank	5.625%
• Investment:	coordination for Germany:	Commerzbank
	coordination for rest of Europe:	Warburgs

In that operation Warburgs was able to use its intermediary role to establish itself as one of the major leaders of an undertaking in which it, like the whole British market, was participating to the tune of very modest amounts. The British merchant banks' lack of placing capacity was thus likely to justify two types of strategies on the part of French banks. Either Franco-British solidarity could be created, or the French institutions could be encouraged to concentrate on the continent again, either by obtaining an opening-up of the French market, which would enable them to develop their placement capacity, or by making use of their European, and particularly their German, connections, perhaps in a European perspective. The Anglo-Saxon option might be preferred by the merchant banks like Paribas and the continental one, with its combination of a national and a European element, by deposit banks like the Crédit Lyonnais.

The continental initiative came from the German banks which, led by Hermann Abs of the Deutsche Bank, were challenging the dominance of their British counterparts who, despite their lack of real placing capacity, ranked themselves above the syndicates. The German banks therefore wanted to increase their placing capacity in their own country in order to offer a serious alternative to the British banks in transaction management.[25] For Abs, the issue of the DM200m. Portuguese loan in 1964 was an opportunity to state the claims of the German establishments, and was presented at a press conference as 'a significant event in the history of German finance';[26] and a syndicate representing fifty German and ten foreign banks was set up. During the day's conversations at Frankfurt he criticized the role of British banks, their claims to manage the syndicates, and the way in which they

Table 13.3. *Cooperation with British and continental banks* (%)

	Underwriting	Placing
Foreign banks	17.5	17.5
Foreign sales group		15
German banks	82.5	67.5

elbowed out establishments with a high placing capacity. The German banks had the lion's share of the Portuguese loan (Table 13.3). The idea for the operation had come from the German banks. It had been intended as a revenge for the first Portuguese loan, issued on the international market and managed by Barings and two British banks, in which the German banks had not been admitted into the underwriting operation until the Portuguese government had insisted on it in view of their placing capacity.[27] The growth in international issues on the German market gave the French banks the opportunity to engage in a series of transactions as sub-participants to their German counterparts, which the Crédit Lyonnais did between 1965 and 1967.[28]

The French banks' reading of the situation largely coincided with that of the Germans. When the European Investment Bank loan was issued in 1964, a senior figure at the Crédit Lyonnais wrote, 'so once again a European institution loan, with largely European investment, has been raised under the management of Anglo-Saxon specialists'.[29] Faced with that situation, Paribas and the Deutsche Bank considered refusing to participate if only American banks figured in the underwriting syndicate. The Germans stood their ground, but Paribas and the French, whose position on their own market was not as strong, backed down.[30] Obviously, the French banks had to be more careful since their freedom of action was still very limited, given the regulations closing the national market. A further chance to point out just how unsatisfactory that situation was was given to the Crédit Lyonnais in July 1967. The bank told the COMIT that it was 'not very happy to have to come lower down the list in the advertising material for the loan than an American firm which in our view has no real claim to be a co-leader in an EIB issue'.[31]

Converging continental interests might have led to a more thought-out joint position. At the beginning of 1966 the Crédit Lyonnais and the Deutsche Bank considered preparing their response in the form of discussions between themselves and the three big Swiss banks before any future major issues, even if the French were unwilling to go as far as refusing to take part.[32] The thinking of the big Swiss banks was fairly close to that of their German colleagues, since they also wanted to make sure that their major placing capacity was recognized by a proper position in underwriting syndicates.[33] The establishment of a cartel of Swiss banks in the summer of 1966 meant that they could adopt a joint attitude with regard to international issues and defend their interests efficiently.[34]

The attempt to found a major continental alliance did not come to full fruition, however. On 18 April, during a meeting of representatives of the Deutsche Bank and the Crédit Lyonnais in Frankfurt, it was accepted in principle to form an agreement to include initially the two first movers of the project, the three major Swiss establishments, and subsequently an institution representing the other three countries of the Common Market. Consultation before major issues was envisaged, even if each establishment was ultimately to keep its freedom of action. The first test was inconclusive. With the Deutsche Bank taking the initiative, there was an attempt to organize a policy of abstention with regard to the forthcoming issue of Bankers' Trust convertible bonds on the European market.[35] It collapsed as a result of the conflicting attitudes of the banks. Although the Deutsche Bank, the Dresdner, the three big Swiss banks, and the Crédit Lyonnais refused to participate for reasons of (for the latter) 'principles of general policy', the other two French banks involved did take part.[36] Despite the relative failure, the Deutsche Bank stood its ground and declared in September 1967 that it was disagreeable to see two great European companies entrusting their transactions to New York houses.[37]

3. Face to face with the state: throwing back the bolts

The situation of the French banks with regard to the international markets was linked to a regulatory context which did not allow them to use their clientele of French depositors or to meet the needs of French institutions on that market. At the fiscal level, what affected non-residents and thus ruled out the French market[38] were the lack of tax credits and the retention of 25 per cent at source. At the regulatory level, it was the need for authorization to subscribe to bonds issued abroad, the fact that foreign bonds were not quoted in France and had to be deposited. In principle, the regulations could even bring the activities of banks almost to a complete standstill by obliging them to apply for prior authorization every time they engaged in underwriting transactions on the international market involving the need to let dollars go out of the country to activate the underwriting. A large degree of tolerance on the part of the administration does, however, seem to have been normal and most banks had stopped applying for prior permission.[39] Issues abroad for loans for French bodies were in fact limited in number and could not be drawn in francs. Once it was no longer possible for French banks to launch international issues based on Paris, they had to make do with a secondary role in managing such transactions and using only a 'tiny fraction' of their placing capacity.[40]

Following Maurice Schlogel's lead, the Crédit Lyonnais resolutely led the banks in their attempt to throw back the bolts that stopped them acting as they saw fit. In July 1964 one of the managing director's chief colleagues discussed his bank's policy regarding placing international loans with the appropriate Treasury officials, pointing out that nothing was invested with French customers and everything went to its international network. The problem of placing international securities with French institutional clients was raised, and the Treasury accepted the placing insofar as it arose from requests from these clients, but would not allow French customers to be approached directly.[41]

A year later, in April 1965, Treasury opinion on international issues in francs was requested. The response was that for both French and foreign borrowers it viewed such transactions 'very unfavorably', since it was government policy to refuse to let the national currency act as a reserve currency.[42] This was still the position when the Crédit Lyonnais was approached by various British dealers in early 1965 regarding international issues in francs.[43] The Germans, however, were less favourable, arguing that the franc was strong, but that it would be better to wait for the outcome of the presidential elections to be held that year.[44] With regard to issues on the Paris market on behalf of foreigners or French nationals with investments abroad, the Treasury's view was more qualified: they were acceptable for French borrowers, but prior agreement was required for foreigners. It did, however, declare itself more in favour of Paris-based Common Market authorities' issues, but not yet with regard to member states' national bodies. The Treasury representative consulted made his hostility to community discussions regarding the opening-up of capital markets within the EEC clear, referring to the 'endless discussions in Brussels', in which France had 'really been largely isolated from her partners'.[45] There was therefore little hope in early 1965 of seeing any changes in the regulations. In March, the Crédit Lyonnais had pointed out to a Samuels representative how little hope there was of investing a tranche of a Mexican loan on the Paris market and was talking of a slow opening-up of the French market. In April his reply to a Deutsche Bank proposal concerning a projected Japanese loan was the same.[46]

In July 1965 the situation caused problems during the issue of a loan to an important Italian body, the ENEL, where it had seemed possible to give a Community dimension to the project by using parallel issues on various European markets. Despite having the authorities' agreement in principle, investing the first tranche in France was difficult, given the obligatory requirement to deposit the securities. The French banks, in fact, found themselves on the verge of having to refuse to take up options on the second tranche and seeing their standing in their partners' eyes slump. They put great pressure on the Treasury, and the office of the Finance Minister in particular, and got a last-minute reprieve: the requirement to deposit securities was lifted.[47]

A further intervention in January 1966 enabled the Crédit Lyonnais to describe its role in international financial transactions to Marc Vienot, the assistant director of the Treasury, and at the same time to express its regret at the obstacles it encountered as a result of current regulations and its ignorance of government views on both the closing of the French market to international issues and the possibility of issues on the international or European markets to the benefit of French issuers. The difficulty of the situation with regard to foreign banks introducing the bank to syndicates and expecting a quid pro quo it could not offer was made clear. Vienot seemed more receptive than his predecessor, and offered some hope of a development that the minister himself seemed to wish for, since he had himself authorized the first issues by French firms on the international market.

A new series of approaches to the Treasury and the Banque de France took place in late April and early May 1966, partly as a result of the Treasury's refusal in connection with the International Harvester subscription of bonds by French customers, deplored by Morgan Stanley of New York, who had approached Maurice Pérouse directly. On the same day a representative of the Crédit Lyonnais was also in discussions with Claude Pierre-Brossolette at the Treasury, asking for a 'proper policy' regarding international issues to be defined. The latter favoured some limited development enabling the clientele of banks to subscribe to international issues in foreign currencies. There was a similar approach to the Banque de France.[48] A further one to Le Guen, one of the Treasury officials, shows just how very hesitant the administration was. Following a request from the Crédit Lyonnais, concerning an American company's bond subscription in France to the tune of $500,000, authorization was finally given at the very last moment and after telephone offers of $250,000, of which $150,000 were for the SICAV Slivam and $100,000 for individuals. Le Guen admitted that at the top levels of the Treasury 'they' did not much like this kind of international issues and indicated that that the breakdown was not taken into account. At the bank, Le Guen's reply was taken as 'an admission of the absurdity of the position that had been taken'.[49]

It is legitimate to see the liberalization measures the government announced in early November 1966 as the result of the steps continuously taken by the Crédit Lyonnais and listed in the *Banque* magazine in January 1967 by its assistant managing director, Maurice Schlogel. It was of course no more than a beginning, and the real effects of the measures would largely depend on the attitude of the Treasury, which left itself plenty of room for manoeuvre in applying them. The main steps taken concerned investments of international loans on the French market benefiting French or foreign lenders which would now follow the same procedures as French issues. This meant that the Treasury kept the possibility of fixing amounts and timing, but also that French banks could place a proportion of the international bonds underwritten by them amongst their French clientele. The securities could also be quoted in Paris, which would develop the secondary market at a lower cost, and the requirement of depositing foreign shares held in France was abolished.[50]

The measures of a general nature taken by the government left it with great freedom of movement with regard to both the opening-up of the Paris market to foreign issues and authorizing French firms to raise loans abroad. The Finance Ministry took some time to work out its position. The success on the international market of the first Électricité de France (EDF) issue, launched in early 1967, seemed to incline the ministry to encourage transactions of this type. The cabinet was 'very excited' by the success (at a rate of around $20,000,000 a month), whereas the Treasury and the Crédit Lyonnais, apparently more concerned about exchange risks, advised greater prudence in order to achieve a 'more even balance'. But the EDF loan had also shown up clear contradictions on the part of the authorities, for instance, the minister's criticism of quotation in Luxembourg when quotation in

Paris and canvassing in France were not allowed.[51] In late 1967, therefore, the ministry's options were still unclear, and the top echelons of the Treasury seemed to 'have no policy', or at least no clearly defined policy, with regard to French transactions on the international market, even though balance of payments considerations and the desire to free the French market seemed to be the dominant concerns.[52] With regard to international loans on the Paris market, Vienot was even more circumspect, despite the numerous overtures made to him, seeking first of all to give priority to international bodies or state, regional, or local authorities with which France had 'affinities' before going any further.[53]

With regard to international loans in francs, reticence was still the order of the day in early 1967. In January, the Crédit Lyonnais offered the option to the Crédit Foncier de France, but the Treasury turned it down.[54] The latter's point of view changed in the autumn of that year, however. A first trial run for Roussel Uclaf, managed by the Crédit Commercial de France, was authorized. The issue was to be 'a test of the possible subsequent use of the franc as a supporting currency for international issues on the same footing as the dollar and the mark'.[55]

The lesson of that first experiment was drawn during a meeting at the Treasury on 15 December 1967. The speaker from the Crédit Lyonnais showed a prudent wish to extend the international role of the franc by urging issues by the most prestigious French providers and at the same time encouraging bodies with dollar receipts at their disposal to use them. As far as issues with exchange options that might help to acclimatize the franc on the international market were concerned, it seemed possible to envisage them on a FF/$ ratio, but indecent to do so in terms of a FF/DM one. In this connection, the many contacts of the Crédit Lyonnais with its colleagues had shown cautious and even reserved attitudes towards issues in francs, particularly since the legislative elections of autumn 1967, while issues with an exchange option were generally deemed to be easier to achieve.[56]

There was something of an upturn in views on issues in francs in early 1968. Despite Lazards' hesitation and a low level of Swiss participation, it was possible to place one issue carried out by the French BP company in February of that year, thanks to a highly concentrated subscription in Belgium and Germany. The Treasury then seemed to want to encourage new transactions of this type exclusively for French participants at the rate of one every two months.[57] In the case of foreigners, it was felt that only private firms in the Common Market should be included. The real world, however, imposed a degree of prudence, and contacts with representatives of foreign firms were inconclusive, for although the franc was strong, it had been so for only a short time.[58]

The events of May 1968 changed prospects radically. The reintroduction of exchange controls cast some doubt on the ability of French banks to operate on the international market. For a time, it was thought that prior Treasury authorization might once more become a prerequisite for banks participating in underwriting syndicates, but this did not materialize, since they used their holdings of currencies abroad to support such transactions.[59] On the other hand, investing international issues in France was no longer possible given the cost of foreign currency securities brought in by exchange controls.[60]

Conversely, the Treasury sought to profit from the opportunities offered by foreign markets for facing up to the needs of French undertakings and administrations not covered by national resources, in order to help create a better balance of payments. This business possibility was exploited by French banks. The Crédit Lyonnais was in the forefront and had received Treasury approval to go ahead by 12 August, provided that the transactions were in marks and not dollars, despite the exchange risks involved.[61]

Such transactions meant a considerable amount of business for the banks, which were more than able to share leadership with their German partners. Despite the attitude of the Crédit Lyonnais, which systematically warned potential participants of the risks involved, many transactions (the SNCF, the Caisse Nationale de l'Énergie, the Caisse Nationale des Télécommunications) were carried out on the direct orders of the top echelons of the Treasury.[62]

4. Competition between French banks on the international market

By the beginning of the 1960s, the merchant banks had to some extent taken the lead with regard to European or international issues authorized by the government on the Paris market. A first issue of the BIRD in 1963 had been taken in hand by Paribas and Lazards[63] who, according to information held by the Crédit Lyonnais, had signed an agreement on such transactions.[64] The same situation arose in connection with the EIB rather later, but Paribas and Lazards subsequently agreed to let the Crédit Lyonnais into the syndicate for public sector loans, but not those intended for insurance companies. In fact, the leaders for the 1964 ECSC loan were Paribas and Lazards, along with the Société Générale as well as the Crédit Lyonnais.[65]

By October 1966, even before the nature of the liberalization measures the government had decided on were known, the Crédit Lyonnais informed various partners that it would now be in a better position to act on the Paris market, although a week or two later it had to admit that the opening-up would be gradual and that initially it was not possible to envisage large sums. In addition, the question of the cost of issues was still a major obstacle, given the level of taxation and the large commissions on the French market.[66] The new situation was welcomed by certain of those engaged in discussions with the bank, however, and one of the directors of Air Liquide declared how happy he was 'that it was no longer necessary to use a British or American bank to launch an issue on the international market'.[67]

The rather small number of French concerns on the international market was a major problem for those French banks about to improve their relations with initially captive customers in that area for the first time and to be able to act as leaders for relatively large amounts on a more regular basis. There was consequently increased competition between French and a foreign bank, but even greater competition between the French banks themselves.

The first signs of tension became apparent during the earliest operations in 1965 and 1966, that is, the CFP issue, managed by Paribas and Morgan and Co., and the Lafarge issue, managed by the CCF, the Société Générale, and the Crédit Lyonnais.[68] A new issue, the Pechiney, in early 1966, aroused fierce argument. Pechiney's choice of Morgan Stanley and Lazard Frères New York as leaders provoked a sharp reaction in the Crédit Lyonnais and Paribas, with the former describing itself as 'deeply wounded' and the latter expressing its 'indignation'. The Crédit Lyonnais was ultimately reinstated as co-leader and Paribas given a 'special bracket'.[69]

The market had been very lightly regulated and hardly subject to trials of strength between French firms, but competition became increasingly severe once it broadened, and a series of splits occurred. Canvassing had become a current practice in early 1967. On 30 January 1967 Air France was sought out by the Crédit Lyonnais, having been preceded by Lazards Rothschilds, the CCF, and a nationalized firm, and the Crédit Lyonnais talked about 'longing for the leadership'.[70] In earlier weeks it had canvassed the City of Paris and the Crédit National,[71] and had been beaten to Sud Aviation by Paribas and an American securities firm.[72]

The 1967 EDF loan, the first issue of a major French firm on the international market, sparked off very lively competition. The earliest discussions in this connection had been initiated by Lazards at the very beginning of 1966, but at that stage the project had not been supported by the Treasury.[73] At that time, however, a split between merchant and nationalized banks had already become apparent. It worsened at the end of the year when the prospects of a loan took clearer shape in the wake of the government's decisions to open up the market. Initial consultations instigated by Lazards, who had been entrusted with exploratory investigations by Pierre Massé, brought the matter to the attention of the Crédit Lyonnais. In this matter, the directors of EDF had preferred the merchant banks, whose job was managing international transactions, whereas domestic transactions were more the affair of deposit banks. From this point of view, it certainly seems that Massé had taken on commitments with Lazards and Jean Reyre, for Paribas, for services to EDF at the international level rendered by the two establishments. The Crédit Lyonnais sprang to the defence of both the nationalized bank and its own expertise:

> It seems strange that the nationalized banks, and in particular the Crédit Lyonnais, the leader in 1967, should not play a leading part in the first international operation of a major issuing institution in the public sector ... Our competence in this field is now recognized and we are quite able to handle the matter as well as, if not better than, any other French establishment.

At this stage, the discussions brought in the directors of these establishments at the highest level, as is shown by President Wiriath's observations to Pierre Massé on 22 December 1966. The Crédit Lyonnais soon managed to get approval for the two biggest nationalized banks to act alongside the merchant banks as rotating joint leaders, a solution which it then rejected. Resistance paid off, and the bank on the Boulevard des Italiens succeeded in being appointed one of the leaders from those first operations with the Banque Nationale de Paris (BNP).[74] With the agreement of the EDF and the Treasury, however, the merchant banks managed to keep ahead of the nationalized banks, so much so that they figured on the opening line of the issue prospectus. Some months later their pre-eminent position was confirmed by the chairman of the EDF's financial committee when a new initiative by the Crédit Lyonnais was being launched. The nationalized undertaking wanted to keep domestic and international issues separate, and asked the Crédit Lyonnais not to underestimate the merchant banks' expertise in international transactions.[75] The steps taken by the Crédit Lyonnais clearly seem to have upset Lazards.

The importance of this first issue had been fully appreciated at the Boulevard des Italiens, as the merchant banks' victory might well determine future developments and perpetuate current positions. Competition speeded up, with the SNCF being canvassed from all sides for its first international issue.[76] The projected SNCF loan discussed from January 1967 enabled the deposit banks to put things back on an even keel. Once again the merchant banks had been quicker off the mark, with the Crédit Lyonnais beginning canvassing on 17 January 1967, after Lazards and Rothschilds. Once again it boasted of its strengths—'funds at least matching those of the merchant banks'—in its attempt to achieve leadership, and pointed out that Lazards' situation was exceptional as far as the EDF issue was concerned.[77] All these moves achieved something, for on 14 April it was decided that the five big banks would be co-leaders, and that the Crédit Lyonnais would contact the nationalized banks directly, with the SNCF management doing the same with the merchant banks. The choice of the SNCF was based on the evidence of the part played by the merchant banks in the first EDF issue, the services they had rendered to the SNCF at the international level, and the wish to associate the operation with its usual bankers in France. Paribas got permission for the financial servicing of the loan, quoted in Luxembourg, to be carried out by Paribas-Luxembourg.

What had happened was that the concrete experience of EDF had led the nationalized banks to an unofficial understanding. The overtures came both from the Crédit Lyonnais, which approached the BNP, and the Société Générale, which contacted the Boulevard des Italiens. The aim was 'to oppose the merchant banks as effectively as possible' in the international issues area. The principle of the agreement was simple: the major nationalized banks were to come together in issues involving the main public sector undertakings in order to create a tripartite leadership and to act as signatory in turn. In other cases, there would be mutual support to obtain the best situation possible for colleagues, depending on the context of each issue. The Société Générale would have liked to go further and had thought of a 'non-aggression agreement' with regard to other issuers, with the leader in domestic transactions keeping the position for international ones.[78] The agreement was in force for a CNT loan negotiated in August 1967, with the nationalized banks appearing on the first line of the prospectus, in accordance with the spirit of the tripartite agreement just signed.[79]

Despite the agreements, there was conflict at another level, namely between the nationalized banks, in particular the Crédit Lyonnais, and the BNP. These tensions arose from the creation of the BNP and its wish to move quickly into leadership in major international issues ahead of its sister banks. There was opposition to this ambition in late 1966, when the BNP was designated leader for France in an Austrian government issue, when it had hitherto never 'taken part in any major issue'.[80] There was further conflict between the Crédit Lyonnais and the BNP in April 1967 regarding the SNCF loan before an overall agreement had been reached.[81] The Crédit Lyonnais also declared its 'serious reservations' when it was proposed to include the BNP in an offer concerning the Inter-American Development Bank it was piloting with the two merchant banks. It also resurfaced during talks about a Michelin loan.[82]

In spite of the big deposit banks' counter-offensive, the merchant banks managed to remain ahead in French companies' international issues, partly because of their links with them through, for example a Citroën loan to the tune of $20,000,000, which had Paribas as leader, along with Lazard-Paris, Kuhn Loeb, Lehmans, and Warburgs.[83] But the rush of French establishments onto the market happened when it was nearing saturation. The slump in late 1967, with its rise in rates and reluctant buyers, slowed the movement down, causing, for example, the postponement of a GdF issue.[84]

5. Conclusion

When we consider the way and the conditions in which the French banks played their part on the issues market during the 1960s, the only possible conclusion is that the extremely honourable results they achieved were to a very small extent due to the action of the public authorities.

Since they could not, as they had done in the good old days, rely on the rock of the traditional French virtue of saving, they took their chance on an emerging international market outside the regulatory constraints in force at home. Fortunately, they had not broken all the links with foreign countries they had had since the nineteenth century, as can be seen from the speed with which they rebuilt old alliances and learned new skills. Their recovery was rapid: by 1967–8 they had managed to achieve prime entries in issue prospectuses.

There were two paths they could take. One was to rely on a permanently closed national market and an international market with no connections with national ones, and to make full use of Anglo-Saxon alliances. That meant acting as a go-between, relying on financial engineering, and giving priority to Anglo-Saxon alliances. Such a course was better suited to Lazards or Paribas than to the Crédit Lyonnais, the BNP, or the Société Générale. For the latter three banks, opening up the market, particularly within a European framework, would have been the solution. On such a basis, French banks would have been able to depend on their huge clientele and make their mark through their placing capacity, like their German or Swiss counterparts. Herman Abs had shown the way, and Maurice Schlogel had seen clearly where his interests lay.

Treasury resistance has been analysed elsewhere, and Laure Quennouëlle has clearly shown its nature.[85] The archives used here confirm her findings: the

Treasury delayed the opening-up of the French market to capital, to foreign actors, and modernity, and presided over its decline in a rather disorderly way and, after May 1968, with a certain neglect of the interests of nationalized enterprises.

What has been said about the 1967–8 reforms does, however, need modifying. Although the Finance Minister played an essential part with regard to his departments, giving competition its due and the desire to develop skills came just as much from the banks, as is shown by the actions of Reyre or Schlogel, and such competition had its roots largely in the skills practised on the international markets, whose virtues the French banks had once again managed to discover.

Notes

1. Crédit Lyonnais, DAF, visit of Samuels of Kuhn Loeb, 22/1064; Paribas, copies of Margerie's letters 6064: 14 Dec. 1960, Margerie to Legorretz, BNM; 14 Dec. 1960, 12 Sept. 1961, Margerie to Cardin; 10 Mar. 1961.
2. Paribas, copies of Margerie's letters 60/64: Margerie to S. Warburg, 26 Sept. 1963.
3. Paribas, copies of Margerie's letters 65/67: Margerie to S. Warburg, 19 May 1967.
4. Paribas, Paribas Ltd., Cardin (?) to X, 27 Nov. 1965.
5. See n. 4.
6. P. Haas, interview in *International Investor*, June 1987.
7. DAF, conversation with J. Guyos, 16 Sept. 1964.
8. DAF, visit of Hambros directors to Schlogel, 15 Mar. 1967.
9. DAF, visit of Champion, Paris representative of WW, 2 Mar. 1966.
10. DAF, meeting at Baring's concerning the Portuguese loan, 14 Apr. 1964: the Crédit Lyonnais could only invest abroad and had to request special authorization for exclusive geographical investment. DAF, visit of Gillis, Samuel and Co.
11. DAF, visit to the Banque Lambert, Brussels, 24 Feb. 1964.
12. DAF, Kockums Mekaniska Verkstads Aktiebolaget, 24–5 Aug. 1965.
13. DAF, visit of Korner of Warburgs to Schlogel, 10 Nov. 1964.
14. DAF, visit of vice-president of the First Boston.
15. DAF, note of 17 Jan. 1966.
16. DAF, City of Copenhagen offer.
17. DAF, First Boston Corporation offer, 22 Dec. 1965.
18. DAF, Tom Clark Equipment issue, 24/166, 11 Feb. 1966; tel White Weld, Paris, 20 Jan. 1966.
19. DAF, working meeting, New York, 14–17 May 1968.
20. DAF, Sumitomo loan, 23 Aug. 1968, 12 Nov. 1968.
21. DAF, note, Kestoy Oy loan, 21 May 1964; note, Japanese Development Bank loan, 9 Sept. 1964.
22. DAF, visit to London, 17–25 Dec. 1964.
23. DAF, Cyanamid loan, 10 Sept. 1965.
24. DAF, Enzo Gutzeit Bond, 5 Jan. 1965.
25. DAF, visit to Germany, 13–15 Oct. 1964.
26. DAF, Portuguese loan in Germany, meeting in Frankfurt at DB, 1 June 1964.
27. See note 20 and DAF, meeting of 14 Apr. 1964 at Barings'.

28. DAF, various participations in issues on the German market, notes 2 Dec. 1965, 15 June 1966, 21 Sept. 1966, 25 Oct. 1966 and 18 Jan. 1967.
29. DAF, tel. Samuel, Schneiter's note of 2 Mar. 1964.
30. DAF, visit of representatives of American banks, EIB loan, 10 Dec. 1964.
31. DAF, tel. Braggiotti, EIB loan, 6 July 1966.
32. DAF, visit of Smolarski to Siebel, DB, 23 Mar. 1966.
33. DAF, visit of J. M. Young of Morgan Stanley and Co., 1966, New York, 28 Mar. 1966; visit to Switzerland to meet directors of the three major banks, 2–3 May 1966.
34. DAF, conversation with a representative of First Boston, 24 Aug. 1966.
35. DAF, meeting at DB, Frankfurt,18 Apr. 1966.
36. DAF, Bankers Trusts issue, 2 May 1966.
37. Visit of Smolarski to Siebel, 22 Sept. 1967.
38. DAF, conversations, 6 Oct. 1965.
39. DAF, ibid, 27 Sept. 1965.
40. M. Schlogel, 'Le Marché financier international et la place de Paris', *Banque* (Jan. 1967), 12–18. DAF, conversation regarding the Monsanto issue, 22 Sept. 1965.
41. DAF, conversation with Guinard, assistant director of the Treasury, 15 July 1964.
42. DAF, conversation with Guinard, Tresury, 1 Apr. 1965.
43. DAF, visit of Gillis, Samuel and Co., 27 Jan. 1965, Smolarski note, 12 Feb. 1965; conversation with L. de Rothschild, 8 Mar. 1965.
44. DAF, conversation with Smolarski, Frankfurt, 9 Mar. 1965.
45. DAF, ibid., 1 Apr. 1965.
46. DAF, visit of Jarvis, Samuel and Co., 19 Mar. 1965; visit of a representative of the Deutsche Bank, 7 Apr. 1965.
47. DAF, conversations, visit of representatives of Morgan Stanley, 27 Apr. 1966.
48. Visit of M. Pierre-Brossolette, 27 Apr. 1966; tel. Bouchet, managing director of foreign services, Banque de France.
49. DAF, tel. with Le Guen, Treasury management, 9 June 1966.
50. Schlogel, 'Le Marché financier', 12–18.
51. DAF, 28 Dec. 1968.
52. DAF, conversation with du Pré, de Saint-Maur, Treasury management, 15 Dec. 1967.
53. DAF, visit of Chauvin to Vienot, assistant director of the Treasury, 10 Feb. 1967.
54. DAF, CFF approach to DAF, 6 Jan. 1967; CFF note, international loan, 11 Apr. 1967.
55. DAF, Roussel UCLAF, projected international loan in francs, 13 Nov. 1967.
56. DAF, conversation with du Pré de Saint-Maur, Treasury management, 15 Dec. 1967.
57. DAF, visit to the Treasury, 20 Mar. 1968.
58. DAF, CR discussions in London, 6 Dec. 1967. German banks visit, 9–10 Jan. 1968; journey to Geneva, Zurich, and Milan, 3–5 Jan. 1968.
59. DAF, commitment of Crédit Lyonnais to underwriting international loans, 29 Nov. 1968.
60. DAF, meeting at Ministry of Finance Crédit Lyonnais, BNP, Société Générale, 7 June 1968.
61. DAF, visit to Vienot, 12 Aug. 1968.
62. DAF, visit of Schlogel to Martial-Simon, 23 Sept. 1968.
63. DAF, visit of Reyre and Guyot to Wiriath, 21 June 1963.
64. DAF, EIB loans, 6 Nov. 1963, 20? 1963.
65. DAF, ESCS loan, 23 Nov. 1963.

66. DAF, 27 Oct. 1966, 3 Nov. 1966; discussions in London, Oct. 1966; 18 Nov. 1966, 15 Dec. 1966. 16 Feb. 1967.
67. DAF, lunch with Vaugelas, Air Liquide, 6 Dec. 1966.
68. DAF, 27 Aug. 1965, 5 Oct. 1965.
69. DAF, visit to Pechiney, 27 Jan. 1966.
70. DAF, visit to Air France, 30 Jan. 1967.
71. DAF, visits, 16 Jan. 1967.
72. DAF, visits 13 Mar. 1967.
73. DAF, 26 Jan., 3 Feb. 1966.
74. DAF, EDF, projected international loan, various discussions, 22–3 Dec. 1966.
75. DAF, visit of representatives of the three deposit banks to the chairman of the finance committee of EDF.
76. DAF, SNCF international loan, 14 Apr. 1967.
77. DAF, approach to Bernard, SNCF, by Crédit Lyonnais.
78. DAF, cooperation between the nationalized banks, 15 Feb., 2 Mar. 1967.
79. DAF, CNT international loan, 3 Aug. 1967.
80. DAF, visit of Korner, director of Warburs.
81. DAF, BID, meeting at Lazards, 1 June 1967.
82. DAF, tel. with BNP concerning a Michelin loan, 17 Apr. 1968.
83. DAF, 17 Feb. 1967.
84. DAF, projected Gaz de France international loan, 4 Dec. 1967, 8 Jan. 1968.
85. L. Quennouëlle, *La Direction du Trésor, 1947–1967. L'État banquier et la croissance* (Paris, 2000), 518–22.

PART V

Internationalization and Globalization, 1980–2000

14

London as an International Financial Centre, 1980–2000: Global Powerhouse or Wimbledon EC2?

RICHARD ROBERTS

'London is the potent force in global finance', crowed *The Global Powerhouse: thecityofLondon*, a distinctly triumphal publication of the Corporation of London to mark the turn of the millennium. But in truth there was much to be triumphant about—by almost any yardstick (and *The Global Powerhouse* was full of them) London was the world's leading international financial centre.

London's resumption of the position of top international financial centre was a development that preceded the decades discussed in this chapter. Writing in the early 1980s, McRae and Cairncross observed that: 'On almost any measure you care to take, the City of London is the world's leading international financial centre . . . if anything in the 1960s and 1970s London's dominance increased.'[1] What happened in the 1980s and 1990s was that the City maintained its 'dominance' and even enhanced it in some activities. What was the evidence for these claims? And how was London's lead sustained in the final decades of the twentieth century?

'As the world's foremost financial centre, London is a vital asset to the British and European economies, attracting investment and boosting competition,' declared UK Chancellor Gordon Brown.[2] Indeed, he deemed its contribution to be so significant that one of the 'five tests' he set in 1997 for the UK's readiness to join the euro was that it should not harm the City to do so. The City was also a key factor in the London economy, boosting employment and prosperity. But the highly paid City workforce skewed London's income distribution and contributed to social distortions, notably the high cost of living and the shortage of affordable housing for low-paid workers in essential services. Moreover, as the City loomed ever larger in the London economy so did its host's vulnerability to a downturn in international financial services activity or the erosion of its leading position. What was the balance between the benefits and costs of hosting this cuckoo in the nest?

Another paradox of the growth of the size and significance of the City in the 1980s and 1990s was the waning significance of British financial firms in the international financial services sector. By the beginning of the twenty-first century more than half of the City's workforce worked for foreign banks or foreign financial firms, and amongst the top international investment banks not one was British.[3] It was a state of affairs sometimes compared to the Wimbledon tennis tournament, for which the UK provides the venue and sells the strawberries and cream but where most of the players, and winners, are foreigners. How and why was the City transformed into Wimbledon EC2? Did it matter?

The prosperity of the international financial services industry in the 1980s and 1990s stimulated other financial centres to try to boost, or just retain, their share of activity. Challenges were mounted by Frankfurt and Paris, taking advantage of the opportunity that appeared to be offered by the UK's non-participation in the launch of the European single currency. There were also internal challenges that threatened to erode the City's competitive standing, notably congested local transport, creeping taxation, and increasingly bureaucratic regulation. How serious were these challenges? And what was the City's outlook for the twenty-first century?

1. Expansion of City Activity

Two types of financial services activity are conducted in any financial centre—'retail' and 'wholesale'. Retail financial services serve a mostly domestic customer base, accommodating the financial needs of individuals and small businesses. Wholesale financial activities—what goes on in the City—serve the requirements of corporations, governments, public agencies, and the financial services industry itself. In the City's case, they are also predominantly international.

Traditionally, *the City* was also a geographical area—the medieval City of London, sometimes known as *the Square Mile*. But from the 1980s, some international banks and other firms conducting wholesale financial business have dispersed to other neighbourhoods, notably Canary Wharf. Despite the diaspora, the traditional term 'the City' continues to be used as shorthand for London's wholesale financial activities; it is in this economic sense—referring to wholesale financial services activities in London, both inside and beyond the Square Mile—that it is used here.

No figures are available for the output of the wholesale financial services sector in the UK prior to the late 1990s. However, there are estimates of employment in 'City-type' wholesale financial activities from the early 1970s, and even a couple of benchmark numbers for earlier years. Michie has calculated City employment in commercial and financial services in 1911 as 194,000, while an estimate by Dunning and Morgan for 1964/6 was 195,000 (these numbers are useful reference points but must be treated with considerable caution because of the changing structure of City activity).[4] In 1971 the wholesale financial services workforce was 178,000 (Fig. 14.1). Most years of the subsequent three decades saw an increase in City employment with particularly rapid rates of expansion in the early 1970s, the mid-1980s, and from the mid-1990s. But there were also short-term reverses in the mid-1970s and the early 1990s, resulting from international recessions and stock market

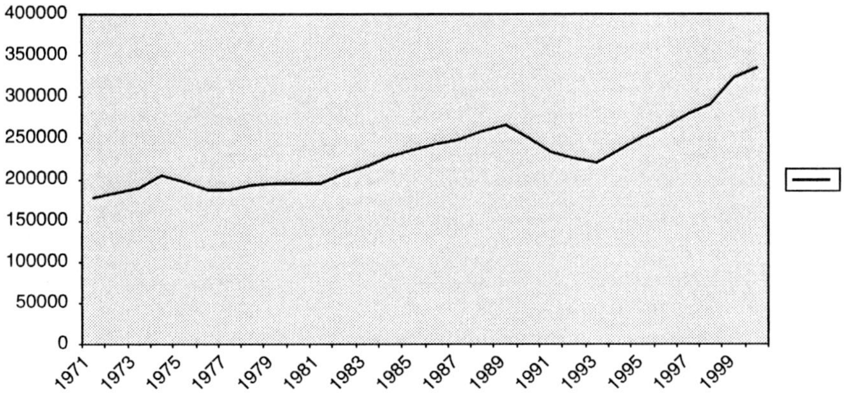

Figure 14.1. Employment in wholesale financial services in London, 1971–2000
Source: Richard Roberts & David Kynaston, *City State: A Contemporary History of the City of London and How Money Triumphed* (Profile Books, 2002), 61.

slumps. The benchmark numbers for 1911 and 1964/6 were surpassed in the early 1980s and, even with the shedding of 50,000 City jobs in the downturn of the early 1990s, employment in wholesale financial services remained at historic highs. Then the upsurge from the mid-1990s set a series of new records, peaking at 335,000 jobs in 2000, almost double the number of thirty years earlier.

Underlying the expansion of City employment from the 1960s was a set of fundamental forces driving the expansion of international financial services. It is a well-known feature of long-term economic development that the stock of financial assets—deposits, loans, shares, bonds, mortgages, etc.—grows faster than the rate of increase of overall output; that is, as a society becomes more prosperous and economically more sophisticated, the ratio of financial assets to national product rises.[5] The management of financial assets is the activity performed by the financial services sector; thus as an economy grows, typically the financial services sector increases faster than national output. This dynamic relationship between economic development and the expansion of the financial services sector also applies to the international economy and to international financial services; as the international economy grows, the international financial services industry expands even more rapidly.

Since 1945, the world economy and world trade have grown more or less continuously. The buoyancy of world trade has provided a direct boost to several City activities—trade finance, foreign exchange dealing, ship and aircraft broking, and international insurance—and a general stimulus overall.

International financial flows have increased even faster than international trade. As the leading international banking centre and the foremost location of the international capital (Eurobond) market, London benefited greatly from these developments. The internationalization of investment was fostered by the abolition of bureaucratic barriers to free financial flows and advances in communications. Following the collapse of the Bretton Woods system in the early 1970s, many countries scrapped the exchange controls they had maintained to protect fixed parities, allowing their citizens to invest their funds wherever they wished and boosting international flows.

Advances in telecommunications radically expanded the quantity and quality of financial information and slashed the cost. Improvements in aviation technology reduced the time and price of air travel, making it easier for fund managers and private investors to visit financial centres in foreign countries. Extended horizons led to the international diversification of assets. The rapid expansion of international financial flows and the internationalization of investment boosted the City's international banking and investment banking activities.

From the 1960s, there was a rapid expansion in the volume of financial transactions conducted 'offshore'—that is, subject to a regulatory and legal framework chosen by the contracting parties, not simply those of their domicile. The 'offshore revolution' had three main strands—offshore banking; offshore bond issuance, underwriting, and trading; and the swaps and derivatives markets.[6] The offshore markets mushroomed as they trounced onshore counterparts by providing a greater range of product types, more dynamic product innovation, and lower costs. In theory, offshore financial facilities could be located anywhere and everywhere. But in reality, the principal centre for the conduct of offshore financial activities and the foremost beneficiary of the general expansion of international financial services from the 1960s was London. But why London?

2. Economies of Scale and Scope

Amongst financial centres, an established leader enjoys advantages over aspiring challengers. Firms that operate from larger financial centres tend to enjoy significant competitive advantages over those in smaller centres because of the operation of *external economies of scale* and *external economies of scope*. External economies of scale accrue to firms when a positive relationship exists between efficiency and the size of the industry (financial centre) in which they operate. There are many reasons why a larger financial centre provides a more advantageous operating environment than a smaller centre. The quality of financial markets—that is, their liquidity and efficiency—is strongly correlated with the scale of operations. These are highly desirable features, meaning lower dealing costs and diminished likelihood of market failure. The most important market of all is the labour market, London possessing an unrivalled critical mass of skills in financial and related services.

Economies of scale also apply to the operations of individual international financial services firms. The concentration of key staff in a single location where they are in face-to-face contact with colleagues, clients, and rivals adds value to a firm's operations. A larger number and greater range of activities of other financial firms produces a more innovative environment, which may generate new business opportunities and demand from other practitioners. Competition between firms stimulates keener pricing for transactions, product innovation, and perhaps the development of bespoke products for individual clients. Such factors advantage larger firms operating from bigger centres in winning business.

Financial firms operating in large financial centres with a wide range of complementary activities also enjoy external economies of scope. The ready availability of commercial lawyers, accountants, specialist printers, information technology experts, financial public relations consultants, and many other specialist services, enhances a firm's efficiency and competitiveness. The bigger the centre, the more extensive and more varied the range of complementary activities.

The 1980s and 1990s also saw the continuation of a variety of institutional, social, and cultural factors that had worked in London's favour since the 1960s.

- The deft regulatory framework operated by the UK authorities over the wholesale financial markets and the international banks that participated in them. Traditionally the Bank of England was the leading regulator, but from 1997 a new unitary body, the Financial Services Authority, assumed the role.
- Financial infrastructure: the quality of payments and settlements systems.
- The volume of international transport links (though not London's internal transport, which deteriorated in the 1990s). In 2000, Heathrow processed more international traffic than any other airport in the world and together London's five airports handled 100 million international passengers.
- Telecommunications, benefiting from the early deregulation and privatization of the UK telecoms industry in the early 1980s. In a survey of European business executives conducted in 2000 about the quality of telecommunications, London scored 1.43 compared with 0.87 for Paris and 0.83 for Frankfurt.[7]
- Flexibility in working practices and favourable personal and corporate tax environment.
- Language, law, learning, and culture. English is the language of international finance; the common tongue was one of the reasons why in the 1960s most US banks decided to establish their Euromarket operations in London, rather than elsewhere. English law is much used in commercial contracts, with disputes resolved principally in English courts or through London-based arbitration and mediation. The presence of leading academic centres for the study and teaching of finance, and specialist financial training companies. And the personal appeal of living in a vibrant cosmopolitan city.

3. Docklands

A new factor in the 1980s and 1990s was the development of a site in derelict Docklands, a mere three miles from the Square Mile, into a second international financial services node. The development of Canary Wharf began in 1985 when the London head of Crédit Suisse First Boston, Michael von Clemm, put together a consortium to pioneer the largest real-estate development in Western Europe, comprising 8.5 million square feet of office space on a 71-acre site.[8] Von Clemm's initiative was prompted by his frustration at being unable to rent the state-of-the-art accommodation his firm needed for the massive open-plan trading floors required by modern investment banks. The same frustration, stemming partly from conservationist planning regulations in the City, led other international banks to look elsewhere in London and to constitute eager potential tenants for the new buildings at Canary Wharf.

Construction began in 1988 and the first tenants arrived in 1991. Despite substantial central government financial support, transport links remained poor and it was not until the completion of an underground link in 2000 that there was an adequate mass transit system. By then the number of people working at Canary Wharf was about to reach 35,000, with 50,000 projected for the mid-2000s.

The Square Mile also saw some new office developments, notably Broadgate where construction began in 1985, the largest building project in the City since the Great Fire of 1666. Alarmed by the success of Canary Wharf at attracting firms away from the Square Mile, the Corporation of London, the City's local government entity, relaxed planning restrictions, thus encouraging a surge of redevelopment projects from the mid-1990s. The outcome of the building at Canary Wharf and in the Square Mile was a rapid expansion in up-to-date office accommodation sufficient to meet the needs of the 1990s boom and even act as an incentive to shift activities to London from European centres.

4. City Activities in 2000

The pattern of City activities in 2000, as mirrored in the distribution of the workforce engaged in wholesale financial services activities, is shown in Table 14.1.

Commercial and investment banking constituted the core of City activity, generating almost half of total jobs. At the beginning of the 1980s, different aspects of banking and securities business were conducted by a set of specialist British-owned institutions, the UK clearing banks, 235 stock exchange brokers, 60 merchant banks, 17 stockjobbers (market-makers), and 11 discount houses.[9] The 1980s and 1990s saw the dismantling of this traditional structure of specialist, modestly sized, British-owned firms due to the deregulation of the securities industry and the acquisition of UK firms by foreign banks; by 2000 City business was dominated by a score of massive, mostly globally active banks undertaking the full range of banking and securities activities, and another score of large firms of financial lawyers and accountants, insurance companies, and fund managers.

Wholesale Commercial Banking

Most of the half-dozen big UK commercial (clearing) banks, the core of the UK's domestic financial system, and many other indigenous financial institutions had their head offices in the City. Around 25,000 people undertook head-office type domestic banking activities in London, mostly in UK banks though some foreign banks also serviced UK corporate and retail customers.

Table 14.1. *London wholesale financial services activities, 2000*

	Number of people	%
Commercial and investment banking		
Domestic commercial banking	25,000	7
International commercial banking	40,000	12
Foreign exchange trading	10,000	3
Corporate finance	15,000	4
Securities		
Bonds	25,000	7
International equities	10,000	3
UK equities	25,000	7
Derivatives	5,000	2
Total bank activities	155,000	
Fund management	40,000	12
Insurance	50,000	15
Marine services, commodities markets, other	20,000	6
Professional and specialist services	70,000	21
Total	335,000	

Sources: Lombard Street Research, *Growth Prospects of City Industries* (London, 1998), 30; Centre for Economic and Business Research, *The City's Importance to the European Union Economy* (London, 2000), 10; (2001), 7. These estimates have been adjusted in the light of a variety of other evidence.

London was host to 481 foreign banks, a larger number than any other financial centre. Some 40,000 people worked in international commercial banking (Table 14.2).

The principal reason for their presence in London was to participate in the thriving offshore financial markets, providing access to these vast pools of funds to foreign corporations, banks, and governments. As a result, London was the leading centre for international cross-border bank lending (Table 14.3).

Foreign Exchange

Most City banks conducted foreign exchange dealing, an activity supporting around 10,000 jobs. A survey conducted by the Bank for International Settlements in 1998 revealed that London had a daily turnover of $637bn., 32 per cent of the global total, making it the world's leading foreign exchange market by a long lead (Table 14.4). It had the largest number of foreign exchange market participants, some 340 dealing firms, and offered the greatest array of spot and forward market contracts.[10]

Corporate Finance and Securities

The leading globally active banks provided advisory services to corporations, notably on mergers and acquisitions, and to governments and other

Table 14.2. *Number of foreign banks, 2000*

London	481
New York	287
Frankfurt	242
Paris	187
Tokyo	92

Source: International Financial Services London, *International Financial Markets in the UK* (Apr. 2001).

Table 14.3. *International cross-border bank lending, market share, 2000*

	%
UK	19.5
Japan	11.5
Germany	8.9
US	8.7
France	6.0

Source: International Financial Services London, *International Financial Markets in the UK* (Apr. 2001).

Table 14.4. *Foreign exchange trading volume, 1998*

	Average daily turnover	
	$bn.	%
London	637	32
New York	350	18
Tokyo	148	8
Singapore	139	7
Frankfurt	94	4
Switzerland	81	4
Hong Kong	78	4
Paris	71	4
Other centres	373	18
Total	1,971	

Source: Bank for International Settlements, *Central Bank Survey (Apr. 1998).*

Table 14.5. *Number of foreign companies listed on selected exchanges, 1999*

London	499
Nasdaq	429
New York	406
Luxembourg	223
Frankfurt	195
Switzerland	173
Paris	169

Source: London Stock Exchange. *Fact File: Key Statistics 2000* (2001), 19.

public bodies. They also undertook the raising of funds for these clients through the capital markets, organizing and underwriting issues of equities and bonds (primary market activity). Around 15,000 people were employed in these activities (known as investment banking). Secondary market trading in securities for clients and on banks' own account (proprietary trading) employed around 60,000.

Securities trading focused on the London Stock Exchange, the world's third largest exchange by equity capitalization. Trading was conducted in a variety of UK securities, and in international equities—the shares of foreign companies with a listing in London as well as on their domestic market. More foreign companies were listed on the London Stock Exchange than on any other exchange, turnover accounting for three-fifths of trading in all international equities around the world.[11] Transactions in international equities substantially surpassed business in UK shares.

Eurobonds

The biggest securities market of all is the offshore Eurobond market. Eurobonds were invented in London in 1963 and the market has been focused there ever since. Eurobonds comprised 90 per cent of international bond issues, 60 per cent of issuance taking place in London. London was also the focal point of the secondary market conducting 70 per cent of Eurobond trading.[12]

Derivatives

Derivative products—options, futures, and swaps—are used for hedging financial risks or for betting on movements in securities and commodities prices, currencies and interest rates. The 1980s and 1990s saw a spectacular expansion of the global derivatives market, which became one of the City's most buoyant growth areas. In 2000 the London International Financial Futures and Options Exchange (LIFFE), founded in 1982, was Europe's largest derivatives exchange and third in the world for exchange traded business.[13] London hosted the highest volume of trading of over-the-counter derivatives, 36 per cent of the global total, substantially ahead of the USA (Table 14.6). Derivatives business generated around 5,000 jobs in London.

Fund Management

London was the world's leading centre for fund management, an activity employing around 40,000 people. The City managed a greater volume of investment funds than the next seven European centres combined (Table 14.7).

Table 14.6. *Average daily turnover of OTC derivatives, 1998*

	OTC turnover ($bn.)	Global share (%)
UK	171	36
USA	91	19
France	46	10
Japan	42	9
Germany	34	7
Switzerland	16	3
Singapore	11	2

Source: Bank for International Settlements, *Central Bank Survey* (Apr. 1998).

Table 14.7. *Holdings of institutional equities in leading financial centres, 1999*

	$bn.
London	2,461
New York	2,363
Tokyo	2,058
Boston	1,871
San Francisco	726
Los Angeles	569
Paris	458
Philadelphia	419
Zurich	491
Denver	340

Source: Thomson Financial, *International Target Cities Report 2000*.

Insurance, Marine Services, Commodities Markets

Insurance was a major City activity, supporting 50,000 jobs.[14] The London market was the world's largest market for internationally traded insurance and the main international centre for reinsurance business, which was focused on the Lloyd's of London wholesale insurance market. Between 1990 and 2000, net worldwide premiums generated by the UK insurance industry more than doubled from £66bn. to £174bn. London was the leading centre for aviation insurance, with 39 per cent of the global market share, and marine insurance, with 19 per cent. The latter reflected London's centuries-old pre-eminence as a centre for marine services focused at the Baltic Exchange. The City was also host to several important commodity markets, notably the London Metal Exchange, the London Commodity Exchange, the International Petroleum Exchange, and the bullion market.

Professional and Specialist Services

The City's banking, securities, fund management, and insurance sectors were serviced by specialist professional firms of lawyers and accountants. Other specialist services included financial public relations, recruitment consultancies, and information services, such as Reuters, Bloomberg, the *Financial Times*, and *Euromoney*. In total these professional and specialist support services employed around 70,000 people.

Round-Up

In 2000, at the end of the two decades under review, the volume of business conducted in London surpassed other centres in a wide range of wholesale international financial services activities. In most banking and trading activities London maintained an established lead during the 1980s and 1990s, though in insurance the length of the lead shortened substantially. The data available about total employment in wholesale financial services in other major financial centres, though incomplete and unsatisfactory, confirm London's leading position. An estimate for New York's wholesale financial services workforce in 2000 was around 360,000, while informed guesswork suggests a figure of 300,000–350,000 for Tokyo.[15] Although these numbers were somewhat higher than London's 335,000, in both cases a much higher proportion of the workforce was engaged in domestic activities. The comparable workforce in other centres was much smaller than in the three global centres: Hong Kong 167,000 (1997); and Frankfurt 75,000–80,000 (both figures include persons undertaking retail activities).[16] This variety of data substantiates London's claim to pride of place in the provision of international financial services.

5. Benefit to UK and EU Economies

In the 1980s and 1990s, the City made an increasingly important contribution to the UK economy in a variety of ways. In 2000, its 335,000–strong workforce comprised 1 per cent of UK employment but their output of £22bn. constituted 3 per cent of UK GDP.[17] Moreover, these modest-sounding macroeconomic statistics did not capture its full significance to the British economy. First, because the City contributed £10bn. in tax towards the public purse, about 4 per cent of central government tax revenues.[18] Secondly, because the City's overseas earnings played a vital part in the UK's balance of payments; in 2000 the financial sector's trade surplus was £14bn. offsetting almost half the £30bn. deficit in trade in goods.[19] Finally, because the City was a dynamic and successful sector of the UK economy with a leading position in a fast-growing global industry—promising still more jobs, greater output, and higher tax revenues.

In 2000, the City's output of wholesale financial services constituted 52 per cent of the EU total of £42.2bn.[20] This concentration of activity resulted in significant economies of scale bringing about an estimated saving in the cost of the provision of wholesale financial services for EU customers of 16 per cent.

London's efficiency, deriving from its critical mass of activity and cost competitiveness, attracted use of its services by clients, particularly multinational corporations, which might otherwise have placed their business in New York or Tokyo or another non-EU financial centre, and by wealthy individuals, who could seek provision of their investment requirements in Switzerland.

Quantitative estimates of the contribution of the City's efficiency as a supplier of wholesale financial services to the EU economy have been undertaken by the Centre for Economic and Business Research, an economic consultancy—an exercise requiring some 'heroic assumptions' and bold estimates of missing data.[21] This was done by comparing the actual situation in the year 2000 and a hypothetical model—the 'fragmented market model'-in which money-centre services were spread evenly across the countries of the EU proportionate to their respective gross domestic products.

Under the fragmented market model, the City's output fell from £22bn. to £7.1bn., a 70 per cent reduction, and about half of City employment disappeared, some 150,000 jobs. It was estimated that the increased costs deriving from the loss of economies of scale would lead many customers to seek services outside the EU. The modelling suggested that only 48 per cent of the business lost by the City would go elsewhere in the EU. Of the remainder, half would migrate to financial centres outside the EU, mostly New York or Switzerland, while the other half of transactions would simply become uneconomic and disappear. As a net result, the EU would be £7.3bn. worse off with a total GDP lower by 0.17 per cent and the overall loss of 110,000 jobs. 'The City of London', the study concluded, 'is a vital component of the whole EU economy that boosts its efficiency and competitiveness and hence its GDP and employment.'[22]

6. The City and the London Economy

The City and its well-paid workforce played a vital role in the economy of its host city, London. In 2000, the 335,000-strong workforce generated 13 per cent of London's GDP and comprised 8 per cent of total employment in the capital.[23] In New York it has been estimated that each job on Wall Street supports two more jobs in the city.[24] Applying this ratio to London suggests that the City may have supported 20–24 per cent of London employment. In 2000 on average each City worker generated output of £63,000 a year. Since this average included a substantial number of support staff—clerks, messengers, secretaries, receptionists, chauffeurs, etc.—it meant that the output generated by the executive echelon was much higher. High levels of output resulted in high levels of remuneration: between 1970 and 2000 the average salary of male City staff rose from £2,256 to £47,673, compared to national average white-collar incomes of £1,856 and £27,762 respectively (Fig. 14.2).

The earnings of City women workers traced a similar path, rising from an annual average of £1,138 at the start of the 1970s to £30,638 in 2000, compared to national averages of £915 and £18,590 respectively (Fig. 14.3). Although at the end of the 1990s, City men's average earnings were 80 per cent higher than those of City women, a gender discrepancy far larger than the nation as a whole, the gender

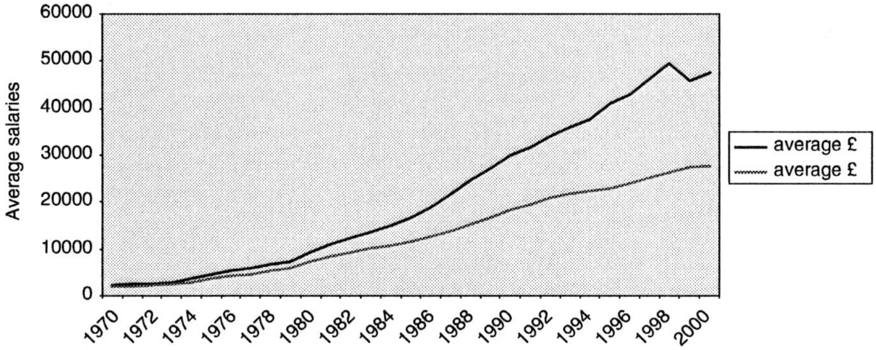

Figure 14.2. Male city salaries, 1970–2000
Source: *New Earnings Survey*, annual data.

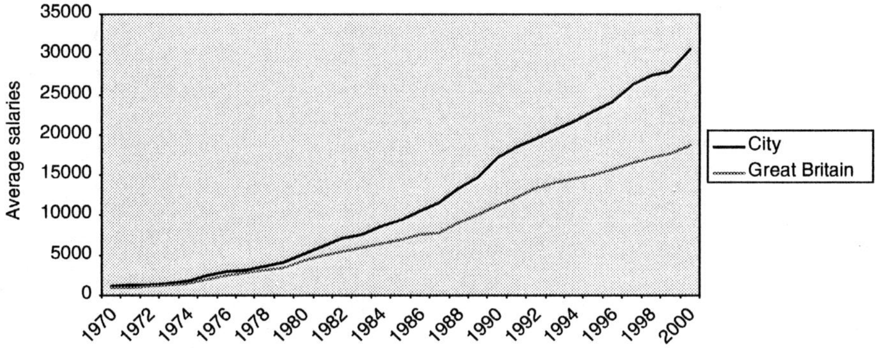

Figure 14.3. Female City Salaries, 1970–2000
Source: *New Earnings Survey*, annual data.

gap had closed a little over the three decades due to the advance of women into highly paid executive positions.

Not only were City staff better paid than workers in other sectors, over the years the pay premium grew wider and wider. In the 1970s the average incomes of City staff were around 20 per cent higher than national average white-collar earnings. The City earnings premium grew rapidly in the 1980s, rising for men from 25 per cent in 1980 to 60 per cent in 1988. These were the years of 'Big Bang', which resulted in a fundamental restructuring of the way many City firms did business and an influx of foreign banks and securities houses into London. Both processes had the effect of bidding up City salaries—the so-called 'yuppie boom'. In the wake of the October 1987 stock market crash, many City firms shed staff and the salary premium stabilized. But City salaries took off again from the mid-1990s; by 2000 the average City salary (full-time adult employees of both sexes) was £45,419, more than double the national average of £21,842.[25]

The fivefold increase since 1970 in the premium of City salaries over the national average, from 20 per cent to more than 100 per cent, was a reflection of the dynamism and efficiency of the wholesale financial services sector. It was consistent with estimates based on national income data that the output of City workers rose by at least 7 per cent a year in real terms over the decades of the 1970s, 1980s, and 1990s.[26] This was a much faster rate of growth than the rate of increase of City employment, which averaged around 1.5 per cent. The outcome was the advance of City remuneration and the ever-widening premium over national average earnings.

The City's well-remunerated workforce was a significant factor in the capital's economy. It has been estimated that the total wages and salaries of London's money-centre workforce in the year 2000 were £11.5bn. in wages and salaries, plus £1.5bn. in bonuses, making total earnings of £13bn.[27]

The bonus system was considerably more widespread in the City than in most other UK business sectors. In theory it provided City firms with a flexible cost base that allowed them to weather the ups and downs of a cyclical revenue stream without having to undermine their effectiveness by laying off staff. In 1980 bonuses in UK banks and merchant banks were around 3 or 4 per cent of salary and sometimes even took the Dickensian form of a turkey or food hamper.[28] Performance-related bonuses were a feature of the remuneration package at stock exchange firms, and one reason for the increase in the bonus dimension of City remuneration was the acquisition of firms of brokers and jobbers by banks with deregulation of the securities industry in 1983–6. Even more important from the mid-1980s was the competition for staff from US banks, where bonuses formed a much greater part of remuneration.

Substantial bonuses were paid in the boom years 1986 and 1987, but payouts were much smaller in the doldrums years of the late 1980s and early 1990s. During the 1990s the bonus dimension of City remuneration increased by leaps and bounds—star performers began to earn payouts several times their annual salary. The rise of big bonuses began in 1993, the year in which more than 100 top partners at the London offices of Goldman Sachs received year-end bonuses of more than $1 m. each. In 1996, the next bumper year, City bonuses totalled £750m. and the following year they hit £1bn. for the first time. The unprecedented largesse of the 1996 and 1997 bonus rounds made a few conscience-stricken City souls uneasy about the size of their remuneration packages. In January 1998 a debate was held at the Mansion House on the motion: *This house believes that City salaries are totally fair and justified.*[29] The motion was defeated, but there is no record of anyone returning their bonus.

The big City bonus payouts of 1996 and 1997 prompted speculation as to whether something more fundamental than a market cycle was afoot in the financial services industry. One proposition was that with the breakdown in national boundaries to investment, the big European and US investment banks had started to compete with each other on a global basis. This had created a single elite labour market, and London pay was catching up with Wall Street pay levels and US remuneration practices.[30]

The East Asia financial crisis, the Russian default, and the near-collapse of Long-Term Capital Management cast a pall over the financial services sector in 1998. The gloomy outlook and a downturn in profits led to layoffs and a fall in bonus payouts, which tumbled to £600m. in 1998. But in 1999 a takeover boom and the dot.com bubble led to record bonus payments aggregating more than £1bn. And 2000 saw another record bonus round totalling in excess of £1.5bn.

City Affluence—Benefits and Costs

In the 1990s, inner London had the highest per capita GDP of any urban region of the European Union. While the media, fashion, and technology sectors were major wealth generators, the City was the single most important source of this prosperity. City salaries and big bonuses were the foremost driving force behind London's boom of the 1980s and 1990s.

Prices in London's prime residential housing market were propelled by City earnings. The central London prime residential rental sector was highly City driven—more than four-fifths of tenants were from overseas, a high proportion of whom worked in the financial services sector.[31] In the purchase market, property consultants F. P. D. Savills estimated that 40 per cent of buyers of prime central London properties had City jobs; in some areas, such as Chelsea, Kensington, and Notting Hill, 70–80 per cent of transactions were for City clients. The late 1990s even saw the phenomenon of an annual upsurge at bonus time, house prices reportedly leaping 20 per cent in prime neighbourhoods.

Hundreds, maybe thousands, of top-of-the-range retailers, travel agents, car showrooms, and restaurants were beneficiaries of the City's high disposable income. Traditionally such emporiums were located in the West End, Knightsbridge, or Chelsea, the City's own streets featuring little more than seedy pubs, newsagents, and sandwich bars. But the late 1990s saw a proliferation of expensive eateries and luxury shops: even the Royal Exchange, where two centuries earlier Nathan Rothschild had made his fortune trading bills of exchange, was converted into a high-class shopping mall. Likewise, a new generation of wine bars sprang up in sumptuously decorated redundant traditional banking halls in the Square Mile. Canary Wharf, with over 500,000 square feet of retail space, was equivalent to a sub-regional shopping mall, attracting almost as many customers from the general public as from Canary Wharf workers.[32]

Underlying the transformation of the City and Canary Wharf from consumer deserts to shopping oases was the affluence of City workers, particularly the growing number of well-paid women. 'Money-rich but time-poor', they were too busy earning money to travel to spend it. So the shops and restaurants came to them, transforming the physical and social fabric of the financial district. A more accommodating attitude on the part of the City planning authorities, rattled by the challenge from Canary Wharf, was a further contributory factor.

During the 1980s and 1990s, London house prices rose by 3.9 per cent a year while average wages grew by only 2.7 per cent. From the mid-1990s there were reports of high property values—City driven—pricing essential service workers out of central London. And surrounding areas too, prices there being pushed up by the arrival of affluent households displaced from the centre by even more affluent bankers. Even in relatively deprived inner London areas, gentrification meant that the rise in the average price of houses outstripped the rise in average salaries by a ratio of seven to one.

For nurses, teachers, police, fire-fighters, social workers, bus crew, and other lower- or middle-income public sector employees, living near one's place of employment became financially impossible and the prospect of owning a home increasingly remote. This led to a mounting problem of staff recruitment and retention and deteriorating public services. Although a variety of policy initiatives were proposed, often based on US experiences of the same phenomenon, little progress was made. Thus, paradoxically, a counterpoint to the City's high average earnings and big bonuses was a deterioration in aspects of the quality of life in London—a crisis of affluence.

7. Deregulation and Strategic Dilemmas

The City of 1980 and the City of 2000 were very different financial communities. The former was populated by British-owned, modestly sized specialist firms, many of which had been around for centuries. By the turn of the millennium a majority of the City's workforce worked for foreign firms and business was dominated by the US bulge-bracket investment banks and other large global players. But where were the British?

The starting point in the story of the decline and disappearance of most of the British merchant banks, securities firms, and discount houses is the abolition of exchange controls on 23 October 1979. This decision, which had profound consequences for London's financial services industry, was taken almost without consultation with the City and with no analysis of its impact on City business.[33] It was driven by the government's desperation to halt the rise of sterling, which was soaring on account of its new status as a petro-currency, inflicting pain on manufacturing industry.

The removal of exchange controls exposed the insularity and uncompetitiveness of the UK securities sector. The surge in the purchase of overseas securities by UK investors following the removal of exchange controls ought to have been a bonanza for UK stockbrokers, but, in fact, the bulk of the business was handled by foreign firms. According to one calculation, 95 per cent of the investments made by the top twenty British pension funds were undertaken by foreign brokerage firms.[34]

This was one of the pieces of evidence that persuaded the Bank of England and government ministers that the British securities industry was in need of a radical overhaul. The outcome was the deal arrived at in July 1983 between the stock exchange and the government, which led to the abolition of fixed commissions and the end of the separation of the functions of stockbroking and market-making. At the same time restrictions on the ownership of stock exchange firms were relaxed, allowing them to be purchased by banks for the first time. This package of changes transforming the UK securities industry became known as 'Big Bang'.

Between 1983 and October 1986, when the new trading arrangements became operational, all the leading securities firms, with only two exceptions, were acquired by outside parties. In total 77 of the by then 225 stock exchange firms were bought, turning more than 500 of their former partners into millionaires: 16 were purchased by UK merchant banks; 27 by UK clearing banks and other UK financial firms; 14 by US banks; and 20 by other foreign, mostly European, banks.[35]

The entry of overseas competitors banks into the hitherto protected domestic UK securities and investment banking markets led to increased competition. This pressure plus the new opportunities offered by deregulation presented the UK merchant banks with a strategic dilemma: should they stick with their traditional client-based, low-risk advisory activities; or should they diversify into securities, following the 'integrated' business model of the US investment banks?[36]

The US investment banks' approach to business was transaction driven rather than relationship based. In other words, they bid aggressively for each mandate as a one-off piece of business, rather than as part of an ongoing client–adviser relationship. Moreover, the US investment banks derived substantial, but very variable, revenues from speculative proprietary trading. This pattern of business was riskier and required more capital, but it could be highly profitable, especially in a bull market.

Most of the UK merchant banks, including the four largest firms of the mid-1980s, S. G. Warburg, Morgan Grenfell, Hill Samuel, and Kleinwort Benson, went for the integrated approach based on the US model. So did Barclays, NatWest, and Midland amongst the major clearing banks. The opposite strategy of sticking to their traditional pattern of business was adopted by Schroders, Lazards, and Flemings amongst the merchant banks, and the stockbroker Cazenove. Rothschilds hedged its position by acquiring a minority interest in Smith New Court, the other significant independent UK stockbroking firm.

At first everything went well for everyone. Business boomed in 1985, 1986, and the first three quarters of 1987, disguising the massive overcapacity created during Big Bang and the decline in margins due to keener price competition. The stock market crash in October 1987 put a stop to the party and brought down Hill Samuel. A second casualty was Morgan Grenfell, which made big losses in equities. Its management was further discredited due to its involvement in the Guinness scandal, making it vulnerable to a takeover bid. In 1989, it became the first merchant bank to pass into foreign ownership when an offer was accepted from Deutsche Bank.

Deutsche Bank's acquisition of Morgan Grenfell was a strategic response to the expansion of the presence of the Wall Street investment banks in London in the late

1980s. The Wall Street firms believed that the process of European economic integration (with the single market due to be completed in 1992) would generate a bonanza for their corporate finance and capital market capabilities and London was their base for the build-up of their European operations.[37] The expansion of US investment banking operations in London was checked by the recession at the beginning of the 1990s, but business revived in New York in 1992, and 1993 saw record profits. On the back of these earnings the Wall Street firms launched a worldwide expansion drive, targeting London in particular as the bridgehead for Europe.

Death of Gentlemanly Capitalism

The burgeoning activity of the Wall Street investment banks in London squeezed the UK merchant banks from two directions. First, competition for talent sent compensation costs soaring. Second, competition for business led to keener pricing and deprived them of mandates they would traditionally have expected to win. The US firms were in a position to bid aggressively for people and business because of the profits generated by their Wall Street operations, which enjoyed higher fee levels than were customary in London and were booming. Continental banks were also able to subsidize their London operations, thanks to the infinite patience of their shareholders. The squeeze on profits led some of the integrated merchant banks to attempt to boost profits from proprietary securities trading, like the US investment banks. One of them was Barings, which went spectacularly bust in February 1995. It was acquired by Dutch bank ING for £1. Another victim of proprietary trading losses, plus a botched merger with Morgan Stanley, was Warburgs, which was acquired by Swiss Bank Corporation in spring 1995 for just its net asset value; in other words the Warburgs brand name, a year earlier the City's foremost franchise, had been rendered virtually valueless.

Between 1995 and 2000, almost the whole sector was sold to overseas owners (Table 14.8).

Some, Morgan Grenfell, Barings, Warburgs, and Hambros, ended up with new owners because they got into trouble. Others, Kleinworts, Smith New Court, MAM, Schroders, and Flemings, came to the conclusion that they were too small to compete with the global players and sold out to one of the European or US banks that was itching to enter the business or expand its presence.

The UK commercial banks Barclays and NatWest did have the capital to compete in the global market place, but to compete effectively with the US investment banks necessitated buying a presence on Wall Street. Still smarting from losses from earlier forays into the USA, not to mention the salutary nightmare of Midland's disastrous acquisition of Crocker Bank in 1980, the directors balked at the cost and the risk. But if they were not prepared to place a firm footprint in New York they were out of the global game. Accordingly, in 1997 both UK banks took the strategic decision largely to pull out of investment banking business and focus on commercial banking. With the sale of Schroders and Flemings in 2000, all that

Table 14.8. *Sale of UK merchant banks, 1989–2000*

Date	Merchant bank	Purchaser	Price (£m.)
1989	Morgan Grenfell	Deutsche Bank	950
1995	Barings	ING	—
1995	S. G. Warburg	Swiss Bank Corporation	860
1995	Kleinwort Benson	Dresdner Bank	1,000
1995	Smith New Court	Merrill Lynch	526
1997	BZW (Barclays) (part)	CSFB	100
1997	NatWest Markets (part)	Bankers Trust/Deutsche Bank	129
1997	Hambros	Société Générale/Investec	738
1997	Mercury Asset Management	Merrill Lynch	3,100
2000	Schroders (part)	Citigroup	1,350
2000	Flemings	Chase Manhattan	4,800

Source: Richard Roberts and David Kynaston, *City State: A Contemporary History of the City of London and how Money Triumphed* (London, 2002), 96.

was left of the independent UK wholesale financial services merchant bank and securities sector was the privately owned firms Rothschilds, Cazenove, and Lazards, and some small niche players.

As the investment banking business globalized, the UK merchant banks found themselves struggling because of the huge advantage enjoyed by the US firms, whose domestic market constituted half the world market. Hence the imperative to establish a substantial presence on Wall Street, a challenge flunked by all the UK firms. As the larger European corporate clients began to shed medium-sized advisers in favour of the top US investment banks, the writing was on the wall for the middle-rank firms. 'The demise of the UK investment banks', commented the *Financial Times* on the sale of Schroders, 'is a natural part of the process of international specialisation that results from globalisation.'[38]

But others blamed parochial shortcomings rather than global processes. Philip Augar, a practitioner during the 1990s and author of *The Death of Gentlemanly Capitalism* (2000), ascribed considerable culpability to amateurish management at the merchant banks. As for the failure of the clearing banks to stay in the game, he blamed irresolute and short-termist senior executives, class-based internal warfare, and failure at the political level, as would surely have been forthcoming in France or Germany, to defend a national interest.

Yet it could be argued that far from being a national humiliation, the City sell-off was a triumph of economic rationality: that the sales of stock exchange firms in the 1980s and of UK merchant banks in the 1990s were shrewd cash-outs at the top of the market cycle from an industry which had been artificially cosseted by barriers to entry and cartel-like practices. Furthermore, it was a sector with highly cyclical and thus poor-quality earnings, in which UK banks would always be at a disadvantage relative to those with much larger domestic economies. In short it was better— not just for the owners but also for the national interest—to get out while the going was good rather than suffer a lingering decline and attrition of value like the UK motor and shipbuilding industries.

Wimbledon EC2

At the end of the 1960s, the staff of the 163 foreign commercial banks which had established a presence in London to conduct Euromarket activities numbered 12,000. The foreign bank presence in London rose rapidly during the Euromarket boom of the 1970s: by 1980 there were 453 foreign banks with 31,000 staff. By the end of the 1980s they had increased to 521 while their staffing had risen to 60,000. During the 1990s the number of foreign banks grew to 537, before declining to 481 in 2000 due to amalgamations and the withdrawal of Japanese banks for domestic reasons. About 50,000 people were added to their payrolls in the 1990s, making an overall total in 2000 of around 110,000 foreign bank staff in London.[39] Thus by the beginning of the twenty-first century, two-thirds of those engaged in wholesale commercial and investment banking activities in London worked for foreign institutions. There were also significant foreign acquisitions in the fund management and insurance industries. Even the set of highly successful City-based accountancy and financial services law firms were becoming cosmopolitan confections as they achieved international expansion through mergers with foreign firms which diluted their Britishness.

The foreign ownership of much of the City gave rise to comparisons with the Wimbledon tennis championship, a tournament hosted by Britain but dominated by foreign players. Some, led by the Bank of England, took the view that ownership did not matter—that liberalized markets maximize economic efficiency and hence wealth creation. After all, Britain got the benefits from hosting the event: the jobs, both direct and indirect, the taxes, and the contributions to invisible earnings. 'Show me', demanded Sir Edward George, governor of the Bank of England, 'a single statistic where the City is in decline.'[40]

But others were uneasy with a free-market stance. 'The fact remains that key decisions about the future of once British-owned merchant banks and securities houses will be made in Frankfurt or New York,' financial journalist Hamish McCrae wrote as early as 1995. 'It is hard to feel completely comfortable with this. There is the obvious fear that if the going gets tough, foreign owners are more likely to withdraw than home-based ones.'[41] 'Ownership brings influence,' argued Philip Augar, 'that's why branch offices always feel different to head offices.'[42] He contended that the domination of international investment banking by US firms cast New York in the role of the industry's global head office, with all other financial centres, including London, as subordinate satellites. He predicted that the brunt of the cutbacks resulting from future downturns would be borne by the satellite financial centres—notably London. 'What will emerge is a hub-and-spoke model run out of New York with a number of subsidiary centres on the rim. London will be just another city at the end of a spoke. It will be no worse off than

Frankfurt, Paris or Zurich but as the current number two after New York, its relative status will be much diminished.'[43]

Yet by 2000 there was no evidence of the fundamental reconfiguration of the relationship between New York and London suggested by Augar. If London really was an investment banking 'branch office', it was a very big branch office where significantly more people worked on the international side of the business than at 'head office'. Indeed, as a senior investment banker with a Wall Street firm put it: 'When the downturn comes, it's New York that will take the brunt of the firings. Europe is where the action is and London is where that business is done.'[44]

It is inconceivable that the City could have become the 'Global Powerhouse' of wholesale financial services without the presence of the major US, European, and Japanese banks and investment banks. Originally they set up shop in London to operate in the offshore Euromarkets, constituting in the 1960s and 1970s a parallel wholesale financial services sector to the traditional British domestic City. Deregulation in the 1980s led to the integration of the offshore and domestic sectors, allowing the increasingly global players from overseas to operate a full range of activities out of London and thereby ensuring that they had no reason to do this business from New York, Switzerland, Paris, Frankfurt, or wherever else. As they built up their London-based European time zone operations, they naturally started to compete for domestic business too and the UK brokerage firms, discount houses, and merchant banks got elbowed into oblivion. Wimbledon EC2 was the other side of the coin of the Global Powerhouse.

7. Challenges

For centuries City business was founded on transatlantic and global ties, European connections being of lesser significance. Stronger links began to be forged from the 1960s when many leading Western European banks established a presence in London—more than 160 of them by the mid-1980s—to undertake Euromarket business. In the 1980s and 1990s, some of them entered the securities and investment banking markets through the acquisition of a UK stockbroker or merchant bank, as in the case of Deutsche Bank, Dresdner Bank, ING, SBC (later UBS), and Société Générale. Others, notably ABN Amro, BNP, Commerzbank, and Paribas enhanced their presence through hirings. By raising their commitment in London, they were able to enter the global market place and to compete with the American banks without having to establish a major presence on Wall Street, though Crédit Suisse, Deutsche Bank, and UBS took this step too.

In the 1990s London emerged more and more as Europe's leading financial and business city. Throughout the decade it consistently topped the annual survey of senior executives from Europe's 15,000 largest companies concerning European cities as business locations conducted by commercial real-estate consultants Healey & Baker.[45] The most important factors in London's favour were all forms of international communication (but *not* internal transport), the availability of suitable staff and office space, and foreign languages spoken.

Paris and Frankfurt, with scores respectively of 0.66 and 0.45 (London scored 0.99) rated second and third amongst European cities as 'best cities to locate a business' in the Healey & Baker survey. They occupied these positions in relation to access to markets, availability of qualified staff, and quality of telecommunications. Paris was top city for internal public transport and for international rail and road links, but lagged considerably behind London and Frankfurt for international air links. Frankfurt scored highest for staff productivity, but poorly for the quality of life of employees (ranked 22 out of 30) and the cost of staff (ranked 25).

In the 1990s both Paris and Frankfurt took steps to challenge London's pre-eminence and to win a greater share of Europe's international wholesale financial business. In Paris a high-powered promotional body, Paris Europlace, was formed with the brief of winning foreign business for the Paris markets. It was backed by the Banque de France, the Paris city council, the Bourse, the big banks, and more than 100 financial institutions, French and foreign. And the French government lent political support. The campaign enjoyed some success in enticing foreign banks and investors to become active in the French markets. But despite its efforts and much to its chagrin, it was German government bonds that were adopted as the benchmark by participants in the new euro-denominated bond market.

Inspired by the example of Paris, in 1996 the Deutsche Börse and the German banks formed Finanzplatz Deutschland, a promotional and developmental body for Frankfurt. Focusing on finding practical solutions to structural weaknesses in the Frankfurt markets, it lobbied the Bundesbank and government about restrictions and imposts that made Frankfurt uncompetitive. It complemented the activities of Wirtschaftsförderung Frankfurt, an entity of the local government authority whose initiatives to promote Frankfurt included the establishment of Japanese and Korean schools to persuade banks and corporations from those countries to locate in the city.

Rivalry between London and Frankfurt was fought out in the mid-1990s in the market for derivatives based on the bund, the German government bond. Initially it was LIFFE, London's bigger and longer-established derivatives exchange, that had the lion's share of the bund market, the biggest of the European derivatives markets, much to the irritation of Frankfurt's Eurex. In London the contracts were traded by the traditional and colourful method of open outcry, but in Frankfurt dealing was screen based. From autumn 1997, as it came to be realized that electronic trading was cheaper and more efficient than open outcry, the volume of contracts traded in Frankfurt began to surge upwards and overtook London. Soon, virtually all bund-based derivatives trading switched to Eurex.

Eurex's triumph in the 'battle of the bund' was hailed as a turning point and a harbinger of a mounting challenge from Frankfurt. It did persuade LIFFE to abandon open outcry in favour of screen trading, but in fact it changed little else. Frankfurt won a significant symbolic victory and got to collect the transaction fees for the trades. However, the bund futures traders remained in London, routing their orders through a computer in Frankfurt rather than one in London. The City was still the place where the banks and the traders wanted to be and to operate from. So London continued to pocket the broking commissions and the UK government to receive the tax on the incomes of the City-based traders, much more valuable prizes than the transaction fees paid to the exchanges.

In 1994 Frankfurt became home to the new European Central Bank (ECB), identifying it with the euro more closely than any other financial centre. Spokesmen for the German banking and securities industry argued that proximity to the institution that sets the euro zone's interest rates conferred advantages on banks with a presence in Frankfurt.[46]

Initially the UK's position of staying out of European monetary union created some anxiety in the City. But by the end of 2000 there was no tangible evidence that the UK's non-participation had had a negative impact on London's role as a global financial centre—in fact, it appeared that the creation of the single currency had consolidated the City's position as Europe's premier financial centre. A Bank of England survey of the key European market participants undertaken almost two years after the introduction of the euro revealed that most such firms concentrated their euro foreign exchange dealing and their treasury and risk management functions in a single centre, mostly London.[47] London was also the principal location of their international bond and equity trading and research, their non-government euro-denominated bond and equity issuance, and their mergers and acquisition advisory businesses. It was estimated that 81,000 City jobs, about a quarter of the total, were dependent in some way on activity originating from clients based in other EU member states. It was a substantially higher headcount than those undertaking wholesale financial services in Frankfurt, Paris, or any other European financial centre.

Despite the efforts to boost Frankfurt, it was a much smaller financial centre than London. In 2000, around 80,000 people worked in banking and insurance (both wholesale and retail) in Frankfurt, less than a quarter of the number of people engaged in wholesale activities alone in London. In truth, Frankfurt's banking leaders entertained few illusions that their city would supplant the City as Europe's leading wholesale financial centre. 'London', commented Rolf Breuer, head of Deutsche Bank and chairman of the Frankfurt Stock Exchange, in 1998, 'will no doubt remain the leading centre in Europe thanks to its advantages of size, excellently qualified personnel, and the attractive tax, legal and cultural environment.'[48] 'Frankfurt's main handicap is, quite simply, Frankfurt,' pronounced Euromarkets veteran Stanislas Yassukovich witheringly. 'The expatriate community that populates an international financial centre has cultural and lifestyle expectations which Frankfurt cannot meet.'[49]

Outlook For The City

Looking forward at the beginning of the twenty-first century, analysts were generally bullish about the outlook for London as an international financial centre. Their optimism was based on the view that the fundamental causes of the City's growth and prosperity in the 1980s and 1990s would continue to operate, despite occasional cyclical downturns. Demand for international financial services was expected to continue to grow rapidly, driven by global economic growth, trade and financial liberalization, and the shift to offshore operations. In fact it was envisaged that these forces might even gather momentum in forthcoming decades as more and more countries, including perhaps Brazil, China, India, and Indonesia, became integrated into the international financial system. The City's leading position, reinforced by the centripetal pull of external economies of scale and economies of scope, would ensure that the lion's share of the growth of international financial services business would accrue to London.

The ongoing dynamic expansion of demand for international financial services, coupled with the City's entrenched advantages as the world's foremost international financial centre, led Lombard Street Research, an economic consultancy, to estimate that the real output of the London money-centre sector would grow by at least 6 per cent per year over the first two decades of the twenty-first century, repeating the performance of the 1980s and 1990s.[50] This would be a much more rapid rate of expansion than the historic trend rate of UK economic growth, suggesting that the City would loom larger and larger as a factor in the economies of Britain and London.

The difference between the 6 per cent per year projected rate of growth of the City's real output and a much lower rate of employment growth, historically 1.5 per cent per annum over the previous thirty years, implied the continuation of substantial increases in real output per head and hence personal incomes. This would be consistent with other factors promoting greater labour productivity, particularly investment in computing and communications equipment and the relentless advance of these technologies. A further factor was the increasing scale of financial transactions in global financial markets—the average size of equity and bond trades, currency deals, or mergers. The predicted outcome was that the already yawning gulf between remuneration levels in the international financial services industry and other employment sectors would continue to grow wider and wider.

But there would certainly be problems and challenges along the way, both domestic and external. Among the domestic clouds on the horizon, the darkest appeared to be the ever worsening state of London traffic and mobility around the city, the threat of yet higher taxation, and the draconian powers of the Financial Services Authority, which gave many practitioners anxiety about the increasing inflexibility and cost of regulation. All three posed a threat to London's competitive advantage.

Externally, there were challenges for business from other European centres and offshore centres. Although neither appeared to pose a serious threat, it was possible that some of the latter might increase their share of offshore activities because of their attractions as tax havens. However, such shifts were often more apparent than real; although deals were booked offshore, much of the high-value-added work would still be done in London. Some saw a concentration of global wholesale financial services in New York as posing a potential threat. But that was before the terrorist attacks on the Twin Towers on 11 September 2001.

The physical devastation and the disruption to business wrought by the terrorist assault on Wall Street posed the question whether concentrated financial centres had had their day. In theory, modern electronic information and trading technologies permitted financial firms to operate from almost anywhere. Maybe the time had come for financial firms to take advantage of technology and disperse, rather than clustering together as trophy targets for terrorists. If it transpired that the 9/11 attacks marked the beginning of the end for the City and other traditional clustered financial centres, the decades of the 1980s and 1990s would not constitute a stepping stone to greater glories but the apogee of a 400-year history.

Notes

1. Hamish McRae and Frances Cairncross, *Capital City: London as a Financial Centre* (London, 1984), 1.
2. Corporation of London, *The Global Powerhouse: thecityoflondon* (London, 2000), 7.
3. Richard Roberts and David Kynaston, *City State: A Contemporary History of the City of London and how Money Triumphed* (London, 2002), 102–4.
4. Ranald Michie, *The City of London: Continuity and Change, 1850–1990* (London, 1992), 17; J. V. Dunning and E. V. Morgan, *An Economic Study of the City of London* (London, 1971), 130–1.
5. See Raymond W. Goldsmith, *Financial Structure and Development* (New Haven, 1969).
6. Lombard Street Research, *Growth Prospects of City Industries* (London, 1998), 14–15.
7. Healey & Baker, *European Cities Monitor* (London, 2000).
8. See Walter Stewart, *Too Big to Fail. Olympia & York: The Story Behind the Headlines* (Ontario, 1993).
9. Nicholas Ritchie, *What Goes on in the City?* (Cambridge, 1981).
10. Corporation of London, *The Global Powerhouse* 10.
11. International Financial Services London, *Key Facts about the City of London* (Nov. 2002), 2.
12. International Financial Services London, *International Financial Markets in the UK* (May 2002), 13.
13. William M. Clarke, *How the City of London Works* (London, 1999), 119.
14. Lloyd's of London, press release, 5 July 1999.
15. Richard Roberts, *Wall Street* (London, 2002), 13, 221–2.
16. Hong Kong Bureau of Census, Mar. 1997; information from Frankfurt Industrie und Handels Kammer.
17. International Financial Services London, *International Financial Markets in the UK*, 3.
18. Centre for Economic and Business Research, *London's Contribution to the UK Economy* (July 2001), 46.
19. International Financial Services London, *International Financial Markets in the UK*, 5–6.
20. Centre for Economic and Business Research, *The City's Importance to the European Union Economy* (Nov. 2000), 14.
21. Ibid. 13–21.
22. Ibid. 6.
23. International Financial Services London, *International Financial Markets in the UK*, 3.
24. Roberts, *Wall Street*, 14.

25. *New Earnings Survey* (2000), table A21: 'Full Time Employees of Both Sexes on Adult Rates'.
26. Lombard Street Research, *Growth Prospects of City Industries*, 9, 40.
27. Roberts and Kynaston, *City State*, 45.
28. Corporation of London. *The City Research Project: Final Report* (London, Mar. 1995), 7.27–7.29.
29. *Evening Standard*, 29 Jan. 1998.
30. *Financial Times*, 1–2 Feb. 1997.
31. F. D. P. Savills, *Residential Research Bulletin* (Autumn 1998).
32. *Financial Times*, 26 Jan. 2001.
33. Richard Roberts, 'Setting the City Free: The Impact of the U.K. Abolition of Exchange Controls', *Journal of International Financial Markets Law and Regulation*, 2/4 (Aug. 2000), 137; Ranald Michie, *The London Stock Exchange: A History* (Oxford, 1999), 545.
34. John Plender and Paul Wallace, *The Square Mile: A Guide to the New City of London* (London, 1985), 47.
35. W. A. Thomas, *The Big Bang* (Oxford, 1986), 157.
36. John Littlewood, *The Stock Market: 50 Years of Capitalism at Work* (London, 1998), 325.
37. *The Banker* (Nov. 1986; Nov. 1989).
38. *Financial Times*, 19 Jan. 2000.
39. *The Banker* plus author's research.
40. Augar, *Death of Gentlemanly Capitalism*, 322.
41. *Independent on Sunday*, 16 July 1995.
42. Augar, *Death of Gentlemanly Capitalism*, 324.
43. Ibid. 326.
44. Author interview, Dec. 2000.
45. Healey & Baker, *European Cities Monitor*, 5.
46. *Financial Times*, 9 June 1997.
47. Bank of England, *Practical Issues Arising from the Euro*, (Nov. 2000).
48. Quoted in David Lascelles, *Confidence in the City outside the Euro* (London, 1999), 1.
49. *Spectator*, 18 Sept. 1999.
50. Lombard Street Research, *Growth Prospects of City Industries*, 40.

15

The Future of the Paris Market as an International Financial Centre from the Point of View of European Integration

ANDRÉ STRAUS

To address this question we need first of all to look briefly at the way the market has developed. An overview of trends over the last half-century in particular will tend to show that Paris has been able to exist as a financial centre only when its financial market has been vigorous, which has clearly been a necessary but not always a sufficient condition.

Initially, then, we should indicate the major stages in the history of the French financial market and in the role it played, or failed to play, in the economic development of the country, and examine the place of international financial relations in it. We shall use the distinction proposed some years ago, chiefly by French economists[1] following a suggestion by Hicks,[2] between what have usually been called 'financial market economies' and 'overdraft economies'.

The first golden age of the Paris financial market was the period 1880–1914, when its international, and mainly European, role was an essential factor in the international allocation of capital flow, partly due to monetary stability and despite a rather archaic regulatory system. The First World War brought about a complete change. France, which had hitherto been a creditor nation, found itself a debtor. Although the government mobilized part of the private portfolio of foreign stocks and shares to finance its outside purchases and avoid outflows of gold as far as possible, it was mainly the failure of foreign debtors (chiefly Russia, which had accounted for a third of the foreign portfolio before 1914) that slashed the value of French capital invested abroad. As a consequence, the Paris Bourse ceased to be an international financial market for a long time.

Similarly, the general context in which financial transactions took place was radically different from what it had been prior to 1914. In particular, the inter-war years saw much greater monetary fluctuation and higher inflation rates then ever before. For most of the time, the financial market was dominated by the foreign exchange market and changes in the purchasing power of the franc. The period was in fact decisive in the history of the financial market. The slump brought about a deep and lasting reduction of its contribution to the financing of the economy, and it was not until a half-century later that the Paris Bourse began to play a significant part on the country's economic stage.

1. The financial market in the period of reconstruction and the early stages of growth

Faced with rebuilding a country ruined by war and financial crisis, the state intervened massively in the financing of the economy by setting out within a planning framework priorities aimed at avoiding a long-lasting weakening of the French economy. There was a great need for financing. Many concerns were highly solvent at the end of hostilities, but their purchasing power was quickly eroded as the galloping inflation of the immediate post-war period increased their need for finance at a time when they were obliged to build up their stocks and modernize their equipment. In such an inflationary context, there were very limited opportunities for recourse to the financial market, given first the rapidly diminishing value of fixed-income securities and the end of quoting representative nationalized-undertaking securities. There was also the low level of savings of households ever more anxious, since the introduction of universal social security, to buy the consumer durables they had been deprived of during the war than to save for a rainy day. Since the major banks were now nationalized and restricted by the government to short-term financing, it was the Treasury and foreign aid, with the help of non-banking financial institutions, which provided most investment credits. The high level of public financing, which increased towards the end of the 1940s, gave rise to several big budget deficits, which were largely made up for by the 'circuit' set up by the Treasury. For all that, however, there was recourse to rapidly growing public savings. The influence of the state on the market at the time is shown by the mass of Treasury loans and loans from major public enterprises and non-banking financial institutions, whose calls on the market still amounted to 60 per cent of bond issues in 1963.

Until the early 1950s, the first loans issued were difficult to place, which brought a general fall in fixed-income bonds despite frequent interventions on the market by the Caisse des Dépôts. The reluctance to save meant that borrowing cost more, lenders shortened the term of their bonds, and from 1952 were having recourse to index-linking or issuing participating or share-convertible bonds. The founding of SICOVAM[3] tended to modernize the way the market worked, particularly in relation to foreign stocks and shares, but on the whole the amount of fresh money raised on a state-dominated bond market was very limited until the early 1950s. Between the 1950s and the early 1960s the favourable outlook for the results of enterprises linked to the higher rate of growth and the renewed fall in interest rates kept share prices high. The boom in oil shares provides an example of the upward trend: after the discovery of Parentis, the price of Esso-Standard shares increased twelvefold in fifteen months.

The rise of variable-income shares during the 1950s gave a new fillip to the financial market and made possible a rapid increase in issues, which was encouraged by new state regulatory measures. Although the private sector benefited greatly from such developments, even if to a lesser extent than the nationalized and mixed-economy industries, the financial market still had a long way to go to achieve its former importance. In terms of real value, issues in 1956 were five times smaller than those in 1928.

2. The financial market in an overdraft economy

The marginalization of the Bourse in the economy became more marked in the 1960s and 1970s, when the French economy was in fact enjoying the highest growth rates in its history and, from 1967, investment was higher than in any other Western European country. Banking credits ousted the financial market because savers preferred to put their money in real estate or liquid financial investments (the Caisses d'Épargne's A books) all of which had tax benefits. A further cause was the leverage benefiting enterprises borrowing from banks. The very largely managed cost of the credits thus obtained made it possible, particularly at a time of rapidly rising prices from the late 1960s, to pay only a very low, and sometimes in fact negative, real interest on capital used to increase their production and profits. The leverage, further increased by tax-deductible interest, consequently rose between the mid-1960s and 1974 and accounts for the increase in the debt level of enterprises. The French economy turned into an overdraft economy, despite reiterated attempts by the public authorities to promote the securities market.

The marginalization of the Bourse was, however, a concomitant of a certain return to the opening-up of trade from 1959[4] with the application of the Treaty of Rome. Trading moved into surplus again, capital that had shifted abroad came back home, and foreign investors flocked in, creating a continuous supply of foreign exchange and a consequent flexibility in exchange controls. French banks took advantage of this favourable development to go back to their oldest traditions and play a large part in issuing and placing major international loans. Like London, Paris attracted the world's major banks, and Chase Manhattan, the Morgan Guaranty Trust, the Bank of America, and the British 'Big Four' set up branches or agencies there. The international nature of the Paris market was confirmed by its role as the financial capital of the franc zone, with the Treasury guaranteeing free convertibility into francs for the currencies of African and Madagascan members of the franc zone. The Paris Stock Market itself started moving towards becoming a real international financial market. Between 1959 and 1967, a series of liberal measures helped to make it more accessible to non-resident traders and to give French investors the opportunity to acquire stocks and shares traded on other markets. The persistence of exchange controls, apart from a short period in 1967–8, and the still closed nature of the French bond market did, however, limit Paris's international ambitions.

The beginning of the slump in the world economy in the early 1970s did not completely wipe out the economic advantages linked to a overdraft economy. The increasing rate of price increases for raw materials, the first oil crisis, and the increase in the share of wages in added value linked to indexing practices reduced enterprises' profit rates, which in turn reduced their investments, and meant a sharp rise in inflation. Although for a short time increasing debt and the rapid erosion of their indebtedness in real terms meant that as a result of a still positive leverage they were able to contain the decline in their financial viability, the situation changed with the second oil crisis.

3. Towards a financial market economy?

Increases in their financial burdens, which became heavier as the effects of deflationary policy on real interest rates began to bite and their financial situation deteriorated, did in fact induce them to modify their financing structure and turn increasingly to the market. At the same time, the recovery policy launched by the state in a context of slower tax receipts gave rise to a considerable growth in public sector loans. The needs of firms and administrative bodies at this juncture explain the rapid recovery of the financial market. Between 1979 and 1984, public issues of shares or participating securities increased fourfold. It was chiefly the bond market, to which the state and the banks mainly turned, that developed spectacularly, with gross issues rising from 235bn. francs in 1984 as against 65.5bn. in 1979, with non-financial undertakings concentrating on consolidating their own funds.

Given such renewed vitality over the last twenty years, the question of the future of Paris as an international financial centre can therefore legitimately be reformulated, since there have been many more attempts to revitalize the market and make it more attractive. This was initially the case at the domestic level, where the rapid growth in the volume of issues is explicable in terms of the relatively brutal shift in the savings of households.

Three factors explain the renewed interest in investments in stocks and shares at a time when the rate of savings of households was falling. The first is the sharp rise in price from 1978, which was scarcely, although notably, interrupted by the results of the 1981 elections, with share prices increasing fourfold between 1981 and 1986, leading savers to hope for much higher returns. Second, there was a return of positive real interest rates along with deflation and the restoration of a hierarchy of rates favouring long-term investments. Finally, the importance of public authority initiatives on behalf of the financial market must be stressed. Although such attempts have a long history (the 1957 law setting up the SICAVs[5] and FCPs[6], tax credits in 1965, the introduction of OPAs[7] in 1966, and the creation of the Commission des Opérations de Bourse in 1967 and SICAV by Monory in 1978), it was not until the 1980s that public initiatives became more frequent and more consistent. Initially their aim was to discourage competing forms of savings, by increasing taxes on term accounts and removing the advantages of investing in real estate (the Quillot law).

Simultaneously, the public authorities kept or strengthened encouragements to buy bonds or shares, originating many new mechanisms for investing which were better adapted to both the needs of issuers and the desires of investors, such as participatory stocks and shares, joint funds for investments involving risk, renewable Treasury bonds, investment certificates, and bonds with share applications. The setting-up of the Second Market in 1982 enabled medium-sized firms to try to attract public savings. New markets were instituted: MATIF[8] in 1986 and MONEP[9] in 1987, which were originally intended to offer better protection to French savers against the increasing risks arising from the considerable imbalances in the world economy and the speed of the transmission of information. This French-style 'big bang' had of course to go hand in hand with a new reorganization of the market. The desire to ensure its liquidity and to develop its international role by giving intermediaries the chance to hold suspense accounts led to a plan aimed at gradually eliminating the monopoly of stockbrokers and changing them into stock exchange companies into whose capital French and foreign banks often had an input.

There is no doubt that this cluster of measures was successful and enabled the Paris financial market place to catch up with its Anglo-Saxon counterparts to some extent. The financial revolution was certainly largely international. An examination of the successive cycles of the world economy since the 1960s shows the series of profound disorders affecting a real economy that was prey to a process of an increasing globalization of trade dominated by ever-increasing competition between nations and economic zones for market shares and standards of living. The changes in the financial sphere were mainly responses to the problems arising from these imbalances, namely an increased need for financing, the need to recycle capital, and protecting agents from fluctuating financial parameters arising from or intended to reduce the imbalances.

The development of national liquidities that led to the gradual integration of markets at world level was fuelled by the USA's deficit of payments, then by the oil-producing countries' dollar surpluses, and later, from 1983, by the appearance of major deficits in the American economy, counterbalanced by surpluses in Japan, the Federal Republic of Germany, and the newly industrialized countries of South-East Asia[10]. In particular, the coexistence at world level of major deficits and surpluses brought about an automatic increase of transactions in the financial sphere and a constant link with the process of innovation, deregulation, and integration of domestic and international markets. Indeed, the considerable increases in the need for financing of the main agents (firms until 1983–4, and particularly since 1975 public financial departments) could not have been met for very long in the old regulatory and operational framework (see Fig. 15.1).

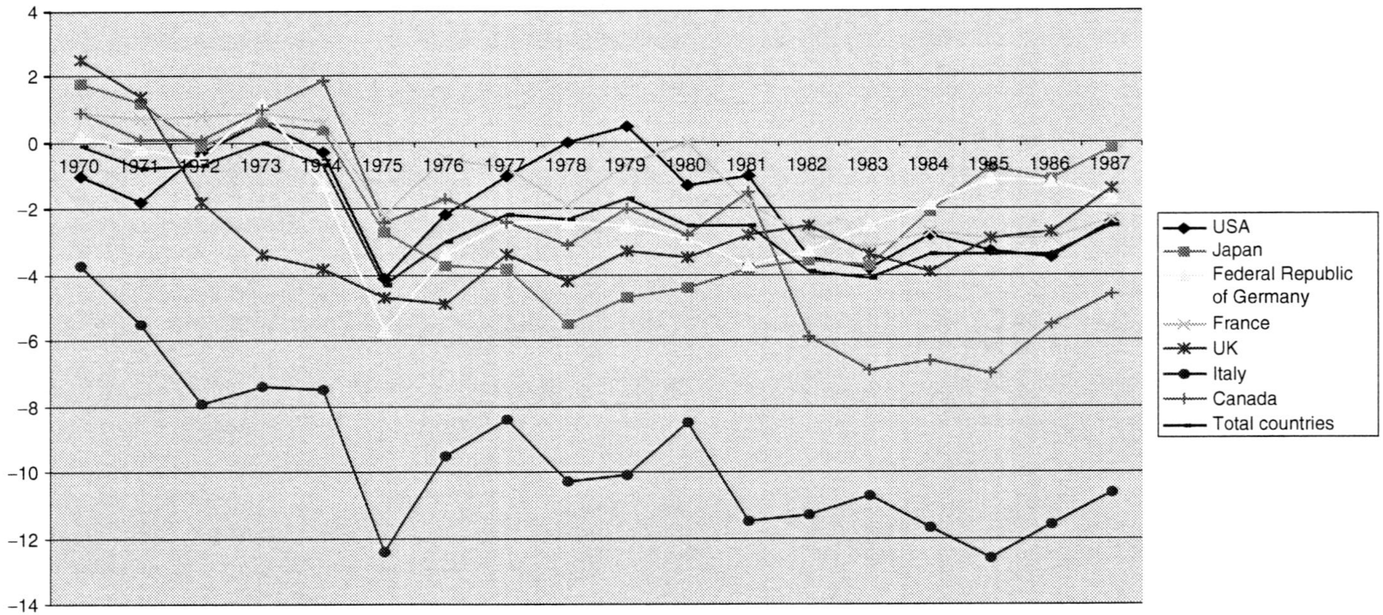

Fig. 15.1. Borrowing requirements of public administrative bodies

4. The limits of the vitality of the Parisian market and of its new international role

Was this real and largely international financial revolution sufficient to give the Paris Bourse the role it had had before the First World War? In the 1970s, the ratio of French market capitalization to GDP was still one of the lowest in Western Europe and it was still very modest in the late 1980s, lying sixth behind Tokyo, New York, London, the German exchanges, and Toronto. In 1986, its capitalization was a fourteenth of New York's and a third of London's. Since then, the Paris market has made great progress. During the 1990s, market capitalization increased fourfold, reaching almost 2,200bn. euros (approximately 14,370bn. francs, with 9,385bn. for shares and 4,985 for bonds) by the end of 1999. Share capitalization reached 107 per cent of GNP as against 35 per cent in 1989,[11] with Paris at the top of the list of continental markets and closing on Anglo-Saxon ones, but still below the noteworthy second place it had occupied in 1914. The long-standing weakening was not due solely to the regression of the French economy in the hierarchy of market economies, but was also the result of the development of the whole of its financial system and the importance of banks in the high-growth period of the 1960s and 1970s.

We should also be on our guard against a starry-eyed view of the international activity of the Parisian market. Although transactions involving foreign shares increased sharply between 1984 and 1992 and then again from 1997, the ratio of foreign share transactions to total transactions makes it quite clear that it was the French share market that the rapid expansion of the Paris financial market chiefly benefited (Fig. 15.2).

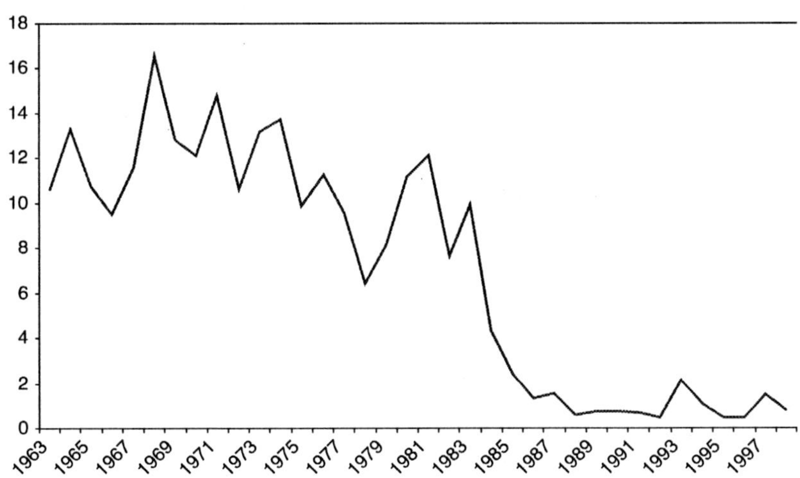

Fig. 15.2. Ratio of foreign share transactions to total transactions

Table 15.1. *Ratio of foreign share transactions to total transactions*

	1981	1982	1983	1984	1985	1986	1988	1989	1990	1991	1993	1994	1995	1996	1997
New York										5.8	8	9.7	8.5	8.3	8.4
London							19.6		48.7	43.5	50.6	54.2	55	58.3	58.1
Brussels	58.8	44.4	46	42.7	40	34.4	22.2	27.5	29.3	25.3	21.3	22.6	16.8	13.9	13.4
Germany	12.2	12.8	15.2	16.6	11	10	5.4	4.8	2.1	2	2.7	2.6	2.3	2.9	4.5
Paris	28.9	25	33.4	24.5	13.6	7.1	5.4	4	3.8	3.4	2.7	1.6	1.5	1.7	2

From the mid-1980s, the percentage of foreign share transactions was below 2 per cent of total transactions. The relatively small proportion of such transactions on the market is confirmed by a comparison with the international activities of other stock exchange markets for which data are available (Table 15.1).

The table shows the great importance of international transactions on the London market, of course, but also on that of Brussels. On the other hand, the German stock exchanges, particularly during the 1990s, developed like Paris. Does this necessarily mean that the Parisian market place has no future? It has disadvantages, of course, but also advantages.

5. Advantages and disadvantages of the Paris market in international competition

The advantages of the Paris market at the dawn of the twenty-first century

First, a certain number of advantages arise from the strengths of the French economy and the modernization of the financial market. The most significant of these is a favourable economic environment, as can be seen in the performance of the national economy, in the agricultural, food processing, aeronautical, automobile, pharmaceutical, or service sectors. The results, which are based on a largely skilled labour force, are commendable and give France a satisfactory ranking in international competition. The favourable economic environment is also due to the stability of the franc over the last fifteen years, and subsequently to the euro. The country's savings capacity should also be mentioned, even if it is still insufficiently directed towards investment in stocks and shares. The lifestyle is favourable, to judge from the level of development of the social and medical infrastructures, or more widely by the quality of life, which is what chiefly accounts for the attractiveness for tourists of the country in general and the capital in particular. More precisely Paris, rather than London or Frankfurt, is the favoured place for the head offices of many national and international companies, a phenomenon which facilitates the growth of negotiable credit notes and mergers and takeovers on the shares market.

Secondly, mention should be made of two further advantages: the internationalization of the economy and France's European vocation. The former can be shown by the increase of the exports/GNP ratio since the 1980s. This rapid opening-up of the economy becomes very significant when the fact that the French economy is open to crossing flows of direct investments is taken into account. This is illustrated by the penetration of manufacturing industry by foreign firms. In the 1980s, France was third in the list of countries attracting foreign investment, but equal first with the United Kingdom in 1992. In parallel, French investment abroad has increased considerably. The current situation is as follows:[12] the 26.7bn. euro financial debit balance in 2001 corresponds, like that of the three preceding years, to the nation's financing capacity with regard to other countries. Resident agents invested more abroad than they went into debt, which is reflected in net capital outflow. With the worldwide slowdown in mergers and takeovers after a record year in 2000 when they reached to 18.9bn. euros, French direct investments fell to 87.9bn. euros. The fall must be considered along with the contraction from 145.4bn. euros in 2001 in portfolio investments by non-residents to 107.5bn. In 2001 the fall in stocks and shares prices made financing by means of share issues more difficult and thus automatically reduced the total transactions. Despite reduced flows, France in 2001 was the second in the world, after the United States, with regard to direct investments abroad, and purchases of foreign debt shares remained steady, mostly concerned, as in 2000, with securities issued by countries in the euro zone.

The trend towards a more international French economy was echoed in financial activities. Since 1986 frontiers had been open to movements of capital, due largely to a more flexible exchange control, which was finally abolished in 1900. For example, at the end of 1992, two-thirds of French bonds and one-fifth of quoted shares were held by non-residents. The franc's performance made it a more international currency, and from 1989 to 1993 international issues in francs increased ninefold. Reflecting this increasingly international nature, the number of

Table 15.2. *Balance of payments finance account (bn. euros)*

	1999	2000	2001
Finance accounts	−37.5	−30.6	−26.7
Direct investments i.e.:	−75.4	−139.2	−32.6
French, abroad	−119.1	−185.9	−687.9
Foreign, into France	43.7	46.7	55.3
Portfolio investments i.e.	−7.1	41.1	27.7
By residents, on securities issued	−117.8	−104.3	−79.8
By non-residents on securities issued by residents	110.6	145.4	107.5
Other investments i.e.:	45.3	59.8	28.8
Assets	−20.1	0.1	−57.3
Commitments	65.3	59.7	28.5

Sources: Banque de France, Ministère de l'Économie, des Finances et de l'Industrie.

foreign banking institutions established in France rose from 200 in 1984 to over 400 in 1993 and to 473 in 1999, placing Paris second in Europe after London, which had 550, and well ahead of Frankfurt's 280. At the same time, French banks had the biggest European network and were fourth in the world with regard to international bank loans.

There are other advantages which would help to place Paris in the forefront of international financial centres, such as the country's high-quality performance as a financial intermediary. A third of the stock exchange companies work hand in hand with major foreign intermediaries and draw funds into the Parisian market. Their financial power means that they can intervene on high-volume markets. State-of-the-art technology at the financial level, such as a fully computerized market and a modernized negotiating system and settling and delivery circuits, provides investors with a high-quality negotiation service which is one of the fastest, most efficient, and cheapest in the world. France is also very strong in management, and is second in the world in the collective management assets for third parties (the OPCVM).[13] The total value of managed funds is estimated at over 1,340bn. euros. It provides a wide base of investors and opportunities for foreign and international financial institutions.

In addition, at the instigation of the Commission des Opérations de Bourse, Paris has undeniably made progress with regard to security and transparency. The quotation system and the increasing number of terminals mean that every operator can follow the precise rates and volumes of transactions, and enjoys a perfect overview of the market, which is practically unique in the world. The Conseil des Marchés Financiers and the Conseil de Discipline de la Gestion Financière complete the machinery of market control.

All in all, this trend has given Paris one or two special market sectors. Its major strength lies in the bond market, the most important Parisian market, with a critical mass that makes it comparable with its most important rivals. In 1994 the total loans issue amounted to 408.5bn. francs (as against 537.7 in 1993) and bond and participatory share capitalization rose to 4,985bn. francs at the end of 1999. The market is mainly aligned on government bonds, especially Treasury securities (OAT)[14] offering very high secondary-market liquidity (thanks to the efforts of Treasury securities specialists), security, and simplicity, with investment following a pre-established calendar, equivalent Treasury bonds, and negotiable Treasury bills. Since the introduction of the euro, the French bond market has doubled in a year and accounts for 20 per cent of the total of private bond issues in the euro zone. Paris is clearly the prime market place for bonds issued by enterprises. In France as in other developed countries, there is a long-term trend towards securitizing enterprise indebtedness, which is towards replacing bank loans with securities.

Derivatives markets were also dynamic in Paris in the early 1990s. Such was the case with MATIF,[15] which in 1993 was fourth in the world, with a market share of 11.7 per cent of contracts negotiated. The high figure was essentially due to contracts on Notionnel (36.9 per cent of firm contracts, 56.3 per cent of options contracts). The CAC 40 contract headed the list of indexed term contracts in

Europe. Overall MATIF covered a very wide range of instruments, within which the Notionnel francs contract was in the first rank in Europe. Since then, however, MATIF has tended to decline to some extent, whereas the German by-products market has become more powerful, and it is still too soon to assess how effective MATIF's attempted revival - a commendable gesture of market solidarity - has in fact been. Finally, Paris ranked third in the world and first in the euro zone for mutual-agreement-rate derivatives and was first in Europe for Treasury notes and certificates of deposit.

2. *Disadvantages of the Paris Market*

There are, however, handicaps to the Paris market's ability to play a part as a leading international financial centre. The first of these is without doubt the fact that this role has not been acknowledged abroad. The internationalization of the French economy is often seen as still insufficient, despite the great leap forward during the last decade. This is the case at several levels. In the first place, French operators still have only limited recourse to foreign markets, and the possibility that in future some major French groups might choose to sell their securities on foreign markets cannot be ruled out. This has already been the case with the Rhône-Poulenc privatization in early 1994, when out of the 4.5bn. shares which were sold, 600m. francs were invested in the United States, 400m. in Japan, and the remainder in Europe. In 1993, when the leading French chemical group issued nearly 2bn. francs' worth of open-term secondary shares, it did so on the American market. Given that enterprises are more highly international than financial institutions, such a trend might become more marked.

In addition, the Paris market does not seem to be a really international one when seen through foreign eyes. It is true that foreign investors account for over 35 per cent of French stock market capitalization and carry out half the number of transactions on it. But that is chiefly a sign of their confidence in the French economy. On the other hand, however, foreign enterprises are not convinced that being quoted on the Paris market really matters much. The proportion of foreign companies of domestic companies quoted is smaller in Paris (22 per cent) than in Germany (47.2 per cent), in Amsterdam (54.7 per cent), and particularly in London (118 per cent). Nor does Paris offer enough offsetting intermediaries to be able to develop all sectors of the market and launch new products.

Generally speaking, in the 1990s the image of France was still suffering from decades of monetary deprivation, financial protectionism, and state intervention as well as from an insufficient control of public spending, all of which adversely affected the credibility of the country's monetary policy. Within France, the role and usefulness of the financial industry and the way the economy works are not understood by the population as a whole. Even those actively involved in finance find it difficult to say what a collective strategy for promoting the Paris market should be. Alongside the British model, which has been very effective in promoting its own market place and creating the image of the City, Frankfurt provides the example of a city of 400,000 inhabitants that, thanks to the stimulus provided by one or two powerful actors, such as banks, insurance firms, and major enterprises, has managed to become an efficient modern market.[16]

Competition between financial institutions is now determined by the quality of men and teams. The success of a financial centre depends more and more on its ability to retain highly mobile traders with highly specialized skills. One disadvantage the Paris market faces is the heavy social and tax burdens affecting market operators and leading to a degree of relocation of financial teams to London. A comparative study of tax and social security factors is difficult because they vary according to income levels and the public services the contributions provide. Social cover, health services, transport infrastructures, the benefits provided by deductions, and the cost of living in the various competing countries also need to be taken into account.

The final negative factor is that from the macroeconomic point of view the trend of household savings is not very favourable. Indeed, although the rate of saving of French households, which is above 15 per cent of disposable income, is the highest in the industrialized world and the rate of financial saving is just as high, savings are still more concerned with debt instruments than with the provision of capital for enterprises. This is because for a long time the public authorities have sought to channel household savings towards financing public deficits by means of tax benefits and savings instruments adapted to savers' preferences. The result is that the number of residents holding shares directly is lower in France than in the Anglo-Saxon countries, whereas it is increasing in Germany, Italy, and even Spain. There are several possible reasons for this. In the first place, the tax system encourages short-, medium-term, or bond investments, with the exception of the plan for saving through shares. Second, life-insurance investments, which are very common in France, are essentially made in bonds meeting the safeguards imposed on insurance companies. Finally, the low level of both pension funds by capitalization and savings from wages in France also contributes to the low rate of financial savings invested in shares. Thus the share of the capital of quoted firms held by non-residents was over 35 per cent in 1999. That percentage, which is certainly a sign that the market is being favourably internationalized, could however reduce the autonomy of French enterprises and deprive French residents of a significant share of the increased wealth linked to rising share prices.

From a macro-financial point of view, it seems that one of the main disadvantages France was still suffering from in 1995, namely the narrowness of its financial market, is on the way to being overcome. The last few years of the 1990s were a decisive turning point that confirmed the rise of Paris among the international financial centres. The stock exchange capitalization of its market increased fourfold in ten years, reaching around 2,200bn. euros at the end of 1999, and share capitalization reached 116 per cent of the GNP, as against 35 per cent in 1989. From that point of view it is now amongst the first rank of continental markets and coming closer to its Anglo-Saxon counterparts. It is certain, however, that in the very long term the relative importance of European economies in the world economy has decreased, and hence that Europe cannot simply play the international part it did before 1914. Yet despite, or because of, its relatively modest growth, the UK has in London an absolutely prime international financial centre with which Paris cannot compete on a world scale.

Thus the future of the Paris market is to be seen in terms of its ability to play a leading part in continental Europe, but it will only be able to do so in alliances with other markets, as the birth of Euronext is trying to do by bringing the Paris, Amsterdam, and Brussels stock markets together. The international exchanges (iX) project, aimed at linking the London and Frankfurt[17] markets, could have been a real challenge if it had materialized, though the Paris market place was able to widen Euronext further to include LIFFE, opening the prospect of a major pan-European euro zone market.

Notes

1. Vivien Lévy-Garboua and B. Weymuller, *Macroéconomie* (Paris, 1981); C. de Boissieu, 'Économie d'endettement, économie de marchés financiers et taux d'intérêt', in *Keynes aujourd'hui, théories et politiques* (Paris, 1985); V. Lévy-Garboua and G. Maarek, *La Dette, le boom, la crise* (Paris, 1985).
2. Sir John Hicks, *The Crisis in Keynesian Economics* (Oxford, 1975). In that work, Hicks develops the contrast between 'auto-sectors' and 'overdraft sectors'.
3. SICOVAM: Société, Interprofessionnelle pour la Compensation des Valeurs Mobilières (Depository Trust Company).
4. See Maurice Schlogel, *Les Relations économiques et financières internationales* (Paris, 1972).
5. SICAV: *société d'investissements à capital variable* (open-ended investment company).
6. FCP: *fonds commun de placements* (unit trust fund).
7. OPA: *offre publique d'achat* (takeover bid)
8. MATIF: *marché à terme des instruments financiers* (futures market).
9. MONEP: *marché des options négociables de Paris* (Paris traded options exchange).
10. Henri Bourguignat, *Les Vertiges de la finance internationale* (Paris, 1987); Isabelle Bouillot, *Économie réelle et sphère financière*, Report of the Conseil Économique et Social, (Nov. 1988).
11. Recommendation adopted by the Conseil Économique et Social at its meeting of 24 May 2000.
12. INSEE, *L'Économie française*, (2002–3 edn.) INSEE, *Rapport sur les comptes de la nation, 2001* (Paris, 2002).
13. OPVCM: *organisme de placement collectif en valeurs mobilières* (organization for collective investment in securities/transferables).
14. OAT: *obligations assimilables du Trésor* (French government/Treasury Bond).
15. Édouard Salustro, 'L'Évolution de la place financière de Paris dans la perspective de la monnaie unique', in *Rapport du Conseil Économique et Social* (Nov. 1995).
16. Cral-Ludwig Holtfrerich, *Frankfurt as a Financial Centre* (Munich, 1999).
17. *Ibid.*

Index

Note: French institutions, e.g. those prefixed 'Banque' and 'Crédit', are indexed alphabetically according to the capitalized word following the first preposition, article or conjunction. Similar ordering is applied to Spanish–, Portuguese–, and English–named institutions. Others are listed under acronym or abbreviation.

Printed in the United Kingdom
by Lightning Source UK Ltd.
115396UKS00001B/30

9 780199 269495